S0-BDL-801

Cracking the

SAT*

Biology E/M
Subject Test

2009–2010 Edition

Cracking the
SAT*

Biology E/M
Subject Test

2009–2010 Edition

Judene Wright, M.S., M.A.Ed.

PrincetonReview.com

Random House, Inc. New York

The Independent Education Consultants Association recognizes The Princeton Review as a valuable resource for high school and college students applying to college and graduate school.

The Princeton Review, Inc.
2315 Broadway
New York, NY 10024
E-mail: editorialsupport@review.com

Copyright © 2009, by The Princeton Review, Inc.

All rights reserved under International and Pan-American Copyright Conventions. Published in the United States by Random House, Inc., New York, and simultaneously in Canada by Random House of Canada Limited, Toronto.

ISBN: 978-0-375-42905-7
ISSN: 1556-8431

*SAT is a registered trademark of the College Board.

Editor: Heather Brady
Production Editor: E. Parker
Production Coordinator: Kim Howie
Illustrations by: The Production Department of
The Princeton Review

Printed in the United States of America.

10 9 8 7 6 5 4 3 2 1

2009–2010 Edition

John Katzman, Chairman, Founder
Michael J. Perik, President, CEO
Stephen Richards, COO, CFO
John Marshall, President, Test Preparation Services
Rob Franek, VP Test Prep Books, Publisher

Editorial
Seamus Mullarkey, Editorial Director
Rebecca Lessem, Senior Editor
Selena Coppock, Editor
Heather Brady, Editor

Production Services
Scott Harris, Executive Director, Production Services
Kim Howie, Senior Graphic Designer

Production Editorial
Meave Shelton, Production Editor
Emma Parker, Production Editor

Research & Development
Ed Carroll, Agent for National Content Directors
Liz Rutzel, Project Editor

Random House Publishing Team
Tom Russell, Publisher
Nicole Benhabib, Publishing Manager
Elham Shahabat, Publishing Assistant
Ellen L. Reed, Production Manager
Alison Stoltzfus, Associate Managing Editor

Acknowledgments

I dedicate this book to my husband Robert, for his unfailing mental, emotional, and physical support; to my children, James, Nicholas, Ian, and Rose, for redefining my role as a teacher; and to my parents, Richard and Barbara Lewandowski, for giving me the faith to believe that I can do whatever I set out to do. I love you all.

Thanks to Paul Kanarek for more help than I can list here.

The Princeton Review would like to acknowledge and thank Kim Howie, Emma Parker, Mary Kinzel, and Effie Hadjiioannou for their work on the 2009–2010 edition of this book.

Special thanks to Adam Robinson, who conceived of and perfected the Joe Bloggs approach to standardized tests and many of the other successful techniques used by The Princeton Review.

Contents

Part I
Orientation

Chapter 1
Introduction

WHAT ARE THE SAT SUBJECT TESTS?

They are a series of one-hour exams administered by Educational Testing Service (ETS). Unlike the SAT, the SAT Subject Tests are designed to measure specific knowledge in specific areas. There are many different tests in many different subject areas, such as biology, history, French, and math. They are scored separately on a 200–800 scale.

HOW ARE THE SAT SUBJECT TESTS USED BY COLLEGE ADMISSIONS?

Because the tests are given in specific areas, colleges use them as another piece of admissions information and, often, to decide whether an applicant can be exempted from college requirements. For example, a certain score may excuse you from a basic English class or a foreign language requirement.

SHOULD I TAKE THE SAT SUBJECT TESTS? HOW MANY? WHEN?

About one-third of the colleges that require SAT I scores also require that you take two or three SAT Subject Tests. Your first order of business is to start reading those college catalogs. College guidebooks, admissions offices, and guidance counselors should have this information as well.

As to which tests you should take, the answer is simple:

1. Take those Subject Tests that you will do well on.
2. Take the tests that the colleges you are applying to may require you to take.
    The best possible situation, of course, is when the two match.

Some colleges have specific requirements, others do not. Again, start asking questions before you start taking tests. Once you find out which tests are required, if any, part of your decision making is done. The next step is to find out which of the tests will show your particular strengths and to contact colleges to see which tests they suggest or require. Evaluate your own strengths and skills. Possibilities range from English literature, U.S. or world history, biology, chemistry, and physics to a variety of foreign languages.

As for when, take tests that are as close as possible to the corresponding coursework you may be doing. If you plan to take the SAT Chemistry Test, for example, and you are currently taking chemistry in high school, don't postpone the test until next year.

WHEN ARE THE SAT SUBJECT TESTS OFFERED?

In general, you can take from one to three Subject Tests per test date in October, November, December, January, May, and June at test sites across the country. Not all subjects are offered at each administration, so check the dates carefully.

HOW DO I REGISTER FOR THE TESTS?

To register by mail, pick up a registration form and *Student Bulletin* at your guidance office. You can also register at the College Board website at www.college-board.com. This site contains other useful information such as the test dates and fees. If you have questions, you can talk to a representative at the College Board by calling 609-771-7600.

You may have your scores sent to you, to your school, and to four colleges of your choice. Additional score reports will be sent to additional colleges for, you guessed it, additional money. The scores take about six weeks to arrive.

WHAT'S A GOOD SCORE?

That's hard to say, exactly. A good score is one that falls within the range of scores the college of your choice usually accepts or looks for. However, if your score falls below the normal score range for Podunk University, that doesn't mean you won't get into Podunk University. Schools are usually fairly flexible in what they are willing to look at as a "good" score for a certain student.

Along with your score, you will also receive a percentile rank. That number tells you how you fit in with the other test takers. In other words, a percentile rank of 60 means that 40 percent of the test takers scored above you and 60 percent scored below you.

WHAT IS THE PRINCETON REVIEW?

The Princeton Review is a test-preparation company based in New York City. We have branches across the country and abroad. We've developed the techniques you'll find in our books, courses, and online resources by analyzing actual exams and testing their effectiveness with our students. What makes our techniques unique is our approach. We base our principles on the same ones used by the people who write the tests. We don't want you to waste your time with superfluous information; we'll give you just the information you'll need to get great score improvements. You'll learn to recognize and comprehend the relatively small amount of information that's actually tested. You'll also learn to avoid common traps, to think like the test writers, to find answers to questions you're unsure of, and to budget your time effectively.

You need to do only two things: trust the techniques, and practice, practice, practice.

CRACKING THE SAT BIOLOGY E/M SUBJECT TEST

This book is for students who want to raise their scores on the SAT Biology E/M Subject Test. At The Princeton Review, we know what standardized test makers are up to. That's because we study their tests. We know how these tests are put together, and we'll use that information to help you raise your score.

How exactly will we do that? In two ways:

1. We'll show you how to approach the test strategically.
2. We'll teach you the biology you need to know to do well on the exam.

TO E OR NOT TO E?

On the day of the test, you will decide to take the Biology E (Ecology) test or the Biology M (Molecular Biology) test. You may not take both tests on the same test day. Here's how you should decide which test to take:

Take the Biology E test if you are more comfortable with questions about energy flow, biological interactions, and populations and communities. This section of the biology test is focused on ecology.

Take the Biology M test if you are more comfortable with topics such as biochemistry, cellular biology, and processes such as photosynthesis and respiration. This section of the test concentrates on molecular biology.

POINT 1: APPROACHING THE TEST STRATEGICALLY

You can improve your score on any multiple-choice exam by knowing a few basic strategies and test-taking techniques. The SAT Biology E/M Subject Test is no different. You should study the types of questions that show up on the exam, you should be wise to their design, and you should be familiar with the techniques that systematically lead to correct answers.

When you sit down to take the SAT Biology E/M Subject Test, you'll see some questions whose answers you don't know right away. Without knowing the techniques that improve your chances of getting the correct answer, you might panic. In Chapter 2 of this book, we'll show you eight strategies that will help you outsmart the SAT Biology E/M Subject Test. Learn our strategies, and if you do see an unexpected question or a question that tests an unfamiliar topic, you won't panic. Why? Because you have the ammunition you need to improve your chances of getting the right answer.

Practice and Practice Tests

This book is interactive. We rehearse you over and over again on the subjects and strategies we teach. We don't present a long array of drill questions at the end of a chapter. Instead, we watch your progress paragraph by paragraph, page by page. We take what you need to know and drive it into your head, word by word, and sentence by sentence.

We also present two full-length practice SAT Biology E/M Subject Tests in Chapters 16 and 18. They're complete with solutions and explanations that don't just give you the right answer but also remind you of the strategies and techniques you should be applying to help you solve the question.

Should I Buy Practice Material from ETS?

It's not a bad idea. If you want to take additional tests beyond the ones we provide, then buy the *Official Guide to the SAT II: Subject Tests*, which is published by the College Board. You can go to the College Board's website, www.collegeboard.com, for more information and practice questions. Take the SAT Biology E/M SAT Subject Test and see how much easier it is after you've read and studied this book.

POINT 2: TEACHING YOU THE BIOLOGY YOU NEED TO KNOW FOR THE EXAM

ETS says its SAT Biology E/M Subject Test covers, among many other topics, aerobic respiration, anaerobic respiration, and the biochemical differences between the two.

If you sat with your biology textbook and read about these subjects, you'd read about a whole lot of information that definitely will not be tested. You'd read about the roles of various enzymes, coenzymes, and cofactors. You'd see pictures like the one on the following page.

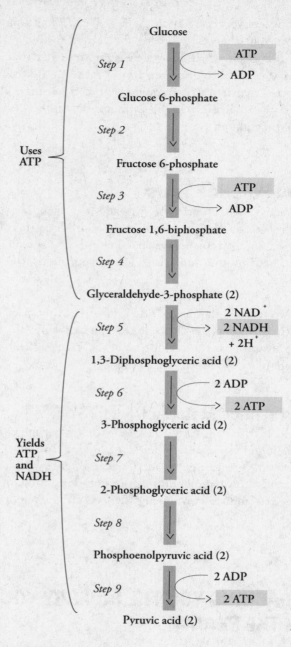

And you'd read text like this:

Glycolysis is a prime illustration of the manner in which vital biochemical processes occur through a series of steps. The complete catabolism of glucose may be considered to embody nine steps. We'll examine the details of glycolysis and notice that the 6-carbon skeleton of the glucose molecule is sequentially degraded, each step being catalyzed by a specific enzyme, to produce adenosine triphosphate (ATP) via the phosphorylation of adenosine diphosphate. Blah, blah, blah . . . acetyl CoA . . . blah, blah, blah . . . NADH and NAD$^+$, blah, blah, blah . . . FADH$_2$ . . . blah, blah, blah . . . cytochrome carrier system, blah, blah, blah . . .

The text would go on and on, scaring and boring you, but offering nothing that would help you raise your test score. You'd become so sick of it that you'd stop reading (which is fine, because reading your textbook might not help you raise your score anyway).

When we teach you about aerobic and anaerobic respiration, we'll tell you exactly what you have to know, and a little bit beyond (just to make sure there are no surprises on test day). As we do that, we drill you with questions and quizzes so you can check your understanding as you go along. The details that won't be tested are left out so that you can focus on understanding and remembering the main points: the material that will be tested. We'll summarize and list these important points for you so that they stand out.

At the end, you'd know that both aerobic and anaerobic respiration involve breaking down glucose to form ATP. You'd also know that aerobic respiration has to do with

(1)   the presence of oxygen,
(2)   more ATP,
(3)   the Krebs cycle,
(4)   the electron transport chain, and
(5)   oxidative phosphorylation.

And you'd know that anaerobic respiration has to do with

(1)   the absence of oxygen,
(2)   less ATP, and
(3)   lactic acid.

Even without completely understanding the biochemical differences between the two processes, these simple associations can help you answer questions. Review the few summary lines above about aerobic and anaerobic respiration, then answer these two SAT Biology E/M Subject Test–like questions:

Among the following, which is associated with
BOTH aerobic and anaerobic respiration?

  I. ATP production
 II. Krebs cycle
III. Oxidative phosphorylation

(A) I only
(B) II only
(C) I and II only
(D) II and III only
(E) I, II, and III

Which of the following substances is produced as a result of anaerobic respiration but NOT of aerobic respiration?

(A) Carbon dioxide
(B) Lactic acid
(C) ATP
(D) Glucose
(E) Glycogen

The answer to the first question is **A**. Both anaerobic and aerobic respiration produce ATP, but only aerobic respiration is associated with the Krebs cycle and oxidative phosphorylation. The answer to the second question is **B**. Anaerobic respiration is associated with the production of lactic acid, and aerobic respiration is not. (Note that on this question, you may not have known about carbon dioxide or glycogen. But you did know that you could eliminate ATP and glucose as choices, and that lactic acid fit the criteria described in the question, making it a better choice than carbon dioxide or glycogen. We'll talk more about this technique later on.)

Our Job and Your Job

This book is designed to help you raise your SAT Biology E/M Subject Test score. It's written, it's published, and you're holding it in your hands. That means our job is done. Your job is to read it, study it, tackle the questions and practice exams, and learn what it has to teach. We had fun doing our job, and believe it or not, you'll have fun doing yours. So, let the fun begin!

For book updates, links to more information, and last-minute test changes, visit our website at **www.princetonreview.com/college-education.aspx**.

Chapter 2
The Exam Format, Question Types, and Strategies

THE FORMAT

The SAT Biology E/M Subject Test consists of a total of 100 questions: a common core of 60 questions followed by 20 questions in each of the two specialty sections. Everyone who takes this exam has to answer the 60 core questions, but you get to choose the specialty section you feel more comfortable with: Ecology or Molecular Biology. Altogether, then, you answer only 80 of the 100 questions: the 60 core questions and the 20 questions from your chosen specialty group. Detailed instructions for choosing your specialty section will be given to you on the day of the exam.

THE QUESTION TYPES

There are three types of questions that are used in the SAT Biology E/M Subject Test:

- Classification questions
- Five-choice questions
- Laboratory five-choice questions

Classification Questions

This type of question is sort of like a little "matching test." A list of five words or phrases is set up, lettered A through E. For each list you get three or four questions, with question numbers next to them. But the questions aren't really questions, they're phrases—half-sentences. Your job is to match the phrase in the question with the word or phrase that appears in the list A through E. Here's an example:

Directions: Each set of lettered choices below refers to the numbered statements immediately following it. Select the one lettered choice that best fits each statement and then fill in the corresponding oval on the answer sheet. A choice may be used once, more than once, or not at all in each set.

Questions 1-3

    (A) Thyroid
    (B) Adrenal cortex
    (C) Pancreas
    (D) Ovaries
    (E) Parathyroid

1. Secretes glucagon

2. Regulates metabolism

3. Structure producing female gametes

The answers are **C**, **A**, and **D**. But don't worry about the answers right now. We just want you to know how this type of question looks. You'll probably get about four of these little "matching tests"—about 16 classification questions in all—when you take the SAT Biology E/M Subject Test.

Five-Choice Questions

The **first type** really is ordinary-looking. Here are a couple of examples:

Directions: Each of the questions or incomplete statements below is followed by five suggested answers or completions. Select the one that is BEST in each case, and then fill in the corresponding oval on the answer sheet.

Which of the following terms describes the process by which the plasma membrane moves substances inward, against a concentration gradient?

    (A) Facilitated diffusion
    (B) Active transport
    (C) Osmosis
    (D) Simple diffusion
    (E) Autotrophism

The endocrine organ that secretes antidiuretic hormone is the

(A) adrenal cortex
(B) pancreas
(C) posterior pituitary gland
(D) kidney
(E) liver

The correct answers are **B** and **C**, but it doesn't matter right now whether you know that. (You *will* know, after you've finished studying this book.) Again, we just want you to know what this type of question looks like.

The **second type** of five-choice question is a twist on the first type, called a LEAST/EXCEPT/NOT question. This is a basic multiple-choice question, except that in this case you're looking for the *wrong* answer—the one that doesn't fit the statement given in the question. Here's an example:

All of the following are functions of the liver EXCEPT

(A) producing bile
(B) storing glycogen
(C) making blood proteins
(D) secreting insulin
(E) storing vitamins

In this question, the wrong statement (and therefore the correct answer choice) is **D**. The liver does everything listed except secrete insulin; that's a function of the pancreas. (You'll know that, of course, after you read Chapter 10.)

The **third type** of five-choice question is a I, II, III question, such as the following:

Which of the following nitrogenous bases are found in DNA?

   I. Thymine
  II. Cytosine
 III. Uracil

(A) I only
(B) II only
(C) I and II only
(D) I and III only
(E) I, II, and III

The correct answer here is **C**, but again, don't worry about that now.

The **fourth type** of five-choice question presents a numbered diagram with two or three questions following it:

Questions 25-26 below refer to the following diagram.

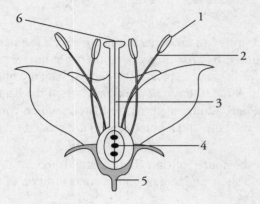

25. Which structure contains female monoploid nuclei?

(A) 1
(B) 2
(C) 3
(D) 4
(E) 5

26. Pollen grains are produced by

(A) 1
(B) 3
(C) 4
(D) 5
(E) 6

The answers for the above questions are **D** and **A**. The core exam will present you with about 10 to 12 of these five-choice questions, and each of the specialty sections may have another four to six.

Laboratory Five-Choice Questions

These questions are designed to see if you can think logically about biological experiments. First you're told about an experiment. You are usually shown a figure, graph, or data table that goes along with it. Then you're asked two to four five-choice questions about the experiment. The questions can be in any of the three formats already discussed. Here's an example:

Questions 30-31 refer to an experiment in which the process of evolution is studied by working with anaerobic bacteria.
A small colony of bacteria is placed on Plate 1, which contains a suitable culture medium. After 10 days, approximately half the bacteria are removed from Plate 1 and transferred to Plate 2, which contains both a suitable culture medium and a potent antibiotic related to penicillin.

30. Over the course of time, both Plates 1 and 2 should show an increase in the concentration of

    (A) ADP
    (B) carbon monoxide
    (C) lactic acid
    (D) Krebs cycle enzymes
    (E) oxygen

31. Which of the following graphs of time versus population is most likely to describe the growth of the colony after inoculating Plate 1?

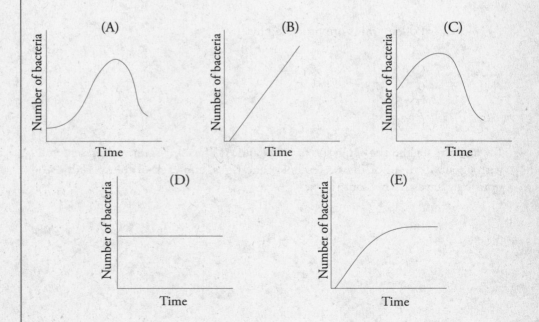

The answers for the previous questions are **C** and **E**. The questions associated with experiments require that you be able to (1) read a graph or data table, and/or (2) exercise a little logic with the biology you know.

The core exam has about 25 to 30 laboratory five-choice questions (about five or six different experiment descriptions) and the specialty sections each have about 14 to 16 of these questions (about three or four different experiment descriptions).

THE STRATEGIES

Strategy 1: Study the Right Stuff in the Right Way

Biology is a vast subject. In other words, there is a LOT that could potentially end up on the SAT Biology E/M Subject Test—like everything that's in your biology textbook and more. So should you sit down and read your textbook cover to cover and memorize all of it? NO!

We've mentioned this before—your textbook goes into a lot of detail that will not be present on the SAT Biology E/M Subject Test. Memorizing it would be a waste of time.

At The Princeton Review, we've studied the SAT Biology E/M Subject Test, and we know the subjects that are most likely to appear on it. In this book, we've taken these topics and explained them in a way that is easy to understand and remember, and we've provided you with summaries of the most important points. Many of the little details that will not be tested are left out. This way you can get the big picture and understand the general concepts, without bogging down your mind with little details. You'll be clear-headed and confident; that's what will help you raise your score, and that's what we provide.

You're probably wondering: "What are the subjects that are likely to appear on the SAT Biology E/M Subject Test?" We'll be glad to list these subjects for you here and now:

- **Cellular and Molecular** Biology, including
  - Biological chemistry
  - Cell structure and organization
  - Enzymes
  - Cellular respiration
  - Mitosis
  - DNA structure and function, including replication
  - RNA structure and function, including protein translation

Percent of the test = 12% (if taking Biology M, 37%)

- **Classical Genetics**, including
  - Meiosis
  - Mendelian genetics
  - Inheritance patterns
  - Pedigrees

Percent of the test = 10%

- **Evolution and Diversity**, including
  - The origin of life
  - Mechanics of evolution
  - Natural selection
  - Patterns of evolution
  - Speciation
  - Classification and diversity of the five-kingdom system (prokaryotes, protists, fungi, plants, and animals)

Percent of the test = 11%

- **Organismal Biology**, including
  - The structure and function of animals (nervous system, endocrine system, circulatory system, blood typing, respiratory system, digestive system, urinary system, skeletal system, muscular system, skin, reproduction, and development)
  - The structure and function of plants (tissues, photosynthesis, transport, and reproduction)
  - Behavior and learning in animals
  - Symbiotic relationships
  - The structure and function of microorganisms (fungi, bacteria, and viruses)

Percent of the test = 30%

- **Ecology**, including
  - Population growth
  - Community interactions
  - Food and energy pyramids
  - Succession
  - Ecosystems
  - Nutrient cycles
  - Biomes

Percent of the test = 12% (if taking Biology E, 37%)

As you look at the list, you're probably thinking two things: first—"Wow, that's a lot"; and second—"That looks like a list of ordinary biology textbook topics." Well, yes, and . . . yes! We agree with you on both counts.

But Here's the Deal

Even though it seems like a lot of material, the test writers cannot possibly cover every single topic that's on that list. More specifically, they cannot cover every topic on that list in great detail. That's good news for you, because it means you don't need an in-depth, detailed understanding of every topic. You just need to know the basic concepts: the "big picture." You're free to study *concepts* without cramming *details*.

And that's good news for us, too, because it means that the *way* we teach you these topics is NOT the way an ordinary biology textbook would teach them. We're free to summarize and elaborate on the major points without hashing through all the details. It's good news all around.

Strategy 2: Practice the Right Stuff at the Right Time

Chapters 3 through 15 of this book teach you the biology you need to know for the SAT Biology E/M Subject Test and include interactive questions all along the way so you can immediately take the knowledge you've gained and practice it. Chapters 16 through 19 provide two full-length practice SAT Biology E/M Subject Tests along with annotated solutions to help you figure out your mistakes and remind you of the strategies you should be using to tackle the questions.

Strategy 3: Easy Stuff First

All the questions on the SAT Biology E/M Subject Test—easy and hard—carry the same credit. The ETS scoring machines don't know the difference between an easy question and a hard question, so answering a hard question correctly doesn't do you one more bit of good than answering an easy question. Therefore, it makes sense not to waste time on the harder questions when you could be answering easy ones.

Start at the beginning of a section and answer as many questions as you can, skipping the ones you find more difficult. When you reach the end of that section, go to the next section and do the same. Once you've answered all the relatively easy questions in all the sections, go back to each section and start answering the harder ones (although after reading this book, hopefully you won't find too many of them very hard). Don't attack the test in the order of its numbered questions, but in the order of its difficulty.

Important: Make sure when you skip questions that you fill in the correct number oval on your answer sheet! We don't want you to lose your hard-earned points because you made a simple numbering error on your answer sheet. Circle the question in your test booklet so you'll be able to find it easily when you go back, and double-check it against your answer sheet.

Strategy 4: Take a Guess, but Guess Smart

You probably know that you get 1 point for each correct answer and lose 1/4 point for each incorrect answer. The ETS says that this is to keep random guessing from increasing your score. It does, and this is why. Each question has five possible answers. If you were to guess randomly, you'd pick the right answer one out of five times. If you guessed randomly on five different questions, you'd answer one correctly and four incorrectly. You'd get 1 point for your correct answer, and lose 1/4 point for each incorrect answer. Because you answered four questions incorrectly, you'd lose one full point. The point you gained by your random correct answer is lost by your random incorrect answers.

However, if you can eliminate some wrong answer choices, guessing from the remaining choices will definitely help you raise your score. Let's say you were able to eliminate two of the five possible choices as wrong. You'd have three remaining choices to guess from and would guess correctly one out of three times. Let's say you did this on six different questions. By eliminating two wrong answer choices from each question and guessing from the rest, you'd answer two of the six questions correctly and four incorrectly. You'd gain 2 points for your correct answers and lose 1 point (1/4 times 4) for your incorrect answers; in other words, you gain 1 net point!

What if you were able to eliminate three of the five possible choices? You'd have a fifty-fifty chance of getting the correct answer. If you were able to do this on four questions, you'd answer two of them correctly and two of them incorrectly. You'd get 2 points for your correct answers and lose 1/2 point (1/4 times 2) for your incorrect answers, a net gain of 1-1/2 points!

Chapters 3 through 15 of this book teach you the biology you will need to help you eliminate wrong answer choices. By "guessing smart" in this way, you will definitely raise your score.

What If I Can't Eliminate Any Wrong Answer Choices?

If you can't cross off any answer choices as wrong and really have no idea what you're doing, leave the question blank. You can leave a number of questions blank and still do well. For instance, omitting about one-third of the questions (that's a raw score of around 55–60) will still get you a score around 600.

And Keep This in Mind

Because the amount of material that could potentially be tested is large, occasionally a question comes up on the exam that was unexpected and therefore might not be covered in this book (although it's rather unlikely, because we do cover a LOT). **Don't be nervous!** If you come across a question that you were completely not expecting and truly have no idea what the answer is, just leave it blank. As we said above, you can leave a number of questions blank and still do well. We just want to let you know of this possibility, so you don't get stressed and blow the test because of one or two unexpected questions.

Strategy 5: Choosing the "Wrong" Answer—LEAST/EXCEPT/NOT Questions

This type of question can easily confuse you because you're being asked to choose the incorrect statement, or the "wrong answer." In other words, every answer choice is true except for one; that's the one you have to pick out.

Actually picking the incorrect statement isn't the hard part. The hard part is remembering that you have to pick the incorrect statement. Often you're so used to picking a true statement for an answer that it becomes very easy to grab the first correct statement you see (more on that later). A good way to remember that you're being asked to choose the exception is to circle the word "LEAST," "EXCEPT," or "NOT" and then draw a vertical line down through the answer choices. This makes a nice visual cue that you should be searching for the answer choice that doesn't fit the question. Here's an example:

All of the following statements are true about taiga EXCEPT

(A) it is found in the northern regions of the globe
(B) it has permanently frozen topsoil
(C) it is primarily made of evergreen trees
(D) fauna include moose and bear
(E) its trees do not drop their leaves in the winter

The correct choice here, by the way, is **B** (choice B is wrong as far as taiga is concerned). Choices A, C, D, and E are all true of the biome known as taiga, but B is true of the biome known as tundra.

Strategy 6: I, II, III—You're Out!

As we said before, some of the questions will look like this:

Which of the following is (are)… ?

    I. blah, blah, blah…
   II. blah, blah, blah…
  III. blah, blah, blah…

(A) I only
(B) II only
(C) I and II only
(D) I and III only
(E) I, II, and III

When you see questions like these, think logically about throwing out wrong answer choices, even if you don't know the right one. Here's how you do that: Forget biology for a minute and look at the question on the following page.

Among the following, which is (are) ordinarily served as a dessert?

    I. Fish filet
   II. Pastry
  III. College ice

(A) I only
(B) II only
(C) I and II only
(D) II and III only
(E) I, II, and III

Never heard of "college ice"? It doesn't matter. You can still use strategy to raise your score. You know that fish (option I) isn't a dessert. Eliminate all answers that mention it. A, C, and E are gone, which means that you're left with just B and D. You've got a fifty-fifty chance of guessing correctly. (Just for your information, "college ice" is an old term for "ice cream sundae," so the correct answer is **D**.) Do that with ten questions and you'll get about five of them right.

Let's try it with the DNA question we presented earlier:

Which of the following nitrogenous bases are found in DNA?

    I. Thymine
   II. Cytosine
  III. Uracil

(A) I only
(B) II only
(C) I and II only
(D) I and III only
(E) I, II, and III

Let's say you know for sure that thymine (option I) and cytosine (option II) are in DNA, but you're unsure of uracil (option III). You can eliminate choices that do not contain both options I and II. That means you eliminate choices A, B, and D. Again, you're left with a fifty-fifty chance. What if you were sure that uracil wasn't in DNA, but didn't know about the others? You could eliminate choices that contain option III—in this case, choices D and E. Not as good as a fifty-fifty chance, but still better than one out of five. (The correct answer here is **C**.) When it comes to the I, II, III type of question, use this strategy. It's a real score-raiser.

Strategy 7: Avoid the Camouflage Trap

When you learn something, whether it's biology or anything else, you usually learn it with certain words in mind. For instance, perhaps you think of an "ovum" as a "haploid gamete produced by an ovary." Okay, that's fine. But suppose you're totally attached to *those* particular words. Think what would happen if you get a question like this:

Which of the following correctly describe(s) an ovum?

    I. It secretes luteinizing hormone.
   II. It is made by a gonad.
  III. It is a monoploid cell.

(A) I only
(B) II only
(C) I and II only
(D) II and III only
(E) I, II, and III

You know what an ovum is, but this question doesn't describe it in a way that's familiar to you. You know your biology but might not know to answer this question with **D**. Why? Because you fell into the camouflage trap.

Don't expect the test writers to use your words. You might express an idea in one way, and they might express it in another. Keep the concepts you know in your mind, and don't get too attached to the words you usually use to express them. In the example above,

> **monoploid**   *is camouflage for* **haploid**
>
> and
>
> **gonad**   *is camouflage for* **ovary**

Let's take another look at the question. First of all, you know that gametes do not secrete hormones (and if you don't now, you will after reading Chapter 10). Already you can eliminate choices A, C, and E, because option I is false. Take a look at choices B and D. Both of them contain option II; therefore, option II must be true. Don't even bother looking at it; go straight to option III. You know that haploid cells have only a single set of chromosomes (again, if you don't know now, you will later), and you should know that *mono* is a prefix that means "one." So it's a good bet that "monoploid" refers to a cell with only a single set of chromosomes—essentially the same meaning as "haploid." You can choose D with confidence.

You Can Avoid the Camouflage Trap

To avoid this trap, keep some simple rules in mind:

1. **Don't take the test with blinders on your brain.** Remember, there's more than one way to say the same thing.
2. **Don't become unglued** just because the right answer to a question doesn't leap out at you, even if it's something you've studied and memorized.

3. **Relax.** Realize that the right answer is probably camouflaged by words that are different from the ones you have in mind. Eliminate as many wrong answer choices as you can, and think logically and calmly about your remaining choices. You may find then that the right answer *does* leap out at you.

Strategy 8: Avoid the Temptation Trap—Predict an Answer

Suppose we gave this question to a seven-year-old child:

> Which of the following best characterizes a
> simple carbohydrate?
>
> (A) It is metabolized without enzymes.
> (B) It serves as an organic catalyst.
> (C) George Washington was the first U.S. president.
> (D) It is the product of multiple peptide bonding.
> (E) It is a molecule containing only carbon,
>   hydrogen, and oxygen in a ratio of 1:2:1,
>   respectively.

The child won't know what any of this means but probably will know that George Washington was the first U.S. president. So, not knowing what else to do, this is the answer that the child will choose; it's something known, so it *seems* right. (The right answer happens to be E. You'll learn about carbohydrates in the next chapter.) The problem is that even though choice C is true, it fails to answer the question.

What's That Got to Do with Me and This Test?

Plenty. When you take the test, there will be a lot of things that you'll know and some things that you won't. When you get a tough question and you think you're lost, you might look for a familiar face and grab at an answer that makes a statement you've heard before, even if that statement doesn't answer the question.

Let's suppose you know all about the human heart and circulatory system. You know that

- most arteries carry oxygen-rich blood
- most veins carry oxygen-poor blood
- the pulmonary artery carries oxygen-poor blood from the right side of the heart to the lungs
- the pulmonary veins carry oxygen-rich blood from the lungs to the left side of the heart

(As usual, if you don't know these facts now, don't worry—you will.)

Now suppose you got this question on test day:

A sample of blood is taken from an unknown site in a human patient. The blood shows an oxygen content equivalent roughly to that of the venous and not the arterial circulation. Among the following, which statement best applies to the blood that was drawn?

(A) It was drawn from the pulmonary vein and is rich in oxygen.

(B) It was drawn from an alveolus and is rich in oxygen.

(C) It was drawn from large branches of the pulmonary artery.

(D) It was drawn from the superior vena cava and will enter the heart at the left ventricle.

(E) It was drawn from the left ventricle and will leave the heart via the aorta.

If the question seems too hard to figure out or the right answer doesn't leap out at you, you might decide to pick choice E because it rings true. Blood that leaves the left ventricle *does* enter the aorta. So E *sounds* right, but E is wrong because it *doesn't answer the question.*

When you find yourself running toward an answer just because it makes a familiar statement, stop and think. Is the question long and confusing? Are you jumping for the first right-sounding statement you see? Are you actually trying to answer the question without knowing what the question *is*?

If the answers are yes, then you're probably *not* really finding the question hard, and you probably *do* know what the answer is. You just don't know what the question is. So what do you do? You swallow hard, you grit your teeth, and you get to know the question. Take it apart piece by piece and figure out what it's asking. Predict an answer, and eliminate choices that contradict your predicted answer. Let's look again at the blood question, piece by piece.

A sample of blood is taken from an unknown site in a human patient.

- We may be asked to determine where the sample was taken from.

The blood shows an oxygen content equivalent roughly to that of the venous and not the arterial circulation.

- So that means that the blood is relatively oxygen-poor.

Among the following, which statement best applies to the blood that was drawn?

Well, we know that it's oxygen-poor. So BEFORE looking at the answer choices, let's see if we can come up with some possible locations for oxygen-poor blood. We know that most veins carry oxygen-poor blood, so veins are probably a good choice. We know that the right side of the heart contains oxygen-poor blood on its way to the lungs, and we know that the pulmonary artery delivers that oxygen-poor blood to the lungs. Keeping this in mind, let's look at the answer choices:

(A) *It was drawn from the pulmonary vein and is rich in oxygen.*
- This can be eliminated because it discusses oxygen-rich blood.

(B) *It was drawn from an alveolus and is rich in oxygen.*
- This can be eliminated for the same reason as choice A—it discusses oxygen-rich blood.

(C) *It was drawn from large branches of the pulmonary artery.*
- Hmm. This is a possibility, because we know that the pulmonary artery carries oxygen-poor blood. Let's look at the other choices to make sure that there isn't a better one.

(D) *It was drawn from the superior vena cava and will enter the heart at the left ventricle.*
- Okay, this choice is false because we know that blood from the superior vena cava enters the heart at the right ventricle, so eliminate it.

(E) *It was drawn from the left ventricle and will leave the heart via the aorta.*
- This statement is true, but is this one of our predicted locations for oxygen-poor blood? *No.* The left side of the heart carries blood rich in oxygen. Eliminate it.

That leaves us with choice C, the correct answer, and you knew that, but you might have chosen something else. Why? Because of the temptation trap. The question and answer choices seemed confusing at first, and choice E seemed safe because it's a true statement. But even a true statement can be wrong if it doesn't answer the question.

You Can Avoid the Temptation Trap
To avoid this trap, keep these simple rules in mind:

1. **Don't pick an answer choice before** you know what the question is asking.
2. **Relax.** Take the question apart piece by piece.
3. **Predict an answer.**
4. **Go through the answer choices systematically**, eliminating those that are false or don't answer the question.

Another Thing to Remember

You may have noticed already that some of the questions on the SAT Biology E/M Subject Test require you to take two or more items of knowledge and put them together to come up with an answer. The last question we considered was like that. You had to know that venous circulation is relatively oxygen-poor compared to arterial circulation, and you had to know that the right side of the heart and the pulmonary artery carry oxygen-poor blood to the lungs. You also had to know a little bit about heart anatomy. It was almost like having three questions in one.

Following the rules for avoiding the temptation trap will help you sort out the separate bits of knowledge you need to correctly answer the question. By taking the question a piece at a time, you can organize your thoughts better to predict an answer. Let's try it on this next question:

> An experimenter subjects a facultative anaerobic bacterium to oxygen-rich conditions between times 1 and 2 and then to oxygen-poor conditions between times 2 and 3. Which of the following changes will most likely take place between the two time periods?
>
> (A) Oxygen consumption will increase.
> (B) ATP production will cease.
> (C) Carbon dioxide production will increase and ATP production will increase.
> (D) Carbon dioxide production will increase and lactic acid production will decrease.
> (E) ATP production will decrease and lactic acid production will increase.

Take the question apart, piece by piece:

> *An experimenter subjects a facultative anaerobic bacterium…*

- This bacterium can survive in both oxygen-rich and oxygen-poor conditions (this information is in Chapter 13). Oxygen-rich means Krebs cycle, more ATP, and carbon dioxide as waste. Oxygen-poor means fermentation, less ATP, and lactic acid as waste.

> *to oxygen-rich conditions…and then to oxygen-poor conditions…*

- Aha! So the bacteria will have to switch from the Krebs cycle to fermentation to survive.

> *Which of the following changes will most likely take place…*

- Before looking at the answer choices, you should predict: ATP will decrease, and lactic acid will increase.

Now let's look at the choices:

  (A) *Oxygen consumption will increase.*
- This is not possible, because oxygen availability is going down.

  (B) *ATP production will cease.*
- No, it will just decrease.

  (C) *Carbon dioxide production will increase and ATP production will increase.*
- We predicted that ATP would decrease, not increase. (Note that the first part of this statement is false, too. Carbon dioxide production will decrease, not increase. But remember, if part of an answer is false, the whole thing is false. You don't need to waste time thinking about the other part.)

  (D) *Carbon dioxide production will increase and lactic acid production will decrease.*
- We predicted that lactic acid production will increase, not decrease. (Same rule as above for the first part of this statement.)

  (E) *ATP production will decrease and lactic acid production will increase.*
- Here, finally, is our predicted answer. E is, in fact, the correct answer choice.

STRATEGY SUMMARY

Let's do a quick review of the eight strategies we've talked about:

- **Strategy 1: Study the Right Stuff in the Right Way**
  You've already begun this strategy—you bought this book.
- **Strategy 2: Practice the Right Stuff at the Right Time**
  Quiz yourself as you move along through the material, not in one lump at the end of a chapter. Use the full-length practice SAT Biology E/M Subject Tests as a final check of your knowledge.
- **Strategy 3: Easy Stuff First**
  Attack the test in the order of its difficulty, doing the easy questions first and skipping the harder ones until later. Make sure to keep this straight on your answer sheet.
- **Strategy 4: Take a Guess, but Guess Smart**
  Eliminate wrong answer choices to increase your probability of choosing the correct answer. Only omit questions for which you cannot eliminate any answer choices.

- **Strategy 5: Choosing the "Wrong" Answer—LEAST/EXCEPT/ NOT Questions**

    Circle the word "LEAST," "EXCEPT," or "NOT" and draw a vertical line through the answer choices. This makes the question stand out so you can remember to choose the statement that does *not* fit the question.

- **Strategy 6: I, II, III—You're Out!**

    On I, II, III questions, eliminate answer choices as you decide whether the options are true or false. For example, if you've decided that option I is false, eliminate all answer choices containing option I. If you've decided that option II is true, eliminate all answer choices that do *not* contain option II.

- **Strategy 7: Avoid the Camouflage Trap**

    Remember that there's more than one way to say something. If a correct answer isn't immediately apparent, calmly look for words that mean the same thing as the words you've memorized.

- **Strategy 8: Avoid the Temptation Trap—Predict an Answer**

    Don't choose an answer before you're sure of the question. Just because a statement is true doesn't mean it's the right answer. Break down difficult questions piece by piece and predict an answer. Then eliminate choices that conflict with your predicted answer.

Special Tips for Laboratory Five-Choice Questions

There are, unfortunately, hundreds and hundreds of potential experiments that could show up on the SAT Biology E/M Subject Test. It would be impossible to list or describe them all. Often the questions for these experiments deal with your ability to evaluate situations, draw conclusions, identify problems, suggest hypotheses, and interpret data. There are, however, some common threads in many of the experiments described on the exam.

1. **The Control:** You should be clear on what a control is and should be able to pick it out from the group of plants, or mosquitoes, or fish, or humans, or cells, or whatever is described in the experiment. The control, or control group, is treated exactly the same as all other groups **except** for the one variable the experiment is designed to test. For example, let's say that an experiment involves testing plants to see if they need nitrogen to grow. One plant, the experimental plant, would be placed in the sun, watered daily, and given a nitrogen-based fertilizer. The other plant, the control, would be placed in the sun, watered daily, and not given the fertilizer. Then the growth of the two plants would be compared to see if nitrogen had an effect.

2. **Graphs and Data Tables:** The experiments almost always contain a graph or data table. You should be able to convert information in a data table into graph form. You should recognize that a steeply sloping line indicates something that is changing rapidly, whereas a gradual slope or a horizontal line indicates a slow change or no

change at all. Finally, you should be able to retrieve data from the graph or table.

3. **Calculations:** You *do* need to be familiar with common algebraic concepts, such as proportions and ratios, and be able to apply them to the data interpretation questions that show up in the laboratory questions. There is nothing more complicated than simple multiplication or division, so you will not need a calculator.

A Word About Scoring

An overview of the scoring system is provided at the end of each practice test in this book. Please turn to pages 401 to 402 or 441 to 442 for more details.

LET'S GET GOING ALREADY!

Now that we've discussed basic strategy, we'll move on to the material! In Chapters 3 through 14, we'll review the biology that is likely to show up on the SAT Biology E/M Subject Test. In addition, each chapter includes Quick Quizzes on key concepts. Answers to those quizzes are provided in Chapter 15. So turn the page and let's get started!.

Part II
Subject Review

Chapter 3
Molecules of Biology

To understand the complex topics covered in the Biology E/M Subject Test, you must first have a general understanding of basic organic chemistry. In this chapter, we will look at organic chemistry at its most basic level—atoms, molecules, compounds—and see how it directly applies to the biological concepts you will learn about.

Atoms, Molecules, and Compounds

Atoms are the fundamental units of the physical world. Individual atoms combine in chemical reactions to form **molecules**:

$$\text{atom} + \text{atom} \rightarrow \text{molecule}$$
$$H + H \rightarrow H_2$$

Thus, a molecule is just a combination of atoms. Molecules can also react with other atoms or other molecules to form larger molecules:

$$\text{reactants} \rightarrow \text{product}$$
$$2\,H_2 + O_2 \rightarrow 2\,H_2O$$

If a molecule contains different types of atoms (as does the molecule above), it is called a **compound**. For example, CCl_4 is a compound because the molecule has both carbon and chlorine in it. On the other hand, H_2 is a molecule but is NOT a compound, because the only atoms in the molecule are hydrogen atoms. (If a molecule contains only a single type of atom, it is an **element**.)

In chemical reactions, the molecules or atoms that are interacting are called **reactants** and are found on the left side of the arrow. The **products** (the results of the interactions) are found on the right side of the arrow.

Biomolecules
Carbon is the main ingredient of organic molecules. Most molecules within a cell, other than water, are carbon based. Therefore, these molecules are sometimes called *biomolecules*. Carbon is common in living things because it has only four electrons in the highest energy level of the electron shells that surround the nucleus. Carbon can therefore form up to four bonds with other atoms.

What Organic Chemistry Means

Organic chemistry is simply the chemistry of molecules and compounds that contain carbon. Molecules and compounds that contain carbon are said to be **organic**, whereas molecules that do not contain carbon are said to be **inorganic**. There's a single exception to this rule: carbon dioxide (CO_2). Even though carbon dioxide contains carbon, it is an inorganic compound.

Quick Quiz #1

Check the appropriate boxes:

1. Water (H_2O) is an [□ **organic** □ **inorganic**] compound.

2. Cl_2 [□ **is** □ **is not**] a compound.

3. H_2O [□ **is** □ **is not**] a compound.

4. Methane (CH_4) is an [□ **organic** □ **inorganic**] compound.

5. Cl_2 [□ **is** □ **is not**] a molecule.

6. Carbon dioxide (CO_2) is an [□ **organic** □ **inorganic**] compound.

7. Products are found on the [□ **right** □ **left**] side of the arrow in a chemical reaction.

There are many organic molecules. Fortunately, as far as biology is concerned, there are only four important types of organic molecules. Most of them are very large, and they're referred to as macromolecules. The four biologically important macromolecules are the only ones you need to worry about for the SAT Biology E/M Subject Test.

The four important organic molecules are

1. proteins
2. carbohydrates
3. lipids
4. nucleic acids

These four macromolecules are **polymers**. Polymers are strings of repeated units. The individual units of polymers are called **monomers**. An example you're probably more familiar with is a string of pearls. Each individual pearl would be a monomer; strung together, the monomers form a polymer: the whole necklace. Let's take a look at the first biologically important macromolecule: protein.

Biologically Important Macromolecule #1: Protein

Proteins are polymers of **amino acids**. In other words, the monomer that makes up a protein is an amino acid. There are 20 different amino acids, and they all have the same basic structure:

The box encloses the backbone of the amino acid. It's called the backbone because this is the part of the molecule that is constant from amino acid to amino acid. All 20 amino acids contain the same backbone structure.

There are two carbon atoms in the backbone. The first is bonded to a hydrogen (H) atom on one side and an NH_2 group on the other side. The NH_2 group is called the **amino group**. The other carbon atom is bonded to an oxygen (O) atom and an OH group. Notice that the oxygen is bonded to the second carbon by a **double bond**. The COOH group is called the **carboxyl group**. If you know what the boxed structure looks like, with its amino and carboxyl group, you'll be able to recognize amino acids on the test. Take a good, long look at the structure in the box, then draw it (three times) on the next page so you'll really be familiar with it.

- Draw it:

- Draw it again:

- Draw it again:

The R-Group
The fourth bond of the central carbon in an amino acid is sometimes called the R-group. It is this side group on an amino acid that gives the amino acid its unique chemical properties.

We've already said that all 20 amino acids contain the same backbone structure. But what about the R part of the molecule? The R part of the molecule makes each amino acid different from all the others. All amino acids have the same basic backbone, but different amino acids differ with respect to R. R could be anything from a simple hydrogen atom to a whole long chain of carbon atoms with different groups bonded to them. The R part of the molecule gives the amino acid its identity.

In the amino acid glycine, R is just a hydrogen atom:

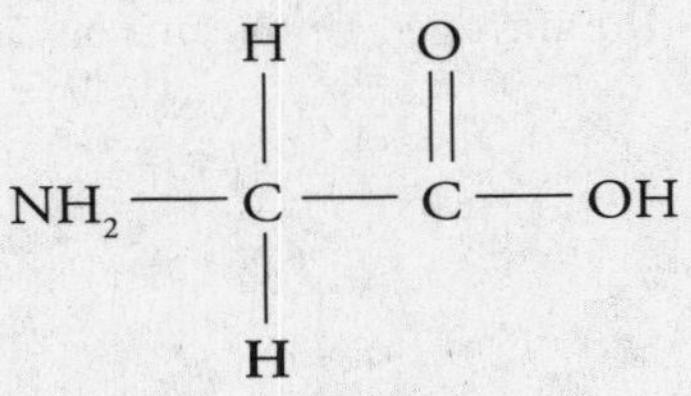

$$
\begin{array}{ccc}
 & H & O \\
 & | & \| \\
NH_2 - & C - & C - OH \qquad \textbf{Glycine} \\
 & | & \\
 & H &
\end{array}
$$

In the amino acid cysteine, R is a carbon atom and a sulfur (S) atom, along with some hydrogen atoms:

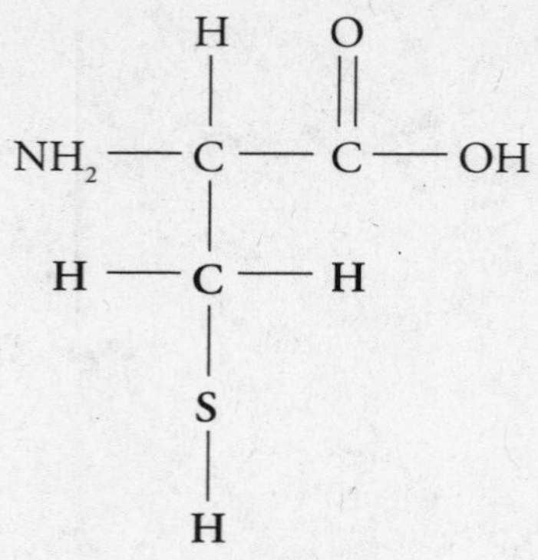

$$
\begin{array}{ccc}
& \text{H} & \text{O} \\
& | & \| \\
\text{NH}_2 \!-\! \text{C} \!-\! & \text{C} \!-\! \text{OH} \\
& | & \\
\text{H} \!-\! \text{C} \!-\! \text{H} & & \quad\text{Cysteine} \\
& | & \\
& \text{S} & \\
& | & \\
& \text{H} &
\end{array}
$$

Again, there are 20 different possibilities for R groups. You don't have to know all of them, but you should be able to recognize the backbone of an amino acid.

Amino Acids Combine to Form Proteins

Amino acids bond together in a chain to form a **protein**. Remember, a long chain of repeated units (monomers; in this case, amino acids) is called a polymer (in this case, a protein). Let's look at how two amino acids join:

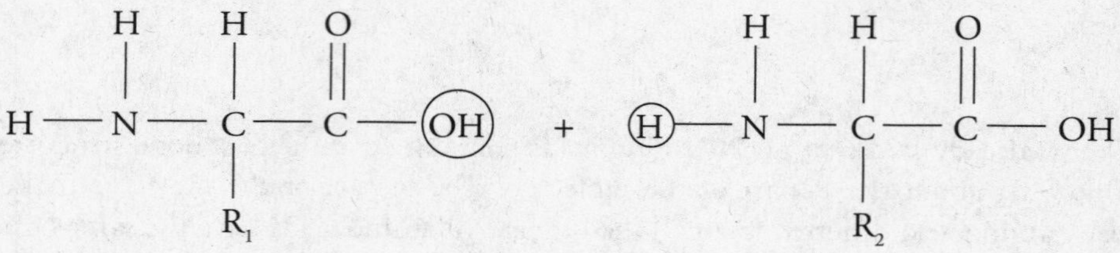

$$
\begin{array}{cccc}
& \text{H} & \text{H} & \text{O} \\
& | & | & \| \\
\text{H} \!-\! \text{N} \!-\! & \text{C} \!-\! & \text{C} \!-\! \boxed{\text{OH}} \quad + \quad \boxed{\text{H}} \!-\! \text{N} \!-\! \text{C} \!-\! \text{C} \!-\! \text{OH} \\
& | & & | \\
& \text{R}_1 & & \text{R}_2
\end{array}
$$

Amino acid #1   Amino acid #2

Notice the circles around the OH group of amino acid #1 and around the H of amino acid #2. The carbon from amino acid #1 loses the OH and bonds instead to the nitrogen on amino acid #2. The nitrogen from amino acid #2 loses one H in the process:

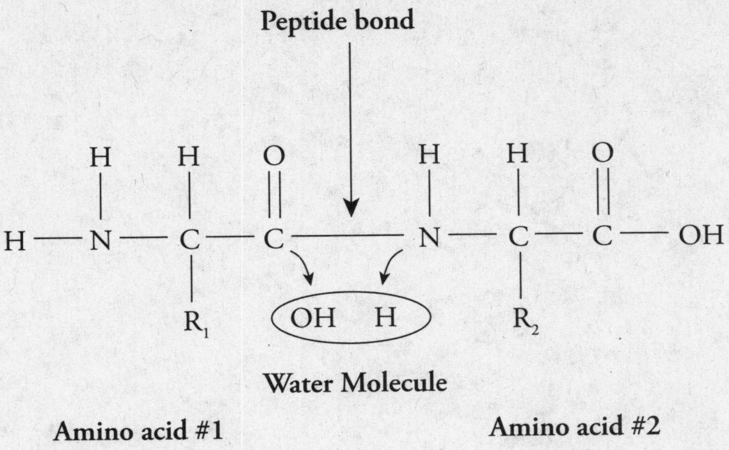

Peptide bond

$$H_2N-C H(R_1)-CO-NH-CH(R_2)-COOH$$

H H O H H O

H—N—C—C—N—C—C—OH

R₁   (OH H)   R₂

Water Molecule

Amino acid #1   **Amino acid #2**

The new bond between the amino acids is called a **peptide bond**. Notice that water (H_2O) is removed. Peptide bonds are said to be formed by **dehydration synthesis**.

When many amino acids join to form a long amino acid chain, this chain is called a protein. Because the amino acids in the chain are all held together by peptide bonds, the protein can also be referred to as a **polypeptide**.

- Peptide bonds are formed by dehydration synthesis in which a molecule of water is removed to join two amino acids.
- Peptide bonds are broken in the reverse process, called **hydrolysis**, when a water molecule is added to the structure.

Amino acid #1   Amino acid #2

Proteins have many different functions. They are enzymes, hormones, channels, structural elements, carriers, messengers, etc. Don't worry yet about these specific functions. They'll come up later as we talk about cells and the body. But do remember that proteins have many different three-dimensional shapes and many different functions.

Quick Quiz #2

Fill in the blanks and check the appropriate boxes:

1. The bond that holds two amino acids together is called a _____ bond.

2. The assembly of a protein from its amino acid constituents involves the [☐ **addition** ☐ **removal**] of water and is called _____ _____.

3. An amino acid is a [☐ **monomer** ☐ **polymer**] of a protein.

4. Because proteins are essentially chains of amino acids linked together by _____ bonds, a protein might also be called a _____.

5. The disassembly of a protein into its component amino acids is called _____ and involves the [☐ **addition** ☐ **removal**] of water.

Biologically Important Macromolecule #2: Carbohydrate

The monomer for a carbohydrate is a **saccharide**. The term *saccharide* refers to "sweetness"; carbohydrates are essentially sugar molecules. All carbohydrates have a common factor: They are made only of carbon, oxygen, and hydrogen.

The carbohydrate is unique among the macromolecules because it is the only macromolecule for which the monomer by itself is considered to be a carbohydrate. A single saccharide can be called a carbohydrate. In fact, there is a whole group of carbohydrates that are made only of a single saccharide. They are called **monosaccharides** (*mono* = one).

Monosaccharides are made of carbon, oxygen, and hydrogen in a fixed ratio. The number of carbon atoms is equal to the number of oxygen atoms, and the number of hydrogen atoms is equal to twice the number of either carbon atoms or oxygen atoms. In other words, the Cs, Hs, and Os exist in a 1:2:1 ratio.

> ## Carbs
> Carbohydrates, or "carbs" as they are sometimes referred to, include the sugar molecules dissolved in a bottle of soda as well as the starch molecules found in pasta and potatoes. Carbohydrates can be used by the body minutes after they are eaten, or they can be stored for use later. Although people involved in athletics seem more concerned with carbs than nonathletes, carbohydrates are an important source of energy for all of us, athlete or not.

> The generic chemical formula for a monosaccharide is
>
> $$C_nH_{2n}O_n$$

The two monosaccharides you need to know for the SAT Biology E/M Subject Test are **glucose** and **fructose**. Glucose and fructose have the same chemical formula: $C_6H_{12}O_6$. So what is different about them?

Glucose and fructose differ in the arrangement of their atoms:

$$
\begin{array}{cc}
\text{Glucose} & \text{Fructose} \\[4pt]
\begin{array}{c}
O \\
\parallel \\
C\!-\!H \\
| \\
H\!-\!C\!-\!OH \\
| \\
HO\!-\!C\!-\!H \\
| \\
H\!-\!C\!-\!OH \\
| \\
H\!-\!C\!-\!OH \\
| \\
H\!-\!C\!-\!OH \\
| \\
H
\end{array}
&
\begin{array}{c}
H \\
| \\
HO\!-\!C\!-\!H \\
| \\
C\!=\!O \\
| \\
HO\!-\!C\!-\!H \\
| \\
H\!-\!C\!-\!OH \\
| \\
H\!-\!C\!-\!OH \\
| \\
H\!-\!C\!-\!OH \\
| \\
H
\end{array}
\end{array}
$$

Glucose   **Fructose**

In the glucose molecule, the double-bonded oxygen is located on the top carbon. In the fructose molecule, it's located on the second carbon from the top.

One last thing you should know about glucose is that it can also form a ring structure:

> ## Glucose and Fructose: A Quick Review
> - Glucose and fructose are both carbohydrates.
> - Both are monosaccharides.
> - Both have the formula $C_6H_{12}O_6$.
> - Glucose and fructose differ in the way the double-bonded oxygen is oriented within the molecule.

Disaccharides

Remember that many carbohydrates are polymers: strings of repeated units. So it makes sense, then, that monosaccharides would link together to form larger carbohydrates. If only two monosaccharides link together, the result is a carbohydrate made of two monomers: a **disaccharide** (*di* = two).

The disaccharides you need to know about for the SAT Biology E/M Subject Test are **maltose** and **sucrose**. Maltose is formed from two molecules of glucose. When the two molecules bond together, a molecule of water (H_2O) is removed. This is dehydration synthesis, just like we saw for peptide bond formation. The chemical formula for maltose **is not** $C_{12}H_{24}O_{12}$ (2 × glucose). Remember that two hydrogen atoms and one oxygen atom disappear, so the chemical formula for maltose is $C_{12}H_{22}O_{11}$.

Sucrose is commonly known as table sugar. It is formed when a molecule of glucose combines with a molecule of fructose in a dehydration synthesis reaction.

The two disaccharides to know are **maltose** and **sucrose**.

glucose   +   glucose   –   water molecule → maltose
$C_6H_{12}O_6$ + $C_6H_{12}O_6$ – H_2O → $C_{12}H_{22}O_{11}$

glucose   +   fructose   –   water molecule → sucrose
$C_6H_{12}O_6$ + $C_6H_{12}O_6$ – H_2O → $C_{12}H_{22}O_{11}$

Polysaccharides

If the number of monosaccharides joined together exceeds two, the molecule is simply known as a **polysaccharide** (*poly* = many). There are three polysaccharides to know about for the SAT Biology E/M Subject Test: glycogen, starch, and cellulose. All three of these are polymers of glucose. In other words, they are formed from many, many, many molecules of glucose bonded together.

If glycogen, starch, and cellulose are all polymers of glucose, what's the difference between them? The difference is in the *way* the glucose molecules are linked together, and that's almost all you have to know.

The other bit of information you need to know about these large polysaccharides is their function. Because they're large chains of glucose, they act as a good storage form for glucose. We will see later that glucose is the primary form of cellular "food," so it makes sense that organisms would want to store it. Different organisms store glucose in different forms:

- **Glycogen:** the form in which animals (including the human animal) store glucose
- **Starch:** the form in which plants store glucose

What about cellulose? Because of the way the glucose molecules are linked together in cellulose, cellulose is a much stronger, more rigid molecule. It is used for plant structures such as stems, leaves, and wood.

- **Cellulose:** a structural polysaccharide that forms the plant's cell walls

Quick Quiz #3

Fill in the blanks and check the appropriate boxes:

1. Starch serves as a means of storing glucose in [☐ **plants** ☐ **animals**].

2. A molecule of maltose is formed from two molecules of _____.

3. Glucose and fructose [☐ **are** ☐ **are not**] identical molecules.

4. A molecule of glucose and a molecule of fructose, both of which are
    _____, combine to form a molecule of
    _____, which is a _____.

5. Cellulose is a _____.

6. Glycogen serves as a means for storing glucose in
    [☐ **plants** ☐ **animals**].

7. The chemical formula for both glucose and fructose is _____.

8. The chemical formula for sucrose is _____.

9. Cellulose and glycogen differ in the way that _____
    molecules are bonded together.

10. The chemical formulas for sucrose and maltose [☐ **are** ☐ **are not**]
    identical.

Biologically Important Macromolecule #3: Lipid

Lipids are fats—oils, butter, lard, and so on. The monomer for a lipid is a **hydrocarbon**. Simply put, this is just a carbon atom with two hydrogen atoms bonded to it.

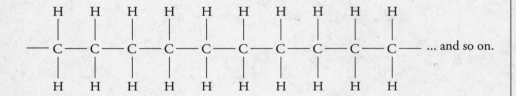

Hydrocarbons can link together to form long chains:

... and so on.

The chains can vary in length and are usually between 12 and 24 carbons long. Hydrocarbon chains are very **hydrophobic**, meaning that they do not interact well with water. Consider what would happen if you put equal amounts of water and cooking oil in a glass and shook it up, then let it sit on the table. The oil and water would begin to separate, and after some time they would be found in separate layers in the glass. The oil (a lipid) is hydrophobic, and it does not want to interact with the water. Another term for hydrophobic is **nonpolar**. Lipids are also referred to as being nonpolar.

The three most common forms in which lipids are found in the body are as **triglycerides**, **phospholipids**, and **cholesterol**. Let's take a look at each of these molecules.

Like Water Off a...
Ever wonder why ducks and geese survive so well in wet environments? A gland just above the tail produces an oily (hydrophobic) substance that the bird spreads over its outer layer of feathers. This helps waterproof the feathers and keeps the thick down underneath dry and warm. In a related manner, humans keep their skin from becoming too dry by spreading moisturizers on it ... these hydrophobic creams keep water in the skin cells by forming an oily barrier that water cannot cross.

Triglycerides

Triglycerides consist of three fatty acids (*tri* = three) bonded to a glycerol molecule (*glyc* = glycerol). A fatty acid is just a long hydrocarbon chain with a carboxyl group at one end. A glycerol molecule is an alcohol that has three carbon atoms in it.

Glycerol   Fatty acids

Most of the fats you eat are in the form of triglycerides, and your body stores fats in the form of triglycerides.

Phospholipids

Phospholipids look very much like triglycerides, except that one of the fatty acid chains is replaced with a phosphate group ($^{-}PO_3^{2-}$).

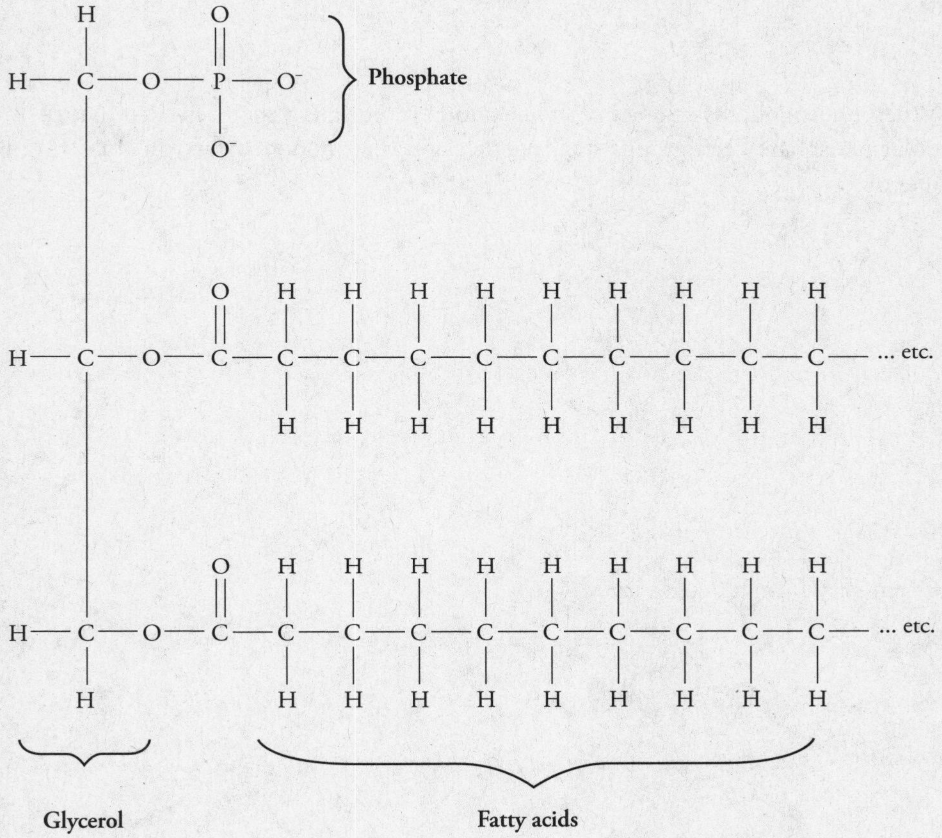

The phosphate group is **hydrophilic** (can interact with water). Another word to describe it is **polar**.

> Phospholipids are polar on one end (the phosphate end) and nonpolar on the other (the fatty acid end).

A common way to represent phospholipids is something like the figure on the next page.

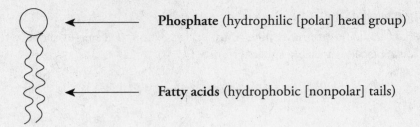

Phosphate (hydrophilic [polar] head group)

Fatty acids (hydrophobic [nonpolar] tails)

When phospholipids interact with one another, they align themselves so that their polar phosphate head groups stay together and their nonpolar fatty acid tails stay together:

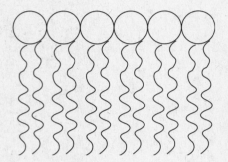

Often they form a double layer:

This double layer of phospholipids is known as a **lipid bilayer**. Lipid bilayers form cell membranes. We'll talk more about cell membranes a little later on.

Cholesterol

Cholesterol is a unique lipid. It is not made of long hydrocarbon chains; instead, the hydrocarbons form rings. Cholesterol is found only in animal cells, in cell membranes along with phospholipids. Additionally, all the steroid hormones in the body (for example, estrogen, testosterone, and progesterone) are derived from cholesterol.

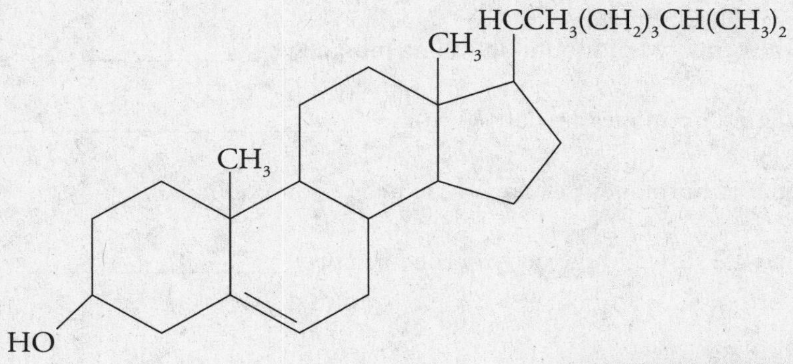

$$HCCH_3(CH_2)_3CH(CH_3)_2$$

CH_3

CH_3

HO

Cholesterol

Cholesterol is probably best known because of its negative reputation. Cholesterol is most infamous for its association with cardiovascular diseases. You may have heard about "good" cholesterol and "bad" cholesterol. "Good cholesterol" is HDL, or a high density lipoprotein. "Bad cholesterol" is LDL, or a low density lipoprotein. Most doctors will recommend that people have an LDL level in their blood of <100 mg/dL, or even considerably less than that for people with a history of heart problems.

Cholesterol does have positive functions. Your body needs cholesterol to build and maintain cell membranes and to produce steroid hormones such as estrogen, testosterone, and progesterone. Cholesterol is found in the body tissues and blood of all animals.

Quick Quiz #4

Fill in the blanks and check the appropriate boxes:

1. Triglycerides are made of one molecule of _____
    and three _____.

2. Lipids in general are [☐ **hydrophilic** ☐ **hydrophobic**].

3. The primary lipid found in cell membranes is _____.

4. Steroid hormones are derived from _____.

5. Steroid hormones [☐ **are** ☐ **are not**] hydrophobic.

6. Fats are stored in the body in the form of _____.

Biologically Important Macromolecule #4: Nucleic Acid

Nucleic acids are acidic macromolecules ("acids") found in the nucleus of the cell ("nucleic"). Specifically, they are **DNA** (deoxyribonucleic acid) and **RNA** (ribonucleic acid). The monomer of a nucleic acid is a **nucleotide**, so nucleic acids are sometimes referred to as **polynucleotides**. A nucleotide is made up of a sugar, a phosphate, and a base:

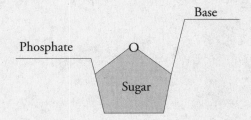

Let's consider the structure of DNA first. RNA is very similar to DNA, so once you understand how DNA is constructed, it will be easy to understand how RNA is constructed.

The "base" in the figure above can be replaced by one of four different chemicals referred to as nucleotide bases.

The four possible nucleotide bases for DNA are

Adenine   **Guanine**   **Cytosine**   **Thymine**

Because there are four types of DNA bases, there are really four types of DNA nucleotides:

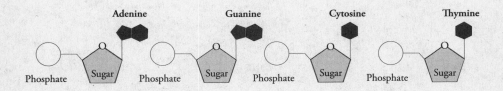

Notice that the sugar and the phosphate are constant from nucleotide to nucleotide. The sugar and the phosphate are known as the backbone of the nucleotide.

When nucleotides bond to form a long chain (a polynucleotide), the chain is a strand of DNA. Because the four types of nucleotides can bond in any order, many different strands of DNA can be made. Here's an example of three possible strands:

Rosalind Franklin
James Watson, Francis Crick, and Maurice Wilkins were awarded the Nobel Prize for discovering the double-helix structure of DNA molecules. However, they were assisted by the pioneering work of Rosalind Franklin. She learned x-ray diffraction techniques while working in Paris as a physical chemist. In 1952 she produced x-ray photographs of DNA strands, which showed the "twisted ladder" structure. Watson and Crick used these photographs when they published their model of the structure of DNA.

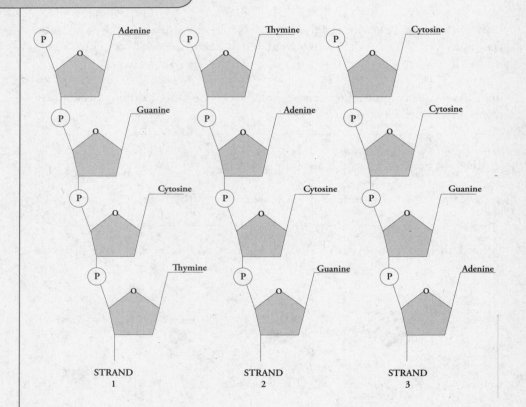

Each is a strand of DNA, and each is a polymer of nucleotides, but each strand differs from the others because of the order in which the nucleotides are bonded together.

DNA Is Double-Stranded

As you may already know, DNA is a double-stranded molecule. Two strands of DNA pair up to form a ladder like structure that twists on itself. This double spiral of DNA strands is known as a **double helix**. The double helix was first discovered in 1956 by two scientists named James Watson and Francis Crick. (They were assisted by the work of Maurice Wilkins and Rosalind Franklin) Here's how the double helix is formed:

1. Two strands of DNA line up next to each other.
2. The sugar-phosphate portions of the two nucleotide chains form the sides of the ladder.
3. The bases bond to each other and form the rungs of the ladder.
4. The ladder twists into a spiral to form the double helix.

Below is a drawing of the DNA ladder before it twists into the double helix.

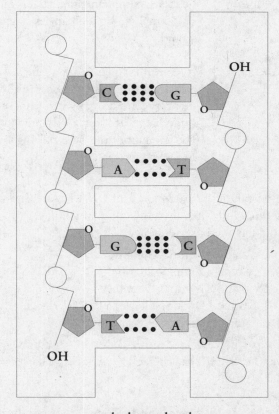

• • • • = hydrogen bonds

Nucleotide Base Pairing

There is one very important thing you should know about the rungs of the ladder: The bases that form the rungs bond to each other very specifically.

> - Adenine and thymine will bond only with each other.
> - Cytosine and guanine will bond only with each other.

Sometimes the bonding of a nucleotide base with its partner is referred to as forming a base pair or, simply, **base pairing**.

Two strands of DNA that can form base pairs with each other at each nucleotide are said to be **complementary**. So the two strands of a double helix are complementary. Each nucleotide base on one strand is bonded to its partner on the other strand.

A common question on the SAT Biology E/M Subject Test involves choosing the correct complementary strand if you're given a sequence of nucleotide bases. It's not a difficult question as long as you remember the base pairing rules. Look at the following example:

Base Pair Memory Trick

Here's a mnemonic device to help you remember who forms a base pair with whom. Write down the bases in alphabetical order:

Adenine   Cytosine   Guanine   Thymine

Then remember that

- the two bases on the ends form a base pair (bond) with each other
- the two bases in the middle form a base pair (bond) with each other

If a particular base sequence in DNA is Adenine-Guanine-Cytosine, then the complementary strand has the base sequence

(A) Cytosine-Adenine-Guanine
(B) Thymine-Adenine-Guanine
(C) Cytosine-Thymine-Adenine
(D) Thymine-Cytosine-Guanine
(E) Guanine-Adenine-Thymine

Following the base pairing rules (adenine pairs with thymine, and guanine pairs with cytosine), we quickly see that choice **D** presents the correct order of bases in the complementary strand.

There is one last thing to remember about DNA base pairing: the number of bonds that hold each pair together. The type of bond that holds the base pairs together is a **hydrogen bond**. Look back at the figure of the "untwisted" ladder. Notice that the A-T base pair is held together by two hydrogen bonds, while the G-C base pair is held together by three hydrogen bonds. What this means is that G-C base pairs are stronger than A-T base pairs. Thus, a DNA double helix that contains many G-C base pairs will be more stable (stronger) than a DNA double helix that contains many A-T base pairs.

RNA

RNA is a polymer of nucleotides that's similar to DNA. The biggest difference between RNA and DNA is that RNA is a single-stranded molecule whereas DNA is double-stranded (a double helix). Another difference is that RNA does not use thymine as a nucleotide base; instead, it uses a base called **uracil**. Uracil can form a base pair with adenine in RNA, just like thymine does in DNA. Below is a summary of the differences between RNA and DNA (RNA can fold on itself to form base pairs).

Characteristic	RNA	DNA
Structure	single-stranded	double-stranded
Bases	adenine, cytosine, guanine, uracil	adenine, cytosine, guanine, thymine
Sugar	ribose	deoxyribose

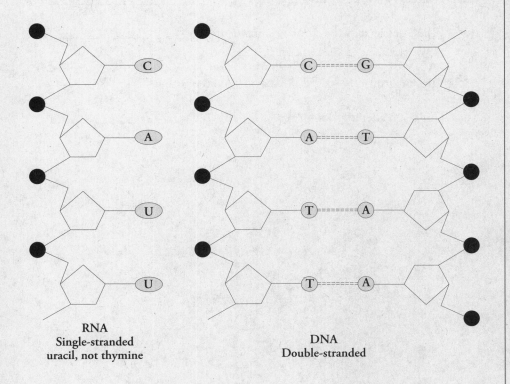

RNA
Single-stranded
uracil, not thymine

DNA
Double-stranded

The fact that RNA is single-stranded allows it to assume various unique shapes. There is no second strand to lock it into a double-helix shape. It can form base pairs with itself, and this allows it to fold up into many different three-dimensional shapes. We'll talk more about RNA later on when we discuss protein synthesis in more detail.

Quick Quiz #5

Fill in the blanks and check the appropriate boxes:

1. The fact that double-stranded DNA forms a double helix was discovered by _____ and _____.

2. The four DNA nucleotide bases are _____, _____, _____, and _____.

3. RNA [☐ is ☐ is not] a double-stranded molecule.

4. RNA nucleotides [☐ do ☐ do not] contain the exact same bases as DNA nucleotides.

5. In DNA, guanine forms a base pair with _____, whereas adenine forms a base pair with _____.

6. The nucleic acid "backbone" is made up of _____ and _____.

7. The sugar in DNA is [☐ ribose ☐ deoxyribose].

8. In RNA, adenine can form a base pair with _____.

Key Words

atoms

molecules

compound

element

reactants

products

organic

inorganic

polymers

monomers

amino acids

amino group

double bond

carboxyl group

protein

peptide bond

dehydration synthesis

protein

polypeptide

hydrolysis

saccharide

monosaccharides

glucose

fructose

disaccharide

maltose

sucrose

polysaccharide

glycogen

starch

cellulose

hydrocarbon

hydrophobic

nonpolar

triglycerides

phospholipids

cholesterol

hydrophilic

polar

lipid bilayer

deoxyribonucleic acid (DNA)

ribonucleic acid (RNA)

nucleotide

polynucleotides

adenine

guanine

cytosine

thymine

double helix

base pairing

complementary

hydrogen bond

uracil

Summary

o   Atoms are the fundamental units of the physical world and combine in chemical reactions to form molecules.

o   An element is any substance that cannot be broken into simpler substances.

o   If two or more elements are combined, they form a compound.

o   The four biologically important macromolecules are proteins, carbohydrates, lipids, and nucleic acids.

o   Proteins are polymers of amino acids. Each of the 20 amino acids has a basic backbone structure with one different R-group.

o   Carbohydrates are made of only carbon, oxygen, and hydrogen. Common carbohydrates include monosaccharides, disaccharides, and polysaccharides.

o   Lipids are composed of hydrocarbons linked to each other. A hydrocarbon is a carbon atom with two hydrogen atoms bonded to it.

o   The most common forms of lipids are triglycerides, phospholipids, and cholesterol.

o   Nucleic acids are biologically important macromolecules that are found in the nucleus of every cell.

o   DNA and RNA are the nucleic acids that make life possible.

Chapter 4
Cell Structure

According to cell theory, every living organism—plant, animal, or otherwise—is made of cells, and all cells arise from preexisting cells. The simplest organisms have one cell; they are **unicellular**. More complex organisms are made of many cells; they are **multicellular**. In this chapter, we will explore the structure of cells—the basic building blocks of life.

EUKARYOTIC CELL STRUCTURE

Look at the following diagram, and think of a cell as having three main areas: the cell wall and/or membrane, the cytoplasm, and the nucleus.

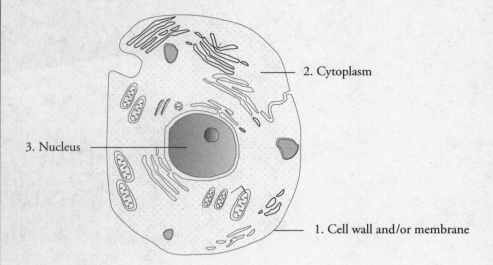

2. Cytoplasm

3. Nucleus

1. Cell wall and/or membrane

Generalized Eukaryotic Cell

1. The **cell wall** and/or **membrane** forms the outer layer.
2. The **cytoplasm** contains the **organelles**.
3. The **nucleus**, which is bounded by a nuclear membrane, contains **chromosomes**.

Notice that in the list, number one says "the cell wall AND/OR membrane." It turns out that plants, bacteria, and fungi have both a cell wall and a membrane (the cell wall is the outermost portion), whereas animal cells have only a cell membrane.

More about Cell Walls

Plants, bacteria, and fungi all have cell walls, but their cell walls are made up of different substances.

- **Plants** have cell walls made of **cellulose**. Remember that cellulose is a polysaccharide.
- **Bacteria** have cell walls made of **peptidoglycan**. *Peptido* refers to protein, and *glycan* refers to sugar, so bacterial cell walls are made of protein and sugar.
- **Fungi** have cell walls made of **chitin**. Chitin is a polysaccharide that's similar to cellulose.

More about the Cell Membrane

Remember: The cell membrane is made of

- lipids
- proteins

We learned about these molecules in the last chapter when we covered basic biological chemistry. The primary lipids found in cell membranes are **phospholipids**; do you remember their special characteristics? If you don't remember, go back and review them now.

Phospholipids have both polar and nonpolar regions and form lipid bilayers:

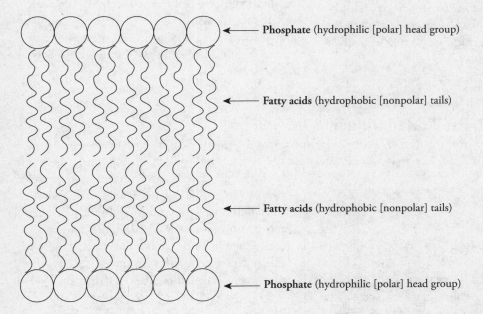

Phosphate (hydrophilic [polar] head group)

Fatty acids (hydrophobic [nonpolar] tails)

Fatty acids (hydrophobic [nonpolar] tails)

Phosphate (hydrophilic [polar] head group)

Cell membranes are just lipid bilayers. They make excellent barriers, because the inside of the cell is **aqueous** (watery), and the external environment of the cell is usually aqueous; so in effect, the lipid bilayer cell membrane forms an "oily" layer between the inside of the cell and the outside of the cell. Substances that are "happy" in an aqueous; medium (in other words, hydrophilic substances) do not like to cross the oily (in other words, hydrophobic) barrier.

However, substances *do* need to get in and out of the cell—oxygen, carbon dioxide, glucose and other nutrients, and waste products, to name a few. The cell membrane lets some things through and restricts the passage of other things. For this reason, it is said to be **selectively permeable**.

Four Ways That Substances Can Cross the Cell Membrane

1. Simple Diffusion

Diffusion is simply the movement of a substance from an area of high concentration to an area of lower concentration. This is called "moving down a concentration gradient." So if there is more of something on one side of the membrane (for example, inside the cell) and less of that same thing on the other side of the membrane (in this case, outside the cell), that substance will simply move across the membrane to the area of lower concentration (again, in this case, outside the cell). Basically, our example substance, whatever it is, relieves some of the crowding inside the cell by moving outside the cell.

Comparisons: Facilitated vs. Simple Diffusion

Facilitated diffusion is like simple diffusion in one important respect: A substance crosses the membrane only if there is a concentration difference on either side of the membrane. Some examples of hydrophilic substances that cross the membrane by facilitated diffusion are sodium, potassium, calcium (in fact, all ions, because they carry a charge, must cross membranes by facilitated diffusion), and glucose.

2. Facilitated Diffusion

Facilitated diffusion is similar to simple diffusion, except that the molecules that cross are not hydrophobic. Because they are not hydrophobic, they cannot interact with the oily barrier and cannot simply cross the membrane. They need help. The proteins that make up the cell membrane can help move substances across the lipid bilayer. Because they help, or facilitate, the movement of substances across the membrane, this type of movement is called **facilitated diffusion**.

Lipid Soluble Substances Only

Because the cell membrane is a lipid bilayer, simple diffusion works only if the substance in question is lipid soluble (hydrophobic) and can interact with that oily barrier. Some examples of substances that cross the cell membrane by simple diffusion are oxygen, carbon dioxide, and cholesterol.

The proteins form specialized channels, sort of like pores, across the membrane. The channels are highly specific for particular substances—for example, a channel might allow sodium to cross but not potassium. Some proteins do not form pores but instead act as carrier molecules that bind to a substance and "pull" it through the membrane.

3. Active Transport

In active transport, the cell must expend energy to move something across the membrane. **Active transport** is different from simple and facilitated diffusion in this important respect: It can move a substance across the cell membrane from an area of low concentration to an area of higher concentration. That's why it requires energy. Another way to describe active transport is to say that it moves substances against their concentration gradients. Simple and facilitated diffusion are considered passive processes because they move substances down their gradients, and this doesn't require energy.

Active transport also relies on membrane proteins to move substances, and it doesn't matter whether the substance is hydrophobic or hydrophilic.

4. Bulk Transport

Bulk transport is what its name implies: the movement of large, bulky items across the cell membrane. There are two possible directions to move the substances: into the cell, called **endocytosis**, and out of the cell, called **exocytosis**.

In endocytosis, the cell takes in some particle by surrounding and engulfing it within a pocket known as a **vesicle**.

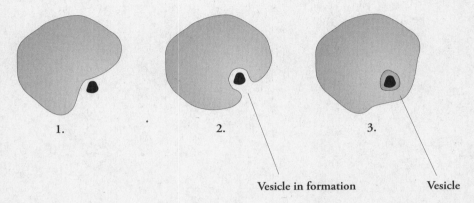

1.   2.   3.

Vesicle in formation   Vesicle

Exocytosis is the exact opposite. A particle in a cell (in a vesicle) is released to the outside by fusing the vesicle with the cell membrane.

Osmosis

Osmosis is simply the movement of water across a cell membrane, down its concentration gradient. The thing to remember, though, is that water's concentration gradient is opposite to the solute (dissolved particles) concentration gradient. In other words, if there is a lot of some particular substance inside a cell and less of that substance outside the cell, then there is less water *inside* the cell and more water *outside* the cell. Basically, the substance takes up some room where water could be, so if there's a lot of the substance present, then there will be less water present. In our example, water will want to move down its concentration gradient, into the cell.

Water is hydrophilic (seems obvious, doesn't it?), so it must cross the membrane by facilitated diffusion. Cells have many water channels in their membranes that allow water to cross easily. This can cause problems if the cells are placed into solutions that are more or less concentrated than they are.

Think about a cell placed into a concentrated solution (a **hypertonic** solution). There are more *particles* outside the cell than inside, so there is less *water* outside the cell than inside. Water will move down its gradient, from inside the cell to outside the cell, and the cell will shrivel up.

Now think about a cell placed into a dilute solution (a **hypotonic** solution). There are now *fewer* particles outside the cell than inside, so there is *more* water outside the cell than inside. Water will move down its gradient, from outside the cell to inside the cell, and the cell will swell up and burst.

If the cell is put into a solution that is exactly the same concentration as the cell itself (an **isotonic** solution), then the cell will neither shrivel nor swell. Human cells are isotonic (equally concentrated) to a 0.9% sodium chloride solution.

Quick Quiz #1

Fill in the blanks and check the appropriate boxes:

1. Animal cells [☐ **do** ☐ **do not**] have cell walls.

2. Bacteria have cell walls made of _____.

3. Engulfing large particles in a vesicle is known as _____.

4. Facilitated diffusion is a way for [☐ **hydrophobic**
    ☐ **hydrophilic**] substances to cross the cell membrane.

5. Fungi have cell walls made of _____,
    and plants have cell walls made of _____.

6. Simple diffusion [☐ **does** ☐ **does not**] require energy.

7. Hydrophobic substances cross the membrane by _____.

8. A type of movement that requires energy and moves substances
    against their concentration gradients is called _____.

9. A human blood cell placed in a 10% solution of
    sodium chloride solution will

    (A) swell
    (B) shrivel
    (C) stay the same
    (D) shrink and then swell
    (E) swell and then shrink

10. Which term best describes a cell membrane?

    (A) Nonpermeable
    (B) Permeable
    (C) Selectively permeable
    (D) Impermeable
    (E) Transparent

More About the Cytoplasm

The cytoplasm is a semiliquid goo that contains a **eukaryotic** cell's organelles. The organelles perform specific functions for the cell. Note that some cells (bacteria) do not have organelles and are **prokaryotic**. We'll talk more about bacteria in Chapter 13.

All of the organelles except the ribosome are bounded by a membrane. Two of the organelles (the nucleus and the mitochondria) are bounded by two membranes.

Study this picture of a eukaryotic cell and its organelles, as well as the list of organelle functions that below.

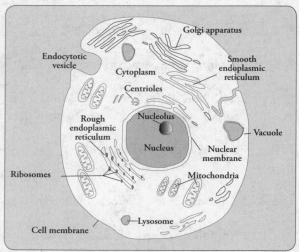

Organelle	Function
Vacuole	Storage of wastes and other material
Ribosomes	Sites of protein synthesis; not bound by membrane
Smooth endoplasmic reticulum	System of membrane and tubes that transports substances around the cell
Rough endoplasmic reticulum	Endoplasmic reticulum with ribosomes bound to it; ribosmomes on the rough ER specifically synthesize membrane proteins (like channels) or secreted proteins
Golgi apparatus	Sorts and packages proteins made by ribosomes on rough ER
Mitochondria	Function in cellular respiration; produce ATP for the cell; bound by a double membrane
Lysosomes	Digest foreign substances and worn-out organelles
Centrioles	Help to form the spindle during mitosis (cell division)
Nucleus	Control center of the cell; contains genetic material (DNA); bound by a double membrane
Nucleolus	Small, dense structure in the nucleus; site of ribosome synthesis
Cell membrane	Outer membrane that regulates what comes into and goes out of the cell

Organelle Function Matching Quiz

Use the following exercise to help you memorize organelle functions.

Match the organelle on the left with its function/description on the right.

1._____ Golgi apparatus

A. contains genetic material (DNA); control center of the cell

2._____ Centrioles

B. holds ribosomes that synthesize membrane or secreted proteins

3._____ Lysosomes

C. sites of protein synthesis

4._____ Rough ER

D. cellular respiration and ATP production; have double membranes

5._____ Cell membrane

E. cellular transport system

6._____ Ribosomes

F. stores waste and other substances

7._____ Nucleolus

G. sorts and packages membrane and secreted proteins

8._____ Vacuole

H. related generally to formation of the spindle during mitosis

9._____ Smooth ER

I. site of ribosome synthesis in the nucleus

10._____ Mitochondria

J. selectively permeable barrier that regulates what enters and exits the cell

11._____ Nucleus

K. contain hydrolytic enzymes; digest foreign substances and worn organelles

Check the answers on the next page to see how you did.

Answers

1. __G__ Golgi apparatus   A.   contains genetic material (DNA); control center of the cell

2. __H__ Centrioles   B.   holds ribosomes that synthesize membrane or secreted proteins

3. __K__ Lysosomes   C.   sites of protein synthesis

4. __B__ Rough ER   D.   cellular respiration and ATP production; have double membranes

5. __J__ Cell membrane   E.   cellular transport system

6. __C__ Ribosomes   F.   stores waste and other substances

7. __I__ Nucleolus   G.   sorts and packages membrane and secreted proteins

8. __F__ Vacuole   H.   related generally to formation of the spindle during mitosis

9. __E__ Smooth ER   I.   site of ribosome synthesis in the nucleus

10. __D__ Mitochondria   J.   selectively permeable barrier that regulates what enters and exits the cell

11. __A__ Nucleus   K.   contain hydrolytic enzymes; digest foreign substances and worn organelles

Now take the test again. (The answers to the test below are in Chapter 15.)

1._____ Golgi apparatus

2._____ Centrioles

3._____ Lysosomes

4._____ Rough ER

5._____ Cell membrane

6._____ Ribosomes

7._____ Nucleolus

8._____ Vacuole

9._____ Smooth ER

10._____ Mitochondria

11._____ Nucleus

A.   cellular transport system

B.   stores waste and other substances

C.   selectively permeable barrier that regulates what enters and exits the cell

D.   site of ribosome synthesis in the nucleus

E.   related generally to formation of the spindle during mitosis

F.   cellular respiration and ATP production; have double membrane

G.   holds ribosomes that synthesize membrane or secreted proteins

H.   contain hydrolytic enzymes; digest foreign substances and worn organelles

I.   contains genetic material (DNA); control center of the cell

J.   sites of protein synthesis

K.   sorts and packages membrane and secreted proteins

What Goes On in the Cytoplasm: Chemical Reactions and Enzymes

Thousands and thousands of different chemical reactions take place in the cytoplasm. Here's an example of a very generic chemical reaction:

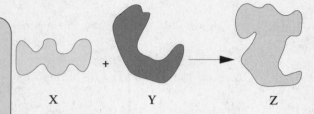

Enzymes: If Ya' Can't Stand the Heat …

One way to accelerate a reaction is to heat up the substances involved. The problem with this is that the heat can potentially cause unintended reactions, which in turn damage the structure of the cell. A more specific way to accelerate a reaction within a cell depends on compounds that speed up chemical reactions. These compounds are called catalysts. Chemical reactions in cells are usually sped up by specific catalysts called enzymes.

In the above reaction, molecules X and Y are the reactants and molecule Z is the product. However, the reaction won't happen unless X and Y get together.

X and Y need a mutual "friend" that will help them get together in the same place at the same time so they can react and form Z. The mutual friend is an **enzyme**. Here's a picture of an enzyme that would work nicely to get X and Y together:

Molecule E

We'll call the enzyme molecule E. If E is around, the reaction between X and Y occurs much more quickly than if E is not around. We call E a **catalyst**. Catalysts simply make chemical reactions occur faster. E's job is to catalyze the reaction between X and Y.

Notice that the spaces on the top of molecule E match up with molecule X's shape. The spaces on the bottom match up with molecule Y's shape.

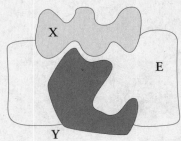

So if molecule E is floating around in the cytoplasm of a cell, X and Y have a good chance of getting together. Once they do, they react to form molecule Z.

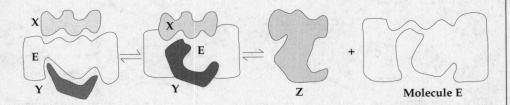

When the reaction is finished, molecule E is still around, and is unchanged. It's now free to go and find another pair of X and Y to catalyze another reaction between them. So here's the first important fact to remember about an enzyme:

> When an enzyme catalyzes a reaction, it is not used up in the reaction.

Remember how precisely molecules X and Y fit into molecule E in our example? Real reactants fit into enzymes just as precisely. This is sometimes referred to as the "lock and key" theory. In other words, the reactants fit into the enzyme as precisely as a key fits into a lock. The places where the reactants bind are called the **active sites** of the enzyme.

Because the fit is so precise, a particular enzyme in a cell can only catalyze a particular reaction. We say that the enzyme is specific for a particular set of reactants and a particular reaction. In our example above, enzyme E is specific to reactants X and Y. E will only catalyze the reaction between X and Y to form Z.

Here's an enzyme called *F*.

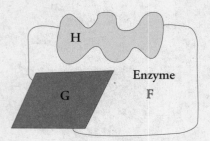

Enzyme *F* is specific to reactants *G* and *H*. It catalyzes only the reaction in which *G* and *H* combine to form some product. So here's the second important fact to remember about an enzyme:

> Enzymes are specific for particular reactions.

One other thing: Reactants in an enzyme-catalyzed reaction are called **substrates**. So molecules *X*, *Y*, *G*, and *H* would be referred to as substrates.

Enzymes Are Proteins

Enzymes are nothing more than proteins, which means they are organic molecules. They have specific three-dimensional shapes (like all proteins), and their shapes are what make them specific for particular reactions. If they lose their shapes (become **denatured**) they can no longer run reactions. One thing that can denature enzymes is heat. Heat destroys an enzyme's three-dimensional shape and prevents it from catalyzing its reaction.

Enzymes are important because they help determine which particular chemical reactions a cell is going to run. Cells are like little bags of chemicals. Enzymes help determine which chemicals will react with one another to carry out the particular functions of a cell.

Sometimes enzymes need help to catalyze reactions. Molecules that help enzymes are called **coenzymes**. Coenzymes can help enzymes work faster, and some enzymes can't work at all without coenzymes. What, specifically, are coenzymes? **Vitamins.** Vitamins are coenzymes. Can you see why getting the right vitamins in your diet is important? Without vitamins, many enzymes would be unable to function properly, and many chemical reactions would not occur. If these chemical reactions were not to occur, your body's cells (and your body!) would not be able to work properly, if at all.

Quick Quiz #2

Fill in the blanks and check the appropriate boxes:

1. The fact that enzymes interact with substrate by physically fitting together has given rise to the phrase "_____ and _____" theory.

2. Enzymes are known as organic _____.

3. When an enzyme has catalyzed a chemical reaction and the products are formed, the enzyme itself [☐ **is** ☐ **is not**] consumed and is [☐ **unavailable** ☐ **available**] to catalyze additional reactions.

4. The location on an enzyme where substrate binds is called the _____.

Key Words

unicellular
multicellular
cell wall
cell membrane
cytoplasm
organelles
nucleus
chromosomes
plants
cellulose
bacteria
peptidoglycan
fungi
chitin
aqueous
phospholipids
semipermeable
diffusion
facilitated diffusion
active transport
bulk transport
endocytosis
exocytosis
vesicle

osmosis
hypertonic
hypotonic
isotonic
eukaryotic
prokaryotic
vacuole
ribosomes
smooth endoplasmic reticulum
rough endoplasmic reticulum
golgi apparatus
mitochondria
lysosomes
centrioles
nucleus
nucleolus
cell membrane
enzyme
catalyst
active sites
substrates
denatured
coenzymes
vitamins

Summary

o   A eukaryotic cell has a cell wall or a cell membrane forming its outer layer, cytoplasm where the organelles are located, and a nucleus where the chromosomes are located.

o   Plants, bacteria, and fungi have cell walls. Animal cells do not. All types of cells have cell membranes.

o   Substances can cross a cell membrane by diffusion, facilitated diffusion, active transport, and bulk transport.

o   Diffusion is the movement of a substance from an area of high concentration to an area of low concentration.

o   In simple diffusion, the molecules must be hydrophobic.

o   In facilitated diffusion, the molecules that move are hydrophilic, and need assistance from special membrane proteins.

o   Active transport requires energy and can move materials from a low concentration to a high concentration.

o   Bulk transport involves the movement of large molecules across the cell membrane.

o   Osmosis is the movement of water across a cell membrane.

o   A eukaryotic cell's organelles are found in the cytoplasm. Each organelle has a unique structure and function within a cell.

o   Enzymes, or special proteins, help speed up the reaction between specific substrates within a cell.

Chapter 5
Cellular Respiration

Cellular respiration is a series of chemical reactions that takes place inside a cell. These chemical reactions produce energy for the cell. This chapter will explore the various molecules and mechanisms involved in cellular respiration.

LET'S TALK ABOUT CELLULAR RESPIRATION

Cellular respiration is nothing more than a series of chemical reactions that occur in a cell. The purpose of these chemical reactions is to produce energy for the cell. Cellular energy comes in the form of a molecule called **ATP**. ATP stands for **adenosine triphosphate**.

A molecule of ATP, as its name indicates, is made of adenosine bonded to three phosphate molecules. There's a lot of energy stored in the bond that holds the third phosphate to the molecule.

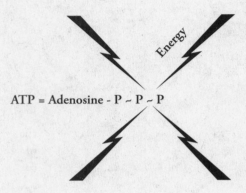

ATP = Adenosine - P ~ P ~ P

When energy is required for some process in the cell (for example, active transport), the cell will **hydrolyze** (break) the bond between the second and third phosphate molecules on ATP. This releases the energy. What remain are a molecule of **adenosine diphosphate (ADP)** and one molecule of phosphate.

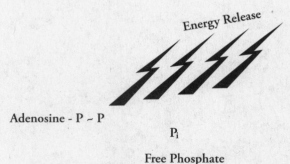

Adenosine - P ~ P

P_i

Free Phosphate

ATP creates the energy to fuel the cell's processes.

ATP → ADP + 1 phosphate molecule + energy

Where the Cell Gets Its ATP: Glycolysis, Krebs Cycle, Electron Transport Chain, and Oxidative Phosphorylation

As we previously mentioned, glucose is the primary source of "cellular food," meaning that this is the molecule that a cell can break down to make ATP. We also talked about glycogen and said it's made of many glucose molecules bonded together; in other words, its purpose is to store energy.

This is the summary equation for cellular respiration:

glucose + oxygen → carbon dioxide + water + ATP

$$C_6H_{12}O_6 + 6\,O_2 \rightarrow 6\,CO_2 + 6\,H_2O + ATP$$

It doesn't occur, however, as a single reaction, in a single step. It occurs in a series of smaller steps designed to maximize the production of energy, as we'll see shortly.

The table on the next page provides a summary of the events that occur in cellular respiration and where in the cell they take place. Remember that this is just a series of chemical reactions that occur on enzymes, so there are substrates and products for each step. This is the MINIMUM amount you need to memorize about cellular respiration. Note that some substrates and some products are left out to keep this table relatively simple. In the following pages, each event will be explained in slightly greater detail.

Cellular Respiration
When it comes to energy, think of it like this:
- ATP is like cash.
- Glucose is like a check.
- Glycogen is like a bank.

When a cell needs ATP, it goes to its glycogen stores and takes out a glucose molecule (a check). Then it cashes the glucose molecule to get ATP (cash). The "check" is "cashed" through cellular respiration.

Event	Location	Substrates	Products	Need oxygen
Glycolysis	Cytoplasm	Glucose, 2 ATP	2 Pyruvate, 2 ATP, 2 NADH	No
PDC (Pyruvate dehydrogenase complex)	Matrix of mitochondria	Pyruvate	Acetyl Co-A, NADH, CO_2	Yes
Krebs cycle	Matrix of mitochondria	Acetyl-CoA, oxaloacetic acid	Oxaloacetic acid, 3 NADH, 1 ATP, 1 $FADH_2$, CO_2	Yes
Electron transport/oxidative phosphorylation	Inner membrane of mitochondria	NADH, $FADH_2$, ADP, P_i	NAD^+, FAD, ATP	Yes

Electron Carriers

There's one last thing to know before the detailed discussion. Basically, cellular respiration is the breakdown of glucose to release energy. Usable energy for the body is ATP. However, the energy released from the breakdown of glucose is not all in the form of ATP. A small amount of ATP is made, but most of the energy is stored as electrons on special molecules called **electron carriers**. When an "empty" electron carrier accepts a pair of electrons, we say it has become **reduced**. When it gives those electrons up later on, we say it has become **oxidized**.

The two most common electron carriers in the body (and the ones that will be used during cellular respiration) are NAD^+ and FAD.

NAD⁺ or FAD?

NAD^+ can accept a pair of electrons (and a hydrogen ion) to become NADH:

$$NAD^+ + H^+ \xrightarrow{2e^-} NADH$$

FAD can accept a pair of electrons (and two hydrogen ions) to become $FADH_2$:

$$FAD + 2\,H^+ \xrightarrow{2e^-} FADH_2$$

These electron carriers will shuttle around the electrons until they can be used at a later time to make usable energy, ATP, for the body.

1. Glycolysis

The word "**glycolysis**" describes what happens during this process. *Glyco-* means "sugar," and *-lysis* means "splitting." So *glycolysis* literally means "sugar splitting," and that's exactly what happens. One molecule of glucose is split in half to produce two molecules of **pyruvate**. A pyruvate molecule is essentially half of a glucose molecule.

Two ATP molecules are needed to start the process of splitting the glucose molecule in half. So before we even accomplish this first step of cellular respiration, we are two ATP "in the hole." However, during the chemical reactions of glycolysis, four ATP molecules are formed, and two NAD^+ molecules accept electrons (become reduced) to become two NADH. So our net end products from glycolysis are two ATP, two NADH, and two pyruvate molecules. The ATP is, of course, immediately usable. The NADH simply carries the electrons until they can be used to make more ATP later on. Here (more or less) is the summary reaction for glycolysis. It's not incredibly detailed, but it will give you an idea of what goes in and what comes out:

$$C_6H_{12}O_6 + 2 \text{ ATP} + 2 \text{ NAD}^+ \rightarrow 2 \text{ Pyruvate} + 4 \text{ ATP} + 2 \text{ NADH}$$

Glycolysis occurs without oxygen. When a process occurs without oxygen, we describe it as **anaerobic**. Glycolysis is an anaerobic process. However, the remaining steps of cellular respiration all require oxygen; they are **aerobic**.

2. The Pyruvate Dehydrogenase Complex (PDC)

If oxygen is available, the pyruvate formed during glycolysis can continue on, through a series of reactions designed to produce more reduced electron carriers and more ATP. The **pyruvate dehydrogenase complex** (PDC) is a group of enzymes that prepares pyruvate to enter the next (third) step of cellular respiration: the Krebs cycle. Pyruvate contains three carbon atoms. However, the Krebs cycle can only accept a molecule that contains two carbon atoms. So the PDC's job is to remove one of the carbons from pyruvate and to attach the remaining two-carbon structure to a coenzyme called **coenzyme A**. In the process, another molecule of NADH is produced, as shown in the following diagram.

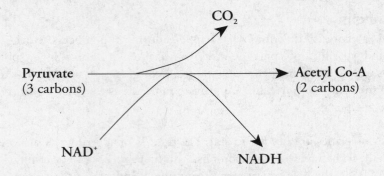

The carbon that is removed leaves in the form of carbon dioxide (CO_2). And don't forget, because there are two molecules of pyruvate at the end of glycolysis, two molecules of acetyl Co-A are produced, two molecules of NADH are produced, and two molecules of carbon dioxide are produced.

Remember, we said earlier that this would occur only if oxygen were available. That's correct, but where's the oxygen? Oxygen is not used directly in this step of cellular respiration, but, as we will see later, if oxygen is not available, this step can't proceed. So this is an aerobic process; it requires oxygen.

Where Does It All Happen?

As you read about the steps of cellular respiration, you may begin to wonder where within the cell this all occurs. Mitochondria are important to the process of cellular respiration. Recall that mitochondria have an outer membrane as well as an intricately folded inner membrane. Glycolysis takes place outside the mitochondria. The enzymes that drive the Krebs cycle are found in the matrix of the mitochondria, and the electron transport chain takes place along the inner membrane of the mitochondria.

Quick Quiz #1

Fill in the blanks and check the appropriate boxes:

1. The process of glycolysis produces ATP and NADH by converting one molecule of _____ to two molecules of _____.

2. The pyruvate dehydrogenase complex is found in the _____ of the mitochondria.

3. The process of glycolysis [☐ **does** ☐ **does not**] require oxygen.

4. _____ is made of many glucose molecules bonded together, and its function is to store energy.

5. When a molecule (such as an electron carrier) accepts a pair of electrons, we say it has become [☐ **reduced** ☐ **oxidized**].

6. During the PDC, a molecule of pyruvate is converted to _____, a molecule of _____ is produced, and _____ is lost.

7. The PDC [☐ **is** ☐ **is not**] an aerobic process.

3. The Krebs Cycle

The **Krebs cycle** is called such because the first molecule is regenerated each time the cycle is completed. That's why, if you look back at the summary table under "Krebs cycle," you see oxaloacetic acid listed as both a substrate and a product.

Here's an overview of what happens in the Krebs cycle. Acetyl Co-A is combined with oxaloacetic acid to form citric acid. (In fact, the Krebs cycle is sometimes referred to as the **citric acid cycle** for this reason.) Citric acid is broken down, one carbon at a time (released as carbon dioxide), then rearranged to form the original oxaloacetic acid molecule. In the process, three molecules of NADH, one molecule of $FADH_2$, and one molecule of ATP are made. Also, carbon dioxide is released.

Here's a picture of the Krebs cycle. You don't need to memorize it, but if you see a picture like this on the SAT Biology E/M Subject Test, you'll know it's the Krebs cycle.

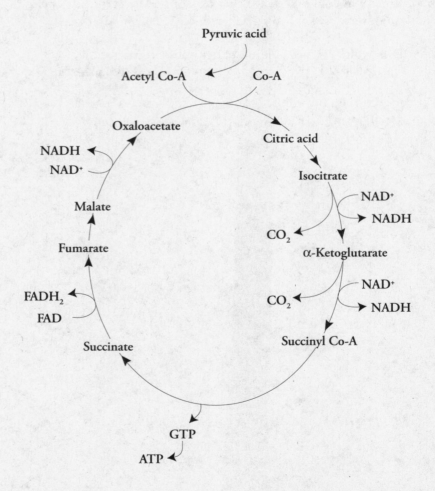

Two last points to remember: First, for every glucose molecule, we get two pyruvate molecules and therefore two acetyl Co-A molecules. So the Krebs cycle runs twice for each glucose molecule. Second, the Krebs cycle requires oxygen. Just like in the PDC, oxygen is not used directly, but if it isn't available, the Krebs cycle can't run. The Krebs cycle is an aerobic process.

So far we've made a little bit of usable energy (ATP). We made two ATP during glycolysis and another two during the Krebs cycle. But most of our energy is stored in the form of reduced electron carriers. It would be great to take these reduced electron carriers and use them to make more ATP . . . and that's exactly what the cell does during electron transport and oxidative phosphorylation.

4. Electron Transport and Oxidative Phosphorylation

Electron transport and **oxidative phosphorylation** have two primary goals:

1. to return the electron carriers to their "empty" state (oxidize them)
2. to use the energy from those electrons to make ATP

If we don't oxidize the electron carriers back to their "empty" states, we can't keep running glycolysis, PDC, or the Krebs cycle. We have to have empty electron carriers so that they can accept electrons during those three processes.

The electron transport chain is a process in which NADH and $FADH_2$ hand down electrons to a chain of carrier molecules. The electrons are passed along the chain until they're given to oxygen, which forms water.

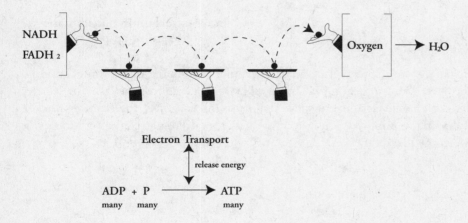

Electron transport is an aerobic process. Oxygen is known as the **final electron acceptor**, because it is the last molecule in the electron transport chain to accept electrons.

So we finally see how oxygen is used. Clearly, electron transport is an aerobic process.

If oxygen is unavailable, it's not there to accept electrons from the transport chain. The transport chain backs up because each member of the chain is "stuck" with its electrons. Ultimately, it backs up all the way to NADH and $FADH_2$, and they're unable to get rid of their electrons (and they become oxidized to "empty"). And if they're unable to be oxidized, there will be no "empty" carriers available for glycolysis, PDC, and the Krebs cycle. Glycolysis, luckily, has another method of acquiring "empty" electron carriers (we'll see it in a minute), but the PDC and the Krebs cycle are stuck. Without empty electron carriers available, these processes shut down. That's why, even though PDC and the Krebs cycle don't use oxygen directly, they still rely on it to run.

So the first goal has been accomplished. But what about the second goal? How can we use the energy of these electrons to make ATP?

Remember where the steps of cellular respiration are taking place:

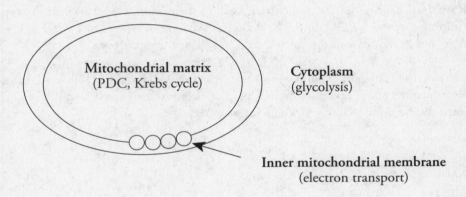

Electron transport takes place along the inner membrane of the mitochondria. Remember that mitochondria are double-membraned organelles. The carrier molecules of the electron transport chain use the energy of the electrons they're transporting to pump H^+ ions out of the mitochondrial matrix and into the space between the membranes.

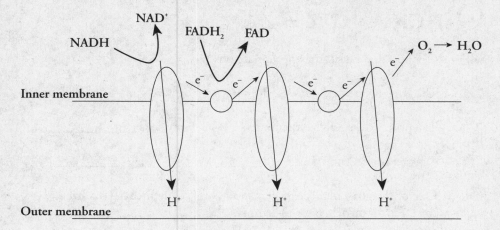

This creates a gradient of H⁺ ions—lots of H⁺ in the space between the membranes, and less H⁺ in the matrix. The H⁺ ions would really like to get back into the matrix, but they can't cross the membrane very easily because they are charged (remember that charged substances can cross membranes only by facilitated diffusion). However, if we provide the H⁺ ions with a method for getting across, they will. And we can use that to our advantage.

The method of getting across the inner membrane is provided by a special protein called an **ATP synthase**. ATP synthase allows the H⁺ ions back into the matrix, and on the way in, that energy is used to phosphorylate an ADP to an ATP. Here's the picture:

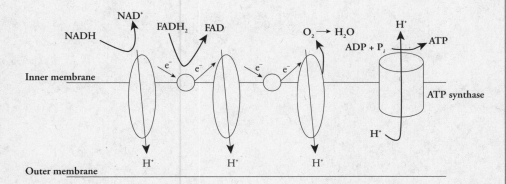

Now both goals have been accomplished. NADH and $FADH_2$ have been oxidized back to NAD^+ and FAD and are free to accept electrons from glycolysis, PDC, and the Krebs cycle. And we've used the energy stored on those electron carriers to make some usable energy for the body in the form of ATP.

> Altogether, the four steps of cellular respiration produce about 36 ATP molecules for each molecule of glucose that's broken down.

Quick Quiz #2

Fill in the blanks and check the appropriate boxes:

1. The Krebs cycle [☐ **does** ☐ **does not**] require oxygen.

2. The principal substance that enters the Krebs cycle is _____.

3. Oxygen is also known as the _____.

4. One of the goals of electron transport is to [☐ **reduce** ☐ **oxidize**] the electron carriers back to "empty."

5. Electron transport occurs along the _____ of the mitochondria.

6. The products of the Krebs cycle are three molecules of _____, one molecule of _____, and one molecule of _____.

7. ATP synthase relies on the facilitated diffusion of _____ ions down their gradient to produce ATP.

8. In the last step of the electron transport chain, oxygen accepts electrons to form _____.

What Happens If Oxygen Is Not Available?

If oxygen is not available, the electron carriers cannot be oxidized back to "empty." Because the PDC and the Krebs cycle absolutely rely on these electron carriers to run, if the electron carriers are not available, PDC and the Krebs cycle shut down. Theoretically, glycolysis should shut down as well, but glycolysis has its own method of creating empty electron carriers that does not rely on oxygen. That's why glycolysis is an anaerobic process.

Regenerating empty electron carriers in the absence of oxygen is called **fermentation**. Remember that in order to "empty" (oxidize) an electron carrier, the electrons must be removed and given to something else (something else must be reduced).

Let's look at what we have at the end of glycolysis:

- **2 ATP**
- **2 NADH**
- **2 pyruvate**

The ATP is, of course, usable energy. The NADH cannot be used to make more ATP, because the electron transport chain is shut down in the absence of oxygen. The pyruvate cannot be converted to acetyl Co-A, because, in the absence of oxygen, the PDC is shut down also. So, because these two substances are not being used, why not take the electrons off the NADH and donate them to pyruvate? That would regenerate an empty electron carrier that can be reused to run glycolysis again, and that's exactly what happens.

The NADH gives its electrons up to pyruvate, thereby becoming NAD^+. Pyruvate, having accepted these electrons, becomes reduced. But to what?

What pyruvate gets reduced to depends upon what organism is running fermentation. In yeast, pyruvate is reduced (in two steps) to ethanol, and carbon dioxide is released as a by-product. In human muscle cells, pyruvate is reduced to lactic acid. Here's the picture:

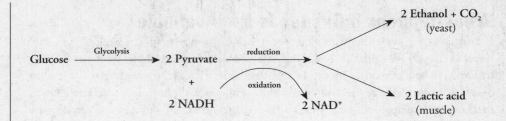

There are only two problems with fermentation. First, the end products, ethanol or lactic acid, are toxic. Yeast die when the ethanol concentration reaches about 12 percent. Muscle cells stop contracting if lactic acid levels get too high (and pH subsequently drops).

Second (and this is the big one to remember for the exam):

The only ATP you get from fermentation are the two net ATP from glycolysis. So instead of a big 36 ATP per glucose from aerobic cellular respiration, only two ATP per glucose are produced.

Two ATP per glucose is enough for yeast, a single-celled organism, to survive. And it's enough for muscle cells to keep functioning for a short while. But it is certainly not enough for large, multicellular organisms like humans, other animals, and plants to survive. This is why humans, other animals, and plants absolutely MUST have oxygen to survive.

Quick Quiz #3

Fill in the blanks and check the appropriate boxes:

1. Fermentation produces _____ in yeast and
    _____ in muscle cells.

2. Anaerobic organisms [☐ **do** ☐ **do not**] conduct glycolysis.

3. Anaerobic respiration (fermentation) produces [☐ **less** ☐ **more**]
    ATP than aerobic respiration.

4. In fermentation, NADH is _____ to NAD^+,
    whereas pyruvate is _____.

5. Anaerobic organisms [☐ **do** ☐ **do not**] conduct the Krebs cycle.

Key Words

adenosine triphosphate (ATP)
hydrolyze
adenosine diphosphate (ADP)
electron carriers
reduced
oxidized
glycolysis
pyruvate
anaerobic
aerobic
pyruvate dehydrogenase
   complex (PDC)

coenzyme A
Krebs cycle
citric acid cycle
electron transport
oxidative phosphorylation
final electron acceptor
inner mitochondrial
   membrane
ATP synthase
fermentation

Summary

○ When glycolysis, PDC, the Krebs cycle, electron transport, and oxidative phosphorylation have all finished, the cell is left with 36 molecules of ATP per glucose.

○ During glycolysis, glucose is converted to two molecules of pyruvic acid. A net total of two ATP and two NADH are formed along the way.

○ During PDC, each molecule of pyruvate is converted to acetyl Co-A. This produces one molecule of NADH per pyruvate and releases carbon dioxide.

○ During the Krebs cycle, the acetyl Co-A from the PDC is combined with oxaloacetic acid to form citric acid, then carbons are removed and rearranged to form oxaloacetic acid again. In the process, three NADH are produced, one $FADH_2$ is produced, and one ATP is produced (per acetyl Co-A). Carbon dioxide is released.

○ During electron transport, NADH and $FADH_2$ give up electrons to the electron transport chain (are oxidized), and the electrons are handed down through a series of carrier molecules and finally to oxygen to form water. As the electrons are passed along the carrier molecules, H^+ ions are pumped out of the matrix and into the space between the inner and outer mitochondrial membranes (an H^+ gradient is formed).

○ During oxidative phosphorylation, the H^+ gradient created during electron transport is used to drive the production of ATP from ADP and P_i. A protein known as an ATP synthase allows the H^+ ions back into the matrix.

○ Without oxygen, fermentation occurs. Fermentation produces toxic by-products and two net ATP. This process is more useful for unicellular organisms than multicellular organisms.

Chapter 6
Transcription and Translation

This chapter deals with the events that take place in
the nucleus of a cell. The nucleus contains the genetic
information, or the DNA, which instructs each of the
cells in the body how to develop. In this chapter you
will learn how DNA replicates and how chromosomes
play a role in creating life as we know it.

THE NUCLEUS

The nucleus contains the cell's **genetic information**—in other words, its DNA. The DNA in eukaryotes is found in several pieces. Each piece is associated with various proteins and is called a **chromosome**. So when we talk about chromosomes, we're really just talking about the pieces of DNA in the nucleus of a cell.

Notice that we specified **eukaryotes**. **Prokaryotes** have DNA, too, even though they don't have a nucleus. Their DNA is found as one large circular chromosome floating around in the cytoplasm. The DNA is still a double helix; the double helix is just joined at both ends to make a circle. We'll talk more about prokaryotes and their chromosomes later.

Even though all chromosomes contain DNA, it is *not* true that all chromosomes are identical. The nucleotide base sequences in two different pieces of DNA—two different chromosomes—can be (and are) different.

DNA Replicates Itself

One of the cool things about DNA is that it is able to make an exact copy of itself—in other words, it's able to **replicate**. This is necessary when cells want to divide. In order for the two new cells to be identical, the original cell first has to replicate its DNA, then divide the replicated DNA evenly between the two new cells. We'll talk about that process a little later. Let's take a look now at how DNA replicates. (You might want to go back and do a quick review of DNA structure first.) There are four simple steps to replication:

All In the Family

An original strand of DNA is called the *parent DNA*. The two new DNA strands that form as a result of replication are called *daughter strands*. Replication begins at specific sites called *origins of replication*. The process of copying the parent DNA occurs in both directions from this origin site.

1. The double helix unwinds, and the two strands separate.
2. Next to each separated strand, an enzyme called **DNA polymerase** lines up nucleotides to form new second strands. The enzyme lines up nucleotides according to the base-pairing rules. Adenines are paired with thymines, and thymines are paired with adenines. Guanines are paired with cytosines, and cytosines are paired with guanines.
3. Hydrogen bonds form between the base pairs, forming the new "rungs" of the DNA ladder. Bonds form between the sugar-phosphate components of the newly aligned nucleotides so that each newly formed ladder has a new side, too.
4. The new double-stranded molecules twist up into double helices.

Let's start with one DNA molecule. The strands separate, and for each strand, the cell makes a new complementary strand, and we end up with two new, but identical, DNA molecules. The original DNA molecule has replicated.

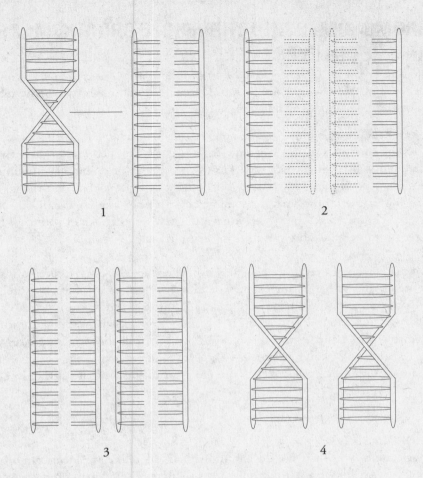

1

2

3

4

An Important SAT Biology E/M Subject Test Word: Template

Think of a replicating DNA molecule. Its strands separate. Now think about one of the separated strands. That strand causes the formation of a new complementary strand with nucleotides that are ordered according to the base-pairing rules. Another way of saying all of that is this:

> Each DNA strand acts as a template for the formation of a new complementary strand.

When we say that one strand acts as a **template** for the formation of another, all we mean is that its nucleotide bases direct the construction of a complementary strand that forms alongside it.

CHROMOSOMES AND THE WHOLE ORGANISM: THE SAME SET IN EVERY CELL

46: The Magic Number
Every cell in the body (excluding sex cells) has 46 chromosomes.

You are an organism. You have cells, your cells have nuclei, and the nuclei contain chromosomes. So if we're going to think about chromosomes, we might as well start by thinking about you and your chromosomes.

You are made up of billions and billions of cells. Every non-sex, or **somatic**, cell has 46 chromosomes sitting in its nucleus. (Sex cells are sperm and ova. They are special and will be discussed later.) Here's the important point: The 46 chromosomes that are sitting in any one of your somatic cells are identical to the 46 that are sitting in every other of your somatic cells. It's not like your skin cells have one set of chromosomes and your kidney cells have another. All of your cells have exactly the same set of chromosomes in their nuclei.

The same is true of every other organism in the whole world. Think about your best friend. His (or her) chromosomes are different from yours, that's for sure. But the 46 chromosomes in any one of his cells is absolutely identical to the 46 chromosomes that are in every other one of his cells. Think about your dog, cat, turtle, or hamster. Think about some tree on your block. Think about any organism you like, and this will always be true: Within any one organism, the chromosomes that are sitting in one cell's nucleus are identical to the set that's sitting in every other cell's nucleus.

An Exception

We just taught you that, within any individual, all cells have identical chromosomes. That's true. We also told you that two different individuals do not have the same sets of chromosomes. That's almost always true. The exception is identical twins. Each identical twin has exactly the same chromosomes as the other.

Chromosomes Come in Pairs: Homologous Chromosomes

We said that human cells have a total of 46 chromosomes. But these 46 chromosomes come in pairs: Each human somatic cell has 23 pairs of chromosomes. Many other species also have their chromosomes situated in pairs. Forty-six just happens to be the number of chromosomes in human cells; hence, human cells have 23 pairs of chromosomes. Another way of saying this is to say that human cells have two sets of chromosomes, and each set consists of 23 different chromosomes.

Think about the set of 23 chromosomes that came from Dad. We'll call them 1A, 2A, 3A . . . all the way to 23A. Now think about the set of 23 chromosomes that came from Mom. We'll call them 1B, 2B, 3B, etc. Chromosomes 1A and 1B are very similar (not exactly alike, but very similar). They form one of the 23 pairs of chromosomes in your cells, and we refer to them as being **homologous**. Chromosomes 1A and 1B form a **homologous pair**. So do chromosomes 2A and 2B, 3A and 3B, 4A and 4B, etc.

One last point: Cells that have two sets of chromosomes (all chromosomes have a homologous partner) are said to be **diploid**. So human cells are diploid, and the cells of any other organism that have two sets of homologous chromosomes are also diploid.

Twins

Identical twins have identical chromosomes. That is because identical twins are the result of a single early-stage embryo splitting in two. You can think of this as natural cloning. Each identical twin carries the same set of chromosomes from the original egg and sperm.

Mom's Eyes, Dad's Nose

One set of your chromosomes came from your father in a sperm cell. One set of those chromosomes came from your mother in an ovum. When the sperm and ovum joined in fertilization, the resulting cell had two sets of 23 chromosomes each, for a total of 46 chromosomes. From that single cell, every other cell in the body was derived, so every other cell in the body has 46 chromosomes.

Quick Quiz #1

Fill in the blanks and check the appropriate boxes:

1. If two individuals are of the same species, then the chromosomes in one individual's cells [□ **are** □ **are not**] identical to the chromosomes in the other individual's cells.

2. The enzyme that runs DNA replication is called _____.

3. Humans have _____ total chromosomes found as _____ sets of _____ chromosomes each.

4. One strand of DNA serves as a _____ for the creation of a complementary strand.

5. If two cells are taken from the same individual, the chromosomes in one cell [□ **are** □ **are not**] identical to the chromosomes in the other cell.

6. Homologous chromosomes [□ **are** □ **are not**] identical.

What Do Chromosomes *Do*?

Okay, we know that the chromosomes found in the nucleus are DNA, and we know that DNA is the genetic information of a cell, but what does that mean, exactly? What is DNA's job?

> DNA's job is to carry the instructions for making proteins.

In other words, it tells the cell in what order to connect amino acids to make proteins. But why just protein instructions? Why not carbohydrate instructions or lipid instructions? The answer is that enzymes are proteins. And if you can make enzymes, the enzymes can then make everything else. The enzymes will run all of the reactions needed to make everything else for a cell.

Human cells contain *a lot* of DNA. And not all of the DNA carries protein-building instructions. Much of the DNA isn't used at all. The portions of DNA that actually carry instructions (and regulatory sequences) for protein synthesis are called **genes**. So the chromosomes contain the genes that tell your body's cells how to make the enzymes (and other proteins) they need to function properly. But you don't go straight from DNA to protein. There's another step in there. Let's take a look below.

How Chromosomes Govern Protein Synthesis: Transcription and Translation

DNA contains genes, and genes tell your cells how to make protein. The step in between is the production of RNA. RNA is the "middleman" between DNA and protein.

DNA ⟶ RNA ⟶ PROTEIN

> This is known as the "central dogma of molecular biology." DNA to RNA to protein. In other words, DNA directs the synthesis of RNA, and RNA directs the synthesis of protein.

To refresh your memory, RNA is a nucleic acid that's similar to DNA. It has a sugar phosphate backbone, but the sugar is **ribose** (not deoxyribose, like in DNA). It is a polymer of nucleotides, but the bases are adenine, guanine, cytosine, and **uracil** (not thymine, like in DNA). And RNA is **single-stranded** (not double-stranded, like DNA).

So DNA is a string of nucleotides, RNA is a string of nucleotides, and proteins are strings of amino acids. We can rewrite the central dogma to look like this:

NUCLEOTIDES ⟶ NUCLEOTIDES ⟶ AMINO ACIDS

Essentially we're going from the language of nucleotides to the language of nucleotides, then from the language of nucleotides to the language of amino acids.

When making RNA from DNA, we're going from the language of nucleotides to the language of nucleotides. Whenever you copy something from one language to the same language, it is called a **transcription**. So DNA to RNA is a transcription.

If you missed class one day and borrowed a friend's notebook to copy over the notes into your notebook, that would be a transcription. Same information, same language, and a few slight differences (different handwriting, maybe a different pen color). Producing RNA from DNA is a similar situation. Same information (how to make protein), same language (nucleotides), slight differences (RNA is single-stranded, uses uracil, etc.).

DNA $\xrightarrow{\text{transcription}}$ RNA ⟶ Protein

Now let's say you have a friend who lives in Russia who just HAS to have a copy of your notes. No problem. You can copy them over for your Russian friend, but what do you have to do first? Translate them. You need to translate them into a new language: Russian. Switching from one language to a new language is a translation. And when you switch from RNA (nucleotide language) to protein (amino acid language), that's a translation.

DNA $\xrightarrow{\text{transcription}}$ RNA $\xrightarrow{\text{translation}}$ Protein

So . . . we can say that RNA is *transcribed* from DNA, and protein is *translated* from RNA. Let's look at these processes in a little more detail.

WHERE RNA COMES FROM: TRANSCRIPTION

Remember DNA replication? The DNA molecule unwinds, then each strand serves as a template for a new complementary strand of DNA. RNA **transcription** is very similar. The DNA molecule unwinds, and an enzyme called **RNA polymerase** creates a complementary strand of RNA, using *one* of the strands of DNA as a template. Guanine (on DNA) is paired with cytosine (on RNA). Cytosine (on DNA) is paired with guanine (on RNA). Thymine on DNA is paired with adenine on RNA. And adenine (on DNA) is paired with uracil (on RNA).

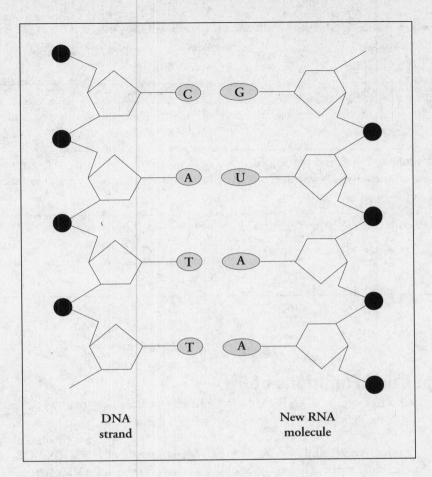

DNA strand

New RNA molecule

The two strands (one DNA and one new RNA) do **NOT** then bond together to form a ladder. Remember: RNA is a **single-stranded** molecule. The new RNA molecule is released, and the DNA strand rejoins with its complementary partner.

One last thing to point out: In replication, the entire DNA molecule (the entire chromosome) is copied over. In transcription, only a portion of the DNA molecule is used (or transcribed) to make RNA. Remember that much of the DNA in human cells does *not* carry instructions for protein synthesis, and that the portions that *do* carry instructions for protein synthesis are called genes. So we need to transcribe only the genes. Furthermore, we need to transcribe only some of the genes—the ones that correspond to proteins needed by the cell at that time.

Here's a summary of the differences between DNA replication and RNA transcription:

DNA Replication	RNA Transcription
Two new molecules of double-stranded DNA are produced.	One new molecule of single-stranded RNA is produced.
Adenine on one strand binds to thymine on the new DNA strand being created.	Adenine on DNA binds to uracil on the new RNA strand being created.
The entire chromosome is replicated.	Only a small portion of the DNA molecule is transcribed to RNA, and this varies based on the cell's needs at the time.

Types and Functions of RNA

There are three types of RNA that can be made, and each of them has a special role in protein synthesis.

1. **mRNA:** *m* stands for "messenger." Messenger RNA is the RNA that actually carries the information for protein synthesis (in the form of a nucleotide sequence).
2. **rRNA:** *r* stands for "ribosomal." Ribosomal RNA interacts with the cell's ribosomes to make them functional. It is thought that rRNA is the catalyst for protein synthesis; if there's no rRNA associated with the ribosomes, then the ribosomes don't work.
3. **tRNA:** *t* stands for "transfer." Transfer RNA carries amino acids from the cytoplasm to the ribosomes during protein synthesis.

Replication and transcription occur in the nucleus. But translation (protein synthesis) occurs in the cytoplasm of the cell. The three types of RNA must leave the nucleus and enter the cytoplasm for protein synthesis to take place.

TRANSLATION

If you were going to translate your notes from English to Russian, you would need a translation dictionary, something that tells you how a word in English is written in Russian. The **translation** of protein is no different. When you move from the language of nucleotides to the language of amino acids, you still need a "dictionary"; something that tells you which nucleotides correspond to which amino acids. More specifically, you need something to tell you which *sequence of three* nucleotides corresponds to which *one* amino acid. A sequence of three nucleotides is called a **codon**, and the order of codons on mRNA specifies the order of amino acids in a protein. The dictionary for protein translation is called the **Genetic Code.**

Because there are four possible nucleotide bases, and codons are groups of three bases, there are 64 (4 × 4 × 4) possible codons. Because there are only 20 different amino acids, some of the amino acids are coded for by more than one codon. The Genetic Code is nothing more, really, than a list of the 64 possible codons and the amino acids to which they correspond. The following chart shows a portion of the Genetic Code.

Codon	Amino Acid
AUG	methionine
CUU	leucine
GCA	alanine
UUG	leucine
CAG	glutamine
CGA	arginine

Cracking the Code
In 1961, Marshall Nirenberg, a chemist, began to explore codons and the amino acids to which they correspond. He made an RNA molecule that contained only nucleotides of uracil. This RNA, therefore, had the codon UUU repeated over and over. He then placed this into a test tube with all 20 amino acids, and found that a single kind of protein was translated: polyphenylalanine.

So, to figure out the order of amino acids in a protein, all you have to do is look at the sequence of codons on the mRNA. Suppose you had a piece of mRNA with the following sequence:

AUGGCACGACUU...

The codons are read in **nonoverlapping sequence**, like this:

AUG   GCA   CGA   CUU...
codon codon codon codon
#1   #2   #3   #4

So, for this piece of mRNA, the amino acid sequence would be:

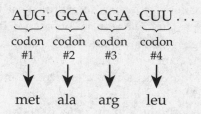

Now you can see how a nucleotide sequence on DNA can specify a nucleotide sequence on RNA, and how that same nucleotide sequence can specify an amino acid sequence in a protein.

Stop and Go
- The codon AUG (methionine) is known as the "start" codon, because it's the first codon on all mRNA, and methionine is the first amino acid in all proteins.
- Three of the 64 possible codons do not specify an amino acid. They specify "stop." In other words, "stop translating, the protein is finished." The three stop codons are **UAA, UGA,** and **UAG.**

Quick Quiz #2

Fill in the blanks and check the appropriate boxes:

1. Production of a strand of RNA from a strand of DNA is called
   _____.

2. The sequence of RNA that is complementary to the DNA sequence
   CAGTATACG is _____.

3. Portions of DNA that carry instructions for protein synthesis are
   called [☐ **genes** ☐ **codons**].

4. _____ carries amino acids from the cytoplasm to the ribosomes during protein translation.

5. The sequence of codons on mRNA is read in [☐ **overlapping**
   ☐ **nonoverlapping**] sequence.

6. The three "stop" codons are _____, _____,
   and _____.

7. Synthesis of protein using a strand of RNA is called _____.

8. The "start" codon is [☐ **AUG** ☐ **UAG**], and it codes for _____.

How Translation Works, Part 1: tRNA

tRNA is the molecule that carries amino acids from the cytoplasm to the ribosomes. It has a specific, three-dimensional shape (it looks somewhat like a pistol), and if it is flattened out, it has a "cloverleaf" shape, something like this (the nucleotide sequence has been eliminated for clarity):

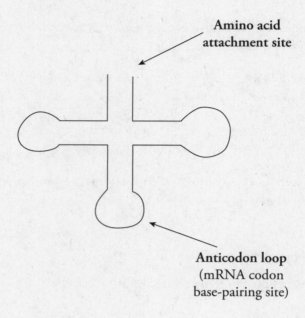

Amino acid attachment site

Anticodon loop (mRNA codon base-pairing site)

> The **anticodon** (contained within the **anticodon loop**) is a special region on the tRNA molecule that can base-pair with codons on mRNA. *The anticodon must be complementary to a codon to base-pair with it.*

For example, if a codon has the sequence AUG, the only tRNA molecules that can base-pair with that codon are the tRNAs that have UAC for an anticodon:

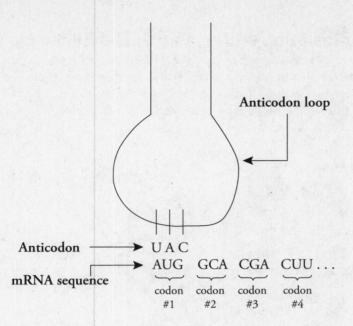

On the other end of the tRNA, an amino acid can attach. The amino acid that attaches corresponds with the codon that the tRNA anticodon can base-pair with. For example, in the situation above, the tRNA anticodon could base-pair with the codon AUG. The codon AUG codes for methionine. So the amino acid that would attach to that particular tRNA would be methionine. Here are some other examples:

mRNA codon	tRNA anticodon	Attached amino acid
AUG	UAC	methionine
CUU	GAA	leucine
GCA	CGU	alanine
UUG	AAC	leucine
CAG	GUC	glutamine
CGA	GCU	arginine

tRNA: A Quick Review
- tRNA molecules carry amino acids from the cytoplasm to the ribosomes.
- tRNA has an "anticodon" that's complementary to mRNA codons and that can base-pair with them.
- The codon that tRNA can base-pair with determines the amino acid that can be carried by the tRNA.

How Translation Works, Part 2: The Ribosome

The **ribosome** is the organelle that synthesizes protein. mRNA binds to ribosomes, and tRNAs carry amino acids to the ribosomes. There are two binding sites on a ribosome: the P-site and the A-site. The mRNA binds to the ribosome so that the first codon is in the P-site and the second codon is in the A-site:

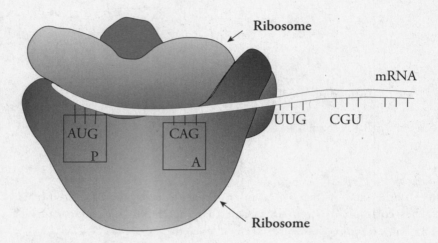

Once the mRNA is bound, tRNA, carrying the appropriate amino acids, comes and base-pairs with the codons on mRNA. Then the ribosome forms a peptide bond between the two amino acids:

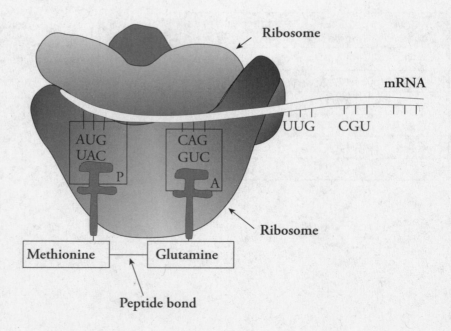

Once the peptide bond is formed, the first (and now empty) tRNA is released from the ribosome. It is free to return to the cytoplasm and bind to another amino acid. The ribosome, meanwhile, slides down one codon, so that the codon that was in the A-site shifts to the P-site, and the next codon in the sequence moves into the A-site:

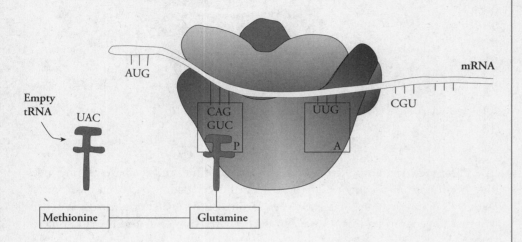

Now the sequence is just repeated. Another tRNA (carrying the appropriate amino acid) moves in and base-pairs with the codon in the A-site. The ribosome forms a peptide bond between the two amino acids (the one attached to the tRNA in the P-site and the one attached to the tRNA in the A-site), and the tRNA in the P-site is now released and returns to the cytoplasm.

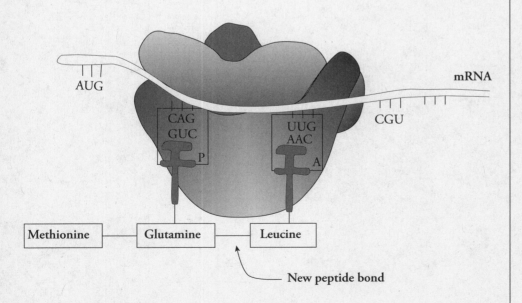

And the ribosome shifts over again:

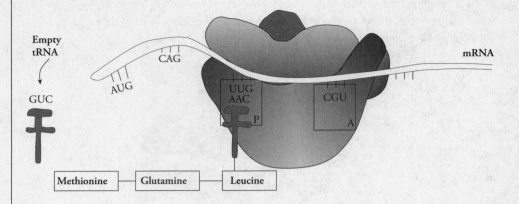

The ribosome continues shifting over a codon at a time, and the base-pairing, peptide bond–forming sequence is repeated until every codon has been base-paired with tRNA and peptide bonds have been formed between all amino acids. We then say that the codons on mRNA have been translated by tRNA and the ribosomes.

When a stop codon (UAG, UGA, or UAA) appears in the A-site, the final tRNA is released from the ribosome, the completed protein is released, and translation is complete.

By the way, the "P" in P-site stands for **peptide**. This is where the growing peptide is attached to the ribosome. And the "A" in A-site stands for **amino acid**. This is where the next amino acid is added to the growing protein.

Quick Quiz #3

Fill in the blanks and check the appropriate boxes:

1. In order to base-pair, the anticodon on a tRNA must be _____ to an mRNA codon.

2. Peptide bonds are formed between [☐ tRNAs ☐ amino acids].

3. The next amino acid for the protein being translated binds (attaches to its tRNA) in the [☐ A-site ☐ P-site].

4. The growing protein is attached to the ribosome through a tRNA in the [☐ A-site ☐ P-site].

5. When a stop codon appears in the [☐ A-site ☐ P-site], the protein is _____ from the ribosome.

Key Words

genetic information
chromosome
eukaryotes
prokaryotes
replicate
DNA polymerase
template
somatic
homologous
homologous pair
diploid
genes
ribose
uracil
single stranded

transcription
translation
RNA polymerase
mRNA
rRNA
tRNA
codon
Genetic Code
nonoverlapping sequence
anticodon
anticodon loop
ribosome
peptide
amino acid

Summary

Here's a brief summary of protein synthesis:

o   A portion of a DNA molecule in the nucleus (a chromosome) unwinds, and an mRNA molecule is transcribed from a gene on that chromosome.

o   mRNA leaves the nucleus and enters the cytoplasm, where it binds to a ribosome (previously transcribed rRNA is associated with the ribosome to make it functional).

o   Previously transcribed tRNA molecules bind to specific amino acids in the cytoplasm according to their anticodons.

o   tRNA anticodons base-pair with mRNA codons, causing amino acids to "line up" in the order their codons appear on mRNA.

o   The ribosome forms peptide bonds between the amino acids and releases the completed protein when a stop codon (UAA, UGA, or UAG) appears in the A-site.

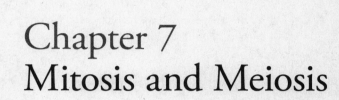

Chapter 7
Mitosis and Meiosis

Cell division is a very important topic in the study of molecular biology for the SAT Biology E/M Subject Test. This chapter will introduce you to the topics of mitosis (cell division) and meiosis (the formation of gametes), as well as to what occurs in the cell before, during, and after these processes.

HOW A WHOLE CELL REPRODUCES ITSELF: MITOSIS

For the SAT Biology E/M Subject Test, you need to know about cell division, which is also called **mitosis**. Before we talk about mitosis itself, let's talk about what happens before mitosis occurs. To make things easy, we'll talk about a human cell.

Most human cells (all, in fact, except for sperm and ova) have 46 chromosomes in their nuclei. The chromosomes are found in pairs, so we can say that the nuclei of the cells have 23 pairs of homologous chromosomes. This should be no surprise to you, because we've already talked about it. Before a cell undergoes mitosis, every single chromosome in its nucleus replicates. In a human cell, all 46 chromosomes have to replicate. We've already discussed how that's done.

Interphase

Interphase is the time during which chromosomes replicate, but a lot of other things happen during interphase; for instance, the cell carries out all of its normal activities. Interphase is sometimes called the resting stage of the cell—not because the cell is taking it easy, but because the cell is not actively dividing.

Once interphase is over, the cell has replicated every one of its 46 chromosomes. How many chromosomes does it have now? Well, the answer would seem to be 46 × 2 = 92. When a cell has finished interphase, you'd think it has 92 chromosomes, and more or less, you'd be right. But the terminology can get confusing.

Watch Out for This Word: Chromatid

After interphase, each chromosome and the duplicate piece of DNA that was just made are held together at their center by a region called a **centromere**. The two chromosomes and the centromere make one united physical structure.

We look at the entire structure—the two chromosomes joined by a centromere—and call the whole thing a **chromosome**. The word **chromatid** is used to describe each of the individual chromosomes.

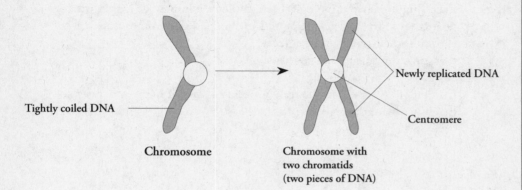

Tightly coiled DNA

Chromosome

Newly replicated DNA

Centromere

Chromosome with
two chromatids
(two pieces of DNA)

When interphase is over, all of the cell's 46 chromosomes have doubled. We might *want* to say the cell has 92 chromosomes, but that's not the way it is described. Instead, we say the cell still has 46 chromosomes, each now consisting of two chromatids.

Quick Quiz #1

Fill in the blanks and check the appropriate boxes:

1. A human cell, after interphase, has a total of _____ chromosomes, each made up of two _____.

2. During the stage called interphase, [☐ **all** ☐ **only some**] of the cell's chromosomes replicate.

3. According to current biological terminology, a human cell, after interphase, has in its nucleus a total of [☐ **92** ☐ **46**] chromosomes, each chromosome having at its center a _____ that joins the chromatids together.

4. DNA replication is [☐ **the only process** ☐ **one of many processes**] that takes place during interphase.

Mitosis Happens in Four Steps

After interphase, mitosis begins. **Step 1** is called **prophase**. In prophase, the centrioles move away from each other to opposite sides of the cell. They form a bunch of fibers called the **mitotic spindle**. These fibers attach to the chromosomes at their centromeres and help to push and pull them around during mitosis. The chromosomes condense (coil up even tighter) and we can see them (under the microscope, of course). The nuclear membrane begins to break up, too.

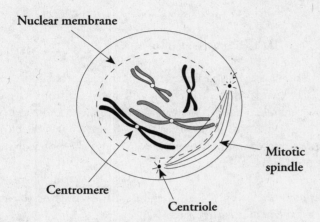

The Cell at Prophase of Mitosis

Note that in the drawing above, and in the ones that follow, the cell has only four chromosomes. That's okay. To simplify things, we have left out the other 42 chromosomes. But everything that's happening to these four chromosomes is happening to the other 42. You'll just have to imagine them. Also notice that one set of the chromosomes is light and one is dark. This is just to clarify that each chromosome has a homologous partner. The long light-colored chromosome and the long dark-colored chromosome are a homologous pair. Likewise, the shorter light-colored chromosome and the shorter dark-colored chromosome are a homologous pair.

Step 2 is called **metaphase**. During metaphase, the chromosomes line up—pushed and pulled by the spindle fibers—at the equator of the cell. The equator of the cell is known as the **metaphase plate**.

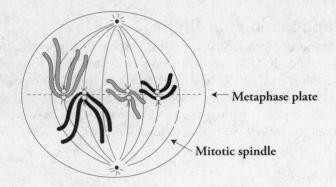

Metaphase plate ←

Mitotic spindle ←

The Cell at Metaphase of Mitosis

Step 3 is called **anaphase**. In anaphase, the centromere that joins each pair of chromatids splits in two so that each chromatid separates from its partner. And guess what? Now each chromatid is once again called a chromosome. So once the centromeres split, you have to admit that the cell briefly has 92 chromosomes. The newly separated chromosomes move toward opposite poles of the cell with the help of the spindle fibers.

Also during anaphase, the cell physically begins splitting in two. The area where it pinches inward is called the **cleavage furrow**.

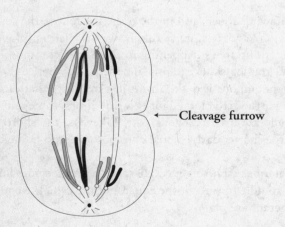

← Cleavage furrow

The Cell at Anaphase of Mitosis

Step 4 is called **telophase**. A nuclear membrane forms in each new cell and two daughter cells result, each of which has 46 chromosomes. The cytoplasm then divides during a process called **cytokinesis**.

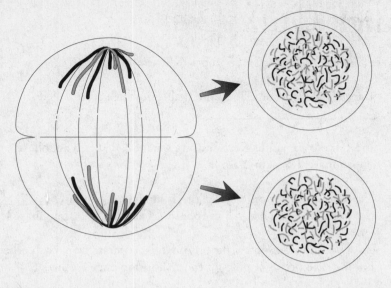

The Cell at Telophase of Mitosis   **Interphase**

Then, of course, the two new daughter cells enter interphase.

The Order of Mitosis
So let's review the order:

- Before mitosis, **interphase**
- **Mitosis:**
  1. Prophase
  2. Metaphase
  3. Anaphase
  4. Telophase

Quick Quiz #2

Fill in the blanks and check the appropriate boxes:

1. The cell's chromosomes become visible during a stage called
    _____.

2. The spindle apparatus forms during a stage called [☐ **anaphase**
    ☐ **prophase** ☐ **metaphase**].

3. The division of the cell's cytoplasm is known as _____,
    and this occurs during [☐ **prophase** ☐ **anaphase** ☐ **telophase**].

4. Duplicate chromosomes (the chromatids) separate from each other
    and move to opposite poles of the cell during a stage called
    _____.

5. During a stage called _____, all of a cell's
    chromosomes replicate.

6. The centromeres divide during a stage called _____.

7. During prophase, the _____ move away
    from one another toward opposite sides of the cell.

GENES, PROTEINS, AND CHROMOSOMES

Each gene corresponds to a single protein. This is known as the **one-gene-one-protein** theory, which means that when we say "gene," we're talking about some portion of a chromosome that gives rise, ultimately, to *one protein molecule*. A gene is any part of any chromosome that is responsible for the creation of one protein molecule.

A chromosome is just a long piece of DNA, and one chromosome contains many, many genes. It takes three nucleotides to make one mRNA codon, and even though one codon codes for only one amino acid, and a single protein is a long, long chain of amino acids, a single chromosome is so very, *very* long that it may give rise to hundreds and hundreds of proteins. That may be difficult to imagine, but it's true.

So remember: When we say "gene," we're talking about one portion of one chromosome. What portion? A portion that ultimately produces—via mRNA and ribosomes—one protein. Also remember that one chromosome contains enough nucleotides to bring about the production of many different proteins. This is another way of saying that *one chromosome contains a large number of genes*.

> ## Remember Why Chromosomes Are Important: They Contain Genes
>
> - Chromosomes are very long strands of DNA.
> - DNA is a chain of nucleotides.
> - A strand of DNA can direct the production of a molecule of mRNA, which is also a chain of nucleotides.
> - mRNA travels from the nucleus to the cytoplasm and binds to a ribosome.
> - A series of three mRNA nucleotides is a codon, which codes for a particular amino acid.
> - Amino acids (carried by tRNA) bind to the ribosome according to the order of the mRNA molecule's codons.
> - Peptide bonds are formed between the amino acids and a polypeptide (a protein) is formed.
>
> This process is known as protein synthesis, or **translation**.
>
> - Not all of the DNA in a chromosome is used to make mRNA.
> - The portions of the chromosome that are transcribed to mRNA, and ultimately translated to protein, are called **genes**.

But Where Did These Chromosomes and Their Genes COME From?

They came from your mom and dad. Remember, we said that all human cells (except for sperm and ova) have 46 chromosomes, and the chromosomes were found as two sets of 23 chromosomes each. One set of 23 chromosomes came from your mom in an ovum, and one set of 23 chromosomes came from your dad in a sperm cell. So that means that sperm and ova (sex cells, or **gametes**) have only 23 chromosomes, half the number of normal (non-sex, or **somatic**) cells. Cells that have two complete sets of chromosomes are described as being **diploid**, and cells that have only one set of chromosomes are described as being **haploid**. So sperm and ova are haploid cells.

Diploid number refers to the number of chromosomes a cell has when it's in a diploid state. For a human cell, the diploid number is 46. Haploid number means the number of chromosomes a cell has when it's in a haploid state. Naturally, the haploid number is always one-half the diploid number. For a human being, the haploid number is 23.

How do sperm and ova come to have only 23 chromosomes? They undergo a special type of cell division called **meiosis**.

THE FORMATION OF GAMETES: MEIOSIS

The gametes—the sperm and ova—are the only human cells that are haploid. Each has 23 chromosomes. When a sperm and an ovum get together—that is, when the sperm fertilizes the ovum—the chromosomes from the sperm join with the chromosomes in the ovum. The newly formed cell—the **zygote**—is diploid. The diploid zygote then undergoes mitosis to begin the new human's development. We'll look at the specifics of how a sperm is formed and how an ovum is formed in just a little while. But first let's go over the basics of meiosis.

During Meiosis

1. The cell undergoes DNA replication during interphase, just as it would if it were about to go through ordinary mitosis. All of the chromosomes replicate, and we're left with a cell that still has 46 chromosomes, each made up of two chromatids joined by a centromere.

2. The replicated chromosomes are split up in the course of two sets of divisions: prophase I, metaphase I, anaphase I, telophase I, and prophase II, metaphase II, anaphase II, and telophase II.

3. The differences between mitosis and meiosis are all found during the first set of divisions: prophase I, metaphase I, anaphase I, and telophase I.

Meiosis I

Meiosis I consists of four phases: prophase I, metaphase I, anaphase I, and telophase I. Remember that the chromosomes have already replicated and are found as two chromatids held together at the centromere. The biggest difference between these four phases and the four phases of mitosis is that at the very beginning, the homologous chromosomes pair up in a process called **synapsis**. This changes everything.

Prophase I

Synapsis occurs during **prophase** I. All the chromosomes have to find their homologous partner and pair up. Chromosome 1-A has to find chromosome 1-B, chromosome 2-A has to find chromosome 2-B, and so on. It takes a while, and prophase I is the longest phase of meiosis. When synapsis is complete, all the chromosomes are paired up with their partners. So instead of finding 46 replicated chromosomes floating around, we find *23 pairs* of replicated chromosomes. Because each pair consists of four chromatids (two chromatids per replicated chromosome, and two replicated chromosomes), this pair is also known as a **tetrad** (*tetra* = four). Notice that, in the drawings below, only four pairs of the 23 pairs are shown.

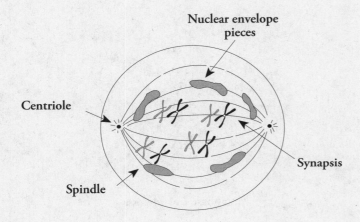

All of the other normal events that occur in prophase still happen. The spindle is formed, the chromosomes condense, and the nuclear membrane disintegrates. After synapsis occurs, an event called **crossing over** takes place. Basically, this means that like segments on homologous chromosomes are exchanged.

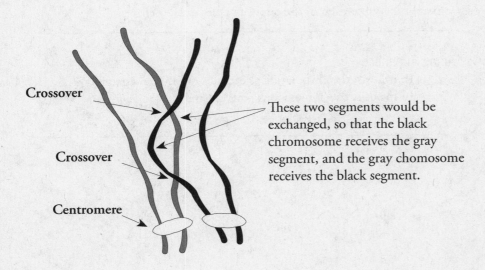

These two segments would be exchanged, so that the black chromosome receives the gray segment, and the gray chomosome receives the black segment.

Metaphase I

During metaphase of mitosis, the chromosomes line up on the equator of the cell. During metaphase of meiosis, the chromosomes also line up on the equator of the cells.

> In meiosis, chromosomes *stay in their homologous pairs*. So instead of 46 individual chromosomes lining up, there are 23 pairs of chromosomes.

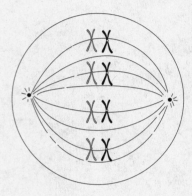

Metaphase I of Meiosis

Anaphase I

During anaphase of mitosis, the 46 replicated chromosomes split at their centromeres, and one chromatid goes to each of the opposite poles of the cell. In anaphase I of meiosis, the centromeres DO NOT divide. Instead, the homologous pairs separate, with one entire replicated chromosome (a pair of chromatids and a centromere) moving to each of the opposite poles of the cell.

> During Anaphase
> - In mitosis, the chromatids of each chromosome separate.
> - In meiosis, the homologous pairs separate.

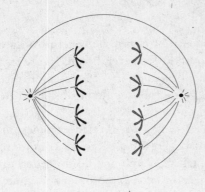

Anaphase I of Meiosis

Telophase I

Telophase I of meiosis is very similar to telophase of mitosis. The two cells finish dividing their cytoplasm (cytokinesis), and nuclear membranes reform around the chromosomes. But this leaves us with a strange situation. The two new cells DO NOT have 23 homologous pairs of chromosomes (46 total chromosomes); they have 23 replicated chromosomes (each chromosome is made of two identical chromatids).

Because there are no homologous pairs, the cells are considered haploid by Telophase I.

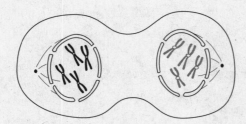

Telophase I of Meiosis

Meiosis II

Meiosis II is virtually identical to mitosis, in terms of how the chromosomes are moved and how they are split. However, because we're starting with the two cells formed in meiosis I, they have only half the number of chromosomes that a cell would have when undergoing mitosis. Remember that, in mitosis, the cell starts with 46 replicated chromosomes. The cells we're starting out with in meiosis II, because of meiosis I, have only 23 replicated chromosomes. But the phases and the chromosome movements are identical to those of mitosis. During prophase II the spindle forms, the nuclear membrane disintegrates, and the DNA condenses (of course, there is no pairing of chromosomes this time, because there is nothing to pair up with—the homologous partners were separated during anaphase I). During metaphase II, the chromosomes line up individually along the equator and, during anaphase II, *the centromere splits and the chromatids divide.* Then the chromatids are called chromosomes again. During telophase II, a nuclear membrane forms around the newly split chromosomes, and we are left with four haploid cells.

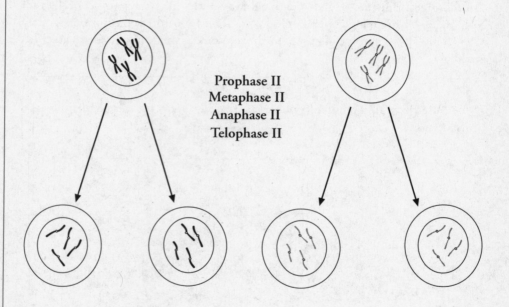

Prophase II
Metaphase II
Anaphase II
Telophase II

The four haploid cells do not replicate any further unless fertilization triggers new cell cycles.

Quick Quiz #3

Fill in the blanks and check the appropriate boxes:

1. If, for a particular organism, the diploid number of chromosomes is 10, then the haploid number is _____.

2. The first metaphase of meiosis (metaphase I) differs from metaphase of mitosis in that a _____ of chromosomes lines up on each spindle fiber.

3. The four cells resulting from meiosis are _____.

4. Crossing over occurs after _____.

5. The word [☐ **haploid** ☐ **diploid**] refers to a cell for which each chromosome does NOT have a homologous partner.

6. The first anaphase of meiosis (anaphase I) differs from anaphase of mitosis in that centromeres [☐ **do** ☐ **do not**] divide.

7. Prophase I of meiosis [☐ **is** ☐ **is not**] similar to prophase of mitosis.

Meiosis and the Formation of Sperm Cells: Spermatogenesis

Because sperm and ova are the gametes, the formation of sperm and ova is called **gametogenesis**. When we talk specifically about the formation of sperm, we call it **spermatogenesis**. Spermatogenesis requires *mei*osis, (not *mit*osis).

We start with a diploid cell called a **spermatogonium** (it's *gon*na become a sperm cell). Spermatogonia live in tiny tubules called **seminiferous tubules**, located in the testes. The testes are the male gonads. One spermatogonium, which is diploid, undergoes meiosis and produces four sperm cells, which are haploid.

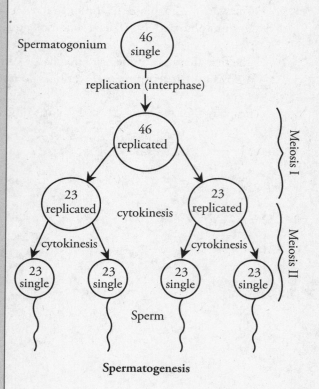

Spermatogenesis

Spermatogenesis

1. The spermatogonium replicates all of its chromosomes during interphase. It now has 46 chromosomes, and each chromosome is made of two chromatids joined by a centromere.

2. The cell undergoes prophase I, the homologous chromosomes pair up (synapsis), and crossing over occurs.

3. The cell undergoes metaphase I in which the paired chromosomes line up on spindles at the equator. We see two centromeres on each spindle fiber.

4. The cell undergoes anaphase I, but the centromeres don't divide. Instead, the homologous chromosome pairs separate.

5. The cell finishes dividing during telophase I, and we now have two cells. Each cell has 23 chromosomes, and each chromosome is made up of two chromatids, still joined by a centromere. These cells are considered haploid.

6. Each of these two cells then goes through prophase, metaphase, anaphase, and telophase II. This second set of divisions DOES resemble mitosis. Chromosomes condense (but do not pair up) during prophase II; they line up individually along spindle fibers during metaphase II, and the centromeres divide during anaphase II. The cells finish dividing during telophase II, and at the end we have four cells, each of which have 23 unreplicated chromosomes (they're still haploid).

One last thing to remember about spermatogenesis: It occurs on a daily basis, beginning at puberty and lasting the entire lifetime of the male. Millions of sperm are produced on a daily basis.

Meiosis and the Formation of Ova: Oogenesis

When we say **oogenesis**, we are talking about the formation of female egg cells, also known as **ova** (singular = **ovum**). We deal, again, with meiosis.

Oogenesis is similar to spermatogenesis: A diploid cell forms haploid cells through meiosis.

Other than the differences in names of the initial and final cell, and the absorption of daughter cells in oogenesis, the overall process is pretty much the same.

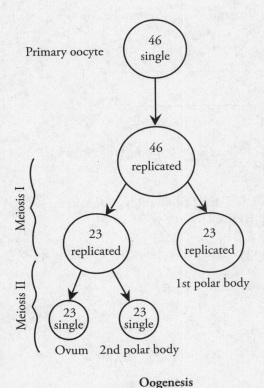

Oogenesis

Oogenesis

1. The initial cell is a **primary oocyte**.
2. Primary oocytes are found in ovaries in the female reproductive system. The ovary is the female gonad.
3. The final cell is called an ovum.
4. Oogenesis results in the production of *a single ovum from a single primary oocyte*. Two of the daughter cells resulting from meiotic division simply disintegrate. These cells are called **polar bodies**. This is very different from spermatogenesis, in which four mature sperm are produced from a single spermatogonium.
5. Oogenesis occurs on a monthly basis, *beginning at puberty and ending at menopause* (the end of regular menstrual cycles, an event that usually occurs between the ages of 46 and 54). A single ovum is produced per month.

Quick Quiz #4

Fill in the blanks and check the appropriate boxes:

1. The cells produced at the end of telophase I are considered to be
    [☐ **haploid** ☐ **diploid**].

2. Spermatogenesis begins at _____ and lasts
    _____.

3. _____ mature sperm are produced from a
    single spermatogonium.

4. The female gonad is the _____.

5. Oogenesis begins at _____ and ends at
    _____.

6. [☐ **Four** ☐ **One**] mature ova (ovum) are (is) produced from a single
    primary oocyte.

7. Spermatogenesis takes place on a [☐ **daily** ☐ **monthly**] basis, whereas
    oogenesis takes place on a [☐ **daily** ☐ **monthly**] basis.

8. The cells that disintegrate during oogenesis are called _____
    _____.

Key Words

mitosis
interphase
centromere
chromosome
chromatid
prophase
mitotic spindle
metaphase
metaphase plate
anaphase
cleavage furrow
telophase
cytokinesis
translation genes
one-gene-one-protein
karyotype
gametes
somatic
diploid
haploid

diploid number
haploid number
meiosis
zygote
synapsis
prophase I
tetrad
crossing over
metaphase I
anaphase I
telophase I
meiosis II
gametogenesis
spermatogenesis
spermatogonium
seminiferous tubules
oogenesis
ova/ovum
primary oocyte
polar bodies

Summary

o Somatic cells undergo a process called mitosis. This is the way that these cells divide.

o Chromosomes replicate during interphase. At the end of interphase, all 46 chromosomes in a cell have been replicated.

o The first stage of mitosis is prophase. The centrioles move away from each other to opposite sides of the cell, and the spindle is formed. The chromosones condense, and the nuclear membrane disintegrates.

o During metaphase, the second stage of mitosis, the chromosomes line up at the equator of the cell.

o During anaphase, the third stage, the centromere splits, separating each chromatid from its partner. The newly seperated chromosomes are pulled to opposite sides of the cell.

o In the last stage, telophase, two daughter cells form, with 46 chromosomes each.

o Gametes form during a process called meiosis.

o In meiosis, as in mitosis, chromosomes are replicated during interphase. At the end of interphase, all 46 chromosomes in a cell have been replicated.

o The replicated chromosomes are split up in the course of two sets of divisions: meiosis I and meiosis II.

o As in mitosis, there are four stages to each set of meiotic division: prophase, metaphase, anaphase, and telophase.

o A main difference between mitosis and meiosis is that at the beginning of meiosis, homologous chromosomes pair up during a process called synapsis.

o The centromeres do not divide in anaphase I; the homologous pairs separate into two cells.

o In anaphase II of meiosis, the centromeres do divide, resulting in four haploid cells with 23 chromosomes each.

o Spermatogenesis is the formation, through meiosis, of 4 haploid sperm cells from a single spermatogonium.

o Oogenesis is the formation, through meiosis, of a single haploid ovum from a single primary oocyte.

Now that you know how sperm and ova come to have only 23 chromosomes each . . .

Chapter 8
Cracking Genetics

The SAT Biology E/M Subject Test will definitely ask you some questions about genetics and inheritance. This chapter will explore what processes in an organism's cells will and will not occur, and how these processes determine what an organism is like: namely, its traits.

BIOLOGY OF INHERITANCE

From studying earlier chapters, you already know that

- genes direct the production of mRNA.
- mRNA contains three-nucleotide-long segments called codons.
- each codon codes for a single amino acid.
- amino acid chains become proteins.
- the primary function of proteins in a cell is to act as enzymes.

The enzymes inside an organism's cells determine which chemical reactions will and will not occur, and that determines what the organism is like. So, an organism's genes determine its features, its characteristics, its appearance—in other words, its traits. The genes determine what traits an organism will possess.

When talking about an organism's traits, we say **phenotype**. If you're a cat and your fur is gray, then we say that, in terms of fur color, your phenotype is gray. If your fur is white, then we say, in terms of fur color, your phenotype is white. If we meet a person who has diabetes, we say that, in terms of diabetes, his phenotype is diabetic. If we meet another person who does *not* have diabetes, we say that in terms of diabetes, her phenotype is nondiabetic, or we might say that her phenotype is normal. So when we say phenotype, we're just talking about the actual traits that an organism does and does not possess.

PHENOTYPE AND GENES

As you'll remember, we said that, generally speaking, chromosomes are arranged in homologous pairs. Each member of the pair is similar to, but also different from, the other member.

Let's look at one pair of chromosomes, and, in particular, let's focus on one part of each chromosome. We want to make the picture easy to look at, so we won't bother with actually shaping the chromosomes like a double helix/twisted ladder.

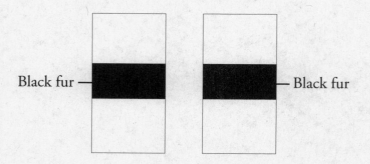

Black fur ─ ─ Black fur

Notice that each of these shaded portions is labeled "black fur." This means that the particular part of the chromosome that we've decided to look at codes for fur color. It's responsible for producing the enzymes that catalyze the chemical reactions that determine the color of the organism's fur. Now, this particular pair of chromosomes codes for enzymes that give rise to black fur. So, when it comes to fur color, what is this organism's phenotype? Simple—it's black.

Now, while we're looking at these two chromosomes, let's introduce another word: **genotype**. For the organism that we're now talking about—the one with the black fur—we'd (1) look at the homologous chromosome pair pictured above, (2) see that the organism has black fur, and (3) say:

> When we say *phenotype*, we're talking about the organism and its traits. But when we say *genotype*, we're talking about the genes responsible for those traits.

Fur Color *Geno*type: black/black (or BB)
Fur Color *Pheno*type: black

More About Genotype and Phenotype: Features That Are Dominant and Recessive

Let's consider another organism with black fur. When it comes to fur, what's the organism's phenotype? It's black.

Now let's look at its genotype. Here are the chromosomes that contain the genes responsible for fur color.

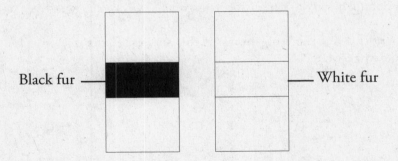

Black fur ——   —— White fur

Notice that the two homologous chromosomes don't agree on what color the organism's fur should be. One codes for black fur, and the other codes for white fur. Yet one member of the pair definitely wins the debate. The organism has black fur. When we want to describe this organism's phenotype and genotype in terms of fur color we say:

> *Geno*type: black / white (or Bb)
> *Pheno*type: black

Why does one of the chromosomes get to express itself in the organism's phenotype while the other one has to keep quiet? Here's the answer: For the species to which this organism belongs, black fur is dominant, and white fur is recessive. That just means that if an organism of this species has one black-fur chromosome and one white-fur chromosome, the organism will have fur that's black. Black fur is **dominant**—a chromosome that codes for black fur dominates a chromosome that codes for white fur. It gets to decide what the *pheno*type will be. White fur is **recessive**—it has to recede—it isn't expressed if one of the pair of homologous chromosomes codes for black fur. That's what we mean when we talk about features that are dominant and recessive.

Notice that we can use a sort of "shorthand" to indicate genotype. We can use letters to represent the genes an organism has. For example, in our first organism, the one in which both chromosomes coded for black fur, we described the genotype as black/black, or BB. The uppercase B represents the gene for black fur. In our second organism, in which one chromosome is coded for black fur and one coded for white fur, we described the genotype as black/white, or Bb. The lowercase b represents the gene for white fur.

> Uppercase letters are used to represent the dominant gene, and lowercase letters are used to represent the recessive gene.

Notice also that the letter chosen to represent the dominant gene is the same letter chosen to represent the recessive gene. In other words, we didn't switch letters and represent the gene for white fur with a lowercase *w*. As long as we're talking about the same trait (in this case, fur color), the letter stays the same; we just use uppercase for dominant and lower case for recessive.

Let's consider a few more organisms of this species. Here's one with fur color genotype: white/white.

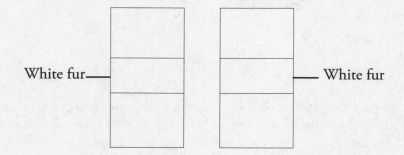

Its fur-color phenotype will be white. Even though white is recessive, both chromosomes agree that the fur should be white. There's no black-fur chromosome around to dominate the matter.

As a matter of fact, if you see an organism of this species and its fur is white, you know that its genotype is white/white, or bb. Because white is recessive, that's the only genotype that can produce a white phenotype. If a black-fur chromosome were around, the phenotype would have to be black. A white-fur phenotype definitely means a bb genotype because white is recessive.

Here's an organism with fur-color genotype: white/black (bB).

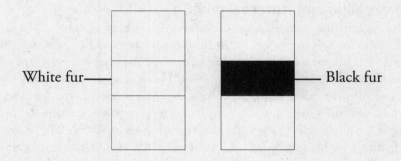

White fur——— ——— Black fur

Its fur-color phenotype will most definitely be black. Why? Because black fur is dominant and white fur is recessive. The black-fur chromosome dominates the white-fur one.

Time Out! Let's Learn Some Simple Biology Subject Test Terms: Allele, Homozygous and Heterozygous, and Codominance

1. Allele

The term **allele** is used to refer to a gene that gives rise to more than one version of the same trait—like, for example, eye color. Just now, for instance, we've been talking about the allele responsible for fur color. The black-fur and the white-fur genes are different alleles of the fur-color gene.

2. Homozygous and Heterozygous

When, for a particular trait, an organism's two alleles are in agreement, we say the organism is **homozygous** for that trait. The organism that has genotype black/black (or BB) is homozygous for fur color. The organism that has genotype white/white (or bb) is also homozygous for fur color. In both cases the two alleles agree on fur color. On the other hand, organisms that had genotypes black/white (Bb) and white/black (bB) were cases in which there was a disagreement within the genotype. One allele codes for white, and the other codes for black. We say that these organisms are **heterozygous** for fur color, which means that their two alleles don't agree on what color the fur should be. (We know, of course, that in both cases the fur will be black because, for this organism, black fur is dominant and white fur is recessive.)

3. Codominance

It is possible, in the case of multiple alleles, for two alleles to exhibit **codominance**. This means that a heterozygote expresses a mixture of the traits of both alleles. This is the case when someone has the blood type AB.

Quick Quiz #1

Fill in the blanks and check the appropriate boxes:

1. Which term refers to an organism's observable traits?

   (A) Phenotype
   (B) Genotype
   (C) Allele
   (D) Homozygous
   (E) Heterozygous

2. The term *allele* [☐ **is**   ☐ **is not**] precisely synonymous with the term *gene*.

3. Which of the following terms refers to the fact that the gene responsible for a particular observable trait might exist in more than one version?

   (A) Phenotype
   (B) Genotype
   (C) Allele
   (D) Homozygous
   (E) Heterozygous

4. If, in a particular organism, one allele on one member of a homologous chromosome pair codes for blue eye color and a corresponding allele on the other codes for brown eye color, the organism is said to be [☐ **homozygous**   ☐ **heterozygous**] for eye color.

5. If an organism is heterozygous for eye color, with one allele coding for green and the other allele coding for gray, the organism will have [☐ **green eyes**   ☐ **gray eyes**] if green is dominant, and [☐ **green eyes**   ☐ **gray eyes**] if gray is dominant.

6. If, for a particular species, the allele that produces a disease called erythema is dominant and the corresponding allele that produces the absence of disease (a normal organism) is recessive, then

   (a) an organism with a genotype that is heterozygous for the trait will have the phenotype: [☐ **normal**   ☐ **erythema**].
   (b) an organism with a genotype that is homozygous for the dominant allele will have the phenotype: [☐ **normal**   ☐ **erythema**].
   (c) an organism with a genotype that is homozygous for the recessive allele will have the phenotype: [☐ **normal**   ☐ **erythema**].
   (d) an organism with a phenotype that is normal must have a genotype that is [☐ **homozygous**   ☐ **heterozygous**].

Mating and Crossing: Predicting the Phenotype and Genotype of Offspring

When you take the SAT Biology E/M Subject Test you'll be asked, in one way or another, to figure out what kind of genotypes and phenotypes to expect from a cross between two organisms that bear offspring. Suppose two organisms decide to have offspring. One has black fur and the other has white fur. Here are the genotypes:

Male Parent	Female Parent
Bb	bb

Go back to Chapter 7 for a few minutes and reread the information about meiosis and fertilization. Realize that, from each pair of chromosomes normally present within the parent cell, the offspring gets one member from its father and another member from its mother. That's because the spermatozoa and ova are haploid cells, each of which contributes one member of a homologous pair to the zygote, which, therefore, is diploid.

Realize also that any offspring gets its particular mix of chromosomes at random, and different offspring get different mixes. Here's what we mean by that. As for the chromosome that carries the fur-color allele, there are four possible mixtures of homologous chromosomes that a particular offspring might receive from its parents.

1. One animal, for instance, might get this combination from his mother and this one from his father:

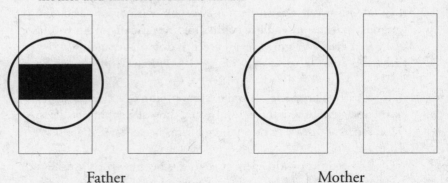

Father   Mother

That means the new organism will have genotype Bb. Its phenotype will be black, because black is dominant.

2. Another possibility is that the animal might get this from his father and this from his mother:

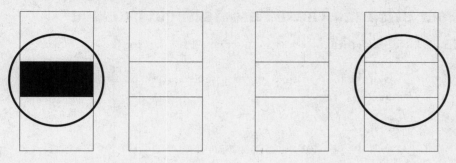

Father · Mother

This new organism will also have genotype Bb. Its phenotype for fur color will be black.

3. In the third possible combination, an animal might get this from his father and this from his mother:

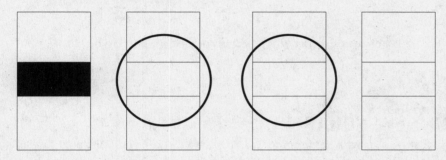

Father · Mother

This new organism will have genotype bb. Its phenotype for fur color will be white.

4. In the last possible combination, an animal might get this from his father and this from his mother:

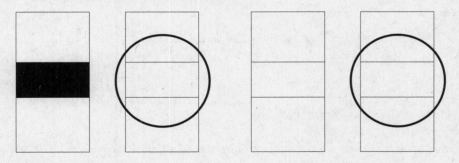

Father · Mother

That means the new organism will have genotype bb. Its phenotype for fur color will be white.

Take a Look at the Genotypes and Phenotypes of the Four Offspring These Parents Might Produce

If you look back at what we've just done, you'll see that for these parents:

- Two of the four possible offspring are genotype bb and phenotype white

  and

- Two of the four possible offspring are genotype Bb and phenotype black

We can say, therefore, that as for *these* parents and the fur color of *their* offspring, the *probability* is that:

- 50% of the offspring will be genotype bb and phenotype white

  and

- 50% of the offspring will be genotype Bb and phenotype black

PUNNETT SQUARES

Before we go on with some more examples, we'll show you a little trick. Draw a four-chambered box, and along the sides of the box indicate the genotypes of the two parents, like this:

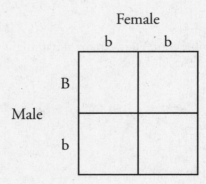

Now, fill in the four segments of the box according to what you've drawn along the sides and you'll easily visualize the four-genotype possibilities. (Knowing which trait is dominant and which is recessive means you can easily figure out the phenotype possibilities.) This is called a **Punnett square**.

Female

	b	b
B	Bb	Bb
b	bb	bb

Male

From this, it's quite easy to calculate the probability of each phenotype.

Once again, you come up with:

- 50% offspring of genotype bb and phenotype white

- 50% offspring of genotype Bb and phenotype black

What can we say about the probability that an offspring's fur will be white? We can say the probability is 50%. What can we say about the probability that its fur will be black? 50%.

Let's Do Some More Predicting

Suppose some species of plant has the possibility of producing flowers that are (1) red or (2) yellow. Suppose we tell you, also, that yellow is dominant and red is recessive. Now let's contemplate a cross between plants with these two genotypes:

Parent A   **Parent B**

Yy   Yy

Take a minute and draw a Punnett square in the space below. Fill it in as we did before. First we'll ask you some questions, and then we'll explain the answers so we're sure you're on top of this stuff.

Refer to your drawing and fill in the blanks and boxes appropriately.

- Parent plant A has phenotype [☐ **red flowers**   ☐ **yellow flowers**].

- Parent plant B has phenotype [☐ **red flowers**   ☐ **yellow flowers**].

- Parent plants A and B [☐ **can** ☐ **cannot**] possibly produce a plant with red flowers [☐ **because**   ☐ **even though**] both A and B have [☐ **red flowers**   ☐ **yellow flowers**].

- The probability that parent plants A and B will produce a plant with red flowers is _____%.

- The probability that parent plants A and B will produce a plant with yellow flowers is _____%.

Here's How to Crack It

If you drew your Punnett square correctly, it probably looks something like this:

Parent B

	Y	y
Y	YY	Yy
y	Yy	yy

Parent A

You might have drawn it with parent A on top and parent B along the side, or vice versa. It doesn't matter. For each parent you might have arranged the y and Y in either order. That doesn't matter either. You'd still get the same overall results.

To begin with, you know that each parent has phenotype yellow. Yellow is dominant. Even though each parent has a chromosome that wants the flowers to be red, each also has one that wants them to be yellow. Yellow wins the fight in both cases. Both parents have yellow flowers.

Your Punnett square shows you that if you make every possible crisscross, your four results are:

1. a plant with genotype YY and phenotype yellow
2. a plant with genotype Yy and phenotype yellow
3. a plant with genotype Yy and phenotype yellow
4. a plant with genotype yy and phenotype red

Of the four possible crisscrosses, two give us genotypes that are heterozygous, which means the phenotypes are yellow, one gives us a genotype that's homozygous for the yellow trait, which means that its phenotype is yellow, and one gives us a genotype that is homozygous for the red trait, which means that its phenotype is red.

Let's Do Another One

Sticking with the red and yellow flowers, let's draw some Punnett squares and make some predictions regarding the offspring of these two parent plants:

Parent A   **Parent B**

Yy   YY

Use the space below to draw this square as before. Make the appropriate markings and labels, and then fill in the blanks and boxes appropriately.

- Parent plant A has phenotype [☐ **red flowers**   ☐ **yellow flowers**].

- Parent plant B has phenotype [☐ **red flowers**   ☐ **yellow flowers**].

- Parent plants A and B [☐ **can**   ☐ **cannot**] possibly produce a plant with red flowers.

- The probability that parent plants A and B will produce a plant with red flowers is _____%.

- The probability that parent plants A and B will produce a plant with yellow flowers is _____%.

Here's How to Crack It

Your Punnett square should look like this:

Parent B

	Y	Y
Y	YY	YY
y	Yy	Yy

Parent A

One parent is homozygous for the dominant trait (yellow), and the other is heterozygous. For both parents, the phenotype is yellow. Your square shows you that the parents might possibly produce these four progeny:

1. a plant with genotype Yy and phenotype yellow
2. another plant with genotype Yy and phenotype yellow
3. a plant with genotype YY and phenotype yellow
4. another plant with genotype YY and phenotype yellow

The parents have a 50% probability of producing offspring with genotype Yy (or yY, however you want to look at it) and a 50% probability of producing offspring with genotype YY. In terms of phenotype, they have a 0% chance of producing offspring with red flowers and a 100% chance of producing offspring with yellow flowers. All of their offspring will have yellow flowers. Half will be heterozygous for the trait.

One More Example

Suppose a certain species of bird has the capacity to be born with oily or nonoily feathers. Suppose that oily is dominant and nonoily is recessive. Fill in the blank lines and boxes appropriately. (Hint: Figure out the genotypes of all organisms first.)

*   If an organism is born with nonoily feathers, it [☐ **is**   ☐ **is not**] possible that *both* of its parents were homozygous for oily feathers.

*   If an organism is born with oily feathers, it [☐ **is**   ☐ **is not**] possible that *both* of its parents were homozygous for oily feathers.

- If an organism is born with oily feathers, it [□ **is** □ **is not**] possible that *one* of its parents was homozygous for nonoily feathers.

- If an organism is born with nonoily feathers and its parent A had oily feathers, then

    (a) the genotype for parent A was _____,
    (b) the genotype for parent B was _____, or _____,
    (c) the phenotype for parent A was _____,
    (d) the phenotype for parent B was _____, or _____.

Here's How to Crack It

- If an organism is born with nonoily feathers, it [□ **is** ■ **is not**] possible that *both* of its parents were homozygous for oily feathers.

If both parents are homozygous for oily feathers, your box would show you that all offspring would also be homozygous for oily feathers. That genotype can't lead to nonoily feathers.

- If an organism is born with oily feathers, it [■ **is** □ **is not**] possible that *both* of its parents were homozygous for oily feathers.

That's because two parents that are homozygous for oily feathers will, in fact, produce offspring that are all oily-feathered. Your Punnett square will show you that.

- If an organism is born with oily feathers, it [■ **is** □ **is not**] possible that *one* of its parents was homozygous for nonoily feathers.

That's because an oily-feathered offspring can result from a parent that is homozygous for nonoily feathers so long as the other parent is either heterozygous or homozygous for oily feathers. Draw a Punnett square and you'll see.

- If an organism is born with nonoily feathers and parent A had oily feathers, then
    (a) the genotype for parent A was <u>Oo</u> (or oO, if you want to look at it that way).

That's because a nonoily-feathered organism can't arise if either parent is homozygous for oily feathers. Because you're told that parent A's phenotype is oily, it's got to be heterozygous: Oo.

    (b) The genotype for parent B was <u>Oo</u> or <u>oo.</u>

That's because a nonoily-feathered creature can result only if both parents have at least one chromosome for nonoily feathers. That means parent B has to be either Oo or oo.

    (c) The phenotype for parent A was <u>oily.</u>

That's because you're told that parent A was oily-feathered.

(d) The phenotype for parent B was oily or nonoily.

That's because a nonoily-feathered creature can result only if both parents have at least one chromosome for nonoily feathers. The right answer to item (b) tells you the right answer to this item (d). Parent B has genotype Oo or oo, which means its phenotype is either oily or nonoily.

Another Thing About Genetics and Inheritance: Sex and Sex-Linked Traits

Gregor Mendel
Almost everything we've just said about dominant traits, recessive traits, and the way they affect offspring was discovered by Gregor Mendel. When you hear the name "Mendel," think, "father of genetics." In the nineteenth century, Gregor Mendel performed experiments on garden peas, and that's how he figured out almost everything we've just learned. Sometimes what we've just learned is called **Mendelian genetics**. Don't forget about Gregor Mendel; he's the father of modern genetics.

A More Complicated Example
A **dihybrid cross** involves the mating of two organisms that differ in two characteristics. Gregor Mendel did experiments to this extent when he bred a round yellow pea that had the genotype *RrYy* with a round yellow pea that had the same genotype (*RrYy*). The offspring that resulted fell into a phenotypic ratio of 9 : 3 : 3 : 1.

Let's think about people. As you know, their cells (other than sperm and ova) have 23 pairs of homologous chromosomes. One of those 23 pairs is the pair that determines whether a person is male or female, and this pair of chromosomes is known as the **sex chromosomes**. All other chromosomes are called **autosomes**.

The sex chromosomes have many genes that determine sexual attributes, as well as some genes that determine nonsexual attributes. A sex chromosome can either be male, in which case we call it a Y chromosome, or it can be female, in which case we call it an X chromosome. A person whose phenotype is male has the sex genotype XY, and a person whose phenotype is female has the sex genotype XX. The male got an X chromosome from his mother (whose genotype is XX) and a Y chromosome from his father (whose genotype is XY). The female got an X chromosome from her mother and an X chromosome from her father. So whether a child is born male or female depends on whether it gets an X or a Y chromosome from its father—because the father can donate either one.

Quick Quiz #2

Fill in the blanks and check the appropriate boxes:

1. A male person receives from his father a(n) [☐ X ☐ Y] chromo-some.

2. A male person [☐ may ☐ must] have the genotype [☐ XY ☐ XX ☐ YY].

3. A female person [☐ may ☐ must] have the genotype [☐ XY ☐ XX ☐ YY].

4. In terms of sex, all persons, male or female, receive from their mothers a(n) _____ chromosome.

5. In terms of sex, all females receive from their fathers a(n) _____ chromosome.

Sex-Linked Traits

The sex chromosomes X and Y, as we said, carry certain genes on them. When we say **sex-linked trait**, we're referring to a trait whose allele is carried on one of the sex chromosomes. Almost all sex-linked traits have alleles that are carried on the X chromosome. The X chromosome is much larger than the Y chromosome and therefore carries more genes. For the purposes of the SAT Biology E/M Subject Test, the only sex-linked traits you need to worry about are ones carried on the X. You can, and should, think of them as being **X-linked**. The fact that some traits are X-linked leads to a few interesting phenotypes, which are very likely to show up on the exam. The three X-linked traits to know for the exam are **hemophilia** (a disorder of blood clotting), color blindness, and male pattern baldness.

Let's consider the disease hemophilia. It's an X-linked trait. In other words, if a person carries the trait, he or she carries it on the X chromosome. It's also recessive, so we can describe hemophilia as being an **X-linked recessive trait**. What does that mean? It means that a female can only get hemophilia if she's homozygous for the X chromosome that carries the allele for hemophilia. For example, take a look at these three female genotypes:

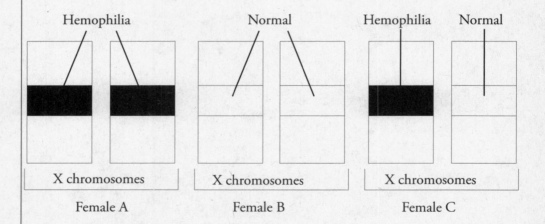

Like all females, Females A, B, and C each have two X chromosomes. For Female A, both X chromosomes carry the allele for hemophilia. That means that she is homozygous for the disease and her phenotype will be hemophilia.

Female B is homozygous for the normal allele. She's not even carrying the allele for hemophilia. Naturally, her phenotype will be normal.

Female C carries the allele for hemophilia on only one of her X chromosomes. Because it is a recessive trait, even though she is carrying the allele, she won't show it in her phenotype. She won't have hemophilia. Her phenotype is normal.

What you've just learned is this: When it comes to X-linked *recessive* traits, a female can express the trait in her phenotype only if her genotype is homozygous for the trait. If she's heterozygous for the trait, then it will not be expressed (it won't show up) in her phenotype. Females who are heterozygous for X-linked recessive traits are known as **carriers**. They don't express the trait, but they do carry the allele for the trait.

Now, what about males? Let's continue discussing hemophilia, and look at these two male genotypes:

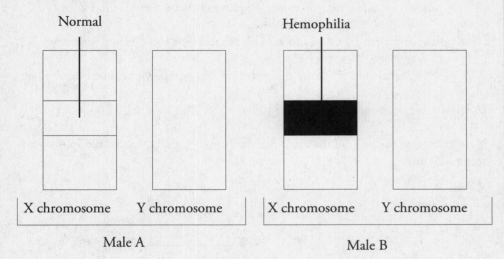

Like all males, Males A and B have an X chromosome (received from their mothers) and a Y chromosome (received from their fathers). Male B is carrying the allele for hemophilia on his X chromosome. Does he have the disease? That is, is his phenotype hemophilia? The answer is yes. Why? Because even though the trait is recessive, there is no normal X chromosome around to dominate it. The male doesn't have a second X chromosome. He has a Y chromosome instead, and that won't suppress the expression of the X chromosome's recessive allele. Male A, of course, is normal. He does not carry the allele for hemophilia.

So, when it comes to an X-linked recessive trait, a female will express the trait in her phenotype only if she is homozygous for it. However, a male will express the trait in his phenotype if he carries the allele on his X chromosome. For this reason, X-linked recessive diseases are much more common in *males* than in females.

Now, still talking about hemophilia, consider these two parents:

Father   Mother

$X_{(normal)}/Y$ $X_{(hemophilia)}/X_{(normal)}$

Draw a Punnett square and figure out, in terms of sex and hemophilia, what kind of children these two parents might produce. After you've done that, fill in the blanks and boxes appropriately.

Genotype Check-In

- With reference to the parents whose genotypes are shown on pages 156–157
  - (a) _____% of children are likely to be male.
  - (b) _____% of children are likely to be female.
  - (c) There is [☐ **no**   ☐ **some**] likelihood that a child will have phenotype hemophilia.
  - (d) There is [☐ **no**   ☐ **some**] likelihood that a female child will have phenotype hemophilia.
  - (e) There is [☐ **no**   ☐ **some**] likelihood that a male child will have phenotype hemophilia.
  - (f) The likelihood that a male child with hemophilia will be born is _____%.

(Answers can be found in Chapter 15.)

Here's how you figure it all out: You draw a Punnett square that would look something like this:

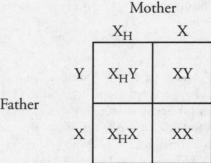

The square shows you that the parents are likely to produce:

1. a male child with genotype X_HY phenotype hemophilia
2. a male child with genotype XY phenotype normal
3. a female child with genotype X_HX phenotype normal
4. a female child with genotype XX phenotype normal

In our talk about X-linked traits, we've discussed only ones that are recessive. You're not likely to be asked questions on the exam about a dominant X-linked trait or a Y-linked trait. Remember, the three X-linked recessive traits you should know about for the SAT Biology E/M Subject Test are hemophilia (which we've already discussed), **color blindness**, and **male pattern baldness** (color blindness and male pattern baldness are inherited in the same way as hemophilia and follow the exact same rules we discussed for hemophilia). Also, you may not be told that these traits are X-linked; instead, you'll be expected to know that—and now you do.

One Last Point About X-linked Recessive Traits: They Can't Go *From* a Male *to* a Male

If the test presents you with a question about an X-linked recessive trait, realize this simple truth:

> An X-linked recessive trait cannot go from father to son.

That's because the allele for an X-linked trait is located on the X chromosome, and a father does not give his son an X chromosome. He gives him a Y chromosome.

Pedigree Analysis

The SAT Biology E/M Subject Test might ask you to determine probabilities by reading (analyzing) a **pedigree**. A pedigree is simply a chart that shows the presence of a particular phenotype in a given family, usually over several generations.

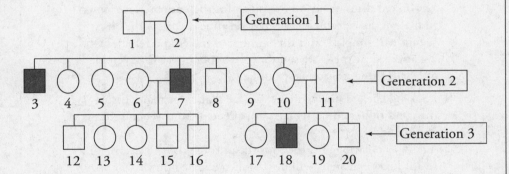

In pedigrees, males are represented by a square, and females are represented by a circle. A horizontal line connecting the two shapes shows the mating between two individuals, and a vertical line connects offspring resulting from that mating. For example, in the pedigree above, individuals 1 and 2 have produced seven offspring: individuals 3, 4, 5, 7, 8, 9, and 10. Individuals 6 and 7 have produced five offspring: individuals 12, 13, 14, 15, and 16. Individuals 10 and 11 have produced four offspring: individuals 17, 18, 19, and 20.

Individuals affected by color blindness are shaded. In our example above, individuals 3, 7, and 18 are affected by the condition. Individuals who marry into the family (in other words, those who are not blood-related) are completely normal and do not carry any abnormal alleles. In our example, these would be individuals 6 and 11.

Questions about pedigrees usually ask you to determine whether a particular individual is heterozygous or homozygous, about the specific genotype of a particular individual, or about the probability of two individuals mating and producing affected offspring. Before attempting to figure out genotypes or probabilities, you must answer two simple questions:

1. **Is the condition dominant or recessive?**
   Recessive conditions skip generations. Pick any affected individual in the pedigree. Look back at that individual's parents. Do they have the condition? Look at that individual's offspring (if present). Do they have the condition? If neither the parents nor the offspring display the condition, the condition is recessive.

   Consider our pedigree. Pick individual 7. He is affected by the condition, but neither his parents nor his offspring are affected. This condition is probably recessive. Let's confirm by looking at another affected individual. Pick individual 18. His parents are not affected and he has no offspring. Because his parents are not affected, this condition is recessive. Of course, if either the parents or the offspring of an affected individual ARE affected, the condition is dominant.

2. **Is the condition sex-linked, or is it autosomal (carried on one of the non-sex chromosomes)?**
   Sex-linked diseases, as we mentioned earlier, are more common in males than in females. So to determine if the condition is sex-linked, simply count the number of males and females who are affected. If there are significantly more males than females affected, the condition is sex-linked.

   Looking back at our pedigree, we see that three males display the condition, and no females are affected. So this condition is sex-linked.
   Again, as mentioned earlier, for the purposes of this exam, all sex-linked conditions will be X-linked (carried on the X chromosome). So this condition is not only sex-linked, but, specifically, X-linked.

So then, the condition shown in our pedigree is an X-linked recessive condition. Knowing that, you can answer some basic questions about the condition. (You might want to review the basics on X-linked conditions first.)

1. **Is individual 2 homozygous or heterozygous for the condition?**
   Individual 2 is female and is not affected by the condition. Therefore, she CANNOT be homozygous, because homozygous females would display a recessive X-linked condition. Furthermore, the fact that she has offspring who are affected by the condition indicates that she must be a carrier for the condition. Therefore, she is heterozygous.

2. **Is individual 13 homozygous or heterozygous for the condition?**
   Individual 13's father (individual 7) is affected by this condition. Because fathers pass their X chromosome on to their daughters, and because individual 7's X chromosome obviously carries the

allele for this condition, his daughter, individual 13, must have received the allele for the condition. However, because she is not affected by the condition (she does not display the affected phenotype), she must be heterozygous and a carrier for the condition.

Notice that the same reasoning can be applied to individual 14. *All daughters of males affected by an X-linked recessive condition are carriers for the condition.*

3. **If individual 13 has a child with a normal male, what is the probability they would produce an affected son?**

We've already determined that individual 13 is heterozygous for the condition. In other words, her genotype is $X_{affected}/X_{normal}$. A normal male would have the genotype X_{normal}/Y. Let's draw a Punnett square to determine the probability.

Female

	$X_{affected}$	X_{normal}
X_{normal}	$X_{affected}/X_{normal}$	X_{normal}/X_{normal}
Y	$X_{affected}/Y$	X_{normal}/Y

Male (labels X_{normal} and Y on left rows)

The genotype of an affected son would be $X_{affected}/Y$. From the Punnett square, we see there is only one such genotype out of the four possible genotypes, so the probability of producing an affected son would be 1/4, or 25%.

4. **If individual 3 has a child with a normal female, what is the probability they would produce an affected son?**

If you remember the rule about father-to-son transmission of an X-linked recessive condition, this question is easy. The probability is zero (0%), because fathers cannot pass X-linked conditions on to their sons. Fathers give their sons a Y chromosome, not an X. Here's the Punnett square to prove it:

Female

	X_{normal}	X_{normal}
$X_{affected}$	$X_{affected}/X_{normal}$	$X_{affected}/X_{normal}$
Y	X_{normal}/Y	X_{normal}/Y

Male (labels $X_{affected}$ and Y on left rows)

As you can see, all male children will be normal. (And all female children will be carriers; see the explanation to question 2, above.)

Following a Trend
The study of the allele frequency distribution and change as a result of migration, natural selection, genetic drift, or mutation is called **population genetics**.

Quick Quiz #3

Consider the pedigree below, then fill in the blanks and check the appropriate boxes:

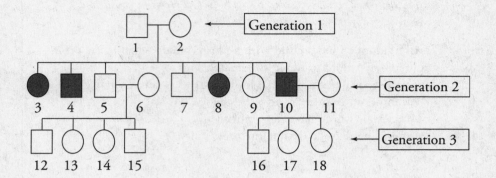

1. This condition is [□ **dominant** □ **recessive**].

2. This condition is [□ **autosomal** □ **X-linked**].

3. The genotype of individual 10 is [□ **homozygous** □ **heterozygous**].

4. The genotype of individual 17 is [□ **homozygous** □ **heterozygous**].

5. The genotype of individual 1 and 2 are [□ **homozygous** □ **heterozygous**].

6. If individual 3 were marry a normal male who does not carry the allele for the condition, the probability they would produce affected offspring would be _____.

7. If individual 4 were to marry a female carrier of the condition (a female heterozygous for the condition), the probability they would produce affected offspring would be _____.

Key Words

phenotype
genotype
dominant
recessive
allele
homozygous
heterozygous
codominance
test cross
Punnett square
dihybrid cross
Mendelian genetics

sex chromosomes
autosomes
sex-linked trait
X-linked
hemophilia
X-linked recessive trait
carriers
color blindness
male pattern baldness
pedigree
population genetics

Summary

○ An allele is an alternative form of a gene.

○ Some alleles are dominant, meaning that they exist in a heterozygous individual and appear to be the only one affecting a trait. Some alleles are recessive. When they exist in a heterozygous individual, the trait that they code for is suppressed.

○ Crosses (such as Punnett squares) can be used to predict the phenotype and genotype of the offspring of two particular parents.

○ One of the 23 pairs of chromosomes in humans determines the gender of the offspring. These are called sex chromosomes. The rest of the chromosomes are called autosomes.

○ Some alleles are passed from generation to generation only on the sex chromosomes.

○ Pedigrees are diagrams that show the presence of phenotypes in several generations of a family.

Chapter 9
Cracking Evolution and Diversity

Evolution and diversity are topics that are at once both easy and difficult: easy, because there is little to understand; difficult, because there is a lot to memorize. In other words, this material is not conceptually difficult, but there is a lot of memorization. So let's start at the beginning.

THE ORIGIN OF LIFE

Life first appeared on this planet around one billion years ago. The atmosphere then was very different from what it is today. Today's atmosphere is mostly nitrogen (about 78%), oxygen (about 21%), and small amounts of carbon dioxide, helium, and neon. The atmosphere on early Earth, however, was mostly made up of hydrogen, ammonia, methane, and water. In addition, the climate of early Earth was fairly intense; there was more lightning, volcanic activity, and UV radiation than we experience today. According to a theory known as the **heterotroph hypothesis**, life began under these conditions.

Many scientists have conducted experiments in which they simulated the gaseous conditions of early Earth's atmosphere in a flask. Sparks of electricity were discharged into the gases to mimic lightning, and it was found that under these artificial conditions, amino acids and other building blocks of life (like RNA) formed spontaneously. You already know how important nucleic acids and proteins are to living organisms, so you can probably imagine that these early proteins and nucleic acids may have run chemical reactions and may have had the ability to replicate themselves. Eventually, the first cells were born. They were **heterotrophs**, meaning that they could not synthesize their own food.

Soon, food became scarce. In other words, the heterotrophs required nutrients at a faster rate than they were being formed spontaneously. This led to the evolution of **autotrophs**, organisms that could make their own food using solar energy.

These early cells were **anaerobic organisms**. Earth's early atmosphere contained little or no oxygen, but oxygen was a waste product of the early autotrophs, and gradually it accumulated. As the heterotrophs and autotrophs evolved, they learned how to use this oxygen to produce energy more efficiently. Eventually over millions of years, the oxygen-using organisms came to be the dominant organisms on the planet.

The most important things to remember about all of this are:

- Today's atmosphere contains mostly nitrogen and oxygen, and the primary organisms on the planet are aerobic.
- Earth's early atmosphere DID NOT contain oxygen. It contained mostly hydrogen, ammonia, methane, and water, and the primary organisms at that time were anaerobic.

Quick Quiz #1

Fill in the blanks and check the appropriate boxes:

1. According to the heterotroph hypothesis, hydrogen
    [☐ **was** ☐ **was not**] a chief component of the atmosphere when
    life began.

2. At present, the gas of highest concentration in Earth's atmosphere is
    [☐ **helium** ☐ **oxygen** ☐ **nitrogen**].

3. According to the heterotroph hypothesis, water [☐ **was** ☐ **was not**]
    a chief component of the atmosphere when life began.

4. The primary organisms on early Earth were
    _____.

5. According to the heterotroph hypothesis, methane
    [☐ **was** ☐ **was not**] a chief component of the atmosphere when
    life began.

6. According to the heterotroph hypothesis, oxygen
    [☐ **was** ☐ **was not**] a chief component of the atmosphere when
    life began.

7. The primary organisms on Earth today are
    _____.

8. According to the heterotroph hypothesis, ammonia
    [☐ **was** ☐ **was not**] a chief component of the atmosphere when
    life began.

EVOLUTION

Consider a large population of people. Now think about all the genes of all the people in the whole population. This is the population's **gene pool**.

Within the population, some people have genes for dark skin and others for light skin. Some have an inborn gift for music and some for running quickly. Some have genes for brown eyes and some for green eyes. Each person in the population has a distinct set of genes, different from all others. This is called **genetic variability**.

The words "genetic variability" tell us that gene pools have many, many different alleles in them. Every person has a set of genes (alleles) that is different from that of every other individual (except for identical twins, who DO have identical genes). What is true for people is true for every species on Earth. All individuals vary in the alleles they possess. For all populations of all species, there is genetic variability.

The Fossil Record

Later in this chapter you will learn how biologists classify organisms. Paleontologists (scientists who study fossils) also classify organisms. All the information that paleontologists have gathered and organized about past life is called the **fossil record**. The fossil record gives evidence about the history of life on our planet. This record of past life also shows how different groups of organisms have changed over time. This is evidence for evolution. Another way to look at evolution is as the gradual change in living things over long periods of time.

How does genetic variability happen? The answer is the **random mutation of DNA**. DNA mutation is the basis for genetic variability. DNA mutation simply means that an error was made during DNA replication. Normally DNA replication is very, very precise. Adenine always pairs with thymine, and guanine always pairs with cytosine. However, very occasionally a mistake is made and adenine may pair with guanine. Or cytosine may pair with thymine. Or some other mistake may occur, which causes base pairs to be mismatched. The point is, the sequence of nucleotide bases in the DNA has been changed.

Remember that the sequence of bases in DNA is used as a template to create the sequence of bases in RNA, and the sequence of bases in RNA is used to create the sequence of amino acids in a protein. This means that if there is a change in the base sequence of DNA, there will be a corresponding change in the base sequence of RNA, and if there's a change in the base sequence of RNA, there's a good chance there will be a change in the order of amino acids in the resulting protein.

Suppose that a particular protein in question was a skin pigment protein. Suppose further that the change in the amino acid sequence caused that pigment protein to appear darker than before the mutation occurred. This would result in a darker skin color than before. If this mutation occurred in a chromosome in a sperm or an ovum, it could be passed on to offspring, and then all future offspring would display the new (darker) skin color.

Of course, not all individuals in the population would display the results of this mutation (darker skin color). Only the offspring of the individuals in which the mutation first occurred would display the results of this mutation. So, looking at the population as a whole, some individuals would have the original skin color, and some individuals would have the new, darker skin color. Through mutation, a new allele of the skin color gene was created. The population as a whole now displays genetic variability.

Quick Quiz #2

Fill in the blanks and check the appropriate boxes:

1. The phrase "_____" refers to the fact that within any population of any species, genotypes vary (i.e., the gene pool features a wide variety of alleles).

2. Genetic variability [☐ **is** ☐ **is not**] caused by a species' ability to adapt to existing environmental conditions.

3. Genetic variability [☐ **is** ☐ **is not**] attributable to random mutation.

4. Once a mutation has occurred, all members of the population [☐ **will** ☐ **will not**] display the results of that mutation.

5. Genetic variability [☐ **is** ☐ **is not**] a property of all populations.

6. If a mutation were to occur in a somatic cell instead of a gamete (sperm or ovum), that mutation [☐ **could** ☐ **could not**] cause genetic variability in the population.

Genetic Variability and Evolution

When we say evolution, we are referring to changing gene pools. Changes in gene pools can occur through random mutation, as we've seen previously, but it can take a long time for this to have a significant effect on the population. More rapid changes in gene pools are caused by competition. More specifically, because of mutations, genetic variability exists. Because of genetic variability (different genotypes), there is physical variability (different phenotypes). And because of physical variability, some members of a population are better equipped to interact with their environment; in other words, they are better competitors.

Consider a population of frogs. Suppose that half of the frogs have alleles for dark skin color and half have alleles for light skin color. Now imagine that an earthquake separates the frogs into two populations. When it's all over, some frogs are left in Place 1 and others in Place 2.

Isolation

The frog populations in this scenario are actually an example of geographic isolation. A new species may form when a group of individuals remains isolated from the rest of the species. One well-known example of geographic isolation is occurring in the southwestern region of the United States. Abert's squirrel and the Kaibab squirrel are from the same species. The two groups became isolated as the Grand Canyon formed. They still belong to the same species, but are beginning to evolve and show some differences. It is possible that in the future these squirrels will evolve into different species.

Places 1 and 2 differ. In Place 1 there are predators that can see light-colored things but *not* dark-colored things. In Place 2 there are predators that can see light and dark colors. What's going to happen?

In Place 1, predators are going to prey happily on light-colored frogs. Many light-colored frogs will be eaten before they're even old enough to reproduce. But the predators won't have much luck with the dark frogs. Many dark frogs will live long enough to reproduce. They'll pass on the alleles for dark skin color to their offspring.

After a few frog generations, the frog gene pool in Place 1 will change. It won't be 50% alleles for light skin color and 50% alleles for dark skin color anymore. It might be 90% alleles for dark color and 10% alleles for light color. Why? The light-colored frogs are dying off—they get eaten before they reproduce. The dark-colored frogs don't have that problem. They're hopping, swimming, jumping— and reproducing.

Meanwhile, what's happening in Place 2? The predators in Place 2 see light-colored and dark-colored frogs equally well, so they eat light-colored and dark-colored frogs in equal numbers. Things are as they were before the earthquake. The gene pool stays 50% alleles for light skin color and 50% alleles for dark skin color.

That's Evolution: The Frogs in Place 1 Evolved

As we said previously, evolution means that a population undergoes a change in the frequency of alleles in its gene pool. If there's a change in the frequency of alleles in a population's gene pool, the population evolves.

The frogs in Place 1 evolved because their environment changed. When it came to surviving in the new environment, dark-colored frogs did better than the light-colored frogs. They competed better. The frogs didn't know they were competing, but they were. They were competing to survive, and the dark-colored frogs were better competitors than the light-colored ones. Why? Their dark color allowed them to escape their predators.

Individuals might compete for food, for water, or for all kinds of things in all kinds of ways and for all kinds of reasons. *The better competitors are better at staying alive, and they have a better chance of reproducing.* This is called **natural selection**. Again, natural selection just means that better competitors are better survivors and have a better chance of reproducing. Nature "selects" them to reproduce.

When organisms reproduce they pass their genes on to their offspring. In each generation more and more individuals resemble the better competitors; fewer and fewer resemble the poorer competitors. So the gene pool changes.

Now let's summarize.

Evolution is a change in a population's gene pool. It happens because

- genetic variability allows some individuals to be better competitors than others. In the "game" of natural selection, they win;
- the winners survive, reproduce, and pass their genes on to their offspring;
- the offspring have genes like those of their parents. Hence, the gene pool changes. With each generation, it has more and more of the alleles that come from the better competitors.

Being Fit

Another way of saying that an organism is a better competitor is to say that the organism is more "fit." **Fitness** describes an organism's ability to contribute to the next generation's gene pool by producing surviving offspring.

Consider two fish, one that swims slowly and one that swims quickly. Each fish lays 100 eggs. When the eggs hatch, the babies of the slow-swimming fish mostly get eaten by predators. Only 8 of the 100 survive. But the babies of the fast-swimming fish escape the predators more easily, and 32 of the 100 survive. We would describe the fast-swimming fish as being more fit than the slow-swimming fish, because it produced more surviving offspring and therefore contributed more to the next generation's gene pool than the slow-swimming fish.

Evolution and Species

Suppose two individuals—such as a bumblebee and a dog—have such different genes that their gametes can't meet and form a new individual. We say the two individuals belong to two different **species**. When we say "different species," we mean individuals that can't produce viable offspring together.

Think again about our frogs, separated by an earthquake. Imagine that over time (hundreds of thousands of years, perhaps) the frogs in Place 1 undergo so much change in their gene pool that they wouldn't be able to mate with the frogs in Place 2, even if they were brought together again. The frogs in Place 1 and the frogs in Place 2 would be considered to be separate species. We would say then that evolution caused **speciation**.

> Speciation is simply the formation of a new species, by evolution or other means. Evolution is the most common cause of speciation.

Another way to describe what happened to the frogs is to say they underwent **divergent evolution**. Divergent evolution is the process by which two populations of the same species end up having different behaviors and traits. They used to have similar traits, but their environments somehow pressured them to change, and over time their behaviors and traits were no longer similar; in other words, they **diverged**. In the case of the frogs, the pressure to change came from the fact that the different environments had different types of predators.

If the evolution of the populations continues, and after a very long time the populations can no longer mate and produce offspring (which is what happened to our frogs), then the two populations are now two separate species—speciation occurred. So speciation is just the extreme form of divergent evolution.

Sometimes, similarities in structure among species give evidence of their evolutionary history. One example is in the forelimbs of all mammals: These all consist of the same skeletal parts. Obviously, the function of a whale's flipper is very different from that of a bat's wing. But these have similar structures, despite their differing functions. **Homologous structures** are common in species that share a common ancestor.

What If Two Populations Become More *Similar* to One Another?

Consider a population of rodents and a population of insects that inhabit the same environment. Suppose that in this particular environment there are many ground-dwelling predators. If the rodents and the insects could somehow get off the ground, they would be safe from the predators. Suppose further that through mutation and genetic variability, and over a long period of time, the insects developed a set of modified legs that could expand to act as glider wings, so that whenever a large gust of wind came around the insects would become airborne. This would keep them off the ground and away from the predators. More of them would survive, and, gradually, the majority of this population of insects would have this "flying" ability.

What about the rodents? What if, also through mutation and genetic variability, over this same long period of time, they developed extensive skin folds between their front and back legs that allowed them to remain airborne when leaping from tree to tree?

Clearly the two populations—the insects and the rodents—could never mate and produce offspring. But they have become more similar to one each other in terms of behaviors and traits. Both populations developed specialized structures that allowed them to "fly." In other words, their traits and behaviors converged. Evolution that results in the production of similar traits and behaviors between two separate populations and/or species is called **convergent evolution**.

Something to remember about convergent evolution is that it NEVER results in speciation (the formation of two separate species). Furthermore, it can NEVER bring two completely different species into a single species.

It is important to recognize that not all similar structures are inherited from a common ancestor, or homologous. In the example above, the insects and rodents both have wings. However, these are not homologous structures, they are analogous. **Analogous structures** are similar adaptations that result from convergent evolution.

One Last Thing to Remember

As a population evolves because of pressures from its environment, sometimes structures that were important at one time become unimportant as the environment, the population, and the population's behaviors change. These useless structures become smaller and smaller and eventually are not seen in the organisms except as remnants of their former selves. These remnants are called **vestigial structures**. Examples of vestigial structures are the appendix in humans and leg bones in snakes.

Quick Quiz #3

Fill in the blanks and check the appropriate boxes:

1. Evolution [☐ **always** ☐ **sometimes**] results in the production of a new species.

2. Speciation [☐ **increases** ☐ **decreases**] biological diversity.

3. In the course of divergent evolution, two populations become [☐ **more** ☐ **less**] similar to each other with regard to behaviors and traits.

4. Evolution means a change in a population's _____.

5. If a population is geographically divided, it [☐ **cannot** ☐ **may**] give rise to two separate species.

6. Evolution that results in two species becoming more similar to each other in terms of behaviors and traits is called _____ evolution.

7. Divergent evolution can result from [☐ **only physical** ☐ **only behavioral** ☐ **both physical and behavioral**] selection pressures from the environment.

8. Convergent evolution [☐ **can** ☐ **cannot**] result in speciation.

GETTING ORGANIZED: PHYLOGENY

When we try to organize people and their addresses, we could think like this:

Country • State • County • Town • Street • Street Number • Person

- The country has many states.
- Each state has many counties.
- Each county has many towns.
- Each town has many streets.
- Each street has many street numbers.
- At each street number, there might be several people.

Think about all the people living in one house. They have a lot in common. They live in the same house, on the same street, in the same town, in the same county, in the same state, in the same country.

Think about all people living on the same street. They have a lot in common, too: street, town, county, state, and country. They don't have as much in common as do the people living in the same house, but they do have a lot in common.

How about people living in the same town? They have a few things in common, too: town, county, state, and country. They have less in common than do the people living on the same street and less still than do the people living in the same house.

So think about it:

- People living in the same house have more in common than do people simply living on the same street.
- People living on the same street have more in common than do people simply living in the same town.
- People living in the same town have more in common than do people simply living in the same county.
- People living in the same county have more in common than do people simply living in the same state.
- People living in the same state have more in common than do all people simply living in this country.

Country • State • County • Town • Street • Street Number • Person

Less in common $\longrightarrow$ $\longrightarrow$ $\longrightarrow$ $\longrightarrow$ More in common

The Same Is True for Species

There are many species on Earth. Biologists assign them "addresses" using this arrangement:

Domain • Kingdom • Phylum • Class • Order • Family • Genus • Species

Less in common $\longrightarrow$ $\longrightarrow$ $\longrightarrow$ More in common

Here's how to remember that:

Dumb King Phillip Came Over From Germany—So?

Domain • Kingdom • Phylum • Class • Order • Family • Genus • Species

Look at the organizational scheme and realize:

- Each domain is made up of one or more kingdoms.
- Each kingdom is made up of many phyla.
- Each phylum is made up of many classes.
- Each class is made up of many orders.
- Each order is made up of many families.
- Each family is made up of many genera (plural of *genus*).
- Each genus is made up of many species.

Realize also that:

- Organisms of the same species have more in common than do organisms simply belonging to the same genus.
- Organisms of the same genus have more in common than do organisms simply belonging to the same family.
- Organisms of the same family have more in common than do organisms simply belonging to the same order.
- Organisms of the same order have more in common than do organisms simply belonging to the same class.
- Organisms of the same class have more in common than do organisms simply belonging to the same phylum.
- Organisms of the same phylum have more in common than do organisms simply belonging to the same kingdom.
- Organisms of the same kingdom have more in common than do organisms simply belonging to the same domain.

What do we actually mean when we say that organisms have things in common? We mean that different organisms came from common ancestors, and they share some traits from those ancestors of long ago. Scientists classify organisms based on their evolutionary relationships (**phylogeny**). **Taxonomy** is the fancy term given to the science of classification.

Remember this man's name: **Carolus Linnaeus**. Carolus Linnaeus came up with what is known as the modern system of classification, called the **binomial system**. The binomial system of classification is based on a two-part name for each organism. The first part is the organism's **genus**, and the second part is the organism's **species**. The genus is capitalized, but the species is not.

Common name:	*Genus*	*species*
Dog:	*Canis*	*familiaris*
Wolf:	*Canis*	*lupis*
Sugar maple:	*Acer*	*sacchaum*
Human:	*Homo*	*sapien*

Quick Quiz #4

Fill in the blanks and check the appropriate boxes:

1. The science of classification is called [☐ **taxidermy** ☐ **taxonomy**].

2. The conventional ordering of phylogeny is domain, kingdom, _____, _____, _____, _____, _____, and _____.

3. The members of a kingdom [☐ **do** ☐ **do not**] have more in common than do the members of an order.

4. The members of an order [☐ **do** ☐ **do not**] have more in common than do the members of a class.

Who Evolved Before Who?

For the exam, not only should you know the main characteristics of the domains and each of the six kingdoms, but you should know something about a few of the phyla within those kingdoms. You should also know the general order in which these organisms evolved.

Generally speaking, life began with unicellular anaerobic organisms and became progressively more complicated as these organisms continued to evolve. The following outline is constructed in the order of evolution of the three domains and their kingdoms.

I. Domain Bacteria

This domain is made up of prokaryotes and includes the bacteria most people are familiar with, from harmful disease-causing organisms (like *E. coli* O157:H7) to the beneficial bacteria used to make yogurt and cheese. They lack a nucleus and any membrane-bound organelles (they have ribosomes, which are not bounded by membranes), and have a circular DNA genome. We will talk more about bacteria in the next chapter.

Domain Bacteria has one kingdom, which is called Eubacteria. This domain (and kingdom) includes the **Cyanobacteria**, which are also known as blue-green algae. The Cyanobacteria contain chlorophyll and can photosynthesize.

II. Domain Archaea

This domain is also made up of prokaryotes, in the kingdom Archaebacteria. Like Domain Bacteria prokaryotes, Archaebacteria lack nuclei and organelles, and have a circular DNA genome; however, they also have some features in common with eukaryotes (such as multiple types of RNA polymerase and methionine as the initiator amino acid, just to name a couple). Domain Archaea organisms often live in extremely harsh environments that most other organisms could not tolerate; for this reason they are described as "**extremophiles**" (think of them as the X-Games enthusiasts of the living world). They include the **extreme halophiles** (that live in extremely salty conditions), the **extreme thermophiles** (that live in extremely hot conditions), and the **methanogens** (extreme anaerobes that release methane gas as a waste product).

III. Domain Eukarya

As its name implies, this domain is made up of eukaryotes. All eukaryotes contain nuclei, membrane-bound organelles, and linear DNA. They are divided into four main kingdoms, the characteristics of which are described on the next page.

A. Kingdom Protista

Protists are eukaryotes and contain organelles and a true nucleus. Most are unicellular, but some form colonies, and some are truly multicellular (algae). This kingdom can be divided into three main groups, or *phyla*: protozoa (animal-like protists), **algae** (plant-like protists)—except for cyanobacteria, blue-green algae—and a few fungus-like protists. When you study these phyla, don't get too concerned about learning the "official" names. Most questions on the exam will refer to these organisms using their more common names, shown here in parentheses.

What's in a Name
It might be helpful to remember that a name ending in *–phyta* refers to plants and one ending in *–mycota* refers to fungi.

1) **Phylum Rhizopoda (Amoebas)**
Amoebas are all unicellular and move about using cellular extensions called pseudopodia. They are found in soils and also in freshwater and marine environments. Some are parasitic, such as those what cause amoebic dysentery in humans.

2) **Phylum Apicomplexa (Sporozoans)**
Sporozoans are all animal parasites. Some cause serious human diseases such as malaria, caused by the parasite plasmodium. Most members of this phylum have life cycles with both sexual and asexual stages that often require two or more different host species for completion. For example, plasmodium requires both humans and mosquitoes to complete its life cycle.

3) **Phylum Ciliophora (Ciliates)**
This group of unicellular organisms is characterized by their use of cilia for movement and feeding. An example is paramecium.

4) **Phyla Myxomycota and Acrasiomycota (Slime Molds)**
These organisms resemble an overgrown amoeba. They contain many nuclei.

5) **Phylum Euglenophyta (Euglena)**
These are unicellular, photosynthetic algae.

6) **Phylum Bacilariophyta (Diatoms)**
These unicellular organisms have unique glasslike walls and live in both freshwater and marine environments. These walls remain behind when the organism dies and form the sediments known as diatomaceous earths. Diatomaceous earth is useful as a filtering medium.

7) **Phylum Phaeophyta (Brown Algae)**
These organisms are commonly known as seaweeds and are the largest and most complex of the plantlike protists. All are multicellular and most live in marine environments. Some are very large, such as the giant kelp.

B. Kingdom Plantae

All plants are multicellular, eukaryotic, and photosynthetic (i.e., autotrophs). Note also that plant biologists use the term **division** instead of phylum; however, the two terms are essentially synonymous. Plants are grouped into two general categories based on how they transport water: the **nonvascular plants** and the **vascular plants**. Vascular plants are further subdivided into **seedless plants** and

seed plants. Seed plants are further divided into nonflowering plants (**gymnosperms**) and flowering plants (**angiosperms**).

1) **Division Byrophyta (Nonvascular Plants)**
   This group lacks the vascular tissue found in most plants, called **xylem** and **phloem**. (Xylem and phloem will be further discussed in the chapter 11.) Therefore they must live in damp areas where water is abundant. Furthermore, they require water for fertilization. These plants do NOT have true stems, leaves, and roots. Examples are mosses, liverworts, and hornworts.

2) **Division Pterophyta (Ferns)**
   Ferns are some of the earliest vascular plants and contain the vascular tissue xylem and phloem, as well as true stems, leaves, and roots. They do NOT, however, have seeds. Instead, ferns have **spores**, which can be scattered by wind.

3) **Division Coniferophyta (Conifers)**
   These are true vascular plants. The term **conifer** refers to the cones that carry the seeds of these plants. Most are large evergreen trees, such as pines, firs, and cedars. Because the seeds are not protected in a seed coat, these are "naked-seed" plants, or gymnosperms. Gymnosperms do NOT produce flowers.

4) **Division Anthophyta (Flowering Plants)**
   This group consists of true vascular plants that produce flowers and pollen. Their seeds are protected by fruits and nuts. Examples are apples, lima beans, tomatoes, melons, etc.

   a) **Class Monocots**
      Monocots are named for their single-seed leaves (*mono* = one) called **cotyledons**. Other characteristics of monocots include parallel veins in their leaves, flower parts in multiples of threes, a complex arrangement of vascular tissue in their stems, and a fibrous root system.

   b) **Class Dicots**
      Dicots have two seed leaves (two cotyledons), netlike veins in their leaves, flower parts in multiples of four or five, vascular tissue arranged in a ring, and a taproot system.

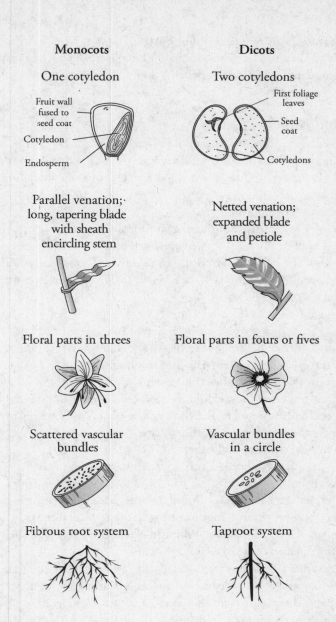

Monocots	Dicots
One cotyledon	Two cotyledons

Fruit wall fused to seed coat
Cotyledon
Endosperm

First foliage leaves
Seed coat
Cotyledons

Parallel venation; long, tapering blade with sheath encircling stem

Netted venation; expanded blade and petiole

Floral parts in threes

Floral parts in fours or fives

Scattered vascular bundles

Vascular bundles in a circle

Fibrous root system

Taproot system

C. Kingdom Fungi

Fungi are all eukaryotic, and almost all are multicellular. One exception is yeast, which is a unicellular fungus. Most fungi have a filamentous structure and are multinucleate. They lack chloroplasts and are therefore heterotrophic (cannot produce their own food). They lack a digestive system and are absorptive feeders. Absorptive feeding is the process of taking up small organic molecules from the environment. Because they often live on decaying material, they are classified as decomposers.

1) **Division Zygomycota**
    This group of fungi reproduces sexually and includes common molds as well as mycorrhizae (mutualistic associations between plant roots and fungi).

2) Division Basidiomycota (Club Fungi)
This group consists of about 25,000 members, including mushrooms, shelf fungi, and puffballs. Some are edible.

D. Kingdom Animalia

Animals are eukaryotic, multicellular, and heterotrophic. This is the most diverse of the six kingdoms. You should *definitely* know the characteristics of each of the following phyla (but again, don't worry too much about the official names).

1) Phylum Porifera (Sponges)
Sponges are **sessile** (nonmoving) animals. They have a perforated body wall made of two layers of cells. Water is drawn through the body wall into the animal, where food in the water is trapped and ingested. Most sponges live in marine environments.

2) Phylum Cnidaria (Coelenterates)
These animals have body walls made of two layers of cells and a central, saclike digestive system. They exhibit radial symmetry. Examples are hydra, jellyfish, and sea anemones.

3) Phylum Platyhelminthes (Flatworms)
Animals in this group exhibit bilateral symmetry and moderate cephalization (a head). They include planaria (nonparasitic), flukes, and tapeworms (both parasitic).

4) Phylum Mollusca (Mollusks)
Mollusks are soft-bodied animals with hard external shells, such as snails, oysters, and clams. Exceptions are octopi and squid, which have only reduced, internal shells. Mollusks have three major body regions: a **foot** for movement; a **visceral mass**, where organs are contained; and a **mantle**, which may secrete a shell.

5) Phylum Annelida (Segmented Worms)
These animals have a closed circulation and a mouth and anus, and they excrete waste through **metanephridia**. The best example is the earthworm; this group also includes leeches.

6) Phylum Arthropoda (Arthropods)
This is the most diverse phylum in the animal kingdom, with nearly one million different species and more than 10^{18} (one billion billion) members. Arthropods have jointed appendages, a hard exoskeleton containing chitin, and a segmented body with a head, thorax, and abdomen. They have an open circulatory system and eliminate wastes through **Malpighian tubules.** Arthropods include crustaceans (e.g., crabs), insects (e.g., moths, ants), and arachnids (e.g., spiders).

7) Phylum Echinodermata (Echinoderms)
These slow-moving or sessile animals exhibit radial symmetry and spiny exoskeletons (*echinoderm* means "spiny skin"). They have a water vascular system ending in tube feet that function in feeding, gas exchange, and movement. Examples are sea stars, sea urchins, and sand dollars.

8) **Phylum Chordata (Chordates)**

Chordates have a hollow notochord, a dorsal nerve cord, and a tail (at some point in their development). Almost all are vertebrates. Chordates include fish, amphibians, reptiles, birds, and mammals.

a) **Class Chondrichthyes** (Cartilaginous Fishes)

These fish have flexible skeletons made of cartilage instead of bone and well-developed jaws and fins. They breathe through gills. Some lay eggs and some bear live young. Examples are sharks and sting rays.

b) **Class Osteichthyes (Bony Fishes)**

These fish have true bone skeletons. They breathe through gills and lay large numbers of eggs, which lack shells. They live in both freshwater and marine environments. Examples are bass, tuna, and trout.

c) **Class Amphibia (Amphibians)**

These animals are well adapted to both land and water. Their eggs lack shells and must be laid in the water. They have an aquatic larval stage and undergo a metamorphosis into a terrestrial adult. They breathe through lungs and/or skin. Examples are frogs and salamanders.

d) **Class Reptilia (Reptiles)**

Reptiles are terrestrial animals with thick, scaly skin adapted to resist water loss. They live well in dry areas, although some inhabit water. Their eggs have shells to resist dehydration, or they bear live young. They breathe through lungs. Examples are crocodiles, lizards, and snakes.

e) **Class Aves (Birds)**

Birds are tetrapods with the forelimbs modified as wings. They breathe through lungs and lay shelled eggs. They are endothermic. Examples are owls, eagles, sparrows, and penguins.

f) **Class Mammalia (Mammals)**

Mammals are endothermic, have hair, and nourish their young from mammary glands. They breathe through lungs. Most bear live young. Examples are rodents, kangaroos, antelope, and humans.

An easy way to remember the order in which phylum Chordata evolved is to remember the word "FARM," but with a "B" stuck in the middle of it—"FARBM."

F: Fish
A: Amphibians
R: Reptiles
B: Birds
M: Mammals

Quick Quiz #5

Fill in the blanks and check the appropriate boxes:

1. Brown algae belong to which kingdom?
   (A) Protista
   (B) Bacteria
   (C) Plantae
   (D) Animalia
   (E) Fungi

2. Soft-bodied animals with hard external shells are classified as
   _____.

3. With respect to the evolution of chordates, fish appeared [☐ **before** ☐ **after**] birds, and birds appeared [☐ **before** ☐ **after**] mammals.

4. Animals with jointed appendages, hard exoskeletons, and segmented bodies are classified as _____.

5. Prokaryotes [☐ **do** ☐ **do not**] have a nucleus.

6. Mushrooms and yeast are
   (A) heterotrophic
   (B) autotrophic
   (C) monocots
   (D) dicots
   (E) angiosperms

7. Amoebas and slime molds belong to which kingdom?
   (A) Archaebacteria
   (B) Plantae
   (C) Animalia
   (D) Protista
   (E) Fungi

8. Having flower parts in multiples of four or five is a characteristic of [☐ **monocots** ☐ **dicots**].

9. Protists [☐ **do** ☐ **do not**] have a nucleus.

10. Mosses and liverworts are examples of _____ plants.

11. Cyanobacteria [☐ **can** ☐ **cannot**] photosynthesize.

12. Earthworms and other segmented worms belong to phylum [☐ **Annelida** ☐ **Arthropoda**].

13. The order in which chordates appeared on Earth is (1) fish, (2)_____, (3) _____, (4) _____, (5) _____.

14. Plants with parallel veins in their leaves, and flower parts in multiples of threes, are classified as [☐ **monocots** ☐ **dicots**].

15. Conifers, such as pine trees, are classified as [☐ **angiosperms** ☐ **gymnosperms**].

Key Words

heterotroph hypothesis
heterotrophs
autotrophs
anaerobic organisms
gene pool
genetic variability
random mutation of DNA
fossil record
evolution
natural selection
fitness
species
speciation
divergent evolution
diverged
homologous structures
convergent evolution
analogous structures
vestigial structures
phylogeny
taxonomy
Carolus Linnaeus
binomial system
genus
species
domain Bacteria
domain Archaea
extremophiles
halophiles

thermophiles
methanogens
domain Eukarya
kingdom Protista
protozoa
algae
kingdom Plantae
division
nonvascular plants
vascular plants
seedless plants
seed plants
gymnosperms
angiosperms
xylem
phloem
spores
conifer
monocot
cotyledon
dicot
kingdom Fungi
kingdom Animalia
sessile
foot
visceral mass
mantle
metanephridia
Malpighian tubules

Summary

○ Each individual in a population has his or her own set of genes. When these gene combinations are all added together, this is called a population's gene pool.

○ Evolution is a changing gene pool.

○ Natural selection is a way in which evolution occurs when the better competitors are more likely to be survivors and therefore will continue to reproduce in future generations.

○ Fitness is an organism's ability to contribute to the next generations' gene pool.

○ If two individuals are members of two different species, they cannot produce viable offspring.

○ Species can be classified according to an organizational scheme, which from least specific to most specific is: domain, kingdom, phylum, class, order, family, genus, and species.

○ Carolus Linnaeus developed a binomial system for naming organisms. By this method humans are *Homo sapiens*.

○ Organisms have been classified into three different domains: Bacteria, Archaea, and Eukarya.

○ Domain Eukarya has been divided into four different kingdoms: Protista, Fungi, Plantae, and Animalia.

Chapter 10
Organ Systems

The human body is made up of eleven different organ systems, each of which is specialized to carry out particular functions. Two systems, the nervous system and the endocrine system, control all the other organ systems, such as the circulatory system, the respiratory system, and the digestive system. This chapter will explore these systems as well as the other systems that make up the human body.

THE ELEVEN SYSTEMS OF THE BODY

This chapter covers the basics of the eleven body systems, which are listed below.

- The nervous system detects and interprets information from the surrounding environment. It essentially controls most body functions.
- The endocrine system controls body functions through the use of chemical messengers called hormones.
- The circulatory system brings needed materials to the cells and carries away waste materials.
- The lymphatic system recaptures and filters fluid from the tissues and returns it to the blood stream.
- The respiratory system takes oxygen into the body and releases carbon dioxide.
- The digestive system takes food into the body, breaks it down, and absorbs the nutrients from the food.
- The urinary system removes wastes from the blood.
- The skeletal system supports the body, protects it, and allows movement (along with the muscular system).
- The muscular system makes it possible for the body to move.
- The skin protects the body and helps regulate body temperature.
- The reproductive system produces the cells necessary to produce offspring.

CONTROL OF THE BODY, PART 1—THE NERVOUS SYSTEM

The **nervous system** consists of billions of nerve cells. Nerve cells are also called **neurons**. Neurons are highly specialized cells that carry impulses—electrical signals—between body parts. Here's a typical neuron:

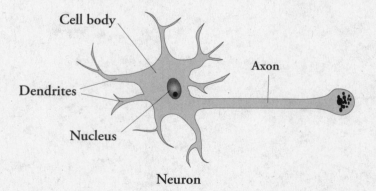

Neuron

The cell body (also called the **soma**) has all the usual cellular material. It has a nucleus, ribosomes, mitochondria, and all the rest of the organelles. Neurons are different from other cells because the cell body has structures sticking off of it in all directions. In the body, anything that sticks off something else is called a

process, so we can say that the neuron has processes extending from the cell body. The processes are called **dendrites** and **axons**. Most neurons have several dendrites but only one axon. To be ready for the test, you should be able to identify the picture on the previous page as a neuron and be able to label the cell body, nucleus, dendrites, and axon.

What Neurons Do

We already said that neurons are specialized to carry impulses from one place to another. The impulse always follows the same path. A neuron *receives* impulses at its dendrites. It *transmits* the impulse through the cell body and down the axon.

> The direction in which an impulse travels through a neuron is dendrite → cell body → axon.

What *Is* This Impulse?

We said that the impulse is an electrical signal. To understand this more completely, we have to take a closer look at the neuron. When a neuron is resting (i.e., not carrying an impulse), we describe it as being **polarized**. That means it's different on one side of its membrane than the other. The inside of the neuron is negatively charged when compared to the outside of the neuron.

The Resting Membrane Potential

All cells establish and maintain a **resting membrane potential** (RMP), wherein the inside of the cell is more negative than the outside. The RMP of most cells is around –70 mV; that is, the inside of the cells is about 70 mV more negative than the outside of the cell. The two membrane proteins that help set up and maintain the RMP are the Na^+/K^+ ATPase and the K^+ leak channel.

How Does the Inside of the Neuron Get More Negative than the Outside?

All cells, including neurons, have protein channels in their membranes (review Chapter 4 if you've forgotten this). The protein channels can act in facilitated diffusion to allow molecules across the membrane down their concentration gradients. They can also act as pumps in active transport to move substances across the membrane against their concentration gradients.

There are two particular membrane proteins we're interested in at the moment. The first is the **sodium-potassium pump** (Na^+/K^+ **ATPase**), which uses a molecule of ATP to move three sodium ions *out* of the cell and (simultaneously) two potassium ions *into* the cell. After these pumps run for a while, there is plenty of sodium outside the cell (and not much inside) and plenty of potassium inside the cell (and not much outside). Remember, because these molecules are charged (they're *ions*), they cannot simply cross the membrane. So once the sodium is out, it's *out*. And once the potassium is in, it's *in*. Unless of course, there's a sodium or potassium **channel** that can allow them to cross the membrane again, according to their gradients.

There are no sodium channels in the membrane, but there *are* potassium channels. This is the second protein we're interested in. These particular potassium channels are referred to as **leak channels**, because they are always open and will always allow potassium to leak out of the cell, according to its gradient. (Remember, because of the ATPase, there is more potassium *inside* the cell than outside, so potassium will leak *out* of the cell.)

The bottom line is that many positively charged ions are being let out of the cell. Sodium ions are being pumped out, and potassium ions are leaking out. Many negatively charged things are left behind, inside the cell. Things like DNA and RNA and proteins. *Because a lot of positive stuff is leaving the cell and a lot of negative stuff is staying behind, the cell is more negative on the inside, compared to the outside;* 70 millivolts more negative, in fact, so that when we look at a cell we say that it rests at –70 mV.

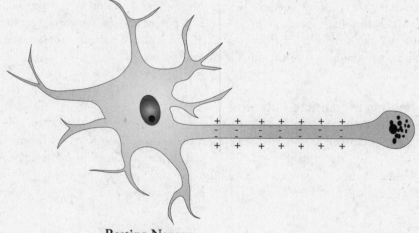

Resting Neuron

Quick Quiz #1

Fill in the blanks and check the appropriate boxes:

1. The _____ is a membrane protein that pumps three sodium ions out of the cell and two potassium ions into the cell.

2. Sodium ions [☐ **can** ☐ **cannot**] cross back into the cell after being pumped out.

3. Dendrites [☐ **receive** ☐ **transmit**] an electrical impulse.

4. The direction in which an impulse travels through a neuron is _____ to _____ to _____.

5. Potassium concentration is [☐ **higher** ☐ **lower**] inside the cell than outside.

6. The resting membrane potential of the cell is _____.

7. Sodium concentration is [☐ **higher** ☐ **lower**] inside the cell than outside.

8. The axon of a neuron carries the nerve impulse [☐ **toward** ☐ **away from**] the cell body.

What's Different About Neurons

Neurons, in addition to the two membrane proteins we discussed above (the Na$^+$/K$^+$ ATPase and the potassium leak channels), have **voltage-gated channels** in their membranes. Voltage-gated channels are channels that open when the cell membrane reaches a particular voltage. At the normal resting potential of the cell, –70 mV, the voltage-gated channels are closed. But if the cell membrane could reach –50 mV, these channels would open. This potential, the potential at which the voltage-gated channels open, is known as the **threshold potential**. (Don't worry just yet about how the cell reaches threshold; we'll talk about this a bit later.) There are two types of voltage-gated channels in neuron cell membranes: **sodium voltage-gated channels** and **potassium voltage-gated channels**.

So What?

Imagine the scene: A barrier separates the inside of the cell from the outside. Sodium ions, plentiful on the outside, long to get in. But they can't cross the barrier. Potassium ions, plentiful on the inside, long to get out. Some of them do, through the leak channels. But many potassium ions stay behind. All of a sudden, the cell potential reaches –50 mV! Sodium voltage-gated channels slam open, and now sodium has a way to get across the barrier. Sodium ions flood into the cell from the outside! The inside of the cell gets very positive, until finally, at around +35 mV, the sodium channels close. Now the potassium voltage-gated channels open! Potassium has a way to get across the barrier, and potassium ions flood out of the cell, carrying a positive charge out of the cell and making the inside of the cell more negative again. At around –90 mV, the potassium voltage-gated channels close, and the only channels left running are the Na$^+$/K$^+$ ATPase and the potassium leak channels. The pump restores the balance of sodium and potassium, and the cell membrane potential again rests at –70 mV.

The sequence of events we've just described is known as an **action potential**. An action potential occurs at only a small portion of the neuron's membrane.

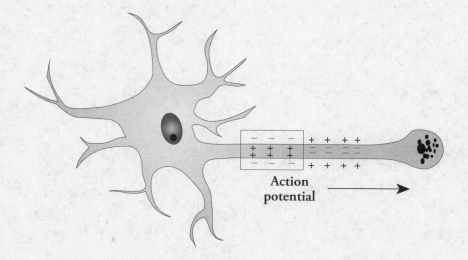

Action potential

Let's take a quick look at some terms and definitions.

> **Polarized:** the state of the membrane at rest, negative on the inside and positive on the outside.
>
> **Depolarization:** the membrane potential moves in the positive direction.
>
> **Repolarization:** the membrane potential returns to its resting value.

So let's describe the scene above again, this time using the appropriate terminology. This might seem a little overwhelming, so let's take it a sentence at a time. Picture in your mind what is going on in the neuron.

1. If a neuron is polarized and at the resting potential (–70 mV), and depolarizes slightly to the threshold potential (–50 mV), voltage-gated sodium and voltage-gated potassium channels will open.
2. The voltage-gated sodium channels open first, allowing sodium to enter the cell according to its concentration gradient (previously established by the Na^+/K^+ ATPase).
3. The entering sodium ions depolarize the cell further, allowing it to reach a maximum of +35 mV before the voltage-gated sodium channels close.
4. Then the voltage-gated potassium channels open, allowing potassium to exit the cell according to its concentration gradient (also previously established by the Na^+/K^+ ATPase).
5. The exiting potassium ions repolarize the cell, actually bypassing the resting membrane potential, to a minimum of –90 mV before the voltage-gated potassium channels close.
6. Finally, the Na^+/K^+ ATPase and the potassium leak channels return the membrane to its resting polarized state.

We said earlier that the function of a neuron is to transmit impulses—electrical signals. This "impulse" is nothing more than a traveling action potential. When one small portion of a neuron's membrane fires an action potential, some of the sodium that rushes in from the opening of the voltage-gated channels travels down the inside of the membrane, bringing the next small portion up to threshold. As soon as threshold is reached, the opening of the voltage-gated channels occurs as we've described, and that portion of the membrane has an action potential. Some of the sodium travels down the inside of the membrane, bringing the next small portion up to threshold and causing it to fire an action potential. And so on, and so on, and so on, all the way down the axon.

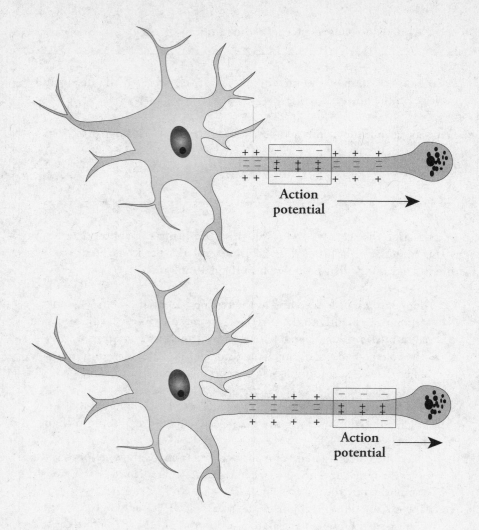

Very Fast Impulse Speeds: Myelin Sheath and Schwann Cells

In some neurons, the axon is wrapped with special cells called **Schwann cells**. This Schwann cell "wrapping" is called a **myelin sheath**. Many Schwann cells can sit on a single axon. The spaces between the Schwann cells are called **nodes of Ranvier**.

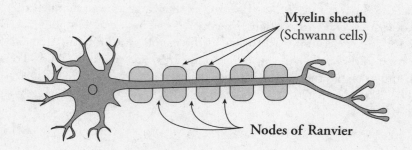

Myelin increases the speed at which an impulse can travel down the axon, because not all portions of the axon have to fire an action potential. The only portions that fire action potentials are the nodes of Ranvier. So the impulse seems to "jump" down the axon from node to node, and this increases the rate at which it reaches the end of the axon. This "jumping" type of conduction is called **saltatory conduction**, from the Latin word *saltar* meaning "to jump." The largest myelinated neurons can conduct impulses at the speed of 100 meters per second (100 m/sec). That's a little more than the length of a football field in one second—virtually instantaneous.

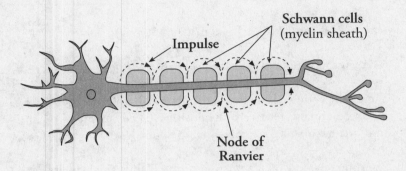

One last thing: For a very short while after firing an action potential, that portion of the membrane is not able to fire a second action potential (that is, until the sodium and potassium channels reset and the membrane is again at the resting potential). In any case, that short period of time is known as the **refractory period**. Having a short refractory period in the portion of the membrane that has just fired an action potential ensures that the action potential (the impulse) will only travel in one direction down the axon—away from the cell body.

Quick Quiz #2

Fill in the blanks and check the appropriate boxes:

1. Depolarization results from an [☐ **influx** ☐ **efflux**] of [☐ **sodium** ☐ **potassium**] ions.

2. Rapid, "jumping" conduction is called _____.

3. Threshold potential is [☐ **–70 mV** ☐ **–50 mV**].

4. A return to the resting, polarized state is called _____.

5. The small portion of a neuron's membrane that is undergoing an action potential is relatively [☐ **positive** ☐ **negative**] on the inside and [☐ **positive** ☐ **negative**] on the outside.

6. The time during which a portion of the membrane is unable to fire an action potential (because of the fact that it has just fired one) is called the _____.

7. In a myelinated axon, action potentials occur only at the [☐ **Schwann cells** ☐ **nodes of Ranvier**].

8. Repolarization results from an [☐ **influx** ☐ **efflux**] of [☐ **sodium** ☐ **potassium**] ions.

9. Ion channels that open at a particular membrane potential are said to be _____.

What Happens When the Impulse (Action Potential) Reaches the End of the Axon?

When the nerve impulse reaches the end of an axon, it will either get transferred to another neuron's dendrites, or it will get transferred to an organ (which will exhibit some effect because of being stimulated by the neuron). The point where the impulse gets transferred is called a synapse. A synapse is nothing more than a neuron-to-neuron junction, or a neuron-to-organ junction.

Most synapses in the body are chemical. In other words, they use a special chemical, called a **neurotransmitter**, to pass the impulse from one neuron to the next. There are many different neurotransmitters in the body. The most common is **acetylcholine** (ACh). Acetylcholine is the neurotransmitter you should remember for the exam.

So how does it work? How does acetylcholine pass a nerve impulse from one neuron to the next? Or from a neuron to an organ? First, let's take a close-up look at the synapse itself.

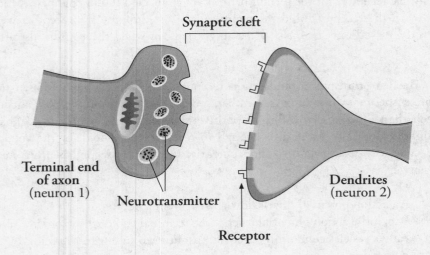

The axon of the first neuron doesn't actually contact the dendrites of the second neuron. There is a small gap between them called the **synaptic cleft**. In the terminal end of the axon are vesicles that contain the chemical neurotransmitter. On the dendrites are receptors that can bind to that neurotransmitter.

When an action potential reaches the terminal end of an axon, it causes the vesicles to fuse with the cell membrane. The neurotransmitter is released into the synaptic cleft by exocytosis. It diffuses instantly across the (very small) synaptic cleft where it binds to the receptors on the dendrites of the next neuron.

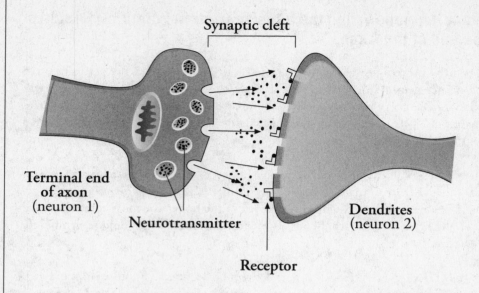

Synaptic cleft

Terminal end
of axon
(neuron 1)

Neurotransmitter

Receptor

Dendrites
(neuron 2)

Usually the receptors on the second neuron are connected to ion channels, which open when the receptors bind the neurotransmitter. Suppose the receptors were connected to sodium channels. What might happen when the neurotransmitter binds?

When the neurotransmitter binds to the receptors, the sodium channels open and sodium rushes into the neuron (remember, sodium concentration is higher outside the cell than inside). This influx of positive ions causes the neuron to depolarize slightly. And if it depolarizes enough to reach the threshold for the voltage-gated channels—BOOM! An action potential fires in the second neuron. Let's summarize:

1. An action potential travels down the axon of a neuron.
2. When the action potential reaches the terminal end of the axon, it causes vesicles containing a neurotransmitter to fuse with the cell membrane.
3. The neurotransmitter is released into the synaptic cleft by exocytosis.
4. The neurotransmitter diffuses across the cleft where it binds to receptors on the dendrites of the next neuron.
5. Binding of the neurotransmitter to the receptors opens ion channels in the next neuron.
6. If the ion channels allow sodium to enter the neuron, it will depolarize.
7. If the neuron depolarizes to threshold, voltage-gated channels will open, causing an action potential to fire.

Not All Neurotransmitters Are the Same

Not all neurotransmitters cause a cell to be **stimulated** (depolarize toward threshold). Some cause a cell to be **inhibited**, in other words, to move away from threshold. And don't forget, a single neuron may receive impulses from many, many other neurons. Some impulses will cause the neuron to be stimulated, some will cause it to be inhibited. The neuron will take all the stimulatory input and all the inhibitory input and "add them up." If there are more stimulatory inputs than inhibitory, the neuron will most likely fire an action potential. If there are more inhibitory inputs than stimulatory, the cell will NOT fire an action potential. This is called **summation**.

Quick Quiz #3

Fill in the blanks and check the appropriate boxes:

1. A neuron whose resting potential is moving away from threshold is said to be [☐ **stimulated** ☐ **inhibited**].

2. The small space between the axon terminus of one neuron and the dendrites of the next neuron is called the _____.

3. A synapse can be found between a [☐ **neuron and an organ** ☐ **neuron and a neuron** ☐ **both of these**].

4. The most common neurotransmitter in the body is _____.

5. A neurotransmitter is released from [☐ **vesicles** ☐ **receptors**] and binds to [☐ **vesicles** ☐ **receptors**].

6. Receptors that open sodium channels would cause the neuron to _____.

7. A neuron will fire an action potential only if its membrane potential reaches _____.

The Nervous System's Job As a Whole

So far we've only looked at the nervous system at the cellular level—the neuron level. But all of an organism's neurons are put together into a complicated network. If an organism were a city's entire electrical system, a neuron would be a single wire. The nervous system would be all of the wires in the whole city—on every street, on every power line and pole, in every wall of every floor of every building and home. In the human nervous system, billions of neurons run every which way, with synapses all over the place, carrying impulses here, there, everywhere.

The brain and the spinal cord are made completely out of neurons. The brain and the spinal cord are referred to as the **central nervous system (CNS)**. Any neurons outside of the brain and spinal cord, like those in our organs and skin, are part of the **peripheral nervous system (PNS)**.

This, then, is the true function of the nervous system as a whole. It receives information from the body's sense organs (eyes, ears, etc.). This sensory information is carried by the PNS to the CNS, where it is processed and integrated with other information. The CNS makes some decisions and sends commands out to the body through the PNS. There are three types of neurons involved here:

> The CNS is like a command station at a military base. Decisions are made here, and information is processed here. The PNS is like a network of phone lines that connect the command station to all other centers on the base. Information from the command station is sent along these phone lines to all other centers so that orders are carried out. New information can be sent to the command station from other centers along these same phone lines. That new information will be processed, decisions will be made, and new orders will be sent along the phone lines.

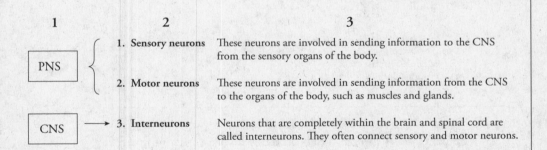

1   **2**   **3**

PNS

1. **Sensory neurons**   These neurons are involved in sending information to the CNS from the sensory organs of the body.

2. **Motor neurons**   These neurons are involved in sending information from the CNS to the organs of the body, such as muscles and glands.

CNS ⟶ 3. **Interneurons**   Neurons that are completely within the brain and spinal cord are called interneurons. They often connect sensory and motor neurons.

Here is something to remember about all of the neurons in the nervous system: They all fire the same type of action potential. In other words, *all action potentials are exactly alike*. There is no such thing as a "big" action potential or a "small" action potential. There is no such thing as a "short" action potential or a "long" action potential. As soon as threshold is reached and the voltage-gated channels open, the action potential occurs automatically, in exactly the same way it did the last time the neuron reached threshold, and in exactly the same way it will the next time the neuron reaches threshold.

However, the sensations picked up by the sensory neurons and sent to the CNS certainly DO differ in strength. We might sense something as a little bit warm or as too hot to touch. The prick of a pin is hardly irritating, but a broken ankle is excruciatingly painful. If all action potentials are the same, how does the CNS "know" when a sensation is strong or weak?

The answer lies in how frequently threshold is reached and, thus, how frequently action potentials are fired. Weak stimuli might cause the neuron to fire two action potentials in a one-second period, while strong stimuli might cause the neuron to fire 20 action potentials in the same one-second period. Very frequent action potentials are interpreted by the CNS as a strong sensation, whereas less frequent action potentials are interpreted as weak sensations.

The Subdivisions of the Nervous System

So far we've looked at two of the subdivisions of the nervous system, the CNS and the PNS. Let's take a closer look at the central nervous system:

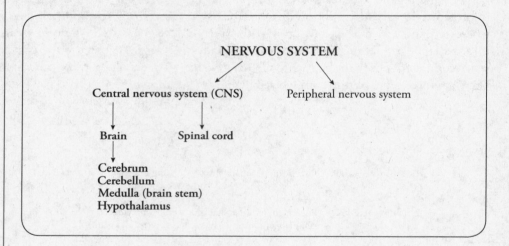

- **Spinal cord:** The spinal cord is primarily involved in primitive, reflex actions.
- **Cerebrum:** The cerebral cortex is our conscious mind. This is where voluntary actions occur, such as movement, speech, and problem solving. This is where we have conscious awareness of sensations, such as smells, sights, hot, and cold.
- **Cerebellum:** The cerebellum coordinates muscle movement and balance, so that movement is smooth and coordinated.
- **Medulla:** Involuntary acts originate here, such as breathing and blood pressure regulation. This is a relatively primitive region.
- **Hypothalamus:** The hypothalamus maintains body homeostasis—a constant internal environment regardless of changing external conditions. It monitors things like hormone levels, electrolyte balance, and temperature.

Now let's take a closer look at the peripheral nervous system (PNS):

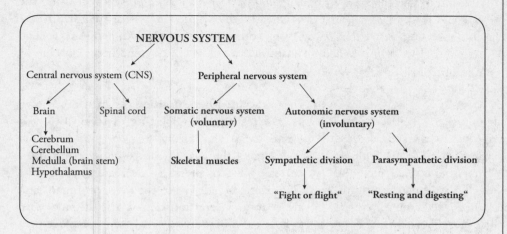

The PNS has two subdivisions: the somatic nervous system and the autonomic nervous system. The **somatic nervous system** is a *voluntary system*, meaning that we have conscious control over the organs that this subdivision controls. The only organs controlled and monitored by the somatic system are the skeletal muscles. The somatic nervous system uses acetylcholine (ACH) as a neurotransmitter. In other words, to stimulate a skeletal muscle, a somatic motor neuron releases a little ACh onto the muscle. The ACh binds to receptors on the muscle, and this causes the muscle to depolarize and contract.

The **autonomic nervous system (ANS)**, as its name implies, is an autonomous, or *involuntary system*. We do NOT have conscious control over the organs controlled by this subdivision. Some examples of the organs controlled by the autonomic nervous system are the heart, the digestive organs, the blood vessels, and the pancreas. The autonomic nervous system can be further subdivided into the sympathetic division (which tends to increase body activity) and the parasympathetic division (which tends to decrease body activity).

The **sympathetic division** is sometimes known as the "**fight or flight**" system. This division of the ANS *helps prepare your body for stress situations* by increasing the rate and force of your heartbeat, increasing blood pressure, increasing breath rate, and diverting blood flow away from your digestive organs and toward skeletal muscles. The primary neurotransmitter used by the sympathetic division is **norepinephrine**.

A Neuro–Endocrine Connection

One of the first things triggered by the sympathetic "fight or flight" system is the release of the hormone *epinephrine* (adrenaline) from the adrenal medulla. Epinephrine is very much like the neurotransmitter norepinephrine, and causes the same effects in the body. However, because it is a hormone, it is released into the bloodstream, where it is present for a much longer time (minutes) than norepinephrine is at a synapse (milliseconds). Thus, it prolongs and enhances the effects of the sympathetic response, making sure that your body is able to deal with a stressful situation for as long as it takes to resolve it.

The **parasympathetic division** is sometimes known as the "**resting and digesting**" system. This division of the ANS is *most active when you are at rest*. It decreases the rate and force of your heartbeat, decreases blood pressure, decreases breath rate, and diverts blood flow to the digestive organs and away from skeletal muscles. It also stimulates activity in the digestive system, such as movement of food through the stomach and intestines and secretion of digestive enzymes. The primary neurotransmitter used by the parasympathetic division is acetylcholine, just like in the somatic (voluntary skeletal muscle) division.

Not Just for Humans

Much of this discussion about the nervous system relates to humans. The nervous system in other organisms of the **vertebrate group,** such as fish, amphibians, and birds, is very similar. In all these organisms, the central nervous system is made up of the brain and spinal cord. Nerves transmit impulses to and from the brain and spinal cord and make up the peripheral nervous system.

The nervous systems of **arthropods** (such as many of the insects we see) and **annelids** (segmented worms) are made up of a ventral nerve cord and a brain. There are a series of **ganglia** (clusters of nerve cell bodies) along the nerve cord and neurons branch from the ganglia.

Quick Quiz #4

Fill in the blanks and check the appropriate boxes:

1. The CNS consists of the _____ and the
    _____.

2. Motor neurons are part of the [☐ **CNS** ☐ **PNS**].

3. Interneurons are part of the [☐ **CNS** ☐ **PNS**].

4. The _____ maintains body homeostasis.

5. Conscious awareness of ourselves and our surroundings is controlled
    by the [☐ **cerebrum** ☐ **cerebellum**] of the brain.

6. The [☐ **somatic** ☐ **sympathetic**] division of the PNS controls the
    skeletal muscles.

7. The primary neurotransmitter used by the parasympathetic division of
    the ANS is
    (A) sympathetic
    (B) parasympathetic
    (C) somatic
    (D) norepinephrine
    (E) acetylcholine

8. The [☐ **sympathetic** ☐ **somatic** ☐ **parasympathetic**] division of
    the PNS is in control of a person watching TV.

9. Which part of the brain smoothes and coordinates body movement?
    (A) Medulla
    (B) Brain stem
    (C) Cerebellum
    (D) Cerebrum
    (E) Spinal cord

10. Neurons of the PNS are [☐ **entirely separated from** ☐ **connected
    to**] neurons of the CNS.

11. Conscious thought processes are carried out by the
    _____.

CONTROL OF THE BODY, PART 2—THE ENDOCRINE SYSTEM

We've seen how the nervous system helps to control body functions. The nervous system is extremely fast. Action potentials last only about two to three milliseconds, so actions controlled by the nervous system are virtually instantaneous. Consider a pain withdrawal reflex (controlled by the nervous system). If you touch something painful, like a hot stove, your hand immediately pulls back, even before you consciously realize you've touched something hot.

The **endocrine system** is also a control system of the body, but it operates on a much slower time scale than the nervous system.

How does the endocrine system control the body? Through the use of **hormones**. Hormones are chemicals made by special glands (called endocrine glands), then secreted (released) into the bloodstream. Once a hormone is in the blood, it goes everywhere in the body; however, it has effects on only some of the organs in the body. What makes some organs respond to a hormone and other organs ignore the same hormone? For a hormone to have an effect on an organ, that organ must have receptors for the hormone. No receptors, no effect. The organs that are affected by a particular hormone are called target organs for that hormone.

> ### Endocrine System
> Consider some of the things controlled by the endocrine system:
>
> - **Ejection of breast milk:** 1–2 minutes
> - **Regulation of blood glucose:** about 15 minutes
> - **Regulation of extracellular sodium:** about 1–2 hours
> - **Female reproductive cycle:** average of 28 days
> - **Puberty:** average of 5 years

Peptides and Steroids

Hormones come in two classes: **peptide hormones** (which are amino acid-based) and **steroid hormones** (which are cholesterol-based). These general classes of hormones act in slightly different ways. Let's take a look.

Peptide hormones are made from amino acids. They are essentially protein molecules, but some are very small and are referred to as peptides. Because they cannot cross cell membranes, peptide hormones must bind to receptors outside the cell (on the extracellular surface). Peptide hormones generally cause their effects rapidly. They do this by turning existing enzymes in the cell on or off. Some examples of peptide hormones are insulin, prolactin, and glucagon.

Steroid hormones are made from cholesterol. They are lipids and can easily cross the cell membrane, so they bind to receptors inside the cell (intracellular). Steroid hormones generally cause their effects more slowly than peptide hormones. They cause their effects by binding to DNA and changing which genes get transcribed. Some examples of steroids are aldosterone, estrogen, and testosterone.

Quick Quiz #5

Fill in the blanks and check the appropriate boxes:

1. Peptide hormones have receptors [☐ **outside** ☐ **inside**] the cell, and steroids have receptors [☐ **outside** ☐ **inside**] the cell.

2. The organs that are affected by a particular hormone are referred to as that hormone's _____.

3. The endocrine system is [☐ **faster** ☐ **slower**] than the nervous system.

4. Peptide hormones cause their effects [☐ **more** ☐ **less**] rapidly than steroid hormones.

5. Steroid hormones cause their effects by _____.

6. Steroid hormones are derived from [☐ **cholesterol** ☐ **amino acids**].

The Endocrine Glands

The endocrine glands (glands that produce hormones) are scattered throughout the body. Hormones are then circulated through the body by blood.

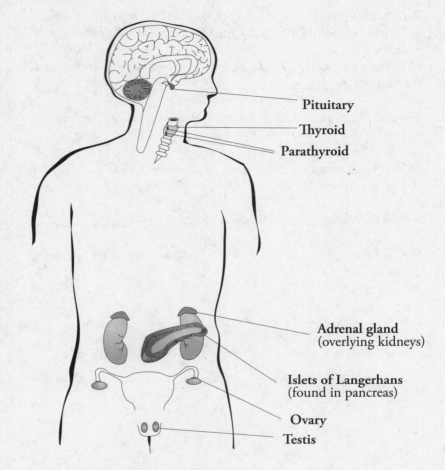

Male and Female Organs

The Pituitary Gland—the "Master" Endocrine Organ

The **pituitary gland** is sometimes referred to as the "master" endocrine organ because its hormones control many of the other endocrine glands in the body. But the pituitary gland itself is controlled by the hypothalamus of the brain, so it really isn't the "master" after all. The pituitary gland has two lobes: the anterior lobe and the posterior lobe.

The **anterior pituitary gland** makes and secretes six different hormones:

1. **Growth hormone (GH):** This hormone targets all tissues and organs in the body and causes them to grow. It is especially important in childhood and adolescence, but in adults it can stimulate the rate at which older cells are replaced with newer cells (called **cell-turnover rate**).

2. **Thyroid stimulating hormone (TSH):** This hormone does exactly what its name implies. It stimulates the thyroid gland to secrete thyroid hormones.

3. **Adrenocorticotropic hormone (ACTH):** This hormone stimulates the adrenal cortex (the outer layer of the adrenal gland) to secrete its hormones.

4. **Follicle stimulating hormone (FSH):** This hormone's target organs are the gonads (the male and female reproductive organs). In the female it stimulates the ovaries, causing maturation of ova and the release of estrogen. In the male it stimulates the testes to make sperm.

5. **Luteinizing hormone (LH):** This hormone also targets the gonads. In the female it stimulates the ovaries, causing development of a corpus luteum (we'll talk more about this later). In the male it stimulates the testes to make testosterone.

6. **Prolactin:** This hormone is released only after childbirth. It stimulates the mammary glands to make breast milk.

The release of these hormones is controlled by special releasing hormones from the hypothalamus. For example, to cause the anterior pituitary to secrete prolactin, the hypothalamus releases prolactin-releasing hormone (prolactin-RH). To cause the anterior pituitary to release thyroid-stimulating hormone (TSH), the hypothalamus releases TSH-releasing hormone (TSH-RH). For every hormone released by the anterior pituitary there is a corresponding releasing hormone from the hypothalamus.

The **posterior pituitary gland** stores and secretes two hormones:

1. **Oxytocin:** This hormone causes the uterus to contract during childbirth and also causes the mammary glands to release milk during breastfeeding.

2. **Antidiuretic hormone (ADH):** This hormone causes the kidneys to retain water. It is also known as **vasopressin.**

The Thyroid Gland

The thyroid gland is located in the anterior part of the neck. It secretes two hormones: thyroid hormone, also known as thyroxine, and calcitonin. **Thyroxine** affects most of the body's cells. It makes them increase their rate of metabolism, meaning that they work harder and use more energy. If you think of the body as a car, thyroxine steps on the gas.

Thyroxine contains **iodine.** If you don't eat enough iodine, you can't make enough thyroxine. If that happens, you develop **hypothyroidism** (*hypo* means "lower than," so hypothyroidism means lower than normal levels of thyroid hormone). A person with hypothyroidism has a low metabolic rate; they can gain weight and become sluggish. The opposite of hypothyroidism is **hyperthyroidism**—an overproduction of thyroxine. This produces a higher than normal metabolic rate, accompanied by symptoms such as weight loss and a fast heart rate.

An Annoying Fact About the Posterior Pituitary Hormones
ADH and oxytocin aren't made in the posterior pituitary. They're actually made by the **hypothalamus,** and then transported to and stored in the posterior pituitary. Release of the hormones is by an action potential from the hypothalamus.

Calcitonin activates special cells in bone that remove calcium from the blood and use it to build new bone. The overall effect is to reduce blood calcium levels (calcitonin "tones down" blood calcium).

The Parathyroid Glands

There are four parathyroid glands. They are very small and are found on the back of the thyroid gland. The parathyroid glands secrete **parathyroid hormone** (also called **parathormone**). Parathyroid hormone functions as the opposite of calcitonin; it activates special cells in bone that dissolve the bone to *release* calcium into the blood, so the overall effect of parathyroid hormone is to increase the amount of calcium in the blood. Calcium is used in many different situations, ranging from nerve impulse conduction to heart contraction to blood clotting, so it is very important to maintain its concentration to be relatively constant.

The Adrenal Glands

The **adrenal glands** sit on top of the kidneys. Even though they are located on top of the kidney, they are not part of the kidney. The adrenal glands have two parts: the adrenal medulla (the inner part) and the adrenal cortex (the outer part).

The **adrenal medulla** secretes two hormones: epinephrine (also known as adrenaline) and norepinephrine (also known as noradrenaline). Most of its output (about 80%) is epinephrine. These two hormones have very similar chemical structures, which means that they can bind to the same receptors and have the same effects on organs.

Remember when we talked about the sympathetic division of the autonomic nervous system? We referred to it as the "fight or flight" system, because it increases body activity, especially the heart rate, in preparation for stressful activity. Remember also that the sympathetic neurons use norepinephrine as a neurotransmitter? In other words, to affect the organs it innervates, the sympathetic system releases a very small amount of norepinephrine onto the organ at a synapse. The norepinephrine binds to receptors on the organ, and this causes the effects of the sympathetic division.

The first thing that gets stimulated by the sympathetic neurons in a stress situation is the adrenal medulla. The effect is to release a lot of epinephrine (and some norepinephrine) into the blood. These hormones can bind to the *same receptors* on organs that norepinephrine from the sympathetic neurons does. The *only difference* is that norepinephrine from a sympathetic neuron is present only for a few milliseconds at a synapse, whereas norepinephrine and epinephrine from the adrenal medulla are present in the blood for a LOT longer: at the very least a few minutes and up to a few hours depending on the situation and the stress level. Otherwise, the effect on the organs is the same.

So . . . bottom line:

> The effect of epinephrine and norepinephrine from the adrenal medulla is to increase and prolong the effects of the sympathetic nervous system.

Imagine you are walking along the side of a road when all of a sudden a car swerves out and almost hits you. You jump quickly out of the way and are safe, but a few minutes after the event your heart rate is still elevated and you still feel "shaky." The stimulation from the sympathetic system came and went in about three milliseconds, but the effect of the epinephrine from the adrenal medulla is prolonged. This is what keeps your heart rate up and keeps your body "on alert" even though the immediate danger has passed. It takes a while for the epinephrine to get cleared out of the blood.

The **adrenal cortex** secretes many different hormones. All are steroids, and they come in three main classes: glucocorticoids, mineralocorticoids, and sex steroids.

One of the targets for the **glucocorticoids** is the liver. The glucocorticoids cause the liver to produce glucose from fats and proteins and to release that "new" glucose into the blood. This is called **gluconeogenesis** (*gluco* = glucose, *neo* = new, *genesis* = formation). Glucocorticoids also target other body cells to use fats for fuel instead of glucose, causing an increase in blood glucose levels and increased body metabolism. These hormones are also strong anti-inflammatory agents. The primary glucocorticoid is *cortisol*. (You've seen this substance in over-the-counter creams available at drug stores to reduce inflammation and itching associated with some skin conditions.)

The targets for the mineralocorticoids are the kidneys. The primary **mineralocorticoid** is **aldosterone**, and aldosterone causes the kidney to retain sodium—in other words, to remove sodium from the urine and return it to the body. When the sodium is returned, water comes with it, so the effect on the body is to retain both sodium AND water. This increases blood volume and blood pressure.

The **sex steroids** from the adrenal cortex (testosterone, etc.) are of little consequence because the primary source of these hormones are the gonads (ovaries and testes) and not the adrenal cortex.

Glands: A Quick Review

Let's quickly review the major glands in the body and their functions:

Gland	Function
anterior pituitary gland	makes and secretes growth hormone, thyroid stimulating hormone, adrenocorticotropic hormone, follicle stimulating hormone, luteinizing hormone, prolactin
posterior pituitary gland	stores and secretes oxytocin, antidiuretic hormone
thyroid gland	secretes thyroxine and calcitonin
parathyroid glands	secrete parathyroid hormones (parathormone)
adrenal medulla	secretes epinephrine and norepinephrine
adrenal cortex	secretes steroids
pancreas	secretes hormones and digestive enzymes
gonads (primary sex organs)	*testes*—produce male steroids called **androgens** *ovaries*—produce female steroids called **estrogens** and **progesterone**

The Pancreas

The **pancreas** has multiple functions; not only does it secrete hormones, it also secretes many digestive enzymes. Secreting enzymes is an exocrine role, which we'll discuss later on. Let's talk now about the pancreas' endocrine role—secreting insulin and glucagon.

Insulin and glucagon are produced by special cells in the pancreas called Islets of Langerhans, or simply **islet cells**. **Insulin** is secreted whenever blood glucose levels are high, such as after a meal. Insulin affects pretty much all the cells in the body; it allows them to take glucose out of the blood so they can use it in cellular respiration (glycolysis, PDC, Krebs cycle, and electron transport) to produce energy. Insulin also stimulates the liver to store glucose as glycogen. Consequently, blood glucose levels go down.

Glucagon has the opposite effect on blood glucose. **Glucagon** is released whenever blood glucose is low, such as between meals, when you haven't eaten in a while. The target organ for glucagon is the liver; it causes the liver to break down glycogen (stored glucose) and to release free glucose into the blood. This is called **glyco-genolysis** (*lysis* = to break). The liver is the only organ that stores glycogen for this purpose. Consequently, blood glucose levels go up. Note that this is different from the effect that cortisol has on the liver. Both cortisol and glucagon cause the liver to release glucose, but cortisol stimulates the production of "new" glucose from fats and proteins (gluconeogenesis), whereas glucagon stimulates the breakdown of glycogen into free glucose (glycogenolysis).

The Gonads

The **gonads** are the male and female primary sex organs. The primary sex organs are those that produce the gametes (the sex cells—sperm and ova). The male primary sex organ—the male gonad—is the **testis** (plural = testes). The female primary sex organ—the female gonad—is the **ovary** (plural = ovaries).

The gonads, in addition to producing gametes, secrete hormones. All the hormones produced and secreted by the gonads are steroids. Because these hormones are involved in maintaining sexual characteristics, they are collectively referred to as the sex steroids.

The testes, as we've already seen in Chapter 7, produce sperm. They also produce male sex steroids, called **androgens**. The primary androgen—the primary male sex steroid—is **testosterone**. Testosterone has many targets in the body. It is responsible for developing the male secondary sex characteristics during puberty and for maintaining them during adulthood. Male secondary sex characteristics include broader shoulders and narrower hips, deeper voice, facial hair, chest hair, axillary hair, pubic hair, and enlarged external genitalia. Testosterone is also necessary for normal and adequate sperm production.

The ovaries, again as we've already seen in Chapter 7, produce ova. They also produce two types of female sex steroids, the **estrogens** and **progesterone**. There are several forms of estrogens; the most common is **estradiol**. Estradiol frequently is simply referred to as "estrogen." Estrogen and progesterone have multiple targets in the female body, just as testosterone does in the male body. They are responsible for developing female secondary sex characteristics during puberty and for maintaining them during adulthood. Female secondary sex characteristics include a narrower waist and wider hips, breasts and mammary glands, axillary and pubic hair, softer skin, and a higher-pitched voice.

Estrogen and progesterone also regulate the menstrual cycle. Estrogen stimulates the growth of the uterine lining in the first half of the cycle, and progesterone enhances and maintains the lining in the second half of the cycle. We'll take a closer look at the menstrual cycle later on.

Whew!

That's a lot of information. For the SAT Biology E/M Subject Test, you need to know which hormones are secreted from which glands, the target organs of the hormones, the specific effects of the hormones on the target organs, and the general effects of the hormones on the body. Go back over all the information we've given you about the different glands and their hormones, and then take these practice quizzes.

Quick Quiz #6

On each blank line place the letter that designates the appropriate hormone.

1. The pancreatic islet cells secrete _____ and _____.

2. The ovaries secrete _____ and _____.

3. The anterior pituitary secretes _____, _____, _____, _____, _____, and _____.

4. The thyroid gland secretes _____ and _____.

5. The adrenal cortex secretes _____ and _____.

6. The posterior pituitary secretes _____ and _____.

7. The adrenal medulla secretes _____ and _____.

8. The testes secrete _____.

9. The parathyroid gland secretes _____.

A.   estrogen

B.   ACTH

C.   aldosterone

D.   epinephrine

E.   prolactin

F.   glucagon

G.   parathormone

H.   LH

I.   insulin

J.   oxytocin

K.   growth hormone

L.   FSH

M.   testosterone

N.   progesterone

O.   cortisol

P.   norepinephrine

Q.   ADH

R.   TSH

S.   thyroxine

T.   calcitonin

Quick Quiz #7

On each blank line place the letter that designates the appropriate target organ. Letters can be used more than once.

1. estrogen / progesterone _____

2. ACTH _____

3. aldosterone _____

4. epinephrine / norepinephrine _____

5. prolactin _____

6. glucagon _____

7. parathormone _____

8. LH / FSH _____

9. insulin _____

10. oxytocin _____

11. growth hormone _____

12. testosterone _____

13. cortisol _____

14. ADH _____

15. TSH _____

16. thyroxine _____

17. calcitonin _____

A. all cells in the body

B. bones

C. male body

D. thyroid gland

E. uterus

F. mammary glands

G. adrenal cortex

H. kidneys

I. female body

J. testes

K. liver

L. ovaries and testes

Quick Quiz #8

On each blank line place the letter that designates the appropriate effect in the body.

1. estrogen _____

2. ACTH _____

3. aldosterone _____

4. epinephrine / norepinephrine_____

5. prolactin _____

6. glucagon _____

7. parathormone _____

8. LH _____

9. insulin _____

10. oxytocin _____

11. growth hormone _____

12. testosterone _____

13. cortisol _____

14. ADH _____

15. TSH _____

16. thyroxine _____

17. FSH _____

18. progesterone _____

19. calcitonin _____

A. produces breast milk

B. contracts uterus, releases breast milk

C. causes gluconeogenesis, increases blood glucose levels

D. maintains male sex characteristics

E. causes release of hormones from adrenal cortex

F. increases body metabolism

G. growth of the body

H. breaks down glycogen, increases blood glucose levels

I. builds bone, decreases blood calcium

J. causes kidneys to retain water

K. maintains female sex characteristics, builds uterine lining

L. releases testosterone in male, forms corpus luteum in female

M. maintains and enhances uterine lining

N. prolongs and enhances "fight or flight" response

O. causes thyroid gland to release thyroxine

P. causes spermatogenesis in male, oogenesis in female

Q. causes kidneys to retain sodium

R. allows cells to take up glucose, decreases blood glucose levels

S. breaks down bone, increases blood calcium

TRANSPORT WITHIN THE BODY—THE CIRCULATORY SYSTEM

The circulatory system is designed to move stuff around the body. It transports oxygen, carbon dioxide, glucose, hormones, waste products, lipids, etc. Essentially, the circulatory system consists of a pump (the heart), a network of tubing (the blood vessels), and a fluid (the blood). Let's start by talking about the blood.

The Blood

Any organism with a closed circulatory system has blood. A closed circulatory system just means that the blood is carried in vessels. But some organisms do not have a closed system; their blood (called **hemolymph** in these organisms) is not carried in vessels; it simply bathes the organs in their body cavities. Examples of organisms with open circulatory systems are the arthropods (insects, etc.).

Blood consists of two main things: (1) fluid and (2) cells that float around in the fluid. The fluid is called plasma, and the cells that float around are red blood cells, white blood cells, and platelets.

Plasma is mostly water. It has a lot of stuff dissolved in it, such as glucose, hormones, ions, and gases. The glucose makes it sticky. It also has a lot of protein in it, like albumin (the most abundant protein in blood), fibrinogen, and lipoproteins. All the blood proteins are made by the liver, and plasma makes up about 50% of the blood volume.

Most of the cells in the plasma are **red blood cells**. In fact, red blood cells make up about 45% of the total blood volume. Red blood cells are shaped like biconcave disks, which look sort of like disks that have been squashed in the center, on both sides. Red blood cells are filled with a protein called **hemoglobin**. There is so much hemoglobin in red blood cells that there is no room for organelles or a nucleus. Red blood cells are the only cells in the body that do not have a nucleus.

Hemoglobin can bind oxygen. Because red blood cells contain hemoglobin, and hemoglobin carries oxygen, we say that *red blood cells carry oxygen and deliver it to cells all over the body*. Really, though, it's the hemoglobin that carries the oxygen.

Hemoglobin is made partly of iron. That means that if you don't get enough iron in your diet, you can't produce enough hemoglobin. Your red blood cells can't bind enough oxygen, and your body's cells get shortchanged. They don't receive all the oxygen they need to carry out cellular respiration to make energy (ATP). When that happens, you have **anemia**. One of the most obvious symptoms of anemia is fatigue. It makes sense—if you can't use cellular respiration to make ATP, you don't have enough energy and you're easily fatigued.

The remaining 5% of the blood volume is made up of white blood cells and platelets. **White blood cells** are very important in fighting off disease. Most of the white blood cells are phagocytes, which means they are very good at phagocytosis (eating stuff). What do they eat? Well, viruses, bacteria, parasites, dead cells, and sick cells, to name a few—anything that's potentially harmful to your body. Some of the white blood cells are **lymphocytes**, which participate in very specific disease defense called immunity. Lymphocytes come in two forms: B-cells and T-cells.

B-cells make antibodies. Antibodies are just markers that can bind to foreign things in the body and mark them for destruction (like by phagocytosis). For example, if you get infected with the chickenpox virus, some of the B-cells in your blood will make antibodies that can bind to the chickenpox virus and mark it for destruction. Because there are millions of different viruses, bacteria, parasites, and other potentially harmful things, you have millions of different B-cells that can make antibodies that are specific for each of the million different potentially harmful things.

T-cells have two jobs. First, they help the B-cells and other T-cells divide and proliferate. T-cells that do this are called **helper T-cells**. Second, they kill any cells that have been infected by viruses. Because viruses are not complete cells they cannot reproduce without some help. So they act as parasites, living *inside* our cells and essentially turning them into virus factories. The easiest way to kill the virus, then, is to kill the cell it has infected. That's what this type of T-cell does, and they are called **killer T-cells**.

Here's another thing to know: AIDS is a disease caused by a virus called **HIV** (Human Immuno-deficiency Virus). HIV infects and lives in helper T-cells, killing the helper T-cells in the process. Because the helper T-cells are so important to B-cells and killer T-cells, without the helper T-cells the other two cell types can't reproduce and fight infection. As a consequence, many, many infections spring up. Patients with AIDS often die of these infections.

Blood Cells: A Quick Review
- All blood cells are made in the bone marrow.
- Blood cells include red cells, white cells, and platelets.
- Red blood cells contain hemoglobin (which contains iron), and hemoglobin binds oxygen and carries it around the body.
- Some white blood cells help to fight infection by phagocytizing harmful things.
- B-cells are a type of white blood cell that makes antibodies against very specific foreign things.
- Helper T-cells help B-cells and other T-cells reproduce, and killer T-cells kill cells that have been infected by a virus.
- AIDS is caused by a virus (HIV) that infects and kills helper T-cells. Without helper T-cells, the body cannot fight infection.
- Platelets are necessary for blood clotting.

Platelets are very, very small structures that are important in blood clotting. If a person is deficient in platelets, the blood does not clot. Platelets secrete a substance that activates a chain of events that ultimately converts a soluble blood protein—fibrinogen—into insoluble threads called fibrin. The fibrin threads form "nets" that trap blood cells and more platelets to form a clot. The process requires calcium, vitamin K, and many other chemicals.

Finally, all blood cells—red, white, and platelets—are made in the bone marrow inside bones.

Quick Quiz #9

Fill in the blanks and check the appropriate boxes:

1. [☐ **Red blood cells** ☐ **White blood cells**] function in the immune system.

2. Hemoglobin contains _____ and can bind
   _____.

3. Approximately what percentage of the blood is made of red blood cells?
   (A) 5%
   (B) 20%
   (C) 45%
   (D) 50%
   (E) 80%

4. B-cells make _____.

5. Insufficient iron in the diet leads to insufficient _____
   and the disease _____.

6. [☐ **Killer** ☐ **Helper**] T-cells are T-cells that help B-cells and other T-cells reproduce.

7. T-cells are [☐ **white** ☐ **red**] blood cells.

8. Blood cells involved in blood clotting are called _____.

9. Plasma is mainly composed of
   (A) glucose
   (B) water
   (C) oxygen
   (D) red blood cells
   (E) white blood cells

Blood Typing

Blood type is determined by the membrane proteins that sit on the surface of red blood cells. You might remember from Chapter 6 that proteins are made by reading codons on mRNA and connecting amino acids in the order specified by the codons, and that the order of codons on mRNA is determined by the sequence of nucleotides in DNA. Do you remember that a portion of a DNA chromosome that gives rise (ultimately) to a protein is called a gene? Well, if you do, it should not surprise you that there are genes that determine which proteins are produced and inserted into the membranes of red blood cells. The gene for the most common form of blood typing (the ABO blood typing system) is called the I gene.

The I gene comes in three versions (three alleles): I^A, I^B, and i. I^A codes for type-A protein, I^B codes for type-B protein, and i codes for the *absence* of protein (no protein). In Chapter 8 you learned that everyone has two copies of each of their genes (two alleles), one on each of a pair of homologous chromosomes. We also said that if both copies of the alleles are the same, the people are said to be homozygous and their phenotype (their trait) is easy to determine. So, if people have two copies of the I^A allele (their genotype is $I^A I^A$), then all they can make is type-A protein and that's all they'll have on their red blood cells. They are said to have blood type A.

The same is true for people who are homozygous for the I^B allele. Their genotype is $I^B I^B$, all they can make is type-B protein, and that's all they'll have on their red blood cells. They are said to have blood type B.

People who are homozygous for i (genotype ii) don't make any protein at all and have no proteins on the surface of their red cells. They have blood type O.

What about heterozygotes? To determine the phenotype of a heterozygote we have to know which alleles are dominant and which are recessive. For this gene, the i allele is recessive to both the I^A allele and the I^B allele, and the I^A allele and the I^B allele are said to be **codominant**. Codominant means that if these two alleles are found together in a heterozygote, neither gene is silent (repressed). They are both expressed independently. So how does this work for blood typing? Let's take a look.

A heterozygote who has the genotype $I^A i$ has one allele that codes for type-A protein and one allele that codes for no protein. Because I^A is dominant to i, the cells make type-A protein and the person has blood type A. The same thing is true for a heterozygote with the genotype $I^B i$. One allele codes for type-B protein, and the other codes for no protein. Because I^B is dominant to i, the cells make type-B protein and the person has blood type B.

A heterozygote who has the genotype $I^A I^B$ has a unique phenotype. Because I^A and I^B are codominant, both will be expressed in this heterozygote. The cells will make both type-A protein AND type-B protein. The person's blood type will be AB.

Here's a summary table of blood types and the genotypes that produce them:

Blood type	Genotype
A	$I^A I^A$ or $I^A i$
B	$I^B I^B$ or $I^B i$
O	ii
AB	$I^A I^B$

What to Expect

There are two types of questions about blood typing that you might see on the SAT Biology E/M Subject Test. The first type of question will ask about blood transfusions—which blood types can donate to other blood types, and which blood types can receive which blood types. The second type is more of a genetics question.

Blood Transfusion Questions

Here's what you have to remember about donating and receiving blood:

> If a person's body does not recognize the proteins on the newly received red blood cells, the newly received red blood cells will clump up and be destroyed.

The clumping of the red blood cells is also called **agglutination**. This clumping is part of a transfusion reaction and it can be fatal.

For example, a person with blood type AB recognizes both types of protein—type-A protein and type-B protein. So people with blood type AB can *receive* blood from *all other blood types*. They can receive type A blood, because their bodies recognize type-A protein. They can receive type B blood, because their bodies recognize type-B protein. And they can receive type O blood, because type O blood has no proteins to be recognized. Blood type AB is sometimes referred to as the universal recipient, because they can receive all other blood types.

People with type A blood can recognize only type-A protein. Type-B protein looks foreign to their bodies. Therefore, people with type A blood can receive type A blood, and they can receive type O blood (no proteins), but they *cannot* receive type B blood. Type B blood given to a type A person will cause a transfusion reaction. They also cannot receive type AB blood, because the red blood cells of type AB blood have both type-A protein AND type-B protein. Type AB blood given to a type A person will also cause a transfusion reaction.

The same is true for people with type B blood. They can recognize only type-B protein, and type-A protein looks foreign to them. A person with type B blood can receive either type B blood or type O blood, but not types A or AB.

Last, people with type O blood can receive only type O blood. Their bodies recognize neither type-A protein nor type-B protein. Therefore, type A blood, type B blood, and type AB blood will all cause transfusion reactions in a type O person. But notice that type O blood can be given to *any other blood type*. That's because its red blood cells have no proteins on them that could cause reactions in the receiving person. For this reason, type O blood is sometimes referred to as the universal donor.

Here's another summary table:

Blood Type	Can Receive from	Can Donate to
AB (universal recipient)	AB, A, B, or O	AB only
A	A or O	A or AB
B	B or O	B or AB
O (universal donor)	O only	O, A, B, or AB

Genetics Questions

The other type of question you might be asked is more like a typical genetics question. You will be asked to determine the probability of blood types in the children of two people whose blood types you are given. Here are a few practice questions. Don't forget to draw a Punnett square if you think it will help you.

Practice Question 1: A man with blood type AB marries a woman who is homozygous for blood type A (genotype $I^A I^A$). What is the probability that they will produce a child with blood type B?

Practice Question 2: Which blood type(s) are NOT possible from a cross between a person with blood type AB and a person heterozygous for blood type B ($I^B i$)?

Practice Question 3: Could a woman with blood type B and a man with blood type A produce a child with blood type O?

(Answers can be found in Chapter 15.)

Quick Quiz #10

Fill in the blanks and check the appropriate boxes:

1. The genotype(s) for blood type O is (are) _____.

2. Blood type AB is sometimes called the [□ **universal donor**
   □ **universal recipient**].

3. Blood type A can receive blood from blood type(s)
   _____.

4. Blood type B can donate blood to blood type(s)
   _____.

5. The probability of a man homozygous for blood type B and a woman
   homozygous for blood type A producing a child with blood type A is
   [□ **0%** □ **25%** □ **50%** □ **75%** □ **100%**].

6. The genotype(s) for blood type A is (are) _____.

7. Blood type AB can donate blood to blood type [□ **AB** □ **A** □ **B**
   □ **O** □ **all of them**].

8. Alleles I^A and I^B are said to be _____.

The Blood Vessels

At the center of the circulatory system is the heart, which acts as a pump. The **blood vessels** lead away from the heart and enter the tissues, then return to the heart. The heart pumps blood through the blood vessels.

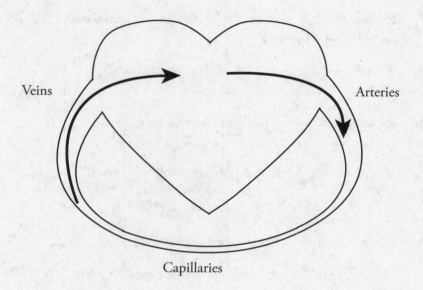

This diagram represents a very basic circuit. Any vessel that carries blood *away from* the heart is called an **artery**. **A**rteries carry blood **A**way from the heart. The blood pressure inside arteries is relatively high, and they have thick, muscular walls that regulate their diameters to regulate blood flow. Blood moves through arteries mostly through momentum, because of the big "push" it gets from the heart. As they travel away from the heart, arteries get smaller and smaller and branch out (not shown above) into arterioles and, ultimately, capillaries.

Capillaries are the smallest blood vessels in the body and are the site of exchange between blood and tissues. Oxygen and nutrients (such as glucose) leave the blood and enter the tissues, and carbon dioxide and other waste products leave the tissues and are picked up by the blood. Blood flow is slow enough here so that there is enough time for this exchange. And, again, even though it's not shown above, **arterioles** branch into thousands and thousands of capillaries. For this reason, blood pressure drops substantially in the capillaries.

Capillaries then merge to form larger vessels, called venules, which merge to form even larger vessels called veins, which carry blood back to the heart. Any vessel that *returns* blood to the heart is called a **vein**. Blood loses most of its forward momentum and pressure as it crosses through the capillaries, so the pressure in the veins is relatively low. As your body moves around and skeletal muscles contract, veins get squeezed, and this pushes the blood along toward the heart. It's just like when you pick up a garden hose and squeeze it and water runs out. But because we want blood to run in only one direction in the veins (water in a hose would run out in both directions) the veins have **valves**, which ensure that the blood keeps moving in the direction we want it to—toward the heart. Veins do not have muscular walls. They do not regulate blood flow. They are passive receivers, taking whatever they get from the capillaries and moving it along to the heart.

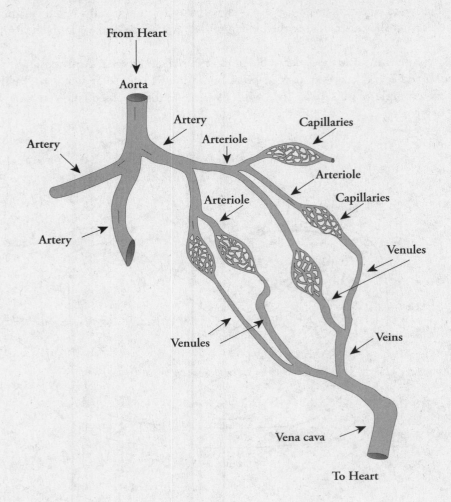

The Blood Vessels: A Quick Review
- Any vessel that carries blood away from the heart is an artery.
- Any vessel that returns blood to the heart is a vein.
- Arteries branch into smaller and smaller vessels, ultimately becoming capillaries.
- Capillaries are the sites of exchange between blood and tissues.
- Capillaries merge into larger and larger vessels, called veins.
- Arteries have higher pressure and muscular walls, can regulate blood flow, and do NOT have valves.
- Veins have lower pressure and no muscle, are passive receivers, and DO have valves.

Oxygen-Rich or Oxygen-Poor?

An important point to note is that the type of blood being carried—oxygen-rich or oxygen-poor—has absolutely nothing to do with the type of vessel carrying it. In other words, arteries and veins are designated as arteries or veins based *only* on the direction they are carrying the blood—either away from or toward the heart.

It is true that most arteries carry blood that is rich in oxygen. And most veins carry blood that is relatively oxygen-poor; but it doesn't have to be that way. We'll see an example of this in a little while, when we discuss blood flow through the heart.

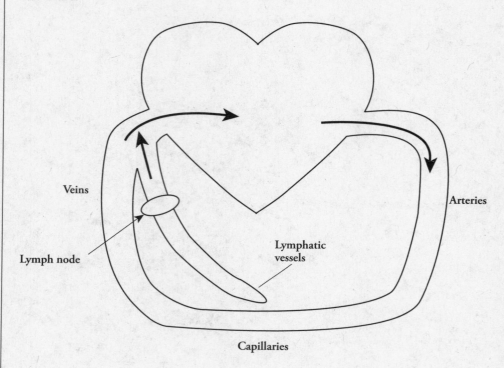

More about the Capillaries

We've mentioned already that capillaries are the sites of exchange between blood and tissues. We've also mentioned that the rate of blood flow and blood pressure both decrease in the capillaries. Here's why: Imagine a river, and imagine that at one place the river gets very narrow. The same amount of water now has to squeeze through a narrower place. What happens? The water speeds up. The water pressure goes up. These areas are sometimes referred to as rapids, or whitewater, because the water moves very fast and white foam forms. Now imagine that a little farther downriver there is a place where the banks widen. What happens here? The water slows down. The pressure is lower. There's more room for the water.

The arteries are like the narrow part of the river. Blood flow is rapid and pressure is high. But as the arteries branch out into smaller and smaller vessels, the combined diameter of all these tiny vessels is actually greater than the diameter of the artery. This is like the wide part of the river. Blood flow slows down and the pressure drops.

On the artery side of a capillary, the blood pressure is higher than on the vein side of the capillary. On the artery side, the pressure forces fluid (essentially blood plasma) out of the capillaries and into the tissues. On the vein side, where pressure is lower, some of the fluid returns to the capillaries, but not all of it; some of it remains in the tissues. So there is a net loss of fluid to the tissues.

The Lymphatic System

Somehow we have to recapture that fluid and return it to the blood vessels. If we don't, blood volume will go down as fluid is lost to the tissues, and the tissues will swell up. Luckily, there is a specialized system of vessels that do just this. The **lymphatic system** is a network of vessels that begins at the tissues and ends at the veins, just before the heart. It recaptures the extra fluid from the tissues, and it filters that fluid to remove anything potentially harmful from it before it gets returned to the blood. The fluid is filtered through structures called **lymph nodes**.

Lymph nodes are just concentrated areas of white blood cells. By passing through the lymph nodes on its way back to the veins, the fluid is exposed to many, many white blood cells. These white blood cells destroy anything harmful before it can get dumped into the general circulation.

The lymphatic vessels are very similar to veins. They have low pressure, no muscle in their walls, and valves that keep the fluid moving in the right direction. Fluid moves through the vessels the same way that blood moves through the veins—by nearby skeletal muscles that squeeze the vessels when they contract. The fluid inside lymphatic vessels is called **lymph**.

Edema

Edema is the swelling of parts of the body due to trapped tissue fluid. Because the flow of lymph through lymphatic vessels depends on nearby muscle contraction, remaining in one position can restrict this flow. The problem can get worse if a person is standing upright because the combination of poor flow and gravity can trap fluid in the lowest parts of the body. This is why people who stand in one place for a long time (e.g. assembly line workers) can have problems with swollen feet and ankles.

Quick Quiz #11

Fill in the blanks and check the appropriate boxes:

1. [☐ **Veins** ☐ **Capillaries** ☐ **Arteries**] are blood vessels that return blood to the heart.

2. _____ return excess tissue fluid to the blood vessels.

3. The type of blood being carried [☐ **does** ☐ **does not**] matter when determining whether a blood vessel is an artery or a vein.

4. Blood pressure in the veins is [☐ **high** ☐ **low**].

5. Blood pressure in the arteries is [☐ **high** ☐ **low**].

6. Blood flow in the capillaries is [☐ **fast** ☐ **slow**].

7. [☐ **Lymph nodes** ☐ **Lymph vessels**] filter potentially harmful things from the lymph before it is returned to the veins.

8. The diameter of an artery is [☐ **larger** ☐ **smaller**] than the combined diameters of the capillaries.

9. Lymphatic vessels [☐ **do** ☐ **do not**] have valves.

10. Blood moves through the veins and lymph moves through the lymphatic vessels when nearby _____ contract and squeeze the vessels.

The Heart

The heart, of course, is the pump that moves the blood through the vessels. It consists of four chambers: two smaller, weaker chambers on the top called **atria** (singular = atrium) and two larger, stronger chambers on the bottom called **ventricles**.

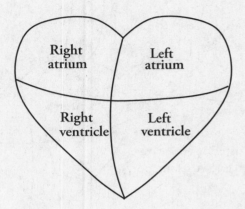

Whenever you think about the heart, you think about it as though it were in a person, and the person is facing you. That person's right side would be on your left side, and the left side would be on your right. That's why in the picture above, the right side of the heart is on your left, and the left side of the heart is on your right. We're thinking about it as though it were in a person.

Blood enters the heart from veins that empty into the atria and leaves the heart through arteries that exit from the ventricles. The heart actually pumps the blood in two separate circuits that run simultaneously. The right side of the heart pumps blood through the **pulmonary circuit**, and the left side of the heart pumps blood through the **systemic circuit**.

Blood Pathway Through the Heart: The Specifics

The pulmonary circuit takes blood that's returning from the tissues of the body and pumps it to the lungs. Blood coming from the tissues is fairly low in oxygen. It has delivered its oxygen to the tissues and picked up carbon dioxide in exchange. It needs to go to the lungs to get rid of the carbon dioxide and pick up a fresh supply of oxygen.

This oxygen-poor blood enters the heart at the right atrium, through the two largest veins in the body, the **anterior vena cava** and the **posterior vena cava**. It passes from the right atrium into the right ventricle, and then from the right ventricle into the **pulmonary artery** on its way to the lungs. (Remember earlier when we said that all arteries carry blood away from the heart and that most arteries carry blood that is oxygen-rich? Here's an example of an artery that carries oxygen-poor blood. It still follows the rule about direction of flow, however; it carries blood AWAY from the heart.)

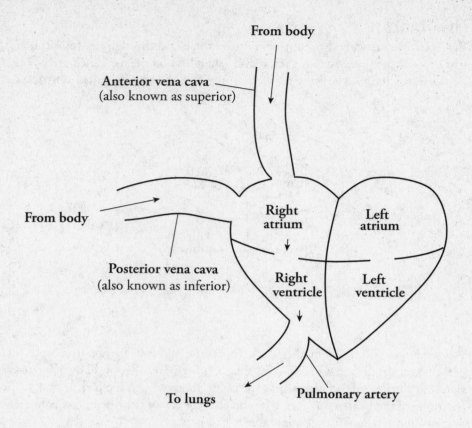

At the lungs, the blood picks up oxygen and delivers its carbon dioxide. It returns to the heart through the **pulmonary veins**, which empty into the left atrium. (Pulmonary veins follow the direction rule also; veins always return blood to the heart. But these are an example of veins that carry oxygen-rich blood, whereas most veins carry blood that is oxygen-poor.) From the left atrium, the blood passes into the left ventricle, then exits the heart through the largest artery in the body, the **aorta**. The aorta carries this oxygen-rich blood to all the tissues of the body. The left side of the heart pumps the blood through the **systemic circuit**. The systemic circuit takes oxygen-rich blood that's returning from the lungs and pumps it to the rest of the body.

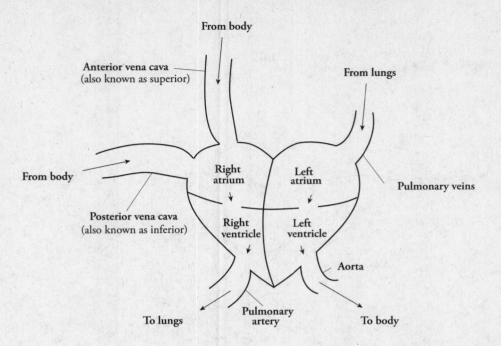

From body

Anterior vena cava
(also known as superior)

From lungs

From body

Right
atrium

Left
atrium

Pulmonary veins

Posterior vena cava
(also known as inferior)

Right
ventricle

Left
ventricle

Aorta

To lungs

Pulmonary
artery

To body

"Lub-Dup, Lub-Dup"

To keep the blood moving in the right direction, the heart has valves. There's a set of valves between the atria and the ventricles, called the **atrioventricular valves** (the AV valves), and there is a set of valves between the ventricles and the arteries, called the **semilunar valves**. The closing of the valves produces the characteristic sound of the heartbeat—"lub-dup, lub-dup, lub-dup." The AV valves close first, at the beginning of heart contraction (producing the "lub" sound) and the semilunar valves close second, at the end of the heart contraction (producing the "dup" sound).

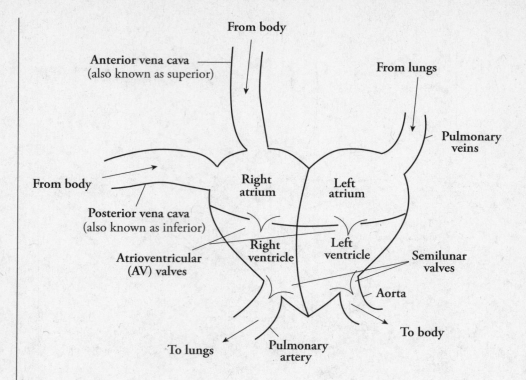

One last thing worth mentioning before we look at the lungs and the pulmonary circuit in a little more detail: The pictures of the heart above are not absolutely anatomically correct. The chambers, the veins, and the valves are all okay, but arteries exit the ventricles at the top of the heart, not out the bottom. We'll see a more correct picture when we look at the heart in conjunction with the lungs.

Not Just for Humans

The circulatory and respiratory systems of other organisms are similar to the human systems. Fish have a two-chambered heart where blood moves in a single circuit. Blood is pumped from the heart to the gills where it receives oxygen.

Amphibians, turtles, and snakes and lizards all have three-chambered hearts. Like humans, these organisms also have two circuits of blood flow. All adult forms of these animals have lungs, for the exchange of gases. It is important to note that in most amphibians, the skin is also a site for the exchange of gas.

Crocodiles, alligators, and birds all have four-chambered hearts with two circuits of blood flow. These animals all have lungs that function like those of mammals.

All arthropods have an open circulatory system. Blood is pumped from the heart to the organs. Arthropods that live in the water have gills. Terrestrial arthropods have tracheae, which lead from the inside of the body to the outside to exchange gases.

VENTILATION AND GAS EXCHANGE— THE RESPIRATORY SYSTEM

The circulatory system's job is to move the blood and the gases, oxygen, and carbon dioxide (as well as anything else that's carried in the blood, like glucose, waste products, and hormones) around the body. But without the respiratory system, there would be no gases to transport. The respiratory system's job is to move air into and out of the lungs. This process is called **ventilation**. The respiratory system also exchanges oxygen and carbon dioxide with the blood. This is **gas exchange**. The respiratory system also plays a role in regulating the pH of the body.

The Conduction Zone—No Gas Exchange

Some parts of the respiratory system are designed for ventilation only and not for the exchange of oxygen and carbon dioxide. Because these parts are designed to conduct air in and out only, they are referred to as the **conduction zone**.

The conduction zone begins at the nose, where air is warmed, filtered, and humidified. The air travels down the throat (called the **pharynx**), past the voicebox (called the **larynx**), and into the windpipe (called the **trachea**). The trachea then branches into two tubes, one that leads to the right lung and one that leads to the left lung. These two tubes are called the **right** and **left primary bronchi**. The primary bronchi continue to branch into smaller and smaller tubes, called **bronchioles**. The walls of the trachea and all of the bronchial tubes are lined with tall cells that secrete mucus. This mucus helps to trap dirt and dust, but it is difficult for gases to diffuse through it. The cells also have cilia, which sweep the "dirty" mucus upward and out of the system.

The Respiratory Zone—Gas Exchange

The smallest bronchioles contain "bubbles" of tissue that have very, very thin walls, and there is very little mucus in these areas. These bubbles are called **alveoli** (singular = alveolus), and this is where gas exchange takes place. The bronchioles actually end in clumps of alveoli that resemble clusters of grapes. Many capillaries surround these clusters of alveoli. Because the walls of the alveoli are so thin, it is very easy for carbon dioxide in the blood to pass through the capillary walls and alveolar walls and into the alveoli. Oxygen travels in the opposite direction—from the alveoli, through the alveolar walls, through the capillary walls, and into the blood. This is **passive diffusion**—the gases are **hydrophobic** (lipid soluble), and they simply move down their concentration gradients. Oxygen concentration is higher in the alveoli than in the blood, so oxygen moves from the alveoli to the blood. Carbon dioxide concentration is higher in the blood than in the alveoli, so carbon dioxide moves from the blood to the alveoli.

Full of Hot Air
A fair amount of water is also exhaled along with carbon dioxide. That's why you can "steam up" a window or a mirror by breathing on it.

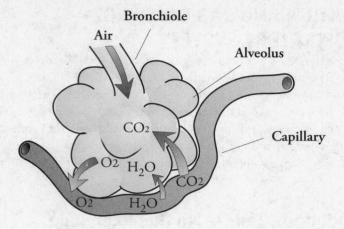

Air
Bronchiole
Alveolus
Capillary
CO₂
O₂ H₂O
CO₂
O₂ H₂O

Where Do the Carbon Dioxide and Water Come From?

Remember the Krebs cycle and electron transport? Well, if you do, then you remember that carbon dioxide is a waste product of the Krebs cycle and that oxygen is the final electron acceptor in the electron transport chain; when it accepts electrons it becomes reduced to water. So carbon dioxide and water are just the natural waste products of your cells as they run the Krebs cycle and electron transport and produce ATP.

This is also the reason we need oxygen in the first place. Remember that these processes are aerobic, which means that they can't occur without oxygen.

The Circulatory and Respiratory Systems Combined: A Quick Review

1. Oxygen-rich blood leaves the left ventricle through the aorta.
2. This blood travels through the aorta, the arteries, the arterioles, and the capillaries.
3. Exchange occurs between the blood in the capillaries and the cells. Oxygen and glucose are delivered to the cells.
4. The cells use the oxygen and glucose in cellular respiration to make ATP. They produce carbon dioxide, water, and other waste products in the process.
5. Exchange occurs between the cells and the blood in the capillaries. Carbon dioxide, water, and other waste products are delivered to the blood.
6. This blood (which is oxygen-poor) passes from capillaries to venules, from venules to veins, and from veins to the largest veins in the body, the superior and inferior vena cavae.
7. The anterior (superior) and posterior (inferior) vena cavae deliver the blood to the right atrium of the heart, which passes it on to the right ventricle.

The Circulatory and Respiratory Systems Combined: A Quick Review (Continued)

8. The right ventricle of the heart sends this oxygen-poor blood through the right and left pulmonary arteries, into the right and left lungs.

9. The pulmonary arteries divide many times to form hundreds of thousands of pulmonary capillaries, which surround the alveoli of the lungs.

10. Exchange occurs between the blood in the pulmonary capillaries and the alveoli. Carbon dioxide and water are delivered to the alveoli (the other waste products are filtered out by the kidney—more on that later). Oxygen is delivered to the blood.

11. The pulmonary capillaries merge to form pulmonary venules, which merge to form pulmonary veins, which merge to form the large left and right pulmonary veins.

12. The pulmonary veins carry this oxygen-rich blood to the left atrium of the heart, which passes it on to the left ventricle.

13. The left ventricle pumps the blood out to the body's cells through the aorta, and the whole cycle starts over again.

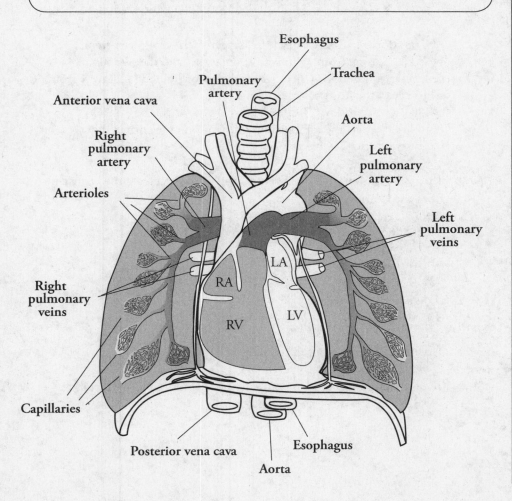

Esophagus

Trachea

Pulmonary artery

Aorta

Anterior vena cava

Left pulmonary artery

Right pulmonary artery

Arterioles

Left pulmonary veins

Right pulmonary veins

LA

RA

RV

LV

Capillaries

Posterior vena cava

Esophagus

Aorta

Quick Quiz #12

Fill in the blanks and check the appropriate boxes:

1. Blood leaves the heart from [☐ **ventricles** ☐ **atria**] and enters the heart at [☐ **ventricles** ☐ **atria**].

2. The aorta carries [☐ **oxygen-rich** ☐ **oxygen-poor**] blood [☐ **away from** ☐ **toward**] the heart, and the two vena cavae carry [☐ **oxygen-rich** ☐ **oxygen-poor**] blood [☐ **away from** ☐ **toward**] the heart.

3. From the right atrium, blood passes immediately to the
    (A) left ventricle
    (B) right ventricle
    (C) left atrium
    (D) pulmonary artery
    (E) posterior vena cava

4. The _____ are the site of exchange between blood and tissue.

5. The pulmonary arteries carry [☐ **oxygen-rich** ☐ **oxygen-poor**] blood [☐ **away from** ☐ **toward**] the heart, and the pulmonary veins carry [☐ **oxygen-rich** ☐ **oxygen-poor**] blood [☐ **away from** ☐ **toward**] the heart.

6. Blood that enters the right atrium after touring the entire body is [☐ **oxygen-rich** ☐ **oxygen-poor**].

7. The [☐ **semilunar** ☐ **atrioventricular**] valves separate the ventricles from the arteries.

8. Where does gas exchange in the lungs occur?
    (A) The aorta
    (B) The capillaries
    (C) The trachea
    (D) Pulmonary arteries
    (E) Alveolus

9. Moving air into and out of the lungs is called _____.

10. The [☐ **pulmonary** ☐ **systemic**] circuit sends blood to the lungs.

11. The _____ zone of the lungs is where gas exchange takes place.

12. The first heart sound is the closing of the [□ **semilunar** □ **atrioventricular**] valves at the [□ **end** □ **beginning**] of heart contraction.

13. From the right ventricle [□ **oxygen-rich** □ **oxygen-poor**] blood is passed to the [□ **pulmonary arteries** □ **pulmonary veins**] and then to the lungs.

14. The larynx is part of the [□ **conduction** □ **respiratory**] zone.

15. Oxygen-rich blood enters the heart at the _____.

16. Blood gases (oxygen and carbon dioxide) are [□ **hydrophilic** □ **hydrophobic**].

pH Regulation by the Respiratory System

It's very important that the body maintain a constant pH, because our cells' enzymes stop working if the pH becomes too acidic or too alkaline. Remember that acidity is measured on the pH scale, which ranges from 1 (really acidic) to 14 (really basic, or alkaline). A neutral pH is 7; our blood pH is approximately 7.4, which is slightly alkaline. Blood pH is maintained in a very narrow range: 7.35 to 7.45. The two systems that regulate blood pH are the respiratory system and the renal (kidney) system. But the respiratory system is by far the faster regulator of the two.

Carbon dioxide, being fairly hydrophobic, does not dissolve well in the plasma, which is mostly water. So carbon dioxide is converted to carbonic acid and then the bicarbonate ion through the following chemical reaction:

$$CO_2 + H_2O \leftrightarrow \underset{\text{carbonic acid}}{H_2CO_3} \leftrightarrow H^+ + \underset{\text{bicarbonate}}{HCO_3^-}$$

Not all of the carbonic acid converts to bicarbonate, so both carbonic acid and bicarbonate are found in the plasma. Because these substances are hydrophilic, they dissolve very easily in the plasma.

What Does This Have to Do With the Respiratory System?

You can think of the carbon dioxide that your body produces as an acid. So if your body gets too acidic (the pH goes down too far), it needs to reverse that by getting rid of some acid. It's very easy and fast to get rid of acid by getting rid of some of the extra carbon dioxide. How do we do that? By breathing faster.

What if your body gets too alkaline (the pH goes up)? That's also very easy to fix. Simply breathe more slowly. Less carbon dioxide will exit the body, and the extra acid will help bring the pH back down to normal.

Of course, you don't consciously have to do this. Your medulla oblongata (in your brain) does it for you. It monitors your pH, and if your pH is out of balance (too acidic or too alkaline), your medulla oblongata will adjust your respiratory rate accordingly.

This is actually the reverse of what most people think. Most people think we breathe faster or slower based on our body's need for oxygen. But really we breathe faster or slower based on our body's need to get rid of, or retain, carbon dioxide (to adjust pH).

How Do We Breathe?

The lungs themselves contain very little muscle, so they cannot expand on their own. All of the muscles that expand and contract the lungs (by expanding and contracting the chest cavity) are found in the chest wall and along the bottom of the lungs (the diaphragm). The lungs are stuck to the inside wall of the chest cavity. So any change in the size of the chest cavity produces a corresponding change in size of the lungs.

The **diaphragm** is the primary muscle of breathing. Other muscles in the chest wall help, too, but the diaphragm does most of the work. When it is relaxed, it curves up under the lungs:

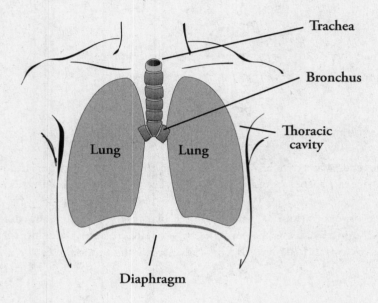

When it contracts, it flattens out, increasing the size of the chest cavity:

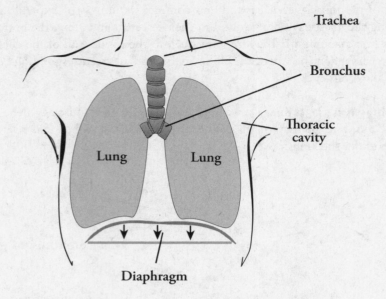

When the chest cavity increases in size, so do the lungs. And when the lungs increase in size, air rushes in to fill the extra space. This is called **inspiration**.

Exhaling, or **expiration**, is accomplished by simply relaxing the diaphragm. The diaphragm returns to its normal, curved state, thereby reducing the size of the chest cavity (and the lungs). This pressure on the lungs forces the air out of the system.

Quick Quiz #13

Fill in the blanks and check the appropriate boxes:

1. Most of the carbon dioxide in the blood is carried as _____ and _____.

2. If your blood is too acidic, your pH is [☐ **higher** ☐ **lower**] and you will breathe [☐ **slower** ☐ **faster**].

3. The system that can change pH more quickly is the [☐ **respiratory** ☐ **renal**] system.

4. The primary muscle of respiration is the _____.

5. Breath rate is adjusted by the _____.

6. When the diaphragm contracts it [☐ **curves upward** ☐ **flattens downward**].

7. Normal blood pH is approximately _____.

8. When the chest cavity gets smaller, air in the lungs rushes [☐ **inward** ☐ **outward**].

BODY PROCESSING, PART 1—THE DIGESTIVE SYSTEM

We've already seen how the body (the body's cells, really) needs glucose to run cellular respiration. We know also that the body's cells need amino acids to make proteins (enzymes, etc.) and fats to make cell membranes and other things. How does the body get these things?

These things are acquired by the consumption of other animals or plants. The carbohydrates, proteins, and fats in the food are broken down into glucose, amino acids, and fats, and these building blocks are used to run cellular respiration or build the specific proteins and fats the body needs. The process of eating (ingesting), breaking down (digesting), and taking up (absorbing) food is managed by the digestive system.

The organs of the digestive system can be divided into two major groups: the **alimentary canal** and the **accessory organs**.

The Alimentary Canal

The alimentary canal is a long, muscular tube that begins at the mouth and ends at the anus. The numbers on the diagram on the following page indicate the order in which food travels through the organs of the alimentary canal.

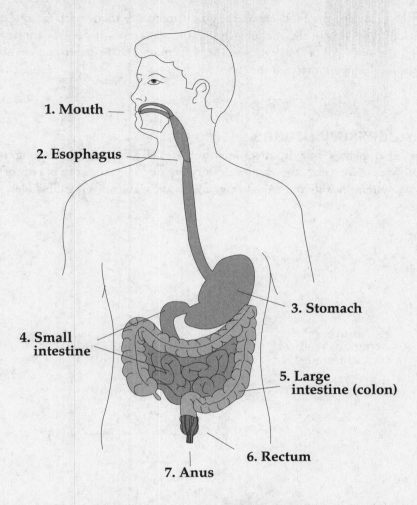

1. Mouth

2. Esophagus

3. Stomach

4. Small intestine

5. Large intestine (colon)

6. Rectum

7. Anus

Food enters the mouth and we swallow it. It enters the esophagus, and the esophagus begins a series of rhythmic, wavelike contractions that push the food down to the stomach. These rhythmic contractions are referred to as **peristalsis**.

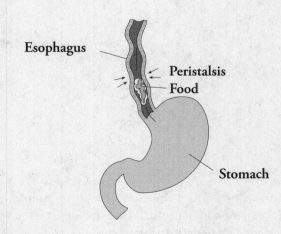

Esophagus

Peristalsis

Food

Stomach

From the stomach, the food enters the small intestine, then the large intestine (the colon), and finally the rectum. Indigestible material—feces—is eliminated through the anus. All of the organs in the alimentary canal perform peristalsis to keep the food moving through the tube.

The Accessory Organs

Organs that play a role in digestion, but are NOT part of the long tube previously described, are known as accessory organs. The accessory organs of the digestive system include the teeth, tongue, salivary glands, liver, gallbladder, and pancreas.

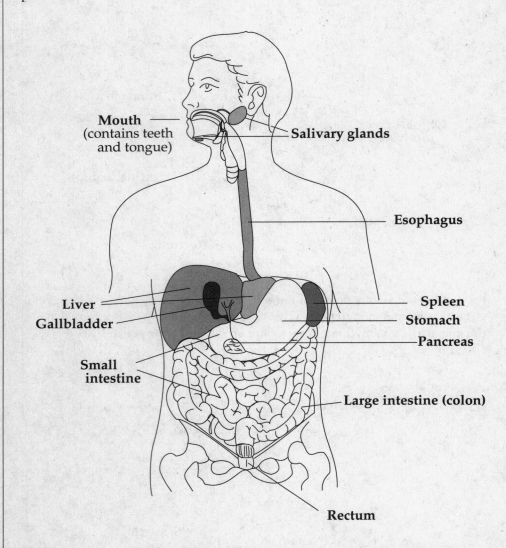

The above illustration shows only a small portion of the pancreas. That's because the pancreas is tucked into a loop of small intestine on its left and extends to the right, behind the stomach where (in this picture) we can't see it. If we were to remove the stomach, we'd see the pancreas tucked into a loop of small intestine like this:

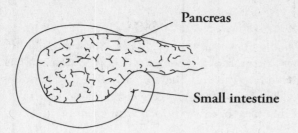

Pancreas

Small intestine

One last note before we look at the functions of the digestive system: Many of the organs are involved in exocrine secretion. We've already talked about *endo*crine secretion. That's the secretion of hormones into the blood (*endo* = inside). *Exo*crine secretion is secretion that occurs outside the blood (*exo* = outside). Exocrine secretions are released *into body cavities* (such as the mouth, the stomach, or the intestines) or onto the body surface (the skin). Some examples of exocrine secretions are digestive enzymes, saliva, mucus, tears, and sweat.

Putting It All Together

Now that we've seen the organs of the digestive system, let's take a trip through the alimentary canal to see how it all works, both the alimentary organs and the accessory organs.

The Mouth

The **mouth** is where it all starts. **Ingestion**, or the intake of food into the system, is accomplished here. The teeth and the tongue are accessory organs that help grind the food and form it into a lump called a **bolus**. Accessory organs called **salivary glands** secrete saliva. Saliva is made up mostly of water and mucus, and it helps to moisten the food and clump it together into the bolus.

Saliva also contains a digestive enzyme called **amylase**. Amylase catalyzes a reaction that breaks long carbohydrate molecules (starch) into little pieces. Amylase helps digest starch.

When you see "amylase," think

- digestive enzyme
- contained in saliva, which is secreted in the mouth
- helps digest starch, which is a carbohydrate

When food leaves the mouth, it's in the form of a bolus, and some of its carbohydrate has been partially digested. It now moves through the esophagus and into the stomach.

The Stomach

The **stomach** is acidic. As you know, acidity is measured on a pH scale, and the lower the number, the more acidic something is. The stomach has a pH between 1 and 2, which is pretty acidic. The stomach is acidic because gastric glands located in the walls of the stomach secrete hydrochloric acid (HCl). This acid helps kill germs that have been swallowed with the food and also helps to break up the food further.

The gastric glands of the stomach secrete not only acid but an enzyme that helps break protein into amino acids (in other words, the enzyme helps digest protein). The enzyme is called **pepsin**. Pepsin is actually released in an inactive form, called **pepsinogen**, and is activated by the acid in the stomach. The stomach itself is prevented from damage by the acid and enzyme by a thick layer of mucus. In cases where there is insufficient mucus lining the stomach, the acid and enzymes can damage the stomach walls, forming **ulcers**.

When food leaves the stomach it is really a pile of mush, and this mush is called **chyme**. The chyme enters the small intestine.

The Small Intestine

The **small intestine** is the site of the most digestion and absorption. The chyme that enters the small intestine is subjected to bile from the liver and gallbladder and many enzymes from the pancreas.

Digestive Processes
The digestive tract carries out the following six processes:

1) **Ingestion**—bringing food into the system
2) **Movement (Peristalsis)**—moving food along the system
3) **Digestion**—mechanical and chemical processes that break down food
4) **Secretion**—release of enzymes and bile into the digestive tract
5) **Absorption**—moving food molecules from the digestive tract into the blood
6) **Defecation**—eliminating solid waste from the large intestine

Bile is produced by the **liver** and stored and concentrated in the **gallbladder**. It is important to remember that the gallbladder doesn't actually make the bile, it just stores (and concentrates) the bile that's made in the liver. Bile is released into the small intestine to help break down fats contained in chyme.

So how exactly does bile do this? Well, before we answer this, we'll tell you what bile does NOT do: It does NOT digest fat. Bile does not digest fat because it is not an enzyme. What it does is **emulsify** fat. *Emulsify* means "to break up." The problem with fats is that they do not mix well with the chyme, which is very hydrophilic. Fats are hydrophobic, and they separate from the chyme like oil separates from water. Bile emulsifies the fats and allows them to better mix in with the chyme. This allows the real fat-digesting enzymes (the lipases) easier access to the fat.

Bile works the same way as soap. Imagine that you've been eating butter-covered popcorn and you want to get the butter off your hands. So you go to the sink and rinse your hands off, but the butter stays. Water all by itself cannot remove the butter, because the butter is hydrophobic and the water is hydrophilic, and they do not mix well. However, if you add some soap, the butter breaks up into tiny pieces that DO mix well with the water. We say that the soap emulsifies the fat on your hands. In exactly the same way, bile emulsifies the fat in your intestines. (In fact, bile is sometimes referred to as "intestinal soap.")

One more thing about the liver—it does a lot more than just make bile. The liver also stores glycogen, produces glucose, metabolizes fats, produces blood proteins, stores vitamins, and detoxifies the blood.

The actual enzymes in the small intestine come mostly from the pancreas. The pancreas secretes at least one enzyme for each type of food that needs to be digested. In other words, the pancreas secretes **amylase** (for carbohydrates), it secretes **lipases** (for fats), and it secretes **proteases** (for proteins). The pancreas also secretes **bicarbonate**, which is a base. The chyme that comes out of the stomach is very acidic, and the enzymes from the pancreas cannot work well in an acidic environment. So the pancreas secretes bicarbonate—a base—to neutralize the acid from the stomach. As a result, the pH in the intestines is close to neutral.

The small intestine is very long—in fact, it's the longest part of the alimentary canal. It also has many internal folds that drastically increase the surface area inside the tube. The length and the relatively large surface area of the small intestine increase the amount of absorption that takes place quite a bit. Think about it this way: If you spilled a cup of water on the floor, would you use a square of toilet paper to mop it up, or would you grab a couple of paper towels? The paper towels, of course, and why? Because they have a greater surface area and therefore absorb more. It's the same deal with the small intestine—the greater the surface area, the more food molecules can be absorbed. So absorption occurs at a fairly high rate in this part of the alimentary canal. The nutrient molecules are absorbed into the blood, which transports them to the liver for processing. The capillaries from the intestines merge to form special veins called **portal veins**, which divide into capillaries again when they reach the liver. This system—called the **hepatic portal system**—is designed to directly deliver nutrients from the intestines to the liver.

Where Does Digestion Really Happen?

One more thing about the stomach and small intestine: When most people think of the stomach, they think "digestion." But the fact of the matter is that the stomach doesn't do much digestion at all. It is mostly a storage tank for food, and it helps grind food up. Very little digestion and absorption occur in the stomach.

> Almost all digestion and absorption occur in the small intestine.

From the small intestine, the chyme moves into the **large intestine**. Not too much happens in the large intestine. The large intestine is also called the **colon**, and it is responsible for reabsorbing water from the chyme. No further digestion takes place in the large intestine. As the water is reabsorbed, the chyme becomes more solid and is referred to as **feces**. Feces is just indigestible, solid waste. It is stored in the large intestine and excreted from the body through the rectum and anus.

The large intestine also contains a large population of bacteria, *E. coli.* These **non-pathogenic** (not harmful) bacteria help keep **pathogenic** (harmful) bacteria from growing, and they also supply us with practically all the vitamin K we need.

> The Alimentary Canal: A Quick Review
> - **Mouth:** The mouth grinds and moistens food, begins starch digestion.
> - **Esophagus:** The esophagus moves food to stomach.
> - **Stomach:** The stomach is responsible for grinding, acid digestion, protein digestion by pepsin, and food storage.
> - **Small intestine:** Chyme is subjected to bile from the liver (emulsifies fats) and digestive enzymes from the pancreas (digests chyme). This is the longest and most extensively folded part of the canal and is the site of almost all the absorption and digestion.
> - **Large intestine:** No further digestion occurs here, but water is reabsorbed from the chyme, leaving behind a solid, indigestible waste product: the feces. Bacteria in the large intestine provide us with vitamin K.

Not Just for Humans

Fish, amphibians, turtles, and snakes and lizards all have a complete digestive tract. They have organs as we do, such as a mouth, pharynx, esophagus, stomach, intestines, liver, pancreas, and anus. Crocodiles, alligators, and birds have those organs listed above but additionally they have a crop to store the food and a gizzard for grinding it in their complete digestive tract.

Vitamins and Minerals

Because we're talking about digestion and nutrition, now is a good time to mention vitamins and minerals. Many vitamins function as coenzymes, and we've already seen how a few minerals are important (iron and iodine, for example). Here are some important things to know about vitamins and minerals.

Name	Vitamin/ Mineral	Function	Deficiency?
A	vitamin	needed to make retinal, a chemical necessary for sight	night blindness
B	vitamin	many different forms (B_1, B_2, B_6, B_{12}); needed for cellular respiration and DNA replication	skin disorders, mental confusion, anemia
C	vitamin	needed to make collagen (fiber in connective tissue)	wounds don't heal, scurvy
D	vitamin	needed for calcium absorption	weak bones and teeth, rickets
E	vitamin	needed to protect cell membranes from damage	anemia
K	vitamin	needed for blood clotting	bruise easily and bleed excessively
iron	mineral	needed in hemoglobin	anemia
calcium	mineral	needed for strong bones and teeth, also for muscle contraction	in children, rickets; in adults, osteomalacia (bone weakening)
iodine	mineral	needed to make thyroxine, a thyroid hormone	decreased metabolic rate (hypothyroidism)

Quick Quiz #14

Fill in the blanks and check the appropriate boxes:

1. The pancreas is [☐ **part of the alimentary canal**
   ☐ **an accessory organ**].

2. The order of the organs in the alimentary canal is _____,
   _____, _____, _____,
   _____.

3. The stomach [☐ **does** ☐ **does not**] secrete a digestive enzyme.

4. The salivary glands secrete an enzyme called [☐ **pepsin**
   ☐ **amylase**] that helps in the digestion of [☐ **carbohydrates**
   ☐ **proteins**].

5. The colon is the [☐ **small** ☐ **large**] intestine.

6. The vitamin needed for blood clotting is vitamin _____, and it
   is made by bacteria in the [☐ **small** ☐ **large**] intestine.

7. What does the liver produce?
   (A) Pepsin
   (B) Collagen
   (C) Bicarbonate
   (D) Bile
   (E) Fats

8. The products of digestion are absorbed through the walls of the
   (A) small intestine
   (B) large intestine
   (C) liver
   (D) kidney
   (E) pancreas

9. The stomach is [☐ **alkaline** ☐ **acidic**], which means that its pH is
   [☐ **low** ☐ **high**].

10. The pancreas produces [☐ **bicarbonate** ☐ **bile**].

11. The function of the large intestine is to _____.

12. Vitamin C is necessary to make [☐ **collagen** ☐ **retinal**].

13. Pepsin is an _____, secreted by the _____.
    It helps in the digestion of _____.

14. Bile [☐ **digests** ☐ **emulsifies**] fats.

15. The _____ produces blood proteins and
    regulates glycogen metabolism.

BODY PROCESSING, PART 2—THE URINARY SYSTEM

The digestive system brings nutrients into the body and breaks them down so that the body's cells have the substances they need to function properly. As the cells run their reactions, waste products are formed and released into the blood. Two of the waste products, carbon dioxide and water, are eliminated by the respiratory system, but what about the others?

Other waste products are filtered from the blood by the **kidneys** and eliminated as **urine**. The three main waste products found in urine are **urea** (from breakdown of amino acids), **uric acid** (from breakdown of nucleic acids), and **creatinine** (a waste product from muscle metabolism).

The functional unit of the kidney is the **nephron**. Kidneys contain about a million nephrons each. Here's what they look like:

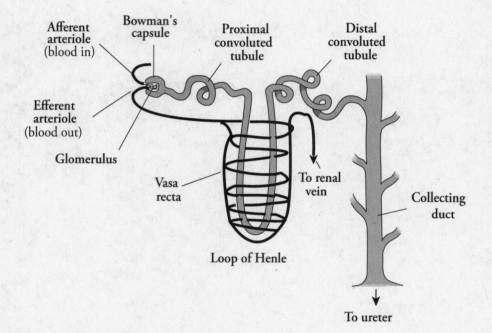

Here's how the nephron sits within the kidney:

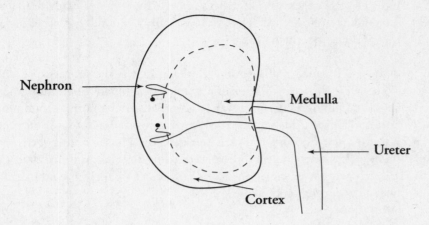

Nephron

Medulla

Ureter

Cortex

Generally speaking, blood enters the kidney through renal arteries that branch into capillaries. The **glomerulus** is a tiny "knot" of capillaries at the beginning of the nephron. It sits inside a cuplike structure called **Bowman's capsule**. These capillaries have pores in their walls and act as tiny sieves. Blood pressure forces the fluid portion of blood (the plasma) through the pores, but because the cells and proteins are too large to fit through, they remain behind, in the capillaries. The plasma enters Bowman's capsule and is now known as **filtrate**. The filtrate begins traveling along the tubules of the nephron, and, along its path, it is modified. Substances that the body needs (like glucose, amino acids, and water) are returned to the blood. Substances that the body wants to eliminate are left in the tubules. When it's all said and done, the filtrate is called urine.

Where does the urine go next? From the kidneys, it travels down the ureters to be stored in the bladder. From the bladder it is eliminated from the body through the urethra.

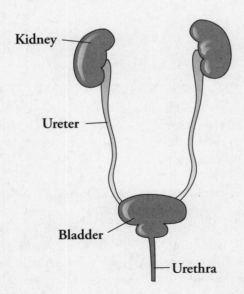

Kidney

Ureter

Bladder

Urethra

Urine Formation—Modifying the Filtrate

There are three processes the nephron uses to make urine. We've already described the first: **filtration**. Filtration just refers to blood pressure forcing plasma out of the capillaries and into Bowman's capsule.

The second process is called **reabsorption**. Reabsorption is the process of taking substances out of the filtrate and returning them to the blood. Some substances, such as glucose and amino acids, are always reabsorbed. Under normal conditions, all the glucose and amino acids that are filtered are reabsorbed. But for some other substances, the amount reabsorbed is regulated according to the body's needs. For example, more or less water is reabsorbed, depending on how well hydrated the body is. The reabsorption of some ions, such as sodium, potassium, and calcium, is also regulated depending on body needs.

The third process is called **secretion**. Secretion is the process of taking substances out of the blood and adding them to the filtrate. Creatinine is always secreted. Some ions, drugs, and toxins are also always secreted.

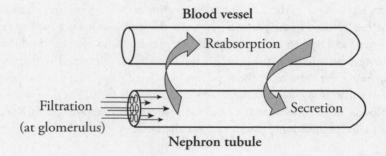

So, by reabsorption and secretion, the filtrate is modified as it travels through the nephron. Now let's take a look at the specific functions of different regions of the nephron.

The Nephron

The first portion of the nephron, after Bowman's capsule, is the **proximal convoluted tubule**. *Proximal* means "close to." *Convoluted* means "twisted up." A *tubule* is just a small tube. So the proximal convoluted tubule is just a small, twisted-up tube that's close to the glomerulus. The proximal convoluted tubule is where most reabsorption and secretion take place.

The next portion of the nephron is the **loop of Henle**, in which a lot of water is reabsorbed. Additionally here, a fair amount of salt is transported out of the filtrate and into the tissues of the kidney. This helps to establish a concentration gradient in the kidney. The inner portions of the kidney (the medulla) are "saltier" (more concentrated) than are the outer portions of the kidney (the cortex). This gradient is important for water reabsorption elsewhere in the nephron. The longer the loop of Henle, the greater the concentration gradient, and the more water that can be reabsorbed. For example, some animals, such as desert rodents and lizards, have very long loops of Henle and reabsorb a lot of water. Their urine is very concentrated. These animals have a great need to conserve water because they live in very dry environments.

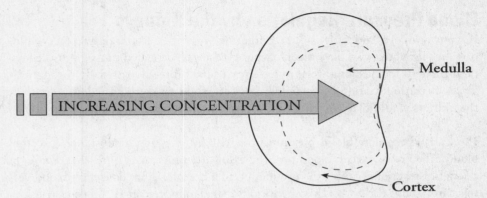

After the loop of Henle is the **distal convoluted tubule** (*distal* = farther away), the small, twisted-up tube that's farther from the glomerulus. Reabsorption and secretion occur here; however, it tends to be more specialized and regulated. You can think of it as "urine fine-tuning." This is the last chance to modify the filtrate before it enters the collecting duct. The distal tubule is where the hormone **aldosterone** has its effect. Aldosterone increases the amount of sodium that's reabsorbed into the blood by the distal tubule. When sodium is reabsorbed, water follows, so water is reabsorbed as well.

The final portion of the nephron is the **collecting duct**. The collecting duct can actually receive filtrate from several nephrons. This is the final location for urine concentration and is where water reabsorption is regulated (all of the water reabsorption we've been talking about so far has been unregulated—the tubules of the kidney have just reabsorbed as much as possible). The collecting duct is where the hormone ADH (antidiuretic hormone) has its effect. ADH causes the walls of the collecting duct to become permeable to water. (In the absence of ADH, the walls are impermeable to water, so water cannot leave the tube—notice that this is one of the few areas of the body that is impermeable to water.) The collecting duct travels inward, toward the center of the kidney along the large concentration gradient established by the loop of Henle. In effect, the duct enters regions that are becoming increasingly "saltier." How does this affect water reabsorption and urine concentration?

If the walls of the duct are permeable to water (if ADH is present), then water can move out of the duct by osmosis and be taken up by the blood. As water leaves the duct, the urine becomes more concentrated. If the walls are impermeable to water (if ADH is absent), water cannot move out of the duct and it must stay in the urine, so the urine stays dilute.

ADH levels are high when the body is dehydrated—for example, after a person has run a marathon. This allows the body to retain water by concentrating the urine.

Filtration Rate

The rate at which healthy kidneys filter blood is approximately 125 mL/min, and the average adult blood volume is about 5 L. This means that the total blood volume can be filtered in about 40 minutes! About 99% of the filtered volume is reabsorbed, making reabsorption critical to the maintenance of normal blood volume.

ADH levels are low when the body is well hydrated—for example, after winning the record for drinking the most water in a 10-minute period. This allows the body to eliminate excess water by keeping the urine dilute.

Blood Pressure Regulation by the Kidneys

If your kidneys suddenly stopped filtering your blood properly, you would only live for about two days. People whose kidneys have failed must go to the hospital three or four times a week to have their blood filtered artificially through dialysis. Because filtration is dependent only on blood pressure, it makes sense that the kidneys would play a role in monitoring and maintaining blood pressure.

The kidneys regulate blood pressure primarily by releasing a substance into the blood called **renin**, when blood pressure is low. Renin is an enzyme that, through a series of reactions, causes the production of a chemical that constricts blood vessels throughout the body. This chemical is called **angiotensin II**. The constriction of the blood vessels causes the blood pressure to go up. Additionally, angiotensin II increases the secretion of aldosterone by the adrenal cortex. Aldosterone causes increased reabsorption of sodium, which causes increased reabsorption of water, which increases the blood volume, which in turn increases the blood pressure.

Not Just for Humans

Most other animals have kidneys to maintain water balance and waste disposal in the body; however, the form in which they eliminate this nitrogen as waste is different. Fish excrete nitrogen wastes in the form of ammonia. Adult amphibians and turtles, as well as humans and other land mammals, excrete waste in the form of urea. Most reptiles and birds excrete waste in the form of uric acid. Worms and insects don't have kidneys, but they still need to eliminate nitrogen wastes. Worms use structures called **metanephridia** to do this, while insects use structures called **malphigian tubules**.

Quick Quiz #15

Fill in the blanks and check the appropriate boxes:

1. The three processes used by the nephron to make urine are _____, _____, and _____.

2. The [☐ **loop of Henle** ☐ **collecting duct**] sets up a concentration gradient in the medulla.

3. [☐ **Secretion** ☐ **Reabsorption**] means taking a substance from the urine and returning it to the blood.

4. Glucose is always [☐ **secreted** ☐ **reabsorbed**].

5. The kidney helps to regulate blood pressure by releasing [☐ **aldosterone** ☐ **renin**].

6. The [☐ **ureter** ☐ **urethra**] carries urine from the bladder to the outside of the body.

7. Filtration occurs at the _____.

8. ADH increases the amount of [☐ **water** ☐ **sodium**] reabsorbed from filtrate.

9. Most reabsorption and secretion occur in the _____.

10. ADH levels are [☐ **high** ☐ **low**] when the body is dehydrated, and this causes the urine to be [☐ **dilute** ☐ **concentrated**].

11. The three main waste products found in urine are _____, _____, and _____.

SUPPORT AND PROTECTION OF THE BODY, PART 1—THE SKELETAL SYSTEM

Many organisms have skeletons. The skeleton is responsible for holding the body together in some recognizable shape. Without a skeleton, an organism's body would be, basically, a pile of mush. So when you see the word *skeleton*, think shape and support.

Some animals, like human beings, have skeletons made of bones, and which are located inside the body. When a skeleton is found inside the body, it's called an **endoskeleton** (remember, *endo* means "inside"). When it comes to endoskeletons, remember this fact:

> All vertebrates (animals with backbones) have endoskeletons.

Fish, amphibians, mammals, reptiles, and birds are all vertebrates, and they all have endoskeletons. In fact, having an endoskeleton is what classifies them as vertebrates.

Some animals, on the other hand, have skeletons outside their bodies. Their skeletons are not made of bones but of hard crusty shells that contain a substance called chitin. Because they're found outside the body, they're called **exoskeletons** (remember, *exo* means "outside"). For the SAT Biology E/M Subject Test, you should know that the arthropods (phylum arthropoda) are organisms with exoskeletons. This includes insects, arachnids, and crustaceans.

Skeletal Tissues

There are two main types of tissue found in the skeletal system—bone and cartilage. **Bone** is a rigid substance made up of cells embedded in a solid calcium-phosphate matrix. It is among the hardest tissues in the body.

> Bones have several functions:
>
> - support the body
> - protect soft organs
> - produce blood cells
> - store minerals

We've already mentioned that the bones provide internal support for the body. They also provide protection for many organs; for example, the brain and spinal cord are almost completely encased in bone. In the same way, the rib cage protects the heart, lungs, and other organs in the chest cavity. Bone marrow is the site of the production of blood cells, and, last, the bones are a supply of calcium that can be dissolved and released into the plasma if the body needs it. (Likewise, if calcium is in excess, it can be stored as bone.)

The other primary skeletal tissue is **cartilage**. Cartilage is also a relatively rigid substance, although it is considerably more flexible than bone. Cartilage is found on the ends of all the bones, at the joints, where it acts as a shock absorber to protect the bone ends from rubbing together. Some structures, such as the end of the nose, the external ear, and the anterior portions of the ribs, are completely made of cartilage. This allows these structures greater flexibility, while still providing them with a defined shape.

One last comment about bones: They are held to other bones (at joints) by **ligaments**. Generally speaking, the more ligaments a joint contains, the stronger the joint is.

The skeletons of other vertebrates include a skull and backbone with vertebrae. Most vertebrae are attached to sets of paired limbs, whether they are wings, legs, or fins. Muscles are attached by tendons to the bones, which move the skeleton, allowing animals to swim, walk, or fly.

SUPPORT AND PROTECTION OF THE BODY, PART 2—THE MUSCULAR SYSTEM

The muscular system works together with the skeletal system to support, protect, and move the body. The muscles pull against the bones to move them around. Postural muscles, such as those around the back and abdominal areas, help support the body in an upright position, and some internal regions of the body—most noticeably the abdominal region—are protected entirely by muscle.

There are actually three different types of muscle tissue in the body: skeletal muscle, cardiac muscle, and smooth muscle. We've already seen two of the types. **Cardiac muscle** is found only in the heart. **Smooth muscle** is found in the walls of hollow organs such as the stomach, intestines, and bladder. Cardiac and smooth muscle are both involuntary muscle, meaning that you do NOT have conscious control over their contraction. Additionally, cardiac muscle is self-excitatory, meaning that it can initiate its own contraction.

Skeletal muscle is attached to the bones; it moves your body around. Skeletal muscle is a voluntary tissue—you have conscious control over its contraction. Skeletal muscle cells are very long and have many nuclei. They are described as being **multinucleate**. Let's take a look at how a skeletal muscle is put together.

Building a Muscle

Muscle tissue is mostly made up of proteins—two types in particular: **actin** and **myosin**. Actin molecules form long, thin chains, while myosin molecules bundle together to form thick fibers. In a muscle cell, actin and myosin are arranged in structures called **sarcomeres**.

actin and myosin → sarcomere

Many sarcomeres line up end to end to form a threadlike structure called a **myofibril**. A myofibril is just a string of sarcomeres.

actin and myosin → sarcomere → myofibril

Many myofibrils bundle together with cytoplasm, organelles, nuclei, and a cell membrane. This is a **muscle cell** (also called a **muscle fiber**). A muscle cell is just a bundle of myofibrils and organelles surrounded by membrane.

actin and myosin → sarcomere → myofibril → muscle cell

Muscle cells are organized into groups called **fascicles**.

actin and myosin → sarcomere → myofibril → muscle cell → fascicle

Fascicles are grouped together to form the whole muscle.

actin and myosin → sarcomere → myofibril → muscle cell → fascicle → whole muscle

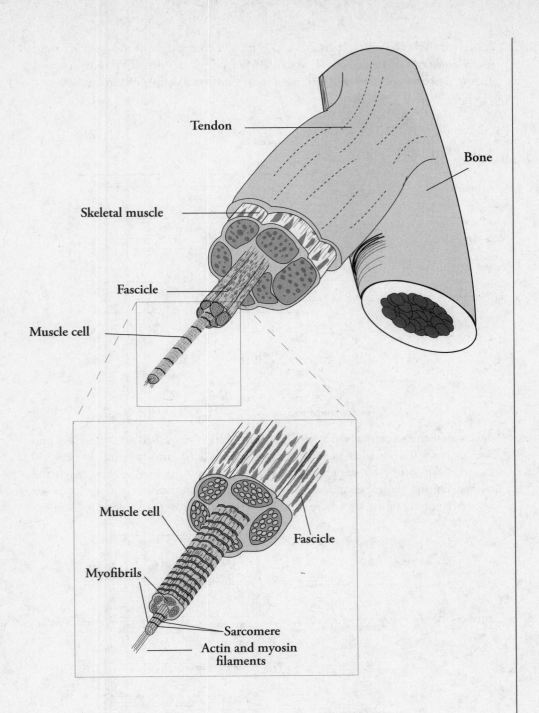

Tendon

Bone

Skeletal muscle

Fascicle

Muscle cell

Muscle cell

Fascicle

Myofibrils

Sarcomere

Actin and myosin
filaments

When a muscle contracts, it gets shorter. The first component of the muscle that actually contracts is the sarcomere. Actin and myosin fibers do NOT change length during muscle contraction. Let's take a look; here are a couple of sarcomeres:

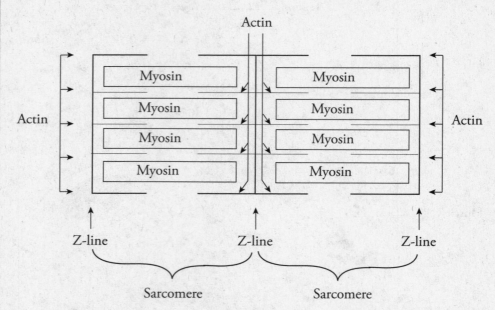

The ends of the sarcomeres are called **Z-lines**. Actin is attached to the Z-lines and extends inward, toward the center of the sarcomere. Myosin is found in between the actin filaments, overlapping with the ends, but myosin does not touch the Z-lines. During muscle contraction, myosin binds to the actin and drags it inward, toward the center of the sarcomere. A fully contracted sarcomere would look like this:

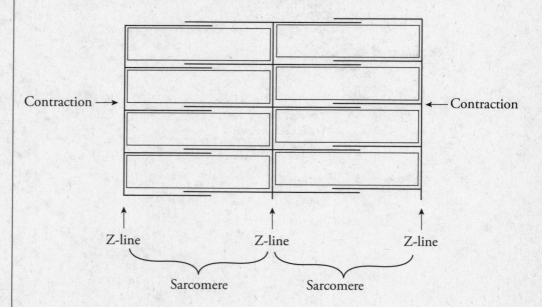

The actin filaments essentially slide over the myosin filaments, dragging the Z-lines with them, and when the sarcomere is completely contracted, the actin filaments actually overlap in the center. Because the sarcomeres get shorter, the myofibrils get shorter, which means that the muscle cell gets shorter, and ultimately the entire muscle gets shorter. The process of contracting, because the filaments appear to slide over one another, is called the **sliding filament theory**.

Miscellaneous Muscle Facts

1. Skeletal muscle is described as being **striated**, or striped. When observed under a microscope, the cells appear to be striped. This comes from the regular arrangement of protein filaments into sarcomers.

2. Skeletal muscles are attached to bones by tendons.

3. Skeletal muscles are stimulated by neurons that release neurotransmitters at special synapses called motor end plates, or neuromuscular junctions. The neurotransmitter used is acetylcholine.

4. Cardiac muscle is also striated. (What does that tell you about its structure?)

5. Muscle contraction requires calcium.

SUPPORT AND PROTECTION OF THE BODY, PART 3—THE SKIN

The skin and all of its associated structures, such as hair, nails, sweat glands, oil glands, and sensory receptors, are collectively considered an organ. Your skin is actually the largest organ in your body. It has a surface area of about 1.5 to 2 square meters and makes up about 7 percent of your total body weight!

The skin is made of three layers of tissue: the **epidermis**, the **dermis**, and the **hypodermis**. The epidermis is a thin layer of cells at the body surface, most of which are dead. The dermis is a relatively thick layer of connective tissue underneath the epidermis that contains blood vessels, nerves, hair follicles, and glands. The hypodermis is a deep layer of fat that helps protect and insulate the body. The hypodermis varies in thickness from person to person.

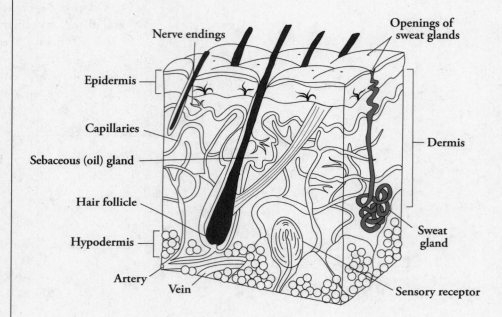

The skin's primary job is to protect the body from:

- abrasion (friction)
- heat loss
- water loss
- infection
- UV radiation

Other functions of the skin include vitamin D production, sensation, and thermoregulation (body temperature control). Let's talk about **thermoregulation**.

Too Hot or Too Cold

Most organisms are unable to regulate their own body temperatures; they are **cold-blooded**. Other terms for cold-blooded include **ectothermic** or **poikilothermic**. The body temperatures of these organisms change with changing external temperature. For example, it's common to see reptiles basking in the sun to raise their body temperatures.

Birds and mammals, however, are **warm-blooded**, or **endothermic**. They are able to maintain a constant body temperature regardless of external temperature. This requires a large expenditure of energy, and birds and mammals have evolved mechanisms to retain heat, such as insulating fat, feathers, and hair. Also, there are various changes that occur in the body when the internal temperature changes.

When your body temperature rises, receptors in your skin and body core monitor the change. They send information to your brain, and your brain sends messages to your body that cause it to cool. Specifically, this is what happens:

1. Blood vessels in the dermis dilate, allowing more blood to come close to the surface of the skin. This allows more heat to leave the body. (It also produces the characteristic red flush of an overheated person.)
2. Sweat glands in the skin become active, secreting sweat. As the sweat evaporates, the body temperature lowers.

When your body temperature falls, again, receptors in the skin and body core monitor the change and send the information to the brain, and the brain sends commands to the body to increase warming. These commands are essentially the reverse of the body-cooling activity. This is what happens:

1. Blood vessels in the dermis constrict, keeping the blood from the surface of the body. This retains more heat near the body core. (It also produces the characteristic bluish color of a very cold person.)
2. Sweat glands in the skin are inactivated.
3. Shivering is initiated. Shivering is rapid, involuntary muscular contractions. Muscle contraction generates a lot of heat, so shivering is an excellent way to raise body temperature.

Quick Quiz #16

Fill in the blanks and check the appropriate boxes:

1. Smooth muscle is found in the _____.

2. The deepest layer of the skin is the [☐ **dermis** ☐ **epidermis** ☐ **hypodermis**].

3. Spiders have [☐ **exoskeletons** ☐ **endoskeletons**].

4. The two proteins found in muscle cell sarcomeres are _____ and _____.

5. When the body gets too warm, dermal blood vessels [☐ **constrict** ☐ **dilate**], and shivering [☐ **is initiated** ☐ **stops**].

6. Muscles are attached to bones by [☐ **ligaments** ☐ **tendons**].

7. In a sarcomere, [☐ **actin** ☐ **myosin**] attaches to the Z-lines.

8. The neurotransmitter used to stimulate muscle contraction is _____.

9. [☐ **Cardiac** ☐ **Skeletal**] muscle is voluntary (under conscious control).

10. Bones are attached to other bones by [☐ **ligaments** ☐ **tendons**].

11. Cardiac muscle is found in [☐ **the heart only** ☐ **both the heart and the blood vessels**].

REPRODUCTION AND DEVELOPMENT, PART 1— THE MALE SYSTEM

Let's start reproduction and development by talking about the male reproductive system. Because we've already covered a fair amount of the important stuff (spermatogenesis in Chapter 7 and hormones earlier in this chapter), and because you're more likely to see questions about the female system on the SAT Biology E/M Subject Test, we won't go into too much detail in this section.

Remember from Chapter 7 that the testes are the male gonads, meaning that they are the organs that produce gametes (sperm) for the male. The testes also produce **testosterone** (the primary male sex hormone) in response to luteinizing hormones (LH) from the pituitary. Testosterone is important for normal sperm development. It also causes the maturation of the sexual organs during puberty and maintains the male sexual characteristics in adulthood. Testes are found outside the body cavity in a sac called the **scrotum**. This keeps them a couple of degrees cooler than normal body temperature, which is also necessary for normal sperm development.

The sperm are produced inside the testes in small tubes—the **seminiferous tubules**—in response to follicle-stimulating hormones (FSH) from the pituitary gland. These tubules merge to form a large duct—the **vas deferens**. The vas deferens ultimately connects with the urethra to carry the sperm out of the body. Along the way, several glands secrete fluid (semen) that carries and provides nutrients for the sperm.

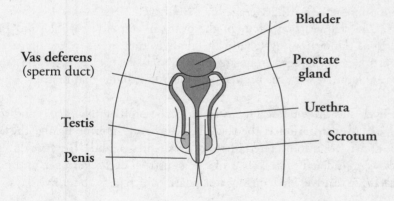

REPRODUCTION AND DEVELOPMENT, PART 2— THE FEMALE SYSTEM

The female system is a little more complex than the male system. Not only does the female reproductive system have to produce gametes, it also has to prepare itself for pregnancy, because the female system (in humans) nurtures developing offspring. That means we have to consider two organs: the ovaries (which produce the gametes) and the **uterus** (which sustains a pregnancy).

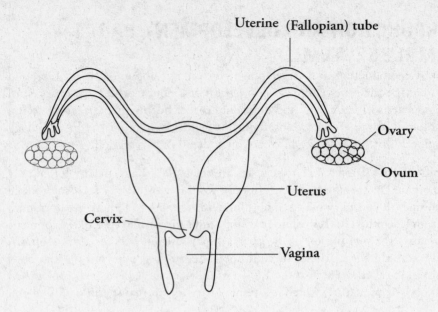

Uterine (Fallopian) tube

Ovary

Ovum

Uterus

Cervix

Vagina

The Menstrual Cycle

Generally speaking, the ovaries are controlled by hormones from the pituitary gland (FSH and LH), and the uterus is controlled by hormones from the ovaries (estrogen and progesterone). The average menstrual cycle lasts 28 days and affects both organs. The changes that occur in the ovary in response to FSH and LH are referred to as the ovarian cycle, and the changes that occur in the uterus in response to estrogen and progesterone are referred to as the uterine cycle. Because more people are familiar with the uterine cycle, let's talk about that first.

The uterine cycle has three phases: menstruation, the proliferative phase, and the secretory phase. **Menstruation** is the shedding of the old uterine lining, the **endometrium**, and is commonly referred to as a woman's period. The first day of menstruation is considered to be Day 1 of the menstrual cycle. Estrogen and progesterone levels are relatively low during this phase, which lasts about five days.

During the **proliferative phase**, a new uterine lining is built. A new endometrium grows on the inside of the uterus. This is under the control of estrogen, which is secreted from the ovary during this phase. The proliferative phase lasts from Day 6 to about Day 13 of the menstrual cycle.

During the **secretory phase**, the new uterine lining is maintained and enhanced in preparation for a possible pregnancy. New blood vessels are added, and glucose and glycogen are secreted into the lining to make it rich and nourishing. This is under the control of progesterone, which is secreted from the ovaries during this time period. The secretory phase lasts from Day 14 to the end of the cycle, Day 28. It ends when progesterone levels fall, and menstrual bleeding begins again, marking the onset of a new cycle.

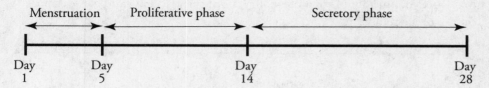

The Uterine Cycle

The ovarian cycle also has three phases: the follicular phase, ovulation, and the luteal phase. The **follicular phase** begins on Day 1 of the cycle and lasts about 13 days. During this phase, FSH from the anterior pituitary gland causes the development of a follicle in the ovary. A **follicle** is just a maturing oocyte and its surrounding cells. As the surrounding cells divide and grow, they secrete estrogen, and as the estrogen level rises, it has its effect on the uterus, as we saw earlier.

Ovulation is the release of the oocyte from the follicle into the uterine (Fallopian) tube. It occurs on or about Day 14, and is caused by a large surge of LH from the anterior pituitary.

Some of the follicle stays behind in the ovary and, under the control of LH, matures into a structure called the **corpus luteum**. This marks the onset of the **luteal phase**. The corpus luteum secretes mostly progesterone (and some estrogen), which then has its effect on the uterus (described earlier). The corpus luteum has a natural life span of about two weeks, after which it degenerates. When it degenerates, the progesterone and estrogen levels fall, and the uterine lining degenerates and sheds off, marking the beginning of the next cycle.

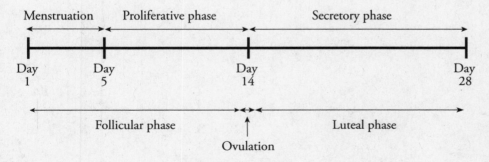

The Ovarian Cycle

But What If . . .

. . . the ovum released on Day 14 of the cycle gets fertilized and implants? Then the resulting embryo secretes a hormone called **human chorionic gonadotropin (hCG)**. hCG has the effect of prolonging the life of the corpus luteum. If the corpus luteum lives longer, it secretes more progesterone; progesterone levels never fall, and the uterine lining never sheds off. This is commonly known as a "missed period" and is usually the first sign of a pregnancy. hCG levels stay high for the first three to four months of a pregnancy, until the placenta can take over production of progesterone.

The Menstrual Cycle: A Quick Review
- The menstrual cycle begins on Day 1, with the onset of bleeding (menstruation). Estrogen and progesterone levels are low. FSH from the anterior pituitary stimulates the growth of a follicle in the ovary (the follicular phase), which, as it grows, secretes estrogen.
- After Day 5, the rising estrogen levels stimulate the uterus to grow a new inner lining (the proliferative phase).
- By Day 14, the lining is thick. A surge in LH from the anterior pituitary gland causes the release of the oocyte and some of the follicular cells from the ovary (ovulation). LH also causes the remaining follicular cells to become the corpus luteum. The corpus luteum secretes progesterone and estrogen (the luteal phase), which further enhance the lining of the uterus (the secretory phase).
- If fertilization and implantation do not occur, the corpus luteum degenerates after about 14 days, and the drop in progesterone and estrogen causes the lining to degrade and shed off, starting the next cycle.

Quick Quiz #17

Fill in the blanks and check the appropriate boxes:

1. Progesterone is secreted during the [☐ **secretory** ☐ **luteal**] phase of the ovarian cycle.

2. Sperm are produced in the
    (A) vas deferens
    (B) semen
    (C) seminiferous tubules
    (D) corpus luteum
    (E) endometrium

3. The ovary is controlled by [☐ **FSH and LH** ☐ **estrogen and progesterone**] from the anterior pituitary, and it secretes [☐ **FSH and LH** ☐ **estrogen and progesterone**] that affect the uterus.

4. _____ prolongs the life of the corpus luteum if fertilization and implantation occur.

5. The _____ is a large duct that conducts sperm from the testes to the urethra.

6. A surge in [☐ **FSH** ☐ **LH**] causes ovulation.

7. The remnants of a follicle after ovulation become the _____.

8. [☐ **Estrogen** ☐ **Progesterone**] causes the uterine lining to grow during the proliferative phase.

9. _____ is a nourishing fluid that carries sperm. It is secreted by glands in the male reproductive system.

10. Estrogen causes growth of the uterine lining during the [☐ **proliferative** ☐ **follicular**] phase of the uterine cycle.

11. What is the lining of the uterus called?
    (A) Estrogen
    (B) Progesterone
    (C) Follicle
    (D) Endometrium
    (E) Corpus luteum

REPRODUCTION AND DEVELOPMENT, PART 3— FERTILIZATION, EMBRYOLOGY, AND FETAL DEVELOPMENT

There is a lot of information concerning the development of a new human. Fortunately, you don't need to know too much of it. Here are the basic steps and events:

1. **Gametes are formed.** We've already discussed spermatogenesis and oogenesis, so we won't repeat that here. Remember that gametes (sperm and ovum) are haploid cells, so they contain only half the number of chromosomes in a normal, somatic cell.

2. **The egg (ovum) is fertilized.** The ovulated egg travels down the uterine tube. The sperm released during copulation swim up through the cervix and the uterus and meet up with the egg in the uterine tube. This is where fertilization occurs. At the top of the sperm is a region called the **acrosome**. The acrosome contains digestive enzymes that help the sperm penetrate the barriers surrounding the ovum.

3. **A zygote is formed.** Once the sperm has penetrated the egg plasma membrane and the sperm and egg nuclei have fused, the resulting cell is called a **zygote**. The zygote has a full set of chromosomes from the sperm and a full set from the ovum, so it is a diploid cell.

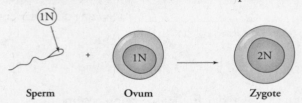

Sperm   Ovum   Zygote

4. **Cleavage.** The zygote starts dividing and dividing and dividing. The first division occurs within 24 to 36 hours of fertilization. As it divides, it continues traveling down the uterine tube toward the uterus. Ultimately it becomes a solid ball of cells called a **morula**.

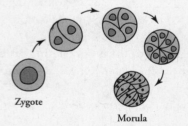

Zygote

Morula

5. **Implantation in the uterus.** Once the morula reaches the uterus, it bumps around for a bit, then implants in the lining of the uterus. While it is bumping around, it continues to divide and starts hollowing out. The resulting structure is called a **blastocyst**. The blastocyst has a mass of cells on one side called the inner cell mass. This group of cells ultimately forms the embryo and all embryonic structures and membranes (like the umbilical cord, and the amniotic sac). The outer ring of cells ultimately forms part of the placenta.

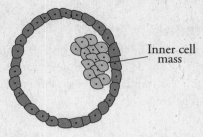

Inner cell mass

Blastocyst (cross section)

6. **The embryonic stage.** Once the blastocyst has implanted, it enters the embryonic stage, which lasts until the eighth week of development. The embryonic stage can be divided into two phases: gastrulation and neurulation.

   a) **Gastrulation.** During gastrulation (the first half of the embryonic stage), the inner cell mass divides into three layers, called the primary germ layers. They are the endoderm, the mesoderm, and the ectoderm, and each is responsible for producing different body structures.

      • **Endoderm:** gives rise to the inner linings of the respiratory system, the digestive system, the reproductive system, and the urinary system; forms glandular organs (such as the liver, pancreas, and salivary glands).

      • **Mesoderm:** gives rise to the "middle" structures, such as bones, blood vessels, muscles, the heart, and non-glandular organs (the kidneys, the ureters, the gonads, etc.)

      • **Ectoderm:** forms external structures (skin, hair, nails, etc.), the linings of the mouth and anus, and all nervous system structures (brain, cord, nerves, eyes, etc.)

   b) **Neurulation.** During neurulation (the second half of the embryonic stage) the organs of the nervous system are formed. To call it neurulation, however, is a little misleading. Not only does the nervous system develop, but every other organ in the body is formed during this period. This is called **organogenesis**. By the time the embryonic period is finished, all the organs and structures that are supposed to be there are formed. From this point on, the organs and structures simply mature and grow larger.

7. **The fetal stage.** This stage lasts from the end of the embryonic stage (about eight weeks of development) until birth. During the fetal stage, the baby simply grows and matures. No new organs are formed during this stage.

Here's a summary of the stages of human development:

> **Gametes → Fertilization → Zygote → Cleavage → Morula → Blastocyst →
> Implantation in the uterus → Gastrulation → Neurulation → Fetus → Birth**

Not Just for Humans

Other vertebrates reproduce sexually as well. Fish and amphibians, for the most part, have external fertilization. The embryo develops in a nonwaterproof egg in an aqueous environment. Thousands of offspring are produced, and parental care is not common with fish or amphibians.

Turtles, snakes, and lizards have internal fertilization and lay eggs that are protected by a watertight shell. There is little parental care with these animals.

Crocodiles, alligators, and birds have internal fertilization and lay eggs with a hard, waterproof shell. There is some degree of parental care with these animals. Most mammals exhibit a prolonged period of parental care.

The Extraembryonic Membranes

"Extraembryonic" simply means "outside the embryo." There are four extraembryonic membranes: the yolk sac, the amnion, the allantois, and the chorion. For clarity, as we discuss the human membranes, we will compare them to a chick embryo.

The **yolk sac** surrounds the yolk of an egg. Egg yolk is essentially food for a developing embryo. Human eggs have very little yolk, because human embryos (and all placental mammals) develop inside the mother's body and receive their nutrition from a placenta. However, bird and reptile embryos develop *outside* the mother's body in an egg, and the nutrition that supports their entire embryonic development must be contained within that egg. Consequently, the eggs of birds and reptiles contain a lot of yolk. Human yolk is the source of the first blood cells.

The **amnion** is a clear membrane that surrounds the developing embryo and is filled with a clear, watery fluid (the amniotic fluid). This fluid acts as a shock absorber to protect the embryo from physical damage.

The **allantois**, in humans, ultimately becomes the umbilical cord, which connects the embryo to the placenta. In birds and reptiles, the allantois forms a disposal site for solid wastes.

The **chorion** is the outermost membrane, and in humans it forms the embryo's part of the placenta. It encloses all the other membranes. In birds and reptiles, the chorion lines the inside of the shell and still encloses all the other membranes.

Quick Quiz #18

Fill in the blanks and check the appropriate boxes:

1. Fertilization takes place in the
    (A) uterus
    (B) fallopian tube
    (C) ovary
    (D) blastocyst
    (E) morula

2. The developmental stage marked by a series of rapid mitotic divisions is called
    (A) gametes
    (B) fertilization
    (C) zygote
    (D) cleavage
    (E) morula

3. The human eye develops from [☐ **mesoderm** ☐ **ectoderm**].

4. Blood vessels develop from [☐ **endoderm** ☐ **mesoderm**].

5. The first eight weeks of development are called the
    (A) fetal stage
    (B) gastrulation
    (C) embryonic stage
    (D) zygote stage
    (E) gamete stage

6. The membrane that most directly surrounds the embryo is the [☐ **chorion** ☐ **amnion**].

7. Organogenesis occurs during [☐ **neurulation** ☐ **gastrulation**].

8. Implantation occurs [☐ **before** ☐ **after**] cleavage.

9. A blastocyst forms [☐ **before** ☐ **after**] a morula.

10. Neurulation occurs [☐ **before** ☐ **after**] the fetal stage.

11. The _____ is the region at the top of the sperm that contains digestive enzymes to help the sperm penetrate the ovum.

12. The nervous system develops from [☐ **endoderm** ☐ **ectoderm**].

13. The kidneys develop from [☐ **mesoderm** ☐ **endoderm**].

Key Words

nervous system
neurons
soma
process
dendrites
axons
polarized
resting membrane potential
sodium-potassium pump
channel
leak channels
voltage-gated channels
threshold potential
sodium voltage-gated channels
potassium voltage-gated
     channels
action potential
polarized
depolarization
repolarization
Schwann cells
myelin sheath
nodes of Ranvier
saltatory conduction
refractory period
synapse
neurotransmitter
acetylcholine
synaptic cleft
stimulated
inhibited
summation
central nervous system
peripheral nervous system
sensory neurons
motor neurons
interneurons
spinal cord
cerebrum
cerebellum
medulla
hypothalamus
somatic nervous system
autonomic nervous system
sympathetic division
fight or flight

norepinephrine
parasympathetic division
resting and digesting
vertebrate group
arthropods
ganglia
endocrine system
hormones
peptide hormones
steroid hormones
pituitary gland
anterior pituitary gland
growth hormone (GH)
cell-turnover rate
thyroid-stimulating hormone
     (TSH)
adrenocorticotropic hormone
     (ACTH)
follicle-stimulating hormone
     (FSH)
luteinizing hormone (LH)
prolactin
posterior pituitary gland
oxytocin
antidiuretic hormone (ADH)
vasopressin
hypothalamus
thyroxine
iodine
hypothyroidism
hyperthyroidism
calcitonin
parathyroid hormone
parathormone
adrenal glands
adrenal medulla
adrenal cortex
glucocorticoids
gluconeogenesis
mineralocorticoid
aldosterone
sex steroids
pancreas
islet cells
insulin
glucagon

glycogenolysis
gonads
testis
ovary
androgens
testosterone
estrogens
progesterone
estradiol
hemolymph
plasma
red blood cells
hemoglobin
anemia
white blood cells
lymphocytes
B-cells
T-cells
HIV
platelets
codominant
agglutination
blood vessels
artery
capillaries
arterioles
vein
valves
lymphatic system
lymph nodes
lymph
atria
ventricles
pulmonary circuit
systemic circuit
anterior vena cava
posterior vena cava
pulmonary artery
pulmonary veins
aorta
systemic circuit
atrioventricular valves
semilunar valves
ventilation
gas exchange
conduction zone
pharynx
larynx
trachea

right and left primary bronchi
bronchioles
alveoli
passive diffusion
hydrophobic
diaphragm
inspiration
expiration
alimentary canal
accessory organs
peristalsis
mouth
ingestion
bolus
salivary glands
amylase
stomach
pepsin
pesinogen
ulcers
chyme
small intestine
bile
liver
gallbladder
emulsify
amylase
lipases
proteases
bicarbonate
portal veins
hepatic portal system
large intestine
colon
feces
nonpathogenic
pathogenic
vitamin A
vitamin B
vitamin C
vitamin D
vitamin E
vitamin K
iron
calcium
iodine
kidneys
urine
urea

uric acid

creatinine

nephron

glomerulus

Bowman's capsule

filtrate

filtration

reabsorption

secretion

proximal convoluted tubule

loop of Henle

distal convoluted tubule

aldosterone

collecting duct

renin

angiotensin II

endoskeletons

exoskeleton

bone

cartilage

ligaments

cardiac muscle

smooth muscle

skeletal muscle

multinucleate

actin

myosin

sarcomeres

myofibril

muscle cell

muscle fiber

fascicles

Z-lines

sliding filament theory

striated

epidermis

dermis

hypodermis

thermoregulation

cold-blooded

ectothermic

poikilothermic

warm-blooded

endothermic

testosterone

seminiferous tubules

vas deferens

uterus

uterine cycle

menstruation

endometrium

proliferation phase

secretory phase

ovarian cycle

follicular phase

follicle

ovulation

corpus luteum

luteal phase

human chorionic
    gonadotrophin

gametes

ovum

acrosome

zygote

morula

blastocyst

embryonic stage

gastrulation

endoderm

mesoderm

ectoderm

neurulation

organogenesis

fetal stage

yolk sac

amnion

allantois

chorion

Summary

o The human body is composed of eleven different organ systems. Each organ system has its own particular function.

o The nervous system carries impulses between body parts.

o The endocrine system controls the body through the use of hormones.

o The circulatory system transports oxygen, carbon dioxide, glucose, hormones, waste products, and other materials around the body. It consists of the heart, a series of blood vessels, and blood.

o The lymphatic system recaptures and filters fluids from the tissues and returns it to the blood stream.

o The respiratory system works to exchange oxygen and carbon dioxide with the blood. It also helps regulate body pH.

o The digestive system manages the process of eating, digesting, and absorbing food.

o The urinary system eliminates nitrogenous waste products from food digestion. It also helps in water and electrolyte balance and blood pressure regulation.

o The skeletal system holds a body together in some regular shape, protects various organs, is a mineral storage site, and produces blood cells.

o The muscular system works with the skeletal system to support, protect, and move the body.

o The skin supports and protects the organs in the body and helps in thermoregulation.

o The reproductive system is responsible for the passing of genetic information to future generations.

Chapter 11
Plants

All the information about plant structure and plant function could fill an entire textbook. Fortunately, this chapter will help you focus in on the material you really need to know for the SAT Biology E/M Subject Test. We will concentrate on leaf structure, photosynthesis, transport, flower structure, and plant reproduction.

LEAF STRUCTURE

Generally speaking, **photosynthesis** involves the use of solar energy (sunlight) to produce food (carbohydrates). It makes sense then that photosynthesis would occur where sunlight is most likely to strike the plant: the leaf. The leaves of a plant provide the plant with a large surface area for sunlight to hit. Here's a cross section of a plant leaf:

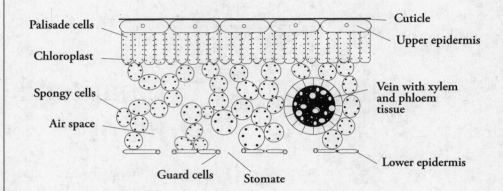

The outer cell layer of a leaf, both top and bottom, is called **epidermis** (just as it is in skin). The epidermis has a layer of wax on it called the **cuticle**. The job of the cuticle is (1) to protect the leaf from attack by things like fungi and (2) to keep water from escaping the leaf. The cuticle is always found on the top surface of a leaf and is often found on the bottom surface as well.

The **palisade layer**, which lies just under the surface, is where most photosynthesis takes place. The **spongy cells** beneath the palisade layer also carry out photosynthesis, but this layer is more important for gas exchange. That's why there are so many air pockets in the spongy layer.

> Photosynthesis requires the intake of carbon dioxide and the release of oxygen. The exchange of these gases, as well as water, occurs through openings on the bottom surface of the leaf, called **stomates**. Stomates are opened and closed by special cells called **guard cells**.

Photosynthesis

Before you start this section on photosynthesis, you should go back and review the information we gave you on cellular respiration in Chapter 5. Many of the ideas and concepts for the two processes are essentially the same, and if you understand cellular respiration, you will find the concepts of photosynthesis easier. Let's start by talking about where the specific reactions of photosynthesis take place. The organelle in which these reactions occur is the **chloroplast**.

The chloroplast is a double-membraned organelle, just like the mitochondria. Here's a look:

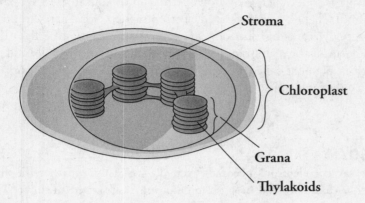

The inner fluid of the chloroplast is the **stroma**. Inside the stroma are flattened membrane structures called **thylakoids**. The inner space of the thylakoid is simply called the **thylakoid space**, and thylakoids themselves are found in stacks called **grana**. The membranes of the thylakoids are filled with green pigments called **chlorophyll**. This is what gives plants their green color.

Basic Reactions of Photosynthesis

In cellular respiration, we basically took some glucose, added some oxygen, and produced energy (ATP). Carbon dioxide and water were released as waste products. Well, photosynthesis is essentially the reverse of cellular respiration. Plants take carbon dioxide, water, and energy and use these substances to produce glucose, and oxygen is released as a waste product.

$$6 \ CO_2 + 6 \ H_2O + energy \rightarrow C_6H_{12}O_6 + 6 \ O_2$$

Even though the overall reaction for photosynthesis looks like the reverse of cellular respiration, the reactions that make up the process are not just those of respiration in reverse. In other words, we can't run the electron transport chain, the Krebs cycle, the pyruvate dehydrogenase complex (PDC), and glycolysis backward to make glucose. The reactions of photosynthesis are a little different. They're split into two main groups: the **light-dependent reactions** and the **light-independent reactions**.

The Light-Dependent Reactions

These reactions get their name from the fact that they require light—solar energy. (Sometimes they're just called the **light reactions**, but light-dependent is more accurate.) The whole point to the light-dependent reactions is to convert solar energy into a usable form of energy—namely ATP and a reduced electron carrier. (Remember from Chapter 5 that reduced electron carriers, which are electron carriers that are actually carrying electrons, are sources of energy.) The light-dependent reactions occur in the membranes of the thylakoids. Remember we said there was a lot of green pigment called chlorophyll there? The chlorophyll absorbs sunlight, and this causes some of its electrons to be excited.

Excited?!

When we say the electrons become "excited," we just mean that they now have more energy than they did before the chlorophyll absorbed sunlight. These energetic electrons are now able to pass down an electron transport chain, just as the electrons did in cellular respiration. At the end of the chain, the electrons are handed off to $NADP^+$, forming a molecule of NADPH. $NADP^+$ is just an electron carrier, and NADPH is its reduced form. You should think of NADPH as usable energy.

The other thing that happens when chlorophyll absorbs sunlight is that a molecule of water is split into hydrogen ions and oxygen. The oxygen is released as a waste product. The hydrogen ions are used to make ATP through an ATP synthase, just as they did in cellular respiration. The ATP synthase is located in the membranes of the thylakoids, and as H^+ ions exit the thylakoids, ATP is made. The ATP is, of course, usable energy.

> **Light-Dependent Reactions**
> Here's a quick summary of what we've learned so far:
> - The light-dependent reactions convert solar energy into usable energy—NADPH and ATP.
> - These reactions occur along the thylakoid membranes.
> - The substance that absorbs sunlight is the green pigment, chlorophyll.
> - This is the part of photosynthesis in which oxygen is released.

> **Calvin Cycle**
> It is important to realize that the Calvin cycle does depend on light, although indirectly. The Calvin cycle is dependent on the input supplied by ATP and NADPH. These are light dependent reactions.

The Light-Independent Reactions (AKA the Calvin Cycle)

The light-independent reactions are sometimes called the **dark reactions**, but this is a bad name, because it makes it sound like the reactions must occur in the dark. They don't *have* to occur in the dark; they just don't need light in order to occur.

> The light-independent reactions take place in the stroma of the chloroplast arc are also known as the **Calvin cycle**.

If this reminds you of the Krebs cycle, it should. The basic concept is the same: We start with a certain molecule that's regenerated each time the cycle takes a turn. In this case, the molecule is **ribulose bisphosphate**. Ribulose bisphosphate is made of five carbon atoms. A molecule of carbon dioxide is added to this, to make a six-carbon molecule that, in a series of reactions, is broken in half to form two three-carbon molecules called **glyceraldehyde-3-phosphate (G3P)**. In each turn of the cycle, one of the G3P molecules formed in this pathway can be used to make glucose and other carbohydrates, and the other G3P molecules are used to regenerate the original ribulose bisphosphate.

The light-independent reactions require energy, and they use the ATP and NADPH produced by the light-dependent reactions. This process (the Calvin cycle), which is used by plants to produce carbohydrates, is also known as **carbon fixation**.

Light-Independent Reactions

- The light-independent reactions are sometimes called the "dark reactions," even though they do not have to occur in the dark.
- They are also known as the Calvin cycle, which is also known as carbon fixation.
- These reactions take place in the stroma of the chloroplast.
- They rely on the energy (ATP and NADPH) from the light-dependent reactions in order to run.
- Their product is a three-carbon carbohydrate called glyceraldehyde-3-phosphate (G3P), which can be used to form glucose and other carbohydrate.

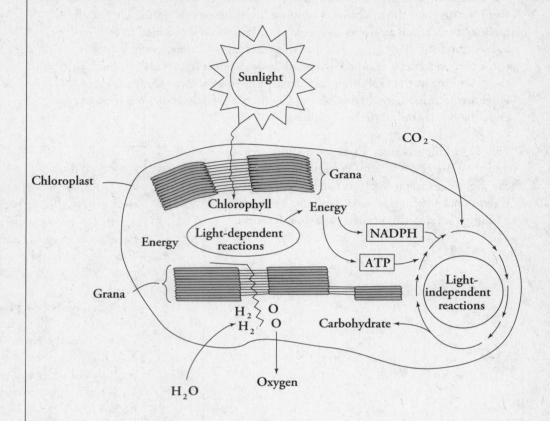

One Last Thing

Organisms that can make (and store) glucose in this way (plants) are essentially making (and storing) their own food. *Troph* is a suffix meaning "related to nutrition," so plants are referred to as **autotrophs** (*auto* means "self"); they are "self-feeders."

Organisms that cannot make their own food are called **heterotrophs**. Heterotrophs rely on the consumption of plants and other animals for nutrition. Humans and other animals are all heterotrophs.

Quick Quiz #1

Fill in the blanks and check the appropriate boxes:

1. The inner fluid of the chloroplast is called [☐ **grana** ☐ **stroma**].

2. The layer of wax on the leaf surface is called the
_____.

3. Most photosynthesis occurs in the [☐ **palisade layer** ☐ **spongy layer**].

4. The Calvin cycle is a series of [☐ **light-dependent** ☐ **light-independent**] reactions.

5. Oxygen is released during the [☐ **light-dependent** ☐ **light-independent**] reactions.

6. The light-dependent reactions convert solar energy to usable energy, namely ATP and _____.

7. The _____ are the membranes inside the chloroplast where the light-dependent reactions take place.

8. Plants are [☐ **autotrophs** ☐ **heterotrophs**] and [☐ **can** ☐ **cannot**] make their own food.

9. Stomates are opened and closed by cells called
_____.

10. Forming carbohydrate from carbon dioxide is also known as
_____.

Transport Within the Plant

Plants, like animals, have a need to transport materials. Water and minerals must be transported through the roots to the rest of the plant. Nutrients from photosynthesis must be transported from the palisade layers of the leaves to the rest of the plant. Water and nutrients are carried through vessels called veins, but they are carried by specific tissues within those veins, called **xylem** and **phloem**.

Let's Start at the Bottom

Which One?

An easy way to remember which type of tissue carries food and which carries water is to remember that the *ph* sound is like the *f* sound, so *ph*loem carries *f*ood. Xylem, then, must carry water.

Roots anchor a plant to the grounds and absorb both water and minerals from the soil. The water and minerals are transported through the xylem upward to the rest of the plant. Xylem tissue is made of several types of cells. The specific cells that transport water are called **tracheids** and **vessel elements**.

Food from photosynthesis (carried out in the palisade layers of the leaves) is transported through the plant in tissue called phloem. Phloem contains two types of cells: **sieve cells** and **companion cells**. Sieve cells are the ones that actually carry out the transport, and companion cells help the sieve cells with their metabolic functions.

Flowers and Reproduction

Flowering plants are called angiosperms, and for the test you should know something about how they reproduce. Here's a typical flower and its parts:

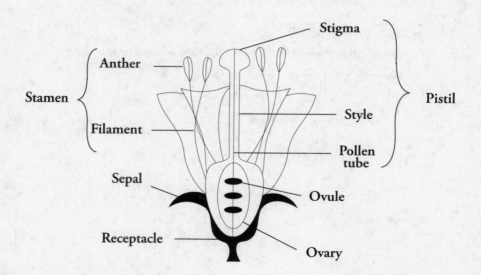

The stamen. The stamen is the plant's male component. It consists of the **anther** and the **filament**. The filament supports the anther, which makes **pollen**. Pollen is made from little cells called **microspores**, and mature pollen grains contain a cell that can divide to form two sperm cells.

The pistil. The pistil is the plant's female component. It consists of the **stigma**, **style**, **ovule**, and **ovary**. Inside the ovary is the ovule, which forms cells called **megaspores**. Megaspores can divide to form eggs and polar bodies.

Here's how a flowering plant reproduces:

1. Some pollen grains fall onto the stigma, which is sticky. There are many ways this can happen. They can be blown there, fall there, be moved there by insects, etc. Once on the stigma, the pollen grains germinate.

2. During germination, a tube called the pollen tube grows down through the style to connect to the ovary.

3. The two sperm (from the pollen) travel down the pollen tube to enter the ovary and the ovule, where they undergo a double fertilization; one sperm fertilizes the egg, and the other sperm combines with the polar bodies.

4. The fertilized egg becomes the plant embryo and the polar bodies become endosperm. Endosperm is a food-storing tissue that surrounds the plant embryo.

5. The entire ovule, which contains the embryo and the endosperm, develops into a seed, and the ovary develops into a fruit. The fruit protects the seed and helps it disperse by wind or animals.

6. The seed is released (the fruit drops, the plant is eaten, etc.), and, when it finds a suitable environment, it develops into a new plant.

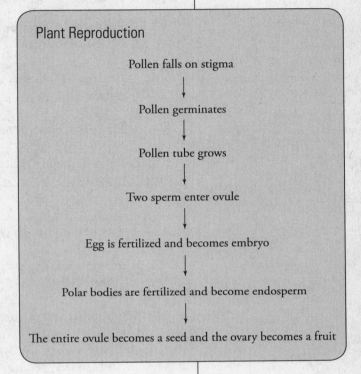

Plant Reproduction

Pollen falls on stigma
↓
Pollen germinates
↓
Pollen tube grows
↓
Two sperm enter ovule
↓
Egg is fertilized and becomes embryo
↓
Polar bodies are fertilized and become endosperm
↓
The entire ovule becomes a seed and the ovary becomes a fruit

Quick Quiz #2

Fill in the blanks and check the appropriate boxes:

1. The female part of a flower is the [☐ **stamen** ☐ **pistil**].

2. The tissue within plant veins that carries water from the roots up to the rest of the plant is the [☐ **phloem** ☐ **xylem**].

3. The specific cells that transport water are the _____ and the _____.

4. The ovary develops into a [☐ **fruit** ☐ **seed**].

5. The polar bodies, when fertilized, become a nutrient-rich tissue called _____.

6. _____ is the type of tissue that carries food from photosynthesis in the leaves to the rest of the plant.

7. The specific cells that transport food are the [☐ **companion cells** ☐ **sieve cells**].

8. The anther and the filament are [☐ **male** ☐ **female**] parts of the flower.

9. In a flowering plant, pollen is produced by and located on the [☐ **stigma** ☐ **anther**].

10. The [☐ **seed** ☐ **fruit**] develops from the ovule.

11. A pollen tube grows down through the [☐ **stigma** ☐ **style**].

Key Words

photosynthesis
epidermis
cuticle
palisade layer
spongy cells
stomates
guard cells
chloroplast
stroma
thylakoids
thylakoid space
grana
chlorophyll
light-dependent reactions
light-independent reactions
light reactions
dark reactions
Calvin cycle
ribulose bisphosphate
gylceraldehyde-3-phosphate
   (G3P)

carbon fixation
autotrophs
heterotrophs
xylem
phloem
tracheids
vessel elements
sieve cells
companion cells
stamen
anther
filament
pollen
microspores
pistil
stigma
style
ovule
ovary
megaspores

Summary

o Photosynthesis is a process in which plants use energy from the sun to produce food.

o Photosynthesis occurs in the part of the plant that sunlight is most likely to hit—the leaves.

o Photosynthetic reactions take place in the chloroplasts of a plant cell.

o Plants take in carbon dioxide, water, and energy and use them to produce glucose and release oxygen.

o The summary equation for photosynthesis:

$$6\,CO_2 + 6\,H_2O + energy \rightarrow C_6H_{12}O_6 + 6\,O_2$$

o There are two types of reactions in the process of photosynthesis: light-dependent reactions and light-independent reactions.

o Minerals, water, and nutrients are transported within a plant by xylem and phloem.

o A flowering plant reproduces in the following way: Pollen falls on the stigma, the pollen then germinates, pollen tubes grow, two sperm enter the ovule, the egg is fertilized and becomes an embryo, the polar bodies are fertilized and become endosperm, and eventually the entire ovule becomes a seed and the ovary becomes a fruit.

Chapter 12
Behavior

In this chapter, you will learn that animals exhibit behavior that is present from birth (instinctive behavior) as well as behavior that is learned. Instinctive behavior comes in two forms: as fixed-action patterns and as imprinting. Learned behavior can be the result of habituation, conditioning, or insight.

Instinctive Behavior

Instinct refers to any type of behavior that is *not* learned—in other words, it exists at the moment of birth; it is inherited behavior. All organisms possess some basic instincts.

Fixed-action patterns are stereotypical behaviors that are triggered by specific stimuli. For example, when a baby bird opens its mouth, a mother bird will put food in it. Another example of a fixed-action pattern is that newly hatched ducks swim when they enter the water. These behaviors are "preprogrammed"; in other words, mother birds don't have to learn to feed their babies; they just do it. Baby ducks don't have to learn to swim; they just swim. Other examples of fixed-action patterns are mating rituals, displays of territoriality, and suckling behaviors, and you can probably think of several more.

Konrad Lorenz

A newly hatched bird will follow the first moving object it sees. Because it has no idea what its parent looks like, it will follow a toy, other animal, or a human. Konrad Lorenz, a scientist from Austria, conducted an experiment in which he was the first thing a set of baby ducks saw after they were born. These ducks became imprinted on Lorenz and continued to follow him around, even as they grew into adults.

Imprinting is the recognition of some object as "mother" when it's seen during a critical time period shortly after birth. Think of a gosling. Imagine that the first thing it sees when it hatches is its mother. Somehow or another the gosling will decide that this creature is its mother. It will follow this creature around and treat it as its mother from then on. That's good, because the creature usually *is* its mother.

Suppose, though, that instead of its mother, the first thing the gosling saw when it hatched was *you*. Believe it or not, the gosling will decide that you are its mother. It will follow you around and treat you as its mother. Even if it sees its real mother after that, it will ignore her and continue to think you are its mother.

An interesting thing about both of these behaviors (fixed-action patterns and imprinting) is that they occur even if the stimulus is not the "real" stimulus encountered in nature. A mother bird will attempt to feed anything that has a gaping mouth, even a decoy. Baby goslings will imprint on anything seen in that critical period, even balloons and ticking clocks.

Learned Behaviors

Learned behaviors are those that require interaction with the environment or with other organisms in order to occur. The simplest form of learning is called habituation. **Habituation** occurs when a non-harmful stimulus is repeated over and over again and the organism learns to ignore it. If you gently poke a dog on the back with a stick, it will turn around to see what's going on. But if you keep on poking it, the dog eventually learns to ignore the poke. Interestingly though, if you poke the dog in a new place, or if you wait a couple of days and poke it in the back again, it will again turn around to see what's going on. In other words, the basic response (turning around, in this case) isn't lost, it's just temporarily modified by learning.

> ## Ivan Pavlov
> You may have heard of Pavlov's dogs. His classical conditioning experiment involved training a dog to associate a ringing bell with food. Soon the dog would salivate whenever he heard a bell, even if no food was available. You probably react in the same way sometimes.

Conditioning is a type of learning in which a stimulus is associated with a particular behavior. Because it involves associations, conditioning is sometimes referred to as **associative learning**.

Imagine some fish in a tank. If we tap on the tank at the same time we drop some fish food into the water, and we do this for several days, the fish learn that a tap on the tank means food. They will swim to the top of the water when they hear a tap even if there is no food present. They have associated tapping with food. This is called **classical conditioning**.

Another form of conditioning is called operant conditioning. Imagine that every time a cat starts scratching on the couch, its owner squirts it with a water gun. The cat soon learns not to scratch on the couch because it knows it will get squirted. Or imagine that a rat learns to press a button because every time it presses the button it gets a food pellet. Learning that occurs because of a reward and punishment system is **operant conditioning**.

The highest form of learning is **insight learning**. Insight refers to the ability to approach new situations and figure out how to deal with them. As animals go, human beings are pretty good at insight. Another word for insight is **reasoning**.

Quick Quiz #1

For each of the situations described below, write:

      (A) if it represents a fixed-action pattern,
      (B) if it represents imprinting,
      (C) if it represents classical conditioning,
      (D) if it represents operant conditioning, or
      (E) if it represents insight learning.

1. _____ A dog learns that if it brings the newspaper into the house each evening, it gets a bone.

2. _____ A bird treats the human it saw when it first hatched as its mother.

3. _____ A frog squeezes the swollen belly of a female frog to release eggs.

4. _____ A cockroach learns to run from light because every time a light comes on someone tries to step on it.

5. _____ A man wishes to turn a screw and, having no screwdriver, realizes that he can use the edge of dull knife as a substitute.

6. _____ A cat runs into the kitchen and looks for food when it hears the electric can opener.

7. _____ A bird puffs up its brightly colored chest to attract a mate.

Turning Behavior in Plants: The Tropisms

The word **tropism** is derived from the Greek word *tropos*, which means "to turn," so tropisms are all turning behaviors in response to particular stimuli. There are three stimuli that can cause turning: light, gravity, and touch.

Plants need light. Suppose a plant sits in a room in which sunlight comes in through one window. The plant will, on its own, bend toward the window. When a plant bends toward light, we call it **phototropism** (*photo* = light).

Plants need minerals and water from the earth. Plant roots therefore like to grow downward, in the direction of the gravitational pull. When roots grow downward, toward the earth, it's called **positive gravitropism**. Plant stems and leaves, on the other hand, grow up, away from the earth. This is called **negative gravitropism**. Gravitropism is sometimes referred to as **geotropism**.

Lastly some plants will grow along a wall or trellis. The physical touch of the plant on the object causes it to grow in that direction. This is known as **thigmotropism** (*thigmo* = touch).

Also, these turning behaviors are induced by plant hormones, called **auxins**. So remember:

Phototropism means . . .	growth of a plant toward light.
Positive gravitropism means . . .	growth of the roots downward, toward the earth.
Negative gravitropism means . . .	growth of the plant stem upward, away from the earth.
Thigmotropism means . . .	growth of the plant along a surface.

Animals and Plants Can Tell Time: Biological Clocks

Think of a plant. Imagine that it predictably opens its leaves at 6 A.M., closes them at noon, opens them again at 6 P.M., and closes them again at midnight. Imagine, furthermore, that the plant does this even if it is kept in the dark all day and all night. This plant seems somehow to know when to open and close its leaves, even without being exposed to changing conditions of sunlight. Something in the plant keeps time.

Circadian Rhythm
Daily cycles of light and dark set an organism's biological clock to approximately 24 hours.

We don't know how plants, animals, or individual cells keep time, but they seem to do it. In other words, living things have biological clocks. The behavior that arises from biological clocks is instinctive; it isn't learned.

When a biological clock makes an organism do something on a daily basis, it is referred to as a **circadian rhythm**. The plant that opens and closes its leaves predictably several times daily exhibits a circadian rhythm. A plant that loses its leaves in the fall and regrows them in the spring does NOT reflect a circadian rhythm. The pattern is seasonal, not daily.

Organisms Communicate: Pheromones

Many animals communicate with other members of their species by releasing chemicals called **pheromones**. A pheromone is any chemical that (1) is released by one member of a species and (2) affects the behavior of other members of the species in a predictable way.

Suppose an ant discovers a food source and wants others of her colony to know about it. She lays down a trail of chemicals, leading from the ant colony to the food source. The other ants know to follow the chemical trail, and so they're led to the food. This chemical is a pheromone.

Some female animals release chemicals that attract males, and these chemicals are also pheromones. On discovering danger, some animals release chemicals that signal others of their species to stay away, and these chemicals, too, are pheromones. In some species, an animal's dead body releases a chemical that causes survivors of the species to bury it. That chemical is a pheromone as well.

Be careful! Do not confuse pheromone with hormone! Hormones are also chemicals, but they are released into the blood of an organism and affect only that organism. Here's a comparison table:

Chemical Signal	Released Where?	Affects Whom?
Pheromone	Outside the body	Other members of the species
Hormones	Into the blood	Only the organism that secreted it

Plants and Animals Coexist: Symbiosis

Organisms of different species sometimes share living space, in arrangements referred to as **symbiosis**. Moss grows on tree trunks, and bacteria live in our intestines. These are both examples of symbiosis. For the SAT Biology E/M Subject Test, you should know the three types of symbiosis: mutualism, parasitism, and commensalism.

In **mutualism**, both organisms in the symbiotic relationship benefit from the association. Humans and their intestinal bacteria are an example of mutualism. The bacteria get a food source (our indigestible material), and they, in turn, provide us with vitamin K.

In **parasitism**, one organism benefits from the association, while the other organism is harmed. Intestinal tapeworms are parasites. The tapeworms benefit—they get food—but the host is harmed, often suffering from nutritional deficiencies.

In **commensalism**, one organism benefits from the association, and the other organism is neither harmed nor helped. In fact, the other organism couldn't care less about the first organism. An example of commensalism is the relationship between buffalo and egrets (birds that live with the buffalo). As the buffalo walk through tall grass, they flush out bugs, which the egrets eat. The egrets benefit from the relationship, and the buffalo don't really care one way or the other.

Relationship	First Organism	Second Organism
Mutualism	☺	☺
Parasitism	☺	☹
Commensalism	☺	😐

Quick Quiz #2

Fill in the blanks and check the appropriate boxes:

1. A chemical released that causes an organism's own heart rate to increase is an example of a [☐ **pheromone** ☐ **hormone**].

2. Roots growing toward the earth is described as [☐ **positive** ☐ **negative**] gravitropism.

3. A rooster crowing in the morning is an example of a _____ rhythm.

4. A fruit tree flowering in the spring is an example of a _____ rhythm.

5. Growth of a plant toward light is called _____.

6. Bacteria that release chemicals to draw other bacteria toward a food source are releasing [☐ **pheromones** ☐ **hormones**].

7. Athlete's foot is the common name that describes a fungal infection of the skin of the feet, especially between the toes. The skin becomes cracked and sore. This is an example of a [☐ **mutualistic** ☐ **commensalistic** ☐ **parasitic**] relationship.

8. Epiphytes are small plants that grow on the branches of big trees. The epiphytes are exposed to sunlight, and the big tree is neither helped nor harmed. This is an example of a [☐ **mutualistic** ☐ **commensalistic** ☐ **parasitic**] relationship.

9. Any two organisms living in an intimate association with each other are said to be in a _____ relationship.

10. An ivy growing along a trellis is an example of _____.

Key Words

instinctive behavior
fixed-action patterns
imprinting
learned behaviors
habituation
conditioning
associative learning
classical conditioning
operant conditioning
insight learning
reasoning
tropism

phototropism
positive gravitropism
negative gravitropism
geotropism
thigmotropism
auxins
circadian rhythm
pheromones
symbiosis
mutualism
parasitism
commensalism

Summary

o   Animals have some behaviors that are present at birth. These are instinctive behaviors.

o   Instinctive behavior can be fixed-action patterns or imprinting.

o   Animals also have learned behaviors, which can be the result of habituation, conditioning, or insight.

o   Plants respond to different stimuli. Specifically, these stimuli are light, gravity, and touch.

o   Animals can communicate by the release of pheromones, chemicals that are released and cause a reaction in another animal.

o   Plants and animals can coexist in arrangements called symbiosis. This includes mutualism, parasitism, and commensalism.

Chapter 13
Microorganisms

There are four types of microorganisms you should know about for the SAT Biology E/M Subject Test: protists, fungi, bacteria, and viruses. Because we've already covered everything you need to know about protists in Chapter 9, in this chapter we'll cover fungi, bacteria, and viruses.

LET'S TALK ABOUT FUNGI

Most **fungi** are multicellular eukaryotes. That means they are made up of many cells, and that their cells have nuclei and other organelles. In some fungi, the cells are not separated by cell walls (fungal cell walls, by the way, are made of **chitin**), and they seem to be one giant cell with many nuclei—in other words, **multinucleate**. In other fungi, the cells are kept distinct. There are many examples of fungi that you are familiar with—molds, mushrooms, etc.

Something to Remember About Yeast

Often people want to classify yeast as prokaryotic because yeasts are unicellular, but don't fall into that trap. Yeasts are fungi, and all fungi are **eukaryotes**—they have nuclei and organelles.

Fungi lack chloroplasts, which means they cannot photosynthesize (produce their own food). Therefore, they are classified as heterotrophs. Furthermore, they are **absorptive feeders.** This means they secrete hydrolytic enzymes that digest their food outside their bodies. This "predigested" food can then be easily absorbed by the fungus. Many fungi feed on dead or decaying material, helping to break it down; they are decomposers.

> Fungi reproduce in several different ways:
>
> 1. **Asexual spores:** These spores are kind of like seeds that can drop off the fungus and grow a new organism.
> 2. **Sexual spores:** Fungi can produce sexual spores (kind of like sperm and ova) that combine to form a new organism.
> 3. **Vegetative growth:** In this type of reproduction, a portion of the fungus breaks off and forms a new fungus.
> 4. **Budding**: A new fungus grows off the side of the old fungus. An example of a fungus that reproduces in this way is yeast.

LET'S TALK ABOUT BACTERIA

Bacteria are single-celled organisms, and these organisms are the only **prokaryotes** around. Prokaryotes have no nuclei and no membrane-bound organelles (they do have ribosomes, which are not membrane-bound). Because they have no nuclei, their DNA is found in the cytoplasm. Bacterial DNA is usually found as a single, circular chromosome. It's still double-stranded, but the ends of the strand are joined in a circle. This helps protect the DNA from damage. Bacteria also have a cell wall, which is made of **peptidoglycan** (proteins and sugars).

Bacteria reproduce in a process called **binary fission**. It's very simple—the bacterium replicates its single chromosome, then splits in half. Each of the new daughter cells gets one of the chromosomes and about half the organelles and cytoplasm. This is a great way of increasing the numbers of bacteria—one becomes two, which become four, which become eight, and so on—but this does not allow for any type of genetic recombination. In other words, there is no chance of mixing up the DNA using this type of reproduction. As we've seen in Chapter 9, being able to mix up the DNA a bit gives a species variability, which can lead to evolution, so it's definitely an advantage to be able to do this.

Bacteria can achieve genetic recombination—mix up the DNA—in three different ways:

1. **Transformation:** In transformation, bacteria can pick up new DNA from the extracellular environment. This is unusual and relatively rare in natural environments but is often used in research for a number of different purposes.
2. **Conjugation:** Conjugation means that a bacterium replicates its DNA and donates some of it to another bacterium through a bridge called a **pilus**.
3. **Transduction:** In transduction, a virus carries DNA from one bacterium to another bacterium during infection.

How This Information Might Show Up on the Test

Bacterial genetics often appears on the SAT Biology E/M Subject Test in an experiment-type question in which one strain of bacteria is being grown, then something happens to it, and suddenly it displays different properties than it did before—it becomes a new strain. For example, perhaps two different strains of bacteria (Strain A and Strain B) were being grown separately, then they were mixed, and a third, new strain (Strain C) resulted. Strain A is **resistant** to the antibiotic ampicillin (it is not killed by ampicillin), but sensitive to tetracycline (tetracycline kills it). Strain A would be denoted *amp^r tet^s*. Strain B is **sensitive** to ampicillin, but resistant to tetracycline, so it would be denoted *amp^s tet^r*. The new strain, Strain C, is resistant to both antibiotics, so it's denoted *amp^r tet^r*.

Antibiotic resistance is determined by the bacterium's DNA, so if the resistance or sensitivity to an antibiotic changes, something has changed in the bacterium's DNA—in other words, genetic recombination has occurred. But how do you know which type of recombination? Was it **transformation? Conjugation? Transduction?** Here's a handy table to help you figure it out.

If This ...	Was Mixed with This ...	And This Resulted ...	Then This Occurred
bacteria	naked DNA	new bacteria	transformation
bacteria	different bacteria	new bacteria	conjugation
bacteria	virus	new bacteria	transduction

So in our example above, Strain A was mixed with Strain B to produce Strain C. Because bacteria were mixed with different bacteria to produce new bacteria, *conjugation* must have occurred. (More specifically, Strain B must have donated the DNA for tetracycline resistance to Strain A, resulting in Strain C.)

Bacteria

Saprobes are bacteria that are decomposers and obtain their nutrients from the breakdown of dead organic matter.
Parasites get their nutrition from living hosts, harming the host in the process.
Symbionts also get their nutrition from living hosts, but they do *not* harm the host in the process.

How Bacteria Get Nutrition

Some bacteria, the cyanobacteria, can perform photosynthesis, which means that they're autotrophs. Most bacteria, however, cannot perform photosynthesis, and they're heterotrophs. The heterotrophs get their nutrition from other organisms.

Most bacteria need oxygen. They're obliged to have oxygen, just as we are, and they are known as **obligate aerobes.** Some bacteria are poisoned by oxygen, and these are known as **obligate anaerobes.** Finally, there are some bacteria that will use oxygen if it's available but can survive by fermentation if it's not. These bacteria are **facultative anaerobes.** Here's a quick summary table for oxygen use by bacteria.

Organism	Oxygen Available	Oxygen Not Available
Obligate aerobes	☺	☹
Obligate anaerobes	☹	☺
Facultative anaerobes	☺	☺

Let's Talk About Auxotrophs

Remember from the discussion on plants that the suffix *troph* refers to nutrition. The prefix *auxo* is derived from the word *auxiliary*, which means "supplementary." So an **auxotroph** is an organism that requires supplementary nutrition.

Most bacteria are *not* auxotrophs and are referred to as **wild type**. These bacteria are perfectly capable of synthesizing all the building blocks they need in terms of nutrition, as long as they are provided with a carbon source such as glucose. They can make all the amino acids, lipids, etc., that they need to build their larger macromolecules (peptidoglycan, carbohydrates, proteins, etc.). For researchers in a laboratory, these bacteria are simple to grow. Wild types grow easily in a petri dish on agar plates with glucose, or in a liquid medium with glucose in a test tube.

Auxotrophic bacteria, however, need a little help. They need additional substances put into their growth medium along with the glucose. What additional substances? That depends on the type of auxotroph you're dealing with. Most auxotrophic bacteria lack the ability to synthesize some amino acid. They are denoted by the amino acid they cannot make, along with a minus sign. For example, if a bacterium could not synthesize arginine, it would be an *arg⁻* auxotroph. If a different bacterium could not synthesize leucine, it would be a *leu⁻* auxotroph.

A single strain of bacteria might have a combination of traits. For example, it might be unable to synthesize leucine but able to synthesize arginine. This strain would be denoted *leu⁻ arg⁺*. Perhaps it is also unable to synthesize histidine. If that were the case, it would be denoted *leu⁻ arg⁺ his⁻*. And so on. Here's an important point to remember:

> If the substance that cannot be synthesized is not added to the growth medium, the auxotroph cannot grow.

However, other bacteria that are not auxotrophic for that particular substance can grow just fine.

How This Might Show Up on the Test

This most often appears as a question in which you are asked to determine the characteristics of a strain of bacteria. A researcher attempts to grow a strain of bacteria in several different media, each containing or lacking some amino acid. Sometimes the bacteria grow and sometimes they don't. You have to figure out if the strain is auxotrophic and what type of auxotroph it is. Here is a simple two-step technique to figure it out:

> **Step 1:** Determine which amino acid is missing from the medium.
>
> **Step 2:** See if the bacteria grow there.
>
> **YES:** The bacteria *are not* auxotrophic for that amino acid (denoted with a plus sign).
>
> **NO:** The bacteria *are* auxotrophic for that amino acid (denoted with a minus sign).
>
> Note that you will have to do this separately for each situation.

Let's Put It Into Practice

The table below contains data from an experiment in which the researcher attempted to grow three different strains of bacteria (Strain A, Strain B, and Strain C) in various types of growth media. Analyze the data, and see if you can figure out the characteristics of each strain.

Test Tube Number	Contains	What Grew
1	glucose, leucine, arginine	Strain B
2	glucose, leucine, histidine	Strains A and C
3	glucose, histidine, arginine	Strains B and C

In this problem, there are three different test tubes and three different strains of bacteria. So you must do Step 1 three times, once for each tube, and Step 2 three times, once for each strain. The first step is to figure out which amino acid is missing. Note that you need to concern yourself only with the amino acids being used—you don't have to worry about all 20! In this experiment, only leucine, arginine, and histidine are being considered.

It's in the Genes

The ability to synthesize an amino acid is coded in the DNA. In other words, this is a genetic trait. These traits might show up in genetic recombination experiments and questions, like the previous example about antibiotic resistance and conjugation.

Tube 1

Step 1:   Missing histidine

Step 2:   Strain A did not grow. Strain A is his⁻. Strain B did grow, so Strain B is his⁺. Strain C did not grow, so Strain C is his⁻.

Tube 2

Step 1:   Missing arginine

Step 2:   Strain A did grow. Strain A is arg⁺. Strain B did not grow, so Strain B is arg⁻. Strain C did grow, so Strain C is arg⁺.

Tube 3

Step 1:   Missing leucine

Step 2:   Strain A did not grow. Strain A is leu⁻. Strain B did grow, so Strain B is leu⁺. Strain C did grow, so Strain C is leu⁺.

So the final summary is:

Strain A: his⁻ arg⁺ leu⁻

Strain B: his⁺ arg⁻ leu⁺

Strain C: his⁻ arg⁺ leu⁺

Remember that if a bacterium can grow in the *absence* of a particular amino acid, it is *not* auxotrophic for that amino acid.

Another Important Thing About Bacteria—They Supply Nitrogen to Soil

Nitrogen is an important component of protein, and plants need nitrogen to grow properly. The atmosphere is about 80 percent nitrogen, but plants cannot use gaseous nitrogen (N_2); they must have it in the form of nitrate (NO_3^-) or ammonium (NH_4^+).

Much of the soil nitrogen comes from the breakdown of dead organic material that releases nitrogen. This nitrogen is converted to ammonium by ammonifying bacteria. Some of the soil nitrogen comes from gaseous nitrogen in the atmosphere, which is converted to ammonia by nitrogen-fixing bacteria. The ammonia is converted to ammonium in the soil. Finally, the ammonium is converted to nitrate by yet another type of bacteria, the nitrifying bacteria.

For the SAT Biology E/M Subject Test, the most important thing to remember about nitrogen and bacteria is that some nitrogen-fixing bacteria form a symbiotic relationship with the roots of certain plants. This relationship is **mutualistic**, meaning that both the plant and the bacteria benefit from the association. The bacteria live in the roots of these plants, in structures called **nodules**. They supply the plant with fixed nitrogen, and the plant supplies them with nutrients. Plants that establish this type of mutualistic relationship with nitrogen-fixing bacteria are **legumes**—beans, peas, peanuts, clover, alfalfa, and soybeans. Sometimes the bacteria fix so much nitrogen that the plant can't use it all, and the extra is secreted into the soil. This is one reason for crop rotation—a legume is planted in the field first and harvested, then a non-legume is planted, which can use the "leftover" nitrogen from the previous legume crop.

LET'S TALK ABOUT VIRUSES

A virus isn't really considered a cell, and it's not even technically considered to be alive. It has only two components: (1) a coat made of protein (only protein) called the **capsid** and, inside the coat, (2) nucleic acid (the **genome**). Depending on the virus, the genome might be DNA or RNA.

Because viruses consist only of a protein capsid and a nucleic acid genome, they have none of the machinery required to reproduce themselves. Therefore, they can reproduce only with the help of another cell, using that cell's enzymes as needed. All types of cells can be infected by viruses—bacteria, fungi, plants, or animals. Let's consider a virus with a DNA genome.

The viral life cycle begins with the following two steps:

1. **Attachment:** The virus attaches itself to the host cell. This is a specific interaction between the virus and the host cell; a virus can attach only to its particular host.
2. **Infection:** The virus injects its genome into the host cell.

Once inside the host, the viral genome enters into one of two possible life cycles, the *lytic* cycle or the *lysogenic* cycle. In the **lytic cycle**, the viral genome is first transcribed and translated (using the host's RNA polymerases and ribosomes) to make viral proteins (for example, the capsid proteins). Host DNA polymerases then replicate the viral genome, and the new viral genomes are packaged into the new viral capsids. Finally, the host is broken open (**lysed**) by a special viral enzyme and the new viruses escape to infect new hosts. Because viruses absolutely *cannot* reproduce outside a host cell, and because the host cell is harmed in the process, viruses are considered to be parasites.

In the **lysogenic cycle**, the viral genome is not immediately transcribed, translated, and replicated. Instead, it is inserted (**integrated**) into the host's genome, where it remains dormant. Every time the host replicates its genome (during cell division) the viral genome is replicated, too. Thus, every daughter cell of the original infected host is also infected; they carry the viral genome integrated with their own. The virus can remain in this dormant state for a long time—years and years in some cases. If the host cell experiences stress of some sort (illness, for example) the virus can remove itself from the host genome and begin the lytic cycle, being transcribed, translated, etc. An example of a virus that follows the lysogenic cycle is the human virus that causes cold sores (HSV 1).

Here's a side-by-side comparison of the two cycles:

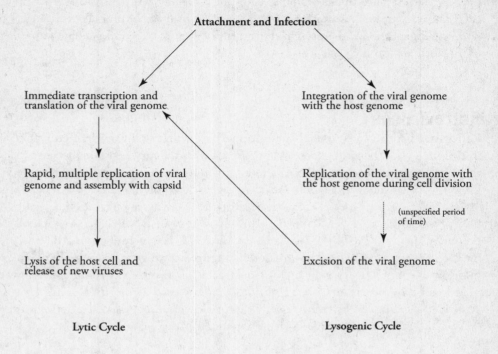

Attachment and Infection

Immediate transcription and translation of the viral genome

Integration of the viral genome with the host genome

Rapid, multiple replication of viral genome and assembly with capsid

Replication of the viral genome with the host genome during cell division

(unspecified period of time)

Lysis of the host cell and release of new viruses

Excision of the viral genome

Lytic Cycle

Lysogenic Cycle

A Special Note About Animal Viruses

Because animal cells do not have a cell wall, viruses that infect these cells do not necessarily have to lyse them to escape. The new viral particles can simply bud out through the plasma membrane. This is an advantage to the virus, because the cell stays alive longer, and ultimately more viruses can be produced (lysing a cell kills it instantly, and if the cell dies, viral production stops). As the virus buds out, it becomes coated in plasma membrane; this layer of membrane around the capsid is called an **envelope**.

Viruses with RNA Genomes

Viruses with RNA genomes have a slight problem when it comes to replicating their genome. Every other organism on the planet has a DNA genome; so they have the DNA polymerases necessary for replication. If a virus also has a DNA genome, it has no problem "borrowing" the host cell's DNA polymerase to replicate itself (recall that viruses rely on host cell enzymes for transcription, translation, and replication).

But an RNA virus cannot use DNA polymerase to replicate (DNA polymerase copies only DNA); the virus needs an *RNA* polymerase. Furthermore, the virus can't use the host's RNA polymerase, because that enzyme makes RNA only by reading a DNA template (transcription). The virus needs a special enzyme that makes a strand of RNA by reading an RNA template—an **RNA-dependent RNA polymerase.** Because this is a unique viral-only enzyme, the virus must either (a) carry the enzyme with it in its capsid and inject it into the host along with its genome or (b) synthesize the protein during translation of the viral genome (a part of the normal viral life cycle).

Retroviruses

Retroviruses are RNA viruses that go through the lysogenic life cycle. Recall that in this life cycle, the viral genome is integrated with the host genome. Because in this case the viral genome is RNA, and all other organisms have a DNA genome, a DNA copy of the viral genome must first be made before integration can occur. Again, this requires a special enzyme, because the host has no enzymes that make DNA by reading an RNA template. This enzyme is an **RNA-dependent DNA-polymerase,** and, as with the RNA-dependent RNA-polymerase discussed above, must either be carried with the virus or synthesized during translation. The common name for RNA-dependent DNA-polymerase is **reverse transcriptase**—normally transcription creates RNA from DNA, and this enzyme runs reverse transcription; it creates *DNA* from *RNA*. The virus that causes AIDS is a retrovirus (HIV), and many cancer-causing viruses are retroviruses.

Decoding Viral Enzyme Names

Okay, you don't want to have to memorize more enzyme names, so here's how you figure them out. Remember it this way: A polymerase makes something by reading something. It is "dependent" on the thing it must read.

- dependent = reads
- polymerase = makes

So if an enzyme is RNA dependent, it reads RNA, and if it is DNA dependent, it reads DNA. If an enzyme makes RNA, it's an RNA polymerase, and if it makes DNA, it's a DNA polymerase.

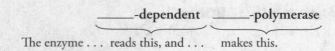

_____-**dependent**   _____-**polymerase**
The enzyme . . . reads this, and . . .   makes this.

To figure out which enzyme a virus needs, first figure out what type of nucleic acid the virus carries: That's what the enzyme has to read. Next, figure out what type of nucleic acid the virus needs to make: That's the type of polymerase needed. Finally, determine if this is an enzyme the host normally has (in which case the virus can "borrow" it), or if this is a special viral enzyme that must be brought in with the genome or created.

Quick Quiz #1

Fill in the blanks and check the appropriate boxes:

1. Fungi are classified as [☐ **eukaryotes** ☐ **prokaryotes**].

2. Bacteria [☐ **do** ☐ **do not**] have mitochondria.

3. Bacteria [☐ **do** ☐ **do not**] have ribosomes.

4. Bacteria [☐ **do** ☐ **do not**] have cell walls.

5. Yeast are [☐ **eukaryotes** ☐ **prokaryotes**] that reproduce by _____.

6. A viral _____ is made of protein.

7. [☐ **Transformation** ☐ **Transduction**] occurs when a virus transfers some DNA from one bacterium to another.

8. Fungi [☐ **can** ☐ **cannot**] photosynthesize.

9. Bacteria that are perfectly happy in the presence OR absence of oxygen are called _____.

10. Number the following steps of the lytic cycle in the order they would occur:

    _____ Virus injects nucleic acid into host cell.

    _____ Host cell is lysed and new viruses are released.

    _____ Viral capsid attaches to host cell.

    _____ New capsids are formed.

    _____ Viral nucleic acids are replicated using host cell machinery.

11. [☐ **Some** ☐ **All**] fungi are eukaryotes.

12. A [☐ **parasitic** ☐ **mutualistic**] relationship exists between some plants and _____ bacteria. These types of plants are called _____.

13. When a bacterium replicates its DNA and gives some of the DNA to another bacterium through a pilus, this is called

    _____.

14. Fungi have a cell wall made of [☐ **proteoglycan** ☐ **chitin**].

15. Bacteria are classified as [☐ **prokaryotes** ☐ **eukaryotes**] and therefore [☐ **do** ☐ **do not**] have nuclei.

16. An enzyme that makes a strand of RNA by reading a strand of DNA is called _____.

17. Retroviruses go through the [☐ **lytic** ☐ **lysogenic**] life cycle.

COOL STUFF: RECOMBINANT DNA TECHNOLOGY

Now that you know about bacteria, viruses, and DNA, let's talk about how these microorganisms can be used in molecular biology research. First, we have to cover a little background information.

Restriction Enzymes

Restriction enzymes are enzymes that recognize a particular short DNA sequence and then cut the DNA strand within that sequence. They were first discovered in bacteria. Bacteria use the enzymes to cut (and thereby destroy) foreign DNA, such as viral DNA. This would *restrict* the growth of the virus, hence the name *restriction enzymes*. The bacterium's own DNA is protected in some way, often by the addition of a methyl group ($-CH_3$) to the sequence recognized by the enzyme, thus preventing the enzyme from binding there.

There have been many, many restriction enzymes discovered. They are named for the strain of bacteria in which they were first found; for example, the restriction enzyme *Eco*RI was found in *E. coli*. Each restriction enzyme recognizes a different DNA sequence. That sequence is usually a *palindrome* (it reads the same from both directions); for example, here is the sequence recognized by *Eco*RI:

5'–G A A T T C–3'
3'–C T T A A G–5'

and here is the sequence recognized by *Pst*I (discovered in *Providencia stuartii*):

5'–C T G C A G–3'
3'–G A C G T C–5'

and here is yet another recognized by *Hpa*I (discovered in *Hemophilus parainfluenzae*):

5'–G T T A A C–3'
3'–C A A T T G–5'

Notice that if you read the sequence (from 5' to 3') in either direction, it is the same.

A "Blunt" Explanation of a "Sticky" Situation

Restriction enzymes cut the DNA sequence in one of two ways, either staggered or blunt. In a staggered cut, short single-stranded tails called **sticky ends** are left at the cut ends of the DNA strand. *Eco*RI and *Pst*I both perform a staggered cut. They cut the DNA strand like this:

5'–G A A T T C–3'   5'–C T G C A G–3'
3'–C T T A A G–5'   3'–G A C G T C–5'

*Eco*RI   *Pst*I

to produce sticky ends like this:

5'–G   A A T T C–3'   5'–C T G C A   G–3'
3'–C T T A   A G–5'   3'–G   A C G T C–5'

*Eco*RI   *Pst*I

If a piece of DNA is cut with a restriction enzyme that produces sticky ends, it can be reattached—ligated—to any other piece of DNA cut with the *same* restriction enzyme. The single-stranded tails must overlap in a complementary fashion.

In a **blunt cut**, the DNA is cut straight across both strands. *Hpa*I performs a blunt cut like this:

5'–G T T A A C–3'
3'–C A A T T G–5

*Hpa*I

to produce blunt ends like this:

5'–G T T   A A C–3'
3'–C A A   T T G–5'

*Hpa*I

If a piece of DNA is cut with an enzyme that produces blunt ends, it can be ligated to any other piece of DNA cut with *any other* enzyme that produces blunt ends, because the ends do not need to overlap in a complementary fashion.

Plasmids

A **plasmid** is a small circular piece of DNA frequently found in bacteria and sometimes in yeast. The plasmid is not considered to be part of the bacterial or yeast genome and can reproduce independently of the microorganism. And because the plasmid is DNA, its sequence contains restriction sites. Let's take a look at how plasmids are used in recombinant DNA research.

Back to Recombinant DNA Technology

Recombinant DNA technology simply refers to the creation of new DNA molecules by cutting and splicing (i.e., *recombining*) the DNA with restriction enzymes. It is used primarily in the study of DNA sequences of species that do not reproduce rapidly.

> ### Antibiotic Resistance
> Some bacteria carry plasmids that contain genes that make the bacteria resistant to antibiotics. These plasmids can be copied, spread throughout the population of bacteria, and even spread to different populations of different bacteria. The result of this process is that many of the bacteria that cause diseases in humans are becoming resistant to certain antibiotics.

Suppose you were a researcher studying a certain mouse gene. As part of your studies, you wish to characterize the DNA for that gene by determining its sequence, or by determining its **restriction map** (a map of the location of various restriction sites within that piece of DNA). In any case, you're going to need quite a bit of that DNA. You could sacrifice a bunch of mice, grind them up (eeww!), and extract the DNA from the tissue. This would be a lot of work, and every time you need a sample of DNA you have to repeat this procedure. Further, this would cost a lot for the mice, not to mention the space for breeding the mice, and the cost of feeding the mice, etc. (Plus, it's hard on the mice!)

But suppose that you obtain a small sample of mouse DNA by sacrificing a single mouse and extracting the DNA from its tissues. And suppose further that you know the particular gene you are interested in is bounded on either side by an *Eco*RI restriction site. Using *Eco*RI, you could cut the gene out of its chromosome and separate it from the remainder of the mouse DNA. In reality, there are several steps involved here, but to keep things simple (after all, we just want to get an idea of the big picture), let's say that these are the only two *Eco*RI sites in the entire mouse genome. Now you have a small (very small!) sample of just the DNA you are interested in, with an *Eco*RI sticky end on each side. The next step is to **amplify** (increase the amount of) that DNA.

So you order a plasmid (custom-made plasmids are commercially available!) that has an *Eco*RI site in its sequence, and you cut that plasmid with *Eco*RI. Then you mix the cut plasmid with your DNA sample (that has the *Eco*RI sticky ends), and because the sticky ends on your DNA are complementary to the sticky ends on the plasmid, they will base-pair with one another and your DNA sample will become inserted into the plasmid. You then add a new enzyme called DNA *ligase* that permanently joins the newly base-paired regions. You now have a plasmid with your DNA of interest inserted.

Now for the Final Part ...

You insert this plasmid into a general strain of laboratory bacteria (okay again, several steps here which, for clarity, will be omitted) and grow gallons of the bacteria. Bacteria are easy and inexpensive to grow, and they reproduce very rapidly, doubling their numbers approximately every 20 minutes. And every time the bacteria reproduce, the plasmid does, too, so you are in effect copying your piece of DNA over and over again. As long as the bacteria are reproducing, you essentially have an endless supply of your DNA of interest. Getting the plasmid out of the bacteria is relatively easy, and removing your DNA of interest is as easy as recutting the plasmid with *Eco*RI.

Yes, this is an oversimplification of the process, but the general idea is sound. Using recombinant DNA technology, plasmids can be custom-made to reproduce in bacteria or in eukaryotes. Sometimes promoter regions can be added so that DNA inserted after the promoter can be transcribed and translated. This allows the cells containing the plasmid to start making the protein coded for by the DNA, creating an unlimited supply of the protein of interest! Using plasmids and cells (prokaryotic or eukaryotic) to reproduce DNA or make protein is a much more efficient method than using live animals for DNA or protein collection.

Here's Another Example

Let's say you have isolated a gene that gives tomato plants the ability to resist attack by certain parasites—perhaps the gene codes for a chemical in the sap of the tomato plant that weakens or kills the parasite. However, the gene is found only in a few isolated tomato plants. If you could somehow get that gene into all the tomato plants on a farm, it would produce a hardier plant and increase crop yield. So, using restriction enzymes, you insert the gene into a lysogenic virus that infects tomato plants, but is relatively harmless (in other words, the virus does not kill the plant or make the plant sick). Then you allow your recombinant virus to infect a field of plants, and as part of its normal life cycle the virus inserts its genome (which now contains the new parasite-resisting gene) into the tomato genome. These new recombinant plants can now resist the effects of the parasite and are minimally affected by the virus.

Here's another definition: a **vector**. A vector is simply a shuttle used to move DNA between species. The plasmid was our vector in the first example, and the virus was the vector in the second example.

Remember This

The examples presented here are an oversimplification, but here's the big picture:

> Restriction enzymes give us the ability to effectively "cut and paste" (recombine) DNA into custom combinations.

Using vectors, these custom DNAs can be moved into other organisms. This allows the DNA to be amplified and studied much more rapidly than it could be in mammalian (or even plant) species. Or, it can provide a new gene (or several genes) to an organism that can give it an advantage. This is the basis for gene replacement therapy as treatment for genetic disorders (although this has not yet been successful in humans).

Quick Quiz #2

1. A _____ cut of DNA by a restriction enzyme produces sticky ends.

2. A piece of DNA cut with a restriction enzyme that produces sticky ends can be ligated to any piece of DNA cut with [□ **the same restriction enzyme** □ **any other restriction enzyme that produces sticky ends**].

3. The enzyme that seals together cut pieces of DNA is called _____.

4. A sequence of DNA that reads the same from both directions is called a _____.

5. [□ **True** □ **False**] A piece of DNA cut with a restriction enzyme that produces blunt ends can be ligated into a plasmid cut with any other restriction enzyme.

Key Words

fungi
chitin
multinucleate
absorptive feeders
asexual spores
sexual spores
vegetative growth
budding
eukaryotes
prokaryotes
peptidoglycan
binary fission
resistant
sensitive
transformation
conjugation
transduction
obligate aerobes
obligate anaerobes
facultative anaerobes
auxotroph
wild type
mutualistic

nodules
legumes
capsid
genome
attachment
infection
lytic cycle
lysed
lysogenic cycle
integrated
envelope
RNA-dependent RNA-polymerase
RNA-dependent DNA-polymerase
reverse transcriptase
restriction enzymes
*Eco*RI
sticky ends
blunt cut
plasmid
restriction map
amplify
vector

Summary

o   There are four types of microorganisms that you need to know for the Biology E/M test: protists, fungi, bacteria, and viruses.

o   Most fungi are multicellular eukaryotes; yeasts are unicellular fungi.

o   Fungi can reproduce by asexual spores, sexual spores, vegetative growth, and by budding.

o   Bacteria are prokaryotes. Some bacteria are autotrophs and some are heterotrophs.

o   Some bacteria supply soil with nitrogen to help plants grow properly.

o   Viruses are not cells and are not alive. They can reproduce only with the help of another cell.

Chapter 14
Cracking Ecology

Ecology is the study of the interactions between organisms and their environments. The environment includes abiotic (nonliving) factors such as light, temperature, nutrients, and water, as well as biotic (living) factors such as other organisms that inhabit the environment. In this chapter we will see how groups of organisms interact with one another and how they interact with their environments.

Before we get into an in-depth discussion of ecology, let's take a look at the levels of biological organization:

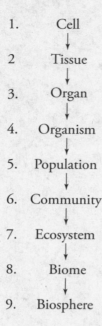

1. Cell
2. Tissue
3. Organ
4. Organism
5. Population
6. Community
7. Ecosystem
8. Biome
9. Biosphere

We've already discussed many of these levels of biological organization (cells, tissues, organs, and organisms) in previous chapters. Let's begin with the fifth level—population.

WHAT IS A POPULATION?

We've mentioned the term **population** before, but we never really defined it, so let's do that now:

> A population is a group of individuals that interbreed and therefore share the same gene pool.

A population is sort of a subset of a species. Think about it this way: A species is a group of organisms that is *able* to interbreed, and a population is a group of organisms that *is* interbreeding. For example, a group of mice on the West Coast of the United States may belong to the same species as a group of mice on the East Coast of the United States, because if they were brought together, they could interbreed. However, because they are separated by such a great distance, they are NOT interbreeding and are NOT members of the same population.

Because a population consists of a group of organisms that are interbreeding, this is the level of organization at which evolution is seen.

> Evolution does not act on an individual; individuals cannot evolve. But populations can evolve, as their individuals (and more important, their individuals' offspring) undergo changes in phenotype and genotype.

Population Growth

There are two types of population growth you should be familiar with for the SAT Biology E/M Subject Test. The first is **exponential growth**, and the second is **limited growth**. The two types are related; a population that starts off growing exponentially will ultimately reach a level at which it is unable to sustain that rapid rate of growth, at which point growth becomes limited.

Consider a single bacterium. This bacterium can divide by binary fission to produce two bacteria. It takes the bacterium about 20 minutes to accomplish this, if all the conditions for growth are ideal. After another 20 minutes, both of the new bacteria would undergo binary fission, and we'd have four bacteria. After another 20 minutes, we'd have 8, then 16, and so on and so on and so on. After just one day—24 hours—we'd have more than 4×10^{12} bacteria. That's 4,000 billion billion bacteria!

In this type of growth the size of the population increases exponentially, and if we graphed it, it would look like this:

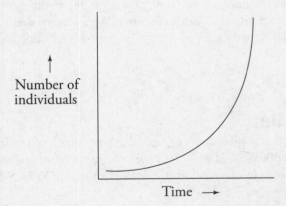

Of course, in reality this could never happen. As the bacterial population continued to grow, nutrients would get used up, space would become scarce, and waste products would accumulate. Some members of the population would die, and the growth curve would flatten out as the population stabilized.

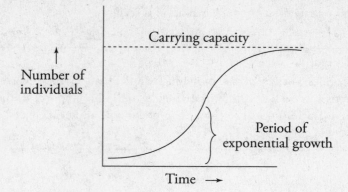

Here, the maximum population size is limited. The maximum population size that a particular environment can sustain is referred to as the **carrying capacity**.

The carrying capacity of an environment can change if the environment changes. For example, if we provide our bacterial population with a larger container and more food, the carrying capacity would increase to reflect this.

Suppose we had a field of grasses that could support a population of 100 mice. Suppose further that a drought reduced the number of grasses that could grow. The field may no longer be able to support all 100 mice. In this case, the carrying capacity of the field would decrease.

WHAT IS A COMMUNITY?

A community is a group of populations that live in a particular environment. These populations can interact with one another in many different ways, including symbiotically, competitively, and predatorily. We already talked about symbiosis in Chapter 12, so we won't cover that again. Instead, let's talk about competition and predation.

Battling It Out

Technically, we've also already mentioned competition, when we talked about evolution in Chapter 9. We said that organisms that were more successful competitors would be better able to survive within their environment. What do we mean when we say "competitors"?

To understand competition fully, we have to introduce a new term: the **niche**. An organism's niche is the way it lives in its environment, including its nesting behavior, what type of food it eats, and when it hunts. You can think of it like this: If an organism's environment is its address, then its niche is its job.

If two populations have similar niches (for example, if they hunt the same food at the same time), there will be a lot of competition between the two populations. The two populations become competitors against each other for the food. Usually, one population will "win out" over the other (it will compete more effectively), and that population will grow in size (to its natural carrying capacity), while the other population will shrink. In extreme cases, the winning population will compete so effectively that it will drive the losing population out altogether. This allows the winning population to be the sole occupant of the niche.

Then What?

Well, we know from Chapter 9 that competition drives evolution. So what happens next is that the populations evolve. Generally, the winning population doesn't have to evolve too much, because the members of the population can keep on doing what they've been doing—they're now the sole owners of the niche. But the losing population has to find another way to survive. Obviously, trying to occupy the original niche was a failure. Perhaps some members of the losing population might begin hunting at a different time. This would allow them to be more successful, because the winning group is temporarily out of the picture. Over time, this would produce distinct differences in the populations' hunting times, and they would occupy different niches.

> ### Populations and Evolution: A Quick Summary
> - Populations occupy different niches within their environment.
> - If two populations have similar niches, they will compete for sole "ownership" of the niche. The more similar the niches, the more intense the competition.
> - The winning population retains the niche and the losing population must evolve to survive.
> - Evolution results in populations that occupy different niches, thereby reducing competition and promoting a more stable community.

Hunt or Be Hunted—Predation

When one organism eats another, we call that **predation**. The organism doing the eating is the predator, and the organism being eaten is the prey. Usually this results in the death of the prey (in the case of a hawk eating a mouse, for example), but it doesn't have to (in the case of a giraffe eating the leaves from the top of a tree—the tree itself usually does not die).

Many times predation causes the prey to evolve. The prey evolves to better escape the predator. Plants evolve to have thorns, mice evolve to have brown fur for better camouflage, etc. In these cases, the evolution of the prey causes the predator to evolve—to better capture the prey. Herbivores evolve tougher mouth skin, hawks evolve to have better eyesight, etc. The alternate evolution of two species based on their interactions with each other is called **coevolution**.

Predators can affect the carrying capacity of an environment. In other words, an environment without predators will have a higher carrying capacity than an environment with predators. A marvelous example of this is the introduction of a species of perch into a lake in east Africa. The intent was to supply the locals living in that area with an additional source of income and food. At the time of introduction, the lake was filled with cichlids, a type of fish that feeds on plants, and fishing was abundant. The only problem (and it was a big one) was that the perch were natural predators of the cichlids. Because prior to this there were no predators, the cichlids had not evolved any defenses against them. The introduced perch completely destroyed the cichlid population, to the point that their own food supply was limited and their population decreased in numbers. In fact, the perch population declined so much that there were not enough perch (or cichlids, for that matter) to support the local fishing industry.

Quick Quiz #1

Fill in the blanks and check the appropriate boxes:

1. The way an organism lives within its environment is called a
    (A) community
    (B) population
    (C) ecosystem
    (D) niche
    (E) species

2. A group of individuals living and interbreeding within the same environment is called a [☐ **population** ☐ **community**].

3. Groups of different species living together and interacting with the same environment is called a
    (A) community
    (B) population
    (C) ecosystem
    (D) niche
    (E) species

4. Unrestricted population growth is called
    (A) carrying capacity
    (B) limited growth
    (C) exponential growth
    (D) ecosystem growth
    (E) community growth

5. Members of the same community are also members of the same [☐ **population** ☐ **ecosystem**].

6. Alternate evolution of two interacting species is called
    _____ .

7. Individuals [☐ **can** ☐ **cannot**] evolve.

8. Hawks and wolves hunting the same population of rabbits is an example of [☐ **competition** ☐ **predation** ☐ **both of these**].

MORE ABOUT THE COMMUNITY—WHO'S WHO

The various populations in a community can be classified based on where they get their food. We've already seen two such divisions—the **autotrophs** and the **heterotrophs**. Autotrophs, of course, are organisms that can make their own food, and heterotrophs are those that must eat other organisms. The groups of heterotrophs in a community can be further subdivided based on which other groups they eat. Sound complicated? Making you hungry? Check out the **food chain**:

1. **The food chain starts with organisms called primary producers.** They're photosynthetic—they take energy from the sun and convert it to carbohydrates. On land, the producers are plants. In water, they can be plants or algae.

2. **The next link in the food chain is made up of the primary consumers.** These are organisms that eat the primary producers. Another word for primary consumer is **herbivore**—an animal that eats plants.

3. **The next link is made up of the secondary consumers.** These are organisms that eat the primary consumers. Secondary consumers are **carnivores**—animals that eat other animals. They can also be herbivorous and eat plants. A word to describe an animal that eats both other animals AND plants is **omnivore**.

4. **The top of the food chain consists of the tertiary consumers.** These are organisms that eat the secondary consumers. Tertiary consumers are carnivores that eat other carnivores.

Don't Forget Decomposers

One way or another, all organisms die. When they do, their dead bodies are broken down (eaten, really) by other organisms called decomposers. Who are they? Bacteria and fungi who live off the dead remains of animals and plants. Bacteria and fungi are decomposers. Remember:

*   Producers (plants) use solar energy to convert carbon dioxide into sugars.
*   Primary consumers (herbivores) eat producers.
*   Secondary consumers (carnivores and omnivores) eat primary consumers (and producers).
*   Tertiary consumers (top carnivores) eat secondary consumers.
*   Decomposers eat the dead.
*   Animals, such as worms, catfish, and vultures, eat the waste and remains of dead organisms. These are known as scavengers.

There are more species and individuals at the bottom of the food chain than at the top. You can think of it as the pyramid on this page.

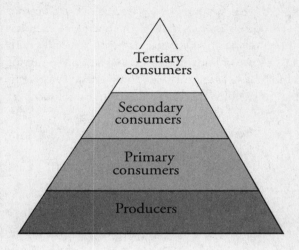

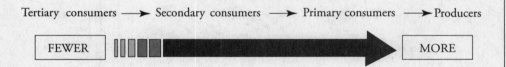

Think about a meadow. Grass and other plants grow in the meadow. Field mice live in the meadow and eat the grass. Insects are found in the meadow and they also eat plants. Sometimes they even eat other insects. Birds fly around eating seeds and insects. Snakes roam the meadow looking for mice. Hawks circle the meadow, pouncing on mice and sometimes snakes. What we're trying to say here is that reality is a lot more complex than a simple food chain, so sometimes it's referred to as a food web.

Here's what it might look like. The arrows show who feeds whom.

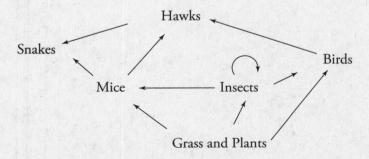

Food Pyramid Energy

There's one last thing to remember about food pyramids, or food chains, or food webs, and that is that there's more energy available at the bottom of the pyramid than at the top. In other words, not all of the energy at each level is available to the next level. Some of the energy is lost as heat (especially with animals), some of the energy is used to run body processes, and so on. So not all of the energy is available as food for the next level. In fact, only about 10 percent of the energy in one level is actually available. That doesn't seem like a lot, does it?

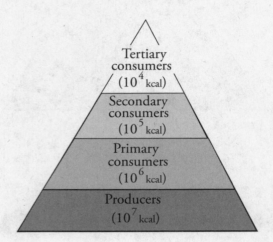

Quick Quiz #2

Fill in the blanks and check the appropriate boxes:

1.   Herbivores eat the [☐ **primary consumers** ☐ **primary producers**].

2.   Organisms that feed off dead and decaying material are called
     _____.

3.   Primary producers are [☐ **autotrophs** ☐ **heterotrophs**].

4.   There are more [☐ **primary producers** ☐ **primary consumers**].

5.   The least amount of energy is available at the [☐ **bottom** ☐ **top**] of
     the food chain.

6.   Organisms that eat both plants and animals are called
     _____.

7.   Decomposers include both _____ and
     _____.

8.   An herbivore is a(n) [☐ **autotroph** ☐ **heterotroph**].

9.   In a food chain consisting of grass, grasshoppers, frogs, and bass,
     grasshoppers are [☐ **more** ☐ **less**] numerous than frogs, and frogs
     are [☐ **more** ☐ **less**] numerous than bass.

LET'S TALK ABOUT ECOLOGICAL SUCCESSION

We've been talking about biological communities and the way their inhabitants live together (and the way in which they eat one another). For the SAT Biology E/M Subject Test you should also know that communities of organisms undergo change over time—just like residential communities of people.

Think first about human beings and an uninhabited area outside a major city. Suppose that in, 1950 a few pioneers decide to build houses in the region and move in. Next, a couple of stores appear. More people become interested in the locality and they move in, too. The region develops slowly into a rural suburb. By 1960 it spawns some housing developments and a few little shopping strips. By 1965 roads widen, traffic increases, and several gas stations appear. The process continues—gradually. By 2000 the whole place is quite different from what it was in 1950. It boasts big shopping malls, wide roads, a lot of traffic, schools, businesses, apartment houses, and a lot of people. It starts to look like a city.

When that process of gradual change takes place in an ecological community, it's called **ecological succession**. Think, for instance, about a rock with no living things on it. Often the first residents to move into the area are organisms called lichen. Lichen are the pioneers, and they are actually referred to as **pioneer organisms** because they're the first to start living in a previously uninhabited area. When you think lichen, think pioneer organism.

As the lichen flourish, they give off substances that corrode the rock. The rock represents an altered environment, and it becomes attractive to other organisms like mosses and herbs. The mosses and herbs further affect the environment to make it suitable for shrubs and grasses. Trees move in next—first pine trees and then deciduous trees, like oaks, beeches, and maple. The rock—formerly lifeless—gave rise to an ecological community; it underwent succession, which begins, always, with some pioneer organism.

Let's run through that succession again:

> rock → lichen → mosses and herbs → grasses and shrubs → pine trees → deciduous trees

We said that the lichen in this succession is the pioneer organism. Does anyone else get a special label? The answer is yes. The deciduous trees—the oaks, beeches, and maples—are called the **climax community**. Once the succession has progressed as far as it can go, what you have left is the climax community. Unlike all of the plant communities that came before it (the lichen, the mosses and herbs, the grasses and shrubs, and the pine trees), the climax community is here to stay. In other words, the climax community is a stable community; it doesn't change. Many things still happen within the climax community—plants and animals come and go, live and die, storms may hit it—but the essential nature of the climax community—that it's made up of deciduous trees and has a characteristic fauna associated with it—stays the same.

Don't Confuse Ecological Succession with Evolution

Ecological succession is NOT about evolution (a whole different ball game). Ecological succession has to do with continuous changes that take place within a community. There are predictable stages to it, as we just saw with our rock-lichen-grass-shrubs-trees example. Another big tip-off that you're dealing with an ecological succession is the time frame involved: It's a lot shorter than the time frame required for evolution to take place. When you think ecological succession, think predictable stages of plant communities usually over a period of decades. (In contrast, evolution takes place over hundreds of thousands or even millions of years.)

Quick Quiz #3

Fill in the blanks and check the appropriate boxes:

1. When a plant community begins on a barren rock, the first organism to colonize the rock is most often [☐ **lichen** ☐ **moss**].

2. In an ecological succession, each new plant community in an area [☐ **coexists with** ☐ **replaces**] the previous plant community.

3. The final community in ecological succession is called the _____ community.

4. Gradual, unpredictable change in plants that occurs over millions of years is called [☐ **ecological succession** ☐ **evolution**].

5. The _____ organism is the one that first appears as the founder of a biological community.

6. The final plant community in ecological succession is made up primarily of _____.

GETTING BIGGER—THE ECOSYSTEM

Okay, we've talked about individual cells, individual organs, organ systems, organisms, groups of organisms (populations), and groups of populations (communities)—now we have to consider the community together with the environment it lives in. This is called an **ecosystem**.

We mentioned before that the environment contains both living (biotic) things and nonliving (abiotic) things. We've just talked about the living things (the organisms, populations, and communities); now let's spend some time discussing a few of the nonliving things, such as water and chemical nutrients.

What Goes Around Comes Around—Nutrient Cycles

Because raw materials on Earth are limited resources, it makes sense to recycle them. Inorganic molecules are taken up by various organisms and converted into biologically useful forms; after these organic versions of the molecules cycle through the community, they are returned to their inorganic forms by decomposers. There are three cycles you should be familiar with: the **water cycle, the carbon cycle,** and the **nitrogen cycle**.

The Water Cycle

Water is obviously essential to living organisms—without it they die. Most of the water on the planet is NOT found in living organisms, however; it is found in the oceans. Because land-dwelling organisms need water, there must be a way to cycle the water from the oceans to the land and back. Here's how it works.

Up, Up, and Away
Transpiration is water escaping as vapor from plants.
Evaporation is water escaping as vapor from a body of water.

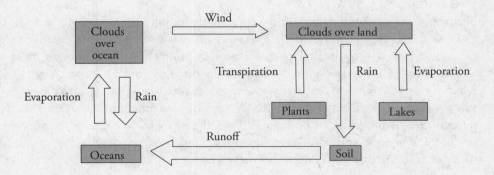

The Water Cycle

To sum up the water cycle, we can say that most water is taken up into clouds by **evaporation** and **transpiration**. The water returns to the oceans, land, and lakes by rainfall. Water that enters the soil returns to the oceans through runoff.

The Carbon Cycle

Carbon is the basic building block of all organic material. Most carbon is found as carbon dioxide in the atmosphere. Carbon is also used by plants to form organic molecules (sugars), which are then eaten by animals. The carbon is recycled to the atmosphere by respiration. Here's the picture.

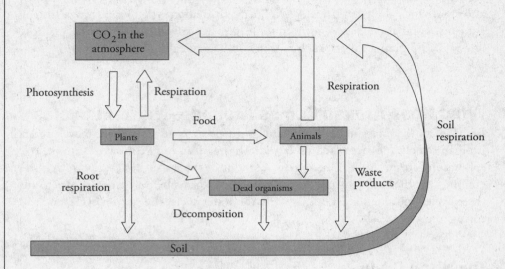

The Carbon Cycle

The Nitrogen Cycle

Nitrogen is an important nutrient for the production of protein—as you may recall, it's found in all amino acids. Every organism—from bacteria to plants to fungi to animals—requires nitrogen for protein production. Even though most of the nitrogen on Earth is found as a gas in the atmosphere, this nitrogen is relatively unavailable for protein synthesis. Most nitrogen is taken up from the soil by plants in the form of nitrates (NO_3^-) and incorporated into protein. These proteins are then consumed by animals, and the nitrogen is ultimately recycled to the soil when the animals die. In the soil, various types of bacteria convert the nitrogen into a usable form. Here's how it works.

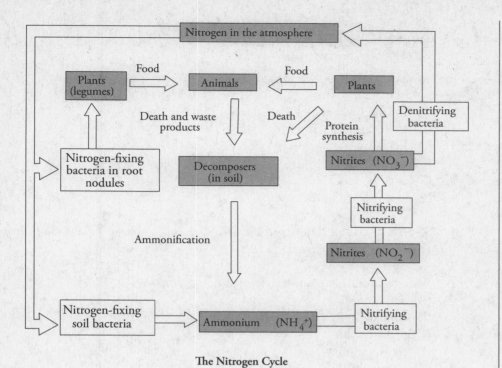

The Nitrogen Cycle

Diagram labels:

Nitrogen in the atmosphere

Plants (legumes) — Food → Animals ← Food — Plants

Death and waste products

Death

Protein synthesis

Denitrifying bacteria

Nitrogen-fixing bacteria in root nodules

Decomposers (in soil)

Nitrites (NO_3^-)

Nitrifying bacteria

Ammonification

Nitrites (NO_2^-)

Nitrogen-fixing soil bacteria → Ammonium (NH_4^+) ← Nitrifying bacteria

Basics of the Nitrogen Cycle

- When animals and plants die, the nitrogen in their bodies is released into the soil.
- The nitrogen in the soil is converted by bacteria into a usable form for plants. Some plants (legumes) have their own "resident" bacteria.
- Some bacteria release nitrogen from the soil into the atmosphere; some take it out of the atmosphere and put it into the soil.
- Plants use the nitrogen from the soil to produce protein.
- Animals eat the plants and use the proteins to make their own proteins.
- When animals and plants die, the cycle begins again.

Quick Quiz #4

Fill in the blanks and check the appropriate boxes:

1. Most carbon is found
    (A) in the atmosphere
    (B) in plants
    (C) in fossil fuels
    (D) as carbon dioxide
    (E) as carbon monoxide

2. Water and chemical nutrients are classified as [☐ **biotic** ☐ **abiotic**] elements of an ecosystem.

3. Water moves from plants to clouds by
    (A) evaporation
    (B) condensation
    (C) precipitation
    (D) transpiration
    (E) decomposition

4. Nitrogen is converted into usable forms in the soil by _____.

5. Carbon is returned to the atmosphere by [☐ **photosynthesis** ☐ **respiration**] and removed from the atmosphere by [☐ **photosynthesis** ☐ **respiration**].

6. Nitrogen-fixing bacteria live in root nodules of
    _____.

GETTING BIGGER AGAIN—BIOMES

Biomes are large areas classified mostly by the ecosystems—the climate and communities—they contain. Most biomes are terrestrial—found on land. Animal life is referred to as fauna, and plant life as flora. Some biomes are aquatic—found in water—and these biomes are the most stable because conditions such as temperature, oxygen, and light availability do not change too much over time.

> All the biomes together make up the **biosphere**—the largest level of organization and, essentially, the planet Earth.

Terrestrial Biomes

Biome 1: The Tundra   A tundra is an area characterized by permanently frozen topsoil. It's found in the northernmost parts of North America, Europe, and Asia. Because the soil is frozen, deep root growth is difficult, so there are very few trees on the tundra. Most plants are short shrubs, grasses, lichen, and mosses. There are several different insects and a few mammals, such as reindeer, caribou, wolves, and bears.

Biome 2: The Taiga   Taiga is found a little bit south of the tundra. Another term for taiga is coniferous forest, because it contains many, many conifers (evergreen trees). Fauna includes many small mammals, such as squirrels and hares; larger herbivores, such as moose, elk, beavers, and deer; and larger carnivores, such as grizzly bears, wolves, and lynxes.

Biome 3: The Deciduous Forests   South of the taiga are the deciduous forests, where there's a lot of rain and a wide variety of plants and animals. The climate has distinct hot and cold seasons. There are many more life forms in the deciduous forests than there are in the tundra or taiga. Examples of fauna are deer, skunk, beavers, raccoon, foxes, black bears, and squirrels. Examples of flora are maple trees, elm trees, oak trees, and chestnut trees. Deciduous trees are characterized by the fact that they drop leaves in the winter and the leaves regrow in the spring.

Biome 4: The Grasslands (Savanna)   Grasslands are characterized by low-growing plants and a few scattered trees. Tree growth is limited by regular periods of drought, grazing, and occasional fires. Tropical savanna (such as those in Africa) support some of the largest herbivores, including antelope, kangaroos, zebras, giraffes, and elephants. Temperate savanna (such as the prairies of North America) support wild horses, bison, and antelope; however, much of the original prairie lands have been converted to farmland because of their especially fertile soil. In both types of grasslands, insects are the dominant herbivores.

Biome 5: The Tropical Rain Forests Tropical rain forests have the highest rainfall of any of the biomes and the greatest diversity in flora and fauna. Animal life includes insects, birds, monkeys, lizards, snakes, and tapirs. The trees grow very tall and many other plants grow around them, such as vines and smaller shrubs. The trees form a canopy above the rest of the vegetation, and sunlight barely reaches the lower regions.

Biome 6: The Desert Deserts are the driest of all the biomes; they receive fewer than 30 centimeters of rainfall per year. Although we mostly associate deserts with hot temperatures, cold deserts also exist. The main thing to remember about deserts is their dryness. Animals and plants that live in deserts must be adapted to live in an arid environment. Desert plants are cacti and other succulents; desert animals are birds, small rodents, lizards, and snakes.

Aquatic Biomes

Aquatic biomes are divided into marine (saltwater) and freshwater biomes.

Biome 1: The Intertidal Zone (Marine) This is the biome where land and water meet. The intertidal zone is subject to alternate periods of dryness and total submersion in water, as tides recede and come in. Organisms that live here include clams, snails, sea urchins, sea stars, crabs, barnacles, mussels, and sponges.

Biome 2: The Neritic Zone (Marine) This biome extends from the intertidal zone, at the shore, to the edge of the continental shelf. Organisms here include kelp and other seaweeds, crustaceans, sea urchins, sea stars, and many species of fish. In warm waters, such as in the tropics, coral reefs are found in the neritic zone, supporting an immense variety of organisms.

Biome 3: The Oceanic Zone (Marine) This biome is essentially open ocean. There is very little nutrient concentration here except for phytoplankton. There are many species of large, free-swimming animals that can search for food, such as fishes, sea turtles, large squids, and marine mammals. They often feed on one another. This biome can be further divided into pelagic (open water) and benthic (ocean bottom) zones. Also, the deepest parts of the ocean are known as abyssal zones.

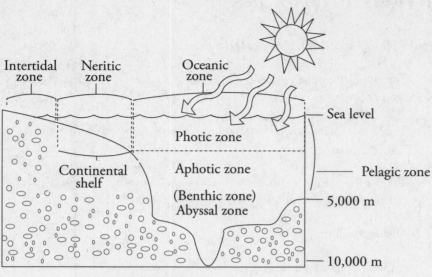

Marine Biomes

Photic vs. Aphotic Zones

The *photic zone* extends from the surface of the water to the depth to which light will penetrate. Obviously, photosynthetic organisms can thrive in this zone. Below the photic zone is the *aphotic zone*, where there is no light at all. Nutrients from the photic zone sink into this area.

Biome 4—The Littoral Zone (Freshwater) This biome is found near the shore of a lake. Many plants grow here and support a wide variety of consumers, such as insects, snails, worms, amphibians, and some fish.

Biome 5—The Limnetic Zone (Freshwater) This zone is farther from the shore and extends downward as far as light will penetrate. Again, because there is light available, many photosynthetic organisms and primary consumers thrive here.

Biome 6—The Profundal Zone (Freshwater) This is essentially the aphotic region of the lake. Nutrients from the limnetic zone float down to support some primary consumers in this area. The primary consumers then become food for secondary consumers.

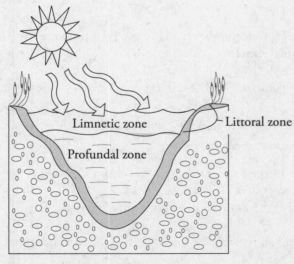

Freshwater Biomes

Quick Quiz #5

Fill in the blanks and check the appropriate boxes:

1.   The tropical rain forest has [☐ **greater** ☐ **lesser**] biological diversity than the tundra.

2.   The biome characterized by large numbers of evergreen conifers is the _____.

3.   The primary plant forms of the [☐ **taiga** ☐ **tundra** ☐ **desert**] are mosses, lichen, and wildflowers.

4.   The ocean floor is known as the _____ zone.

5.   Animals with adaptations for a dry environment would live in the [☐ **savanna** ☐ **desert**].

6.   The deepest zone of the ocean is the [☐ **abyssal zone** ☐ **pelagic zone**].

7.   Permanently frozen soil is a characteristic of _____.

8.   The biome with very fertile soil and many herbivores is the _____ _____.

9.   Deer, bears, and raccoon are found in the [☐ **tundra** ☐ **rain forest** ☐ **deciduous forest**], where as caribou and moose are found in the [☐ **tundra** ☐ **rain forest** ☐ **deciduous forest**].

10. Deciduous trees [☐ **do** ☐ **do not**] lose their leaves during cold seasons.

11. Phytoplankton would thrive well in the [☐ **limnetic zone** ☐ **profundal zone**].

12. Succulent plants are well suited to [☐ **savanna** ☐ **desert**].

13. Areas of water where light does not penetrate are known as _____ zones.

14. The most northern biome is the [☐ **taiga** ☐ **tundra**].

15. The tundra [☐ **does** ☐ **does not**] grow many trees.

16. Coral reefs can typically be found in the [☐ **intertidal zone** ☐ **neritic zone**].

Key Words

abiotic
biotic
population
exponential growth
limited growth
carrying capacity
niche
predation
coevolution
autotrophs
heterotrophs
food chain
primary producers
primary consumers
herbivore
secondary consumers
carnivore
omnivore
tertiary consumers
scavengers
ecological succession
pioneer organisms
climax community
ecosystem
the water cycle

the carbon cycle
the nitrogen cycle
evaporation
transpiration
biomes
biosphere
terrestrial biomes
tundra
taiga
deciduous forests
savanna
tropical rain forests
desert
aquatic biomes
marine biomes
freshwater biomes
intertidal zone
neritic zone
oceanic zone
photic zones
aphotic zones
littoral zone
limnetic zone
profundal zone

Summary

o   Populations are groups of individuals that inter-breed and share the same gene pool.

o   Populations can expand by exponential growth and by limited growth.

o   A community is a population that lives in a particular environment.

o   Food chains, food webs, and food pyramids show the movement of material and energy from one group of organisms to another.

o   Ecological succession is a change that a community will experience over time. It is not the same as evolution, however.

o   Three cycles—the water cycle, nitrogen cycle, and carbon cycle—move nutrients throughout ecosystems.

o   Biomes are the large areas classified by ecosystems.

Part III
Answers to In-Chapter Questions

Chapter 15
Answers to In-Chapter
Questions

CHAPTER 3

Quick Quiz #1

Check the appropriate boxes:

1. Water (H_2O) is an [☐ **organic** ■ **inorganic**] compound.
2. Cl_2 [☐ **is** ■ **is not**] a compound.
3. H_2O [■ **is** ☐ **is not**] a compound.
4. Methane (CH_4) is an [■ **organic** ☐ **inorganic**] compound.
5. Cl_2 [■ **is** ☐ **is not**] a molecule.
6. Carbon dioxide (CO_2) is an [☐ **organic** ■ **inorganic**] compound.
7. Products are found on the [■ **right** ☐ **left**] side of the arrow in a chemical reaction.

Quick Quiz #2

Fill in the blanks and check the appropriate boxes:

1. The bond that holds two amino acids together is called a ___peptide___ bond.
2. The assembly of a protein from its amino acid constituents involves the [☐ **addition** ■ **removal**] of water, and is called ___dehydration___.
3. An amino acid is a [■ **monomer** ☐ **polymer**] of a protein.
4. Because proteins are essentially chains of amino acids linked together by ___peptide___ bonds, a protein might also be called a ___polypeptide___.
5. The disassembly of a protein into its component amino acids is called ___hydrolysis___ and involves the [■ **addition** ☐ **removal**] of water.

Quick Quiz #3

Fill in the blanks and check the appropriate boxes:

1. Starch serves as a means of storing glucose in [■ **plants** ☐ **animals**].
2. A molecule of maltose is formed from two molecules of ___glucose___.
3. Glucose and fructose [☐ **are** ■ **are not**] identical molecules.
4. A molecule of glucose and a molecule of fructose, both of which are ___monosaccharides___, combine to form a molecule of ___sucrose___, which is a ___disaccharide___.
5. Cellulose is a ___polysaccharide___.
6. Glycogen serves as a means for storing glucose in [☐ **plants** ■ **animals**].
7. The chemical formula for both glucose and fructose is ___$C_6H_{12}O_6$___.
8. The chemical formula for sucrose is ___$C_{12}H_{22}O_{11}$___.
9. Cellulose and glycogen differ in the way that ___glucose___ molecules are bonded together.
10. The chemical formulas for sucrose and maltose [■ **are** ☐ **are not**] identical.

Quick Quiz #4

Fill in the blanks and check the appropriate boxes:

1. Triglycerides are made of one molecule of ___glycerol___ and three ___fatty acids___.
2. Lipids in general are [☐ **hydrophilic** ■ **hydrophobic**].
3. The primary lipid found in cell membranes is ___phospholipid___.
4. Steroid hormones are derived from ___cholesterol___.
5. Steroid hormones [■ **are** ☐ **are not**] hydrophobic.
6. Fats are stored in the body in the form of ___triglycerides___.

Quick Quiz #5

Fill in the blanks and check the appropriate boxes:

1. The fact that double-stranded DNA forms a double helix was discovered by ___Watson___ and ___Crick___.
2. The four DNA nucleotide bases are ___adenine___, ___thymine___, ___cytosine___, and ___guanine___.
3. RNA [☐ **is** ■ **is not**] a double-stranded molecule.
4. RNA nucleotides [☐ **do** ■ **do not**] contain the exact same bases as DNA nucleotides.
5. In DNA, guanine forms a base pair with ___cytosine___, whereas adenine forms a base pair with ___thymine___.
6. The nucleic acid "backbone" is made up of ___sugar___ and ___phosphate___.
7. The sugar in DNA is [☐ **ribose** ■ **deoxyribose**].
8. In RNA, adenine can form a base pair with ___uracil___.

CHAPTER 4

Quick Quiz #1

Fill in the blanks and check the appropriate boxes:

1. Animal cells [☐ **do** ■ **do not**] have cell walls.
2. Bacteria have cell walls made of ___peptidoglycan___.
3. Engulfing large particles in a vesicle is known as ___endocytosis___.
4. Facilitated diffusion is a way for [☐ **hydrophobic** ■ **hydrophilic**] substances to cross the cell membrane.
5. Fungi have cell walls made of ___chitin___, and plants have cell walls made of ___cellulose___.
6. Simple diffusion [☐ **does** ■ **does not**] require energy.
7. Hydrophobic substances cross the membrane by ___simple diffusion___.
8. A type of movement that requires energy and moves substances against their concentration gradients is called ___active transport___.
9. B
10. C

Organelle Function Matching Quiz

1. _K_ Golgi apparatus
2. _E_ Centrioles
3. _H_ Lysosomes
4. _G_ Rough ER
5. _C_ Cell membrane
6. _J_ Ribosomes
7. _D_ Nucleolus
8. _B_ Vacuole
9. _A_ Smooth ER
10. _F_ Mitochondria
11. _I_ Nucleus

A. cellular transport system

B. stores waste and other substances

C. selectively permeable barrier that regulates what enters and exits the cell

D. site of ribosome synthesis in the nucleus

E. related generally to formation of the spindle during mitosis

F. cellular respiration and ATP production; has double membrane

G. holds ribosomes that synthesize membrane or secreted proteins

H. contain hydrolytic enzymes; digest foreign substances and worn organelles

I. contains genetic material (DNA); control center of the cell

J. sites of protein synthesis

K. sorts and packages membrane and secreted proteins

Quick Quiz #2

Fill in the blanks and check the appropriate boxes:

1. The fact that enzymes interact with substrate by physically fitting together has given rise to the phrase "____lock____ and ____key____" theory.
2. Enzymes are known as organic _____catalysts_____.
3. When an enzyme has catalyzed a chemical reaction and the products are formed, the enzyme itself [□ **is** ■ **is not**] consumed and is [□ **unavailable** ■ **available**] to catalyze additional reactions.
4. The location on an enzyme where substrate binds is called the _____active site_____.

CHAPTER 5

Quick Quiz #1

Fill in the blanks and check the appropriate boxes:

1. The process of glycolysis produces ATP and NADH by converting one molecule of ___glucose___ to two molecules of ____pyruvate____.
2. The pyruvate dehydrogenase complex is found in the ____matrix____ of the mitochondria.
3. The process of glycolysis [□ **does** ■ **does not**] require oxygen.
4. ____Glycogen____ is made of many glucose molecules bonded together, and its function is to store energy.
5. When a molecule (such as an electron carrier) accepts a pair of electrons, we say it has become [■ **reduced** □ **oxidized**].
6. During the PDC, a molecule of pyruvate is converted to ____acetyl Co-A____, a molecule of ____NADH____ is produced, and _CO_2_ is lost.
7. The PDC [■ **is** □ **is not**] an aerobic process.

Quick Quiz #2

Fill in the blanks and check the appropriate boxes:

1. The Krebs cycle [■ **does** ☐ **does not**] require oxygen.
2. The principal substance that enters the Krebs cycle is ___acetyl Co-A___.
3. Oxygen is also known as the _____final electron acceptor_____.
4. One of the goals of electron transport is to [☐ **reduce** ■ **oxidize**] the electron carriers back to "empty."
5. Electron transport occurs along the _____inner membrane_____ of the mitochondria.
6. The products of the Krebs cycle are three molecules of _____NADH_____, one molecule of _____ATP_____, and one molecule of ___FADH$_2$___.
7. ATP synthase relies on the facilitated diffusion of ___H$^+$___ ions down their gradient to produce ATP.
8. In the last step of the electron transport chain, oxygen accepts electrons to form ___water___.

Quick Quiz #3

Fill in the blanks and check the appropriate boxes:

1. Fermentation produces _____ethanol_____ in yeast and ___lactic acid___ in muscle cells.
2. Anaerobic organisms [■ **do** ☐ **do not**] conduct glycolysis.
3. Anaerobic respiration (fermentation) produces [■ **less** ☐ **more**] ATP than aerobic respiration.
4. In fermentation, NADH is _____oxidized_____ to NAD$^+$, whereas pyruvate is _____reduced_____.
5. Anaerobic organisms [☐ **do** ■ **do not**] conduct the Krebs cycle.

CHAPTER 6

Quick Quiz #1

Fill in the blanks and check the appropriate boxes:

1. If two individuals are of the same species, then the chromosomes in one individual's cells [☐ **are** ■ **are not**] identical to the chromosomes in the other individual's cells.
2. The enzyme that runs DNA replication is called ___DNA polymerase___.
3. Humans have ___46___ total chromosomes found as ___2___ sets of ___23___ chromosomes each.
4. One strand of DNA serves as a _____template_____ for the creation of a complementary strand.
5. If two cells are taken from the same individual, the chromosomes in one cell [■ **are** ☐ **are not**] identical to the chromosomes in the other cell.
6. Homologous chromosomes [☐ **are** ■ **are not**] identical.

Quick Quiz #2

Fill in the blanks and check the appropriate boxes:

1. Production of a strand of RNA from a strand of DNA is called ___transcription___.
2. The sequence of RNA that is complementary to the DNA sequence CAGTATACG is ___GUCAUAUGC___.
3. Portions of DNA that carry instructions for protein synthesis are called [■ **genes** □ **codons**].
4. ___tRNA___ carries amino acids from the cytoplasm to the ribosomes during protein translation.
5. The sequence of codons on mRNA is read in [□ **overlapping** ■ **nonoverlapping**] sequence.
6. The three "stop" codons are ___UAA___, ___UGA___, and ___UAG___.
7. Synthesis of protein using a strand of RNA is called ___translation___.
8. The "start" codon is [■ **AUG** □ **UAG**], and it codes for ___methionine___.

Quick Quiz #3

Fill in the blanks and check the appropriate boxes:

1. In order to base-pair, the anticodon on a tRNA must be ___complementary___ to an mRNA codon.
2. Peptide bonds are formed between [□ **tRNAs** ■ **amino acids**].
3. The next amino acid for the protein being translated binds (attaches to its tRNA) in the [■ **A-site** □ **P-site**].
4. The growing protein is attached to the ribosome through a tRNA in the [□ **A-site** ■ **P-site**].
5. When a stop codon appears in the [■ **A-site** □ **P-site**], the protein is ___released___ from the ribosome.

CHAPTER 7

Quick Quiz #1

Fill in the blanks and check the appropriate boxes:

1. A human cell, after interphase, has a total of ___46___ chromosomes, each made up of two ___chromatids___.
2. During the stage called interphase, [■ **all** □ **only some**] of the cell's chromosomes replicate.
3. According to current biological terminology, a human cell, after interphase, has in its nucleus a total of [□ **92** ■ **46**] chromosomes, each chromosome having at its center a ___centromere___ that joins the chromatids together.
4. DNA replication is [□ **the only process** ■ **one of many processes**] that takes place during interphase.

Quick Quiz #2

Fill in the blanks and check the appropriate boxes:

1. The cell's chromosomes become visible during a stage called _____prophase_____.
2. The spindle apparatus forms during a stage called [☐ **anaphase**
    ■ **prophase** ☐ **metaphase**].
3. The division of the cell's cytoplasm is known as _____cytokinesis_____, and this occurs
    during [☐ **prophase** ☐ **anaphase** ■ **telophase**].
4. Duplicate chromosomes (the chromatids) separate from each other and move to opposite poles of
    the cell during a stage called _____anaphase_____.
5. During a stage called _____interphase_____, all of a cell's chromosomes replicate.
6. The centromeres divide during a stage called _____anaphase_____.
7. During prophase, the _____centrioles_____ move away from one another toward opposite sides
    of the cell.

Quick Quiz #3

Fill in the blanks and check the appropriate boxes:

1. If, for a particular organism, the diploid number of chromosomes is 10, then the haploid number is
    _____5_____.
2. The first metaphase of meiosis (metaphase I) differs from metaphase of mitosis in that a ___pair___
    of chromosomes lines up on each spindle fiber.
3. The four cells resulting from meiosis are _____haploid_____.
4. Crossing over occurs after _____synaspsis_____.
5. The word [■ **haploid** ☐ **diploid**] refers to a cell for which each chromosome does NOT have a
    homologous partner.
6. The first anaphase of meiosis (anaphase I) differs from anaphase of mitosis in that centromeres
    [☐ **do** ■ **do not**] divide.
7. Prophase I of meiosis [☐ **is** ■ **is not**] similar to prophase of mitosis.

Quick Quiz #4

Fill in the blanks and check the appropriate boxes:

1. The cells produced at the end of telophase I are considered to be
    [■ **haploid** ☐ **diploid**].
2. Spermatogenesis begins at _____puberty_____ and lasts _____for the life of the man_____.
3. _____4_____ mature sperm are produced from a single spermatogonium.
4. The female gonad is the _____ovary_____.
5. Oogenesis begins at _____puberty_____ and ends at _____menopause_____.
6. [☐ **Four** ■ **One**] mature ova (ovum) are (is) produced from a single primary oocyte.
7. Spermatogenesis takes place on a [■ **daily** ☐ **monthly**] basis, whereas oogenesis takes place on a
    [☐ **daily** ■ **monthly**] basis.
8. The cells that disintegrate during oogenesis are called _____polar bodies_____.

CHAPTER 8

Quick Quiz #1

Fill in the blanks and check the appropriate boxes:

1. A
2. The term *allele* [☐ **is** ☑ **is not**] precisely synonymous with the term *gene*.
3. C
4. If, in a particular organism, one allele on one member of a homologous chromosome pair codes for blue eye color, and a corresponding allele on the other codes for brown eye color, the organism is said to be [☐ **homozygous** ☑ **heterozygous**] for eye color.
5. If an organism is heterozygous for eye color, with one allele coding for green and the other allele coding for gray, the organism will have [☑ **green eyes** ☐ **gray eyes**] if green is dominant, and [☐ **green eyes** ☑ **gray eyes**] if gray is dominant.
6. If, for a particular species, the allele that produces a disease called erythemia is dominant and the corresponding allele that produces the absence of disease (a normal organism) is recessive, then
    (a) an organism with a genotype that is heterozygous for the trait will have the phenotype [☐ **normal** ☑ **erythemia**].
    (b) An organism with a genotype that is homozygous for the dominant allele will have the phenotype [☐ **normal** ☑ **erythemia**].
    (c) An organism with a genotype that is homozygous for the recessive allele will have the phenotype [☑ **normal** ☐ **erythemia**].
    (d) An organism with a phenotype that is normal must have a genotype that is [☑ **homozygous** ☐ **heterozygous**].

Quick Quiz #2

Fill in the blanks and check the appropriate boxes:

1. A male person receives from his father a(n) [☐ **X** ☑ **Y**] chromosome.
2. A male person [☐ **may** ☑ **must**] have the genotype [☑ **XY** ☐ **XX** ☐ **YY**].
3. A female person [☐ **may** ☑ **must**] have the genotype [☐ **XY** ☑ **XX** ☐ **YY**].
4. In terms of sex, all persons, male or female, receive from their mothers a(n) __X__ chromosome.
5. In terms of sex, all females receive from their fathers a(n) __X__ chromosome.

Genotype Check-In

- With reference to the parents whose genotypes are shown on pages 156–157.
    (a) __50%__ of children are likely to be male.
    (b) __50%__ of children are likely to be female.
    (c) There is [☐ **no** ☑ **some**] likelihood that a child will have phenotype hemophilia.
    (d) There is [☐ **some** ☑ **no**] likelihood that a female child will have phenotype hemophilia.
    (e) There is [☐ **no** ☑ **some**] likelihood that a male child will have phenotype hemophilia.
    (f) The likelihood that a male child will be born with hemophilia is __25%__.

Quick Quiz #3

Consider the pedigree below, then fill in the blanks and check the appropriate boxes:

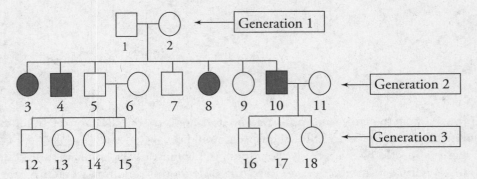

1. This condition is [☐ **dominant** ■ **recessive**].
    Because the condition "skips" generations it is recessive. Look at individual 10. Neither his parents
    nor his offspring have the condition.
2. This condition is [■ **autosomal** ☐ **X-linked**].
    Because equal numbers of males and females display the condition, it is autosomal. X-linked condi-
    tions are seen more frequently in males.
3. The genotype of individual 10 is [■ **homozygous** ☐ **heterozygous**].
    Because the condition is recessive, and individual 10 is affected by the condition (displays the phe-
    notype), then he must be homozygous for the condition.
4. The genotype of individual 17 is [☐ **homozygous** ■ **heterozygous**].
    Individual 17 is the child of an affected (homozygous recessive) parent and an unaffected par-
    ent. Remember that individuals who marry into a family are considered to be completely normal;
    therefore, individual 11 does not carry the allele and is homozygous for the dominant (normal)
    condition. Let's draw a Punnett square to determine the genotypes of their offspring. We'll use N
    to represent the normal allele and n to represent the abnormal allele.

	Female	
	N	N
n	Nn	Nn
n	Nn	Nn

(Male)

As you can see, all offspring would have the genotype Nn (heterozygous) and would not display the
condition.
5. The genotypes of individuals 1 and 2 are [☐ **homozygous** ■ **heterozygous**].
    Individuals 1 and 2 must be heterozygous for the condition. Neither of them display the affected
    phenotype; therefore, they must each have at least one normal allele (genotype N/?). Because they
    have offspring that are affected by the condition, they must also each have one abnormal allele
    (genotype Nn). The only way to produce homozygous recessive offspring is if each parent donates a
    recessive allele. Here's the Punnett square:

                              Female

                         N   n

              N   ┌──────────┬──────────┐
                   │   Nn   │   Nn   │
      Male   ├──────────┼──────────┤
              n   │   Nn   │   nn   │
                   └──────────┴──────────┘

6. If individual 3 were to marry a normal male who does not carry the allele for the condition, the
    probability they would produce affected offspring would be _____ zero _____.
    Individual 3 is affected by this recessive condition, so she must have a homozygous recessive geno-
    type (nn). A normal male who does not carry the allele for this condition would have the homozy-
    gous dominant genotype (NN). All their offspring would be heterozygous and normal. Here's the
    Punnett square:

                              Female

                         n   n

              N   ┌──────────┬──────────┐
                   │   Nn   │   Nn   │
      Male   ├──────────┼──────────┤
              N   │   Nn   │   Nn   │
                   └──────────┴──────────┘

7. If individual 4 were to marry a female carrier of the condition (a female heterozygous for the condi-
    tion), the probability they would produce affected offspring would be ___ 50% ___.
    Individual 4 is affected by the condition and therefore has the homozygous recessive genotype (nn).
    If he were to marry a heterozygous female, the probability of producing an affected child would be
    50%. Here's the Punnett square:

                              Female

                         N   n

              n   ┌──────────┬──────────┐
                   │   Nn   │   nn   │
      Male   ├──────────┼──────────┤
              n   │   Nn   │   nn   │
                   └──────────┴──────────┘

CHAPTER 9

Quick Quiz #1

Fill in the blanks and check the appropriate boxes:

1. According to the heterotroph hypothesis, hydrogen [■ **was** ☐ **was not**] a chief component of the atmosphere when life began.
2. At present, the gas of highest concentration in Earth's atmosphere is [☐ **helium** ☐ **oxygen** ■ **nitrogen**].
3. According to the heterotroph hypothesis, water [■ **was** ☐ **was not**] a chief component of the atmosphere when life began.
4. The primary organisms on early Earth were _____anaerobic_____.
5. According to the heterotroph hypothesis, methane [■ **was** ☐ **was not**] a chief component of the atmosphere when life began.
6 According to the heterotroph hypothesis, oxygen [☐ **was** ■ **was not**] a chief component of the atmosphere when life began.
7. The primary organisms on Earth today are _____aerobic_____.
8 According to the heterotroph hypothesis, ammonia [■ **was** ☐ **was not**] a chief component of the atmosphere when life began.

Quick Quiz #2

Fill in the blanks and check the appropriate boxes:

1. The phrase "_____genetic variability_____" refers to the fact that within any population of any species, genotypes vary (i.e., the gene pool features a wide variety of alleles).
2. Genetic variability [☐ **is** ■ **is not**] caused by a species' ability to adapt to existing environmental conditions.
3. Genetic variability [■ **is** ☐ **is not**] attributable to random mutation.
4. Once a mutation has occurred, all members of the population [☐ **will** ■ **will not**] display the results of that mutation.
5. Genetic variability [■ **is** ☐ **is not**] a property of all populations.
6. If a mutation were to occur in a somatic cell instead of a gamete (sperm or ovum), that mutation [☐ **could** ■ **could not**] cause genetic variability in the population.

Quick Quiz #3

Fill in the blanks and check the appropriate boxes:

1. Evolution [☐ **always** ■ **sometimes**] results in the production of a new species.
2. Speciation [■ **increases** ☐ **decreases**] biological diversity.
3. In the course of divergent evolution, two populations become [☐ **more** ■ **less**] similar to each other with regard to behaviors and traits.
4. Evolution means a change in a population's _____gene pool_____.
5. If a population is geographically divided, it [☐ **cannot** ■ **may**] give rise to two separate species.
6. Evolution that results in two species becoming more similar to each other in terms of behaviors and traits is called _____convergent_____ evolution.
7. Divergent evolution can result from [☐ **only physical** ☐ **only behavioral** ■ **both physical and behavioral**] selection pressures from the environment.
8. Convergent evolution [☐ **can** ■ **cannot**] result in speciation.

Quick Quiz #4

Fill in the blanks and check the appropriate boxes:

1. The science of classification is called [☐ **taxidermy** ■ **taxonomy**].
2. The conventional ordering of phylogeny is domain, kingdom, _____phylum_____, _____class_____, _____order_____, _____family_____, _____genus_____, _____species_____.
3. The members of a kingdom [☐ **do** ■ **do not**] have more in common than do the members of an order.
4. The members of an order [■ **do** ☐ **do not**] have more in common than do the members of a class.

Quick Quiz #5

Fill in the blanks and check the appropriate boxes:

1. A
2. Soft-bodied animals with hard external shells are classified as _mollusks_.
3. With respect to the evolution of chordates, fish appeared [■ **before** ☐ **after**] birds, and birds appeared [■ **before** ☐ **after**] mammals.
4. Animals with jointed appendages, hard exoskeletons, and segmented bodies are classified as _____arthropods_____.
5. Prokaryotes [☐ **do** ■ **do not**] have a nucleus.
6. A
7. D
8. Having flower parts in multiples of four or five is a characteristic of [☐ **monocots** ■ **dicots**].
9. Protists [■ **do** ☐ **do not**] have a nucleus.
10. Mosses and liverworts are examples of _____nonvascular_____ plants.
11. Cyanobacteria [■ **can** ☐ **cannot**] photosynthesize.
12. Earthworms and other segmented worms belong to phylum [■ **Annelida** ☐ **Arthropoda**].
13. The order in which chordates appeared on Earth is (1) fish, (2) _amphibia_, (3) _____reptiles_____, (4) _____birds_____, (5) _____mammals_____.
14. Plants with parallel veins in their leaves and flower parts in multiples of three are classified as [■ **monocots** ☐ **dicots**].
15. Conifers, such as pine trees, are classified as [☐ **angiosperms** ■ **gymnosperms**].

CHAPTER 10

Quick Quiz #1

Fill in the blanks and check the appropriate boxes:

1. The _____NA^+/K^+ ATPase_____ is a membrane protein that pumps three sodium ions out of the cell and two potassium ions into the cell.
2. Sodium ions [☐ **can** ■ **cannot**] cross back into the cell after being pumped out.
3. Dendrites [■ **receive** ☐ **transmit**] an electrical impulse.
4. The direction in which an impulse travels through a neuron is _dendrites_ to _____cell body_____ to _____axon_____.
5. Potassium concentration is [■ **higher** ☐ **lower**] inside the cell than outside.
6. The resting membrane potential of the cell is _____−70 mV_____.

7. Sodium concentration is [□ **higher**   ■ **lower**] inside the cell than outside.
8. The axon of a neuron carries the nerve impulse [□ **toward**   ■ **away from**] the cell body.

Quick Quiz #2

Fill in the blanks and check the appropriate boxes:

1. Depolarization results from an [■ **influx**   □ **efflux**] of [■ **sodium**   □ **potassium**] ions.
2. Rapid, "jumping" conduction is called _____saltatory conduction_____.
3. Threshold potential is [□ **–70 mV**   ■ **–50 mV**].
4. A return to the resting, polarized state is called _____repolarization_____.
5. The small portion of a neuron's membrane that is undergoing an action potential is relatively [■ **positive**   □ **negative**] on the inside and [□ **positive**   ■ **negative**] on the outside.
6. The time during which a portion of the membrane is unable to fire an action potential (because of the fact that it has just fired one) is called the _____refractory period_____.
7. In a myelinated axon, action potentials occur only at the [□ **Schwann cells**   ■ **nodes of Ranvier**].
8. Repolarization results from an [□ **influx**   ■ **efflux**] of [□ **sodium**   ■ **potassium**] ions.
9. Ion channels that open at a particular membrane potential are said to be _____voltage-gated_____.

Quick Quiz #3

Fill in the blanks and check the appropriate boxes:

1. A neuron whose resting potential is moving away from threshold is said to be [□ **stimulated**   ■ **inhibited**].
2. The small space between the axon terminus of one neuron and the dendrites of the next neuron is called the _____synaptic cleft_____.
3. A synapse can be found between a [□ **neuron and an organ**   □ **neuron and a neuron**   ■ **both of these**].
4. The most common neurotransmitter in the body is _____acetylcholine_____.
5. A neurotransmitter is released from [■ **vesicles**   □ **receptors**] and binds to [□ **vesicles**   ■ **receptors**].
6. Receptors that open sodium channels would cause the neuron to _____depolarize_____.
7. A neuron will fire an action potential only if its membrane potential reaches _____threshold_____.

Quick Quiz #4

Fill in the blanks and check the appropriate boxes:

1. The CNS consists of the _____brain_____ and the _____spinal cord_____.
2. Motor neurons are part of the [□ **CNS**   ■ **PNS**].
3. Interneurons are part of the [■ **CNS**   □ **PNS**].
4. The _____hypothalamus_____ maintains body homeostasis.
5. Conscious awareness of our selves and our surroundings is controlled by the [■ **cerebrum**   □ **cerebellum**] of the brain.
6. The [■ **somatic**   □ **sympathetic**] division of the PNS controls the skeletal muscles.
7. E
8. The [□ **sympathetic**   □ **somatic**   ■ **parasympathetic**] division of the PNS is in control of a person watching TV.
9. C

10. Neurons of the PNS are [☐ **entirely separated from** ■ **connected to**] neurons of the CNS.
11. Conscious thought processes are carried out by the ___cerebrum___ .

Quick Quiz #5
Fill in the blanks and check the appropriate boxes:

1. Peptide hormones have receptors [■ **outside** ☐ **inside**] the cell, and steroids have receptors [☐ **outside** ■ **inside**] the cell.
2. The organs that are affected by a particular hormone are referred to as that hormone's ___target organs___ .
3. The endocrine system is [☐ **faster** ■ **slower**] than the nervous system.
4. Peptide hormones cause their effects [■ **more** ☐ **less**] rapidly than steroid hormones.
5. Steroid hormones cause their effects by ___modifying transcription___ .
6. Steroid hormones are derived from [■ **cholesterol** ☐ **amino acids**].

Quick Quiz #6
On each blank line place the letter that designates the appropriate hormone.

1. The pancreatic islet cells secrete ___F___ and ___I___ .
2. The ovaries secrete ___A___ and ___N___ .
3. The anterior pituitary secretes ___B___ , ___E___ , ___H___ , ___K___ , ___L___ , and ___R___ .
4. The thyroid gland secretes ___S___ and ___T___ .
5. The adrenal cortex secretes ___C___ and ___O___ .
6. The posterior pituitary secretes ___- J___ and ___Q___ .
7. The adrenal medulla secretes ___D___ and ___P___ .
8. The testes secrete ___M___ .
9. The parathyroid gland secretes ___G___ .

A. estrogen
B. ACTH
C. aldosterone
D. epinephrine
E. prolactin
F. glucagon
G. parathormone
H. LH
I. insulin
J. oxytocin
K. growth hormone
L. FSH
M. testosterone
N. progesterone
O. cortisol
P. norepinephrine
Q. ADH
R. TSH
S. thyroxine
T. calcitonin

Quick Quiz #7

On each blank line place the letter that designates the appropriate target organ. Letters can be used more than once.

1. estrogen / progesterone __E__
2. ACTH __G__
3. aldosterone __H__
4. epinephrine / norepinephrine __A__
5. prolactin __F__
6. glucagon __K__
7. parathormone __B__
8. LH / FSH __L__
9. insulin __A__
10. oxytocin __E__
11. growth hormone __A__
12. testosterone __C__
13. cortisol __A__
14. ADH __H__
15. TSH __D__
16. thyroxine __A__
17. calcitonin __B__

A. all cells in the body
B. bones
C. male body
D. thyroid gland
E. uterus
F. mammary glands
G. adrenal cortex
H. kidneys
I. female body
J. testes
K. liver
L. ovaries and testes

Quick Quiz #8

On each blank line place the letter that designates the appropriate effect in the body.

1. estrogen __K__
2. ACTH __E__
3. aldosterone __Q__
4. epinephrine / nonepinephine __N__
5. prolactin __A__
6. glucagon __H__
7. parathormone __S__
8. LH __L__
9. insulin __R__
10. oxytocin __B__
11. growth hormone __G__
12. testosterone __D__

A. production of breast milk
B. contract uterus, releases breast milk
C. causes gluconeogenesis, increases blood glucose levels
D. maintains male sex characteristics
E. causes release of hormones from adrenal cortex
F. increases body metabolism
G. growth of the body
H. breakdown of glycogen, increases blood glucose levels
I. builds bone, decreases blood calcium
J. causes kidneys to retain water
K. maintains female sex characteristics, builds uterine lining
L. releases testosterone in male, forms corpus luteum in female

13.	cortisol __C__	M.	maintains and enhances uterine lining
14.	ADH __J__	N.	prolongs and enhances "fight or flight" response
15.	TSH __O__	O.	causes thyroid gland to release thyroxine
16.	thyroxine __F__	P.	causes spermatogenesis in male, oogenesis in female
17.	FSH __P__	Q.	causes kidney to retain sodium
18.	progesterone __M__	R.	allows cells to take up glucose, decreases blood glucose levels
19.	calcitonin __I__	S.	breaks down bone, increases blood calcium

Quick Quiz #9

Fill in the blanks and check the appropriate boxes:

1. [☐ **Red blood cells**   ■ **White blood cells**] function in the immune system.
2. Hemoglobin contains _____iron_____ and can bind _____oxygen_____.
3. C
4. B-cells make _____antibodies_____.
5. Insufficient iron in the diet leads to insufficient _____hemoglobin_____ and the disease _____anemia_____.
6. [☐ **Killer**   ■ **Helper**] T-cells are T-cells that help B-cells and other T-cells reproduce.
7. T-cells are [■ **white**   ☐ **red**] blood cells.
8. Blood cells involved in blood clotting are called _____platelets_____.
9. B

Genetics Questions

Practice Question 1: A man with blood type AB marries a woman who is homozygous for blood type A (genotype $I^A I^A$). What is the probability they will produce a child with blood type B?

The man with blood type AB has the genotype $I^A I^B$. The woman's genotype is given ($I^A I^A$). Let's construct a Punnett square:

	I^A	I^A
I^A	$I^A I^A$	$I^A I^A$
I^B	$I^A I^B$	$I^A I^B$

There are only two possible genotypes for their children: $I^A I^A$ and $I^A I^B$. $I^A I^A$ corresponds to blood type A, and $I^A I^B$ coresponds to blood type AB, so the probability of producing a child with blood type B is 0%.

Practice Question 2: Which blood type(s) are NOT possible from a cross between a person with blood type AB and a person heterozygous for blood type B (I^Bi)?

A person with blood type AB has the genotype I^AI^B. The heterozygous genotype for blood type B is given as I^Bi. Let's construct a Punnett square:

	I^A	I^B
I^B	I^AI^B	I^AI^B
i	I^Ai	I^Bi

The possible genotypes of their children are I^AI^B (blood type AB), I^Ai (blood type A), and I^Bi (blood type B). The only blood type not resulting from this cross is blood type O (genotype ii).

Practice Question 3: Could a woman with blood type B and a man with blood type A produce a child with blood type O?

Yes. A woman with blood type B could have one of the following genotypes: I^BI^B or I^Bi. A man with blood type A could have one of the following genotypes: I^AI^A or I^Ai. Blood type O can only result from the genotype ii, and that genotype could result from a cross between I^Bi (type B) and I^Ai (type A) individuals. Here's the Punnett square:

	I^A	i
I^B	I^AI^B	iI^B
i	I^Ai	ii

Quick Quiz #10
Fill in the blanks and check the appropriate boxes:

1. The genotype(s) for blood type O is (are) _____ _ii_ _____.
2. Blood type AB is sometimes called the [☐ **universal donor**　■ **universal recipient**].
3. Blood type A can receive blood from blood type (s) _____ _A and O_ _____.
4. Blood type B can donate blood to blood type(s) _____ _B and AB_ _____.
5. The probability of a man homozygous for blood type B and a woman homozygous for blood type A producing a child with blood type A is [■ **0%**　☐ **25%**　☐ **50%**　☐ **75%**　☐ **100%**].
6. The genotype(s) for blood type A is (are) _____ _I^AI^A and I^Ai_ .
7. Blood type AB can donate blood to blood type [■ **AB**　☐ **A**　☐ **B**　☐ **O**　☐ **all of them**].
8. Alleles I^A and I^B are said to be _____ _codominant_ _____.

Quick Quiz #11

Fill in the blanks and check the appropriate boxes:

1. [■ **Veins** □ **Capillaries** □ **Arteries**] are blood vessels that return blood to the heart.
2. _____Lymphatic vessels_____ return excess tissue fluid to the blood vessels.
3. The type of blood being carried [□ **does** ■ **does not**] matter when determining whether a blood vessel is an artery or a vein.
4. Blood pressure in the veins is [□ **high** ■ **low**].
5. Blood pressure in the arteries is [■ **high** □ **low**].
6. Blood flow in the capillaries is [□ **fast** ■ **slow**].
7. [■ **Lymph nodes** □ **Lymph vessels**] filter potentially harmful things from the lymph before it is returned to the veins.
8. The diameter of an artery is [□ **larger** ■ **smaller**] than the combined diameters of the capillaries.
9. Lymphatic vessels [■ **do** □ **do not**] have valves.
10. Blood moves through the veins and lymph moves through the lymphatic vessels when nearby _____skeletal muscles_____ contract and squeeze the vessels.

Quick Quiz #12

Fill in the blanks and check the appropriate boxes:

1. Blood leaves the heart from [■ **ventricles** □ **atria**] and enters the heart at [□ **ventricles** ■ **atria**].
2. The aorta carries [■ **oxygen-rich** □ **oxygen-poor**] blood [■ **away from** □ **toward**] the heart, and the two vena cavae carry [□ **oxygen-rich** ■ **oxygen-poor**] blood [□ **away from** ■ **toward**] the heart.
3. B
4. The _____capillaries_____ are the site of exchange between blood and tissue.
5. The pulmonary arteries carry [□ **oxygen-rich** ■ **oxygen-poor**] blood [■ **away from** □ **toward**] the heart, and the pulmonary veins carry [■ **oxygen-rich** □ **oxygen-poor**] blood [□ **away from** ■ **toward**] the heart.
6. Blood that enters the right atrium after touring the entire body is [□ **oxygen-rich** ■ **oxygen-poor**].
7. The [■ **semilunar** □ **atrioventricular**] valves separate the ventricles from the arteries.
8. E
9. Moving air into and out of the lungs is called _____ventilation_____.
10. The [■ **pulmonary** □ **systemic**] circuit sends blood to the lungs.
11. The _____respiratory_____ zone of the lungs is where gas exchange takes place.
12. The first heart sound is the closing of the [□ **semilunar** ■ **atrioventricular**] valves at the [□ **end** ■ **beginning**] of heart contraction.
13. From the right ventricle [□ **oxygen-rich** ■ **oxygen-poor**] blood is passed to the [■ **pulmonary arteries** □ **pulmonary veins**] and then to the lungs.
14. The larynx is part of the [■ **conduction** □ **respiratory**] zone.
15. Oxygen-rich blood enters the heart at the _____left atrium_____.
16. Blood gases (oxygen and carbon dioxide) are [□ **hydrophilic** ■ **hydrophobic**].

Quick Quiz #13

Fill in the blanks and check the appropriate boxes:

1. Most of the carbon dioxide in the blood is carried as _____carbonic acid_____ and _____bicarbonate_____.
2. If your blood is too acidic, your pH is [☐ **higher** ■ **lower**] and you will breathe [☐ **slower** ■ **faster**].
3. The system that can change pH more quickly is the [■ **respiratory** ☐ **renal**] system.
4. The primary muscle of respiration is the _____diaphragm_____.
5. Breath rate is adjusted by the _____medulla oblongata_____.
6. When the diaphragm contracts it [☐ **curves upward** ■ **flattens downward**].
7. Normal blood pH is approximately _____7.4_____.
8. When the chest cavity gets smaller, air in the lungs rushes [☐ **inward** ■ **outward**].

Quick Quiz #14

Fill in the blanks and check the appropriate boxes:

1. The pancreas is [☐ **part of the alimentary canal** ■ **an accessory organ**].
2. The order of the organs in the alimentary canal is _____mouth_____, _____esophagus_____, _____stomach_____, _____small intestine_____, _____large intestine_____.
3. The stomach [■ **does** ☐ **does not**] secrete a digestive enzyme.
4. The salivary glands secrete an enzyme called [☐ **pepsin** ■ **amylase**] that helps in the digestion of [■ **carbohydrates** ☐ **proteins**].
5. The colon is the [☐ **small** ■ **large**] intestine.
6. The vitamin needed for blood clotting is vitamin __K__, and it is made by bacteria in the [☐ **small** ■ **large**] intestine.
7. D
8. A
9. The stomach is [☐ **alkaline** ■ **acidic**], which means that its pH is [■ **low** ☐ **high**].
10. The pancreas produces [■ **bicarbonate** ☐ **bile**].
11. The function of the large intestine is to _____reabsorb water_____.
12. Vitamin C is necessary to make [■ **collagen** ☐ **retinal**].
13. Pepsin is an _____enzyme_____, secreted by the _____stomach_____. It helps in the digestion of _____proteins_____.
14. Bile [☐ **digests** ■ **emulsifies**] fats.
15. The _____liver_____ produces proteins and regulates glycogen metabolism.

Quick Quiz #15

Fill in the blanks and check the appropriate boxes:

1. The three processes used by the nephron to make urine are _____filtration_____, _____reabsorption_____, and _____secretion_____.
2. The [■ **loop of Henle** ☐ **collecting duct**] sets up a concentration gradient in the medulla.
3. [☐ **Secretion** ■ **Reabsorption**] means taking a substance from the urine and returning it to the blood.
4. Glucose is always [☐ **secreted** ■ **reabsorbed**].
5. The kidney helps to regulate blood pressure by releasing [☐ **aldosterone** ■ **renin**].

6. The [□ **ureter**   ■ **urethra**] carries urine from the bladder to the outside of the body.
7. Filtration occurs at the _____ glomerulus _____ .
8. ADH increases the amount of [■ **water**   □ **sodium**] reabsorbed from filtrate.
9. Most reabsorption and secretion occur in the ___ proximal convoluted tubule ___ .
10. ADH levels are [■ **high**   □ **low**] when the body is dehydrated, and this causes the urine to be [□ **dilute**   ■ **concentrated**].
11. The three main waste products found in urine are ___ urea ___ , ___ uric acid ___ , and _____ creatinine _____ .

Quick Quiz #16

Fill in the blanks and check the appropriate boxes:

1. Smooth muscle is found in the _____ walls of hollow organs _____ .
2. The deepest layer of the skin is the [□ **dermis**   □ **epidermis**   ■ **hypodermis**].
3. Spiders have [■ **exoskeletons**   □ **endoskeletons**].
4. The two proteins found in muscle cell sarcomeres are ___ actin ___ and ___ myosin ___ .
5. When the body gets too warm, dermal blood vessels [□ **constrict**   ■ **dilate**], and shivering [□ **is initiated**   ■ **stops**].
6. Muscles are attached to bones by [□ **ligaments**   ■ **tendons**].
7. In a sarcomere, [■ **actin**   □ **myosin**] attaches to the Z-lines.
8. The neurotransmitter used to stimulate muscle contraction is ___ acetylcholine ___ .
9. [□ **Cardiac**   ■ **Skeletal**] muscle is voluntary (under conscious control).
10. Bones are attached to other bones by [■ **ligaments**   □ **tendons**].
11. Cardiac muscle is found in [■ **the heart only**   □ **both the heart and the blood vessels**].

Quick Quiz #17

Fill in the blanks and check the appropriate boxes:

1. Progesterone is secreted during the [□ **secretory**   ■ **luteal**] phase of the ovarian cycle.
2. C
3. The ovary is controlled by [■ **FSH and LH**   □ **estrogen and progesterone**] from the anterior pituitary, and it secretes [□ **FSH and LH**   ■ **estrogen and progesterone**] that affect the uterus.
4. ___ hCG ___ prolongs the life of the corpus luteum if fertilization and implantation occur.
5. The ___ vas deferens ___ is a large duct that conducts sperm from the testes to the urethra.
6. A surge in [□ **FSH**   ■ **LH**] causes ovulation.
7. The remnants of a follicle after ovulation become the ___ corpus luteum ___ .
8. [■ **Estrogen**   □ **Progesterone**] causes the uterine lining to grow during the proliferative phase.
9. ___ Semen ___ is a nourishing fluid that carries sperm. It is secreted by glands in the male reproductive system.
10. Estrogen causes growth of the uterine lining during the [■ **proliferative**   □ **follicular**] phase of the uterine cycle.
11. D

Quick Quiz #18
Fill in the blanks and check the appropriate boxes:

1. B
2. D
3. The human eye develops from [☐ **mesoderm** ■ **ectoderm**].
4. Blood vessels develop from [☐ **endoderm** ■ **mesoderm**].
5. C
6. The membrane that most directly surrounds the embryo is the [☐ **chorion** ■ **amnion**].
7. Organogenesis occurs during [■ **neurulation** ☐ **gastrulation**].
8. Implantation occurs [☐ **before** ■ **after**] cleavage.
9. A blastocyst forms [☐ **before** ■ **after**] a morula.
10. Neurulation occurs [■ **before** ☐ **after**] the fetal stage.
11. The _____acrosome_____ is the region at the top of the sperm that contains digestive enzymes to help the sperm penetrate the ovum.
12. The nervous system develops from [☐ **endoderm** ■ **ectoderm**].
13. The kidneys develop from [■ **mesoderm** ☐ **endoderm**].

CHAPTER 11

Quick Quiz #1
Fill in the blanks and check the appropriate boxes:

1. The inner fluid of the chloroplast is called [☐ **grana** ■ **stroma**].
2. The layer of wax on the leaf surface is called the _____cuticle_____.
3. Most photosynthesis occurs in the [■ **palisade layer** ☐ **spongy layer**].
4. The Calvin cycle is a series of [☐ **light-dependent** ■ **light-independent**] reactions.
5. Oxygen is released during the [■ **light-dependent** ☐ **light-independent**] reactions.
6. The light-dependent reactions convert solar energy to usable energy, namely ATP and _____NADPH_____.
7. The _____thylakoids_____ are the membranes inside the chloroplast where the light-dependent reactions take place.
8. Plants are [■ **autotrophs** ☐ **heterotrophs**] and [■ **can** ☐ **cannot**] make their own food.
9. Stomates are opened and closed by cells called _____guard cells_____.
10. Forming carbohydrate from carbon dioxide is also known as _____carbon fixation_____.

Quick Quiz #2
Fill in the blanks and check the appropriate boxes:

1. The female part of a flower is the [☐ **stamen** ■ **pistil**].
2. The tissue within plant veins that carries water from the roots up to the rest of the plant is the [☐ **phloem** ■ **xylem**].
3. The specific cells that transport water are the _____tracheids_____ and the _____vessel elements_____.
4. The ovary develops into a [■ **fruit** ☐ **seed**].

5. The polar bodies, when fertilized, become a nutrient-rich tissue called __endosperm__.
6. ___Phloem___ is the type of tissue that carries food from photosynthesis in the leaves to the rest of the plant.
7. The specific cells that transport food are the [☐ **companion cells** ■ **sieve cells**].
8. The anther and the filament are [■ **male** ☐ **female**] parts of the flower.
9. In a flowering plant, pollen is produced by and located on the [☐ **stigma** ■ **anther**].
10. The [■ **seed** ☐ **fruit**] develops from the ovule.
11. A pollen tube grows down through the [☐ **stigma** ■ **style**].

CHAPTER 12

Quick Quiz #1

For each of the situations described below, write:

    (A)   if it represents a fixed-action pattern,
    (B)   if it represents imprinting,
    (C)   if it represents classical conditioning,
    (D)   if it represents operant conditioning, or
    (E)   if it represents insight learning.

1. __D__ A dog learns that if it brings the newspaper into the house each evening it gets a bone.
2. __B__ A bird treats the human it saw when it first hatched as its mother.
3. __A__ A frog squeezes the swollen belly of a female frog to release eggs.
4. __D__ A cockroach learns to run from light because every time a light comes on someone tries to step on it.
5. __E__ A man wishes to turn a screw and, having no screwdriver, realizes that he can use the edge of dull knife as a substitute.
6. __C__ A cat runs into the kitchen and looks for food when it hears the electric can opener.
7. __A__ A bird puffs up its brightly colored chest to attract a mate.

Quick Quiz #2

Fill in the blanks and check the appropriate boxes:

1. A chemical released that causes an organism's own heart rate to increase is an example of a [☐ **pheromone** ■ **hormone**].
2. Roots growing toward the earth is described as [■ **positive** ☐ **negative**] gravitropism.
3. A rooster crowing in the morning is an example of a ___circadian___ rhythm.
4. A fruit tree flowering in the spring is an example of a ___seasonal___ rhythm.
5. Growth of a plant toward light is called ___phototropism___.
6. Bacteria that release chemicals to draw other bacteria toward a food source are releasing [■ **pheromones** ☐ **hormones**].
7. Athlete's foot is the common name that describes a fungal infection of the skin of the feet, especially between the toes. The skin becomes cracked and sore. This is an example of a [☐ **mutualistic** ☐ **commensalistic** ■ **parasitic**] relationship.

8. Epiphytes are small plants that grow on the branches of big trees. The epiphytes are exposed to sunlight, and the big tree is neither helped nor harmed. This is an example of a [□ **mutualistic** ■ **commensalistic** □ **parasitic**] relationship.

9. Any two organisms living in an intimate association with each other are said to be in a _____symbiotic_____ relationship.

10. An ivy growing along a trellis is an example of __thigmotropism__.

CHAPTER 13

Quick Quiz #1

Fill in the blanks and check the appropriate boxes:

1. Fungi are classified as [■ **eukaryotes** □ **prokaryotes**].
2. Bacteria [□ **do** ■ **do not**] have mitochondria.
3. Bacteria [■ **do** □ **do not**] have ribosomes.
4. Bacteria [■ **do** □ **do not**] have cell walls.
5. Yeast are [■ **eukaryotes** □ **prokaryotes**] that reproduce by __budding__.
6. A viral ____capsid____ is made of protein.
7. [□ **Transformation** ■ **Transduction**] occurs when a virus transfers some DNA from one bacterium to another.
8. Fungi [□ **can** ■ **cannot**] photosynthesize.
9. Bacteria that are perfectly happy in the presence OR absence of oxygen are called _____facultative anaerobes_____.
10. Number the following steps of the lytic cycle in the order they would occur:
    - __2__ Virus injects nucleic acid into host cell.
    - __5__ Host cell is lysed and new viruses are released.
    - __1__ Viral capsid attaches to host cell.
    - __4__ New capsids are formed.
    - __3__ Viral nucleic acids are replicated using host cell machinery.
11. [□ **Some** ■ **All**] fungi are eukaryotes.
12. A [□ **parasitic** ■ **mutualistic**] relationship exists between some plants and _____nitrogen-fixing_____ bacteria. These types of plants are called _____legumes_____.
13. When a bacterium replicates its DNA and gives some of the DNA to another bacterium through a pilus, this is called _____conjugation_____.
14. Fungi have a cell wall made of [□ **proteoglycan** ■ **chitin**].
15. Bacteria are classified as [■ **prokaryotes** □ **eukaryotes**] and therefore [□ **do** ■ **do not**] have nuclei.
16. An enzyme that makes a strand of RNA by reading a strand of DNA is called __DNA-dependent RNA polymerase__.
17. Retroviruses go through the [□ **lytic** ■ **lysogenic**] lifecycle.

Quick Quiz #2

1. A _____staggered_____ cut of DNA by a restriction enzyme produces sticky ends.
2. A piece of DNA cut with a restriction enzyme that produces sticky ends can be ligated to any piece of DNA cut with [■ **the same restriction enzyme** □ **any other restriction enzyme that produces sticky ends**].
3. The enzyme that seals together cut pieces of DNA is called_____DNA ligase_____.
4. A sequence of DNA that reads the same from both directions is called a _____palindrome_____.
5. [□ **True** ■ **False**] A piece of DNA cut with a restriction enzyme that produces blunt ends can be ligated into a plasmid cut with any other restriction enzyme.

CHAPTER 14

Quick Quiz #1

Fill in the blanks and check the appropriate boxes:

1. D
2. A group of individuals living and interbreeding within the same environment is called a [□ **population** ■ **community**].
3. A
4. C
5. Members of the same community are also members of the same [□ **population** ■ **ecosystem**].
6. Alternate evolution of two interacting species is called ____coevolution____.
7. Individuals [□ **can** ■ **cannot**] evolve.
8. Hawks and wolves hunting the same population of rabbits is an example of [□ **competition** □ **predation** ■ **both of these**].

Quick Quiz #2

Fill in the blanks and check the appropriate boxes:

1. Herbivores eat the [□ **primary consumers** ■ **primary producers**].
2. Organisms that feed off dead and decaying material are called ___decomposers___.
3. Primary producers are [■ **autotrophs** □ **heterotrophs**].
4. There are more [■ **primary producers** □ **primary consumers**].
5. The least amounts of energy is available at the [□ **bottom** ■ **top**] of the food chain.
6. Organisms that eat both plants and animals are called ___omnivores___.
7. Decomposers include both ____bacteria____ and ___fungi___.
8. An herbivore is a(n) [□ **autotroph** ■ **heterotroph**].
9. In a food chain consisting of grass, grasshoppers, frogs, and bass, grasshoppers are [■ **more** □ **less**] numerous than frogs, and frogs are [■ **more** □ **less**] numerous than bass.

Quick Quiz #3

Fill in the blanks and check the appropriate boxes:

1. When a plant community begins on a barren rock, the first organism to colonize the rock is most often [■ **lichen** ☐ **moss**].
2. In an ecological succession, each new plant community in an area [■ **coexists with** ☐ **replaces**] the previous plant community.
3. The final community in ecological succession is called the ____climax____ community.
4. Gradual, unpredictable change in plants that occurs over millions of years is called [☐ **ecological succession** ■ **evolution**].
5. The ____pioneer____ organism is the one that first appears as the founder of a biological community.
6. The final plant community in ecological succession is made up primarily of ____deciduous trees____.

Quick Quiz #4

Fill in the blanks and check the appropriate boxes:

1. D
2. Water and chemical nutrients are classified as [☐ **biotic** ■ **abiotic**] elements of an ecosystem.
3. D
4. Nitrogen is converted into usable forms in the soil by ____bacteria____.
5. Carbon is returned to the atmosphere by [☐ **photosynthesis** ■ **respiration**] and removed from the atmosphere by [■ **photosynthesis** ☐ **respiration**].
6. Nitrogen-fixing bacteria live in root nodules of ____legumes____.

Quick Quiz #5

Fill in the blanks and check the appropriate boxes:

1. The tropical rain forest has [■ **greater** ☐ **lesser**] biological diversity than the tundra.
2. The biome characterized by large numbers of evergreen conifers is the ____taiga____.
3. The primary plant forms of the [☐ **taiga** ■ **tundra** ☐ **desert**] are mosses, lichen, and wild-flowers.
4. The ocean floor is known as the ____benthic____ zone.
5. Animals with adaptations for a dry environment would live in the [☐ **savanna** ■ **desert**].
6. The deepest zone of the ocean is the [■ **abyssal zone** ☐ **pelagic zone**].
7. Permanently frozen soil is a characteristic of ____tundra____.
8. The biome with very fertile soil and many herbivores is the ____grassland____.
9. Deer, bears, and raccoon are found in the [☐ **tundra** ☐ **rain forest** ■ **deciduous forest**] , whereas caribou and moose are found in the [■ **tundra** ☐ **rain forest** ☐ **deciduous forest**].
10. Deciduous trees [■ **do** ☐ **do not**] lose their leaves during cold seasons.
11. Phytoplankton would thrive well in the [■ **limnetic zone** ☐ **profundal zone**].
12. Succulent plants are well suited to [☐ **savanna** ■ **desert**].
13. Areas of water where light does not penetrate are known as ____aphotic____ zones.
14. The most northern biome is the [☐ **taiga** ■ **tundra**].
15. The tundra [☐ **does** ■ **does not**] grow many trees.
16. Coral reefs can typically be found in the [☐ **intertidal zone** ■ **neritic zone**].

Part IV
The Princeton Review Practice SAT Biology E/M Subject Tests and Explanations

Chapter 16
Practice SAT Biology
E/M Subject Test 1

BIOLOGY E/M
SUBJECT TEST 1

Your responses to the Biology E/M Subject Test 2 questions must be filled in on the Test 2 part of your answer sheet (at the back of the book). Marks on any other section will not be counted toward your Biology E/M Subject Test score.

When your supervisor gives the signal, turn the page and begin the Biology E/M Subject Test. There are 100 numbered ovals on the answer sheet. There are 60 questions in the core Biology test, 20 questions in the Biology-E section, and 20 questions in the Biology-M section. Therefore, use ONLY ovals 1-80 (for Biology-E) OR ovals 1-60 plus 81-100 (for Biology-M) for recording your answers.

BIOLOGY E/M SUBJECT TEST 1—*Continued*

FOR BOTH BIOLOGY-E AND BIOLOGY-M,
ANSWER QUESTIONS 1-60

Directions: Each set of lettered choices below refers to the numbered statements immediately following it. Select the one lettered choice that best answers each question or best fits each statement, and then fill in the corresponding oval on the answer sheet. A choice may be used once, more than once, or not at all in each set.

Questions 1-3

    (A) Mitochondria
    (B) Cytoplasm
    (C) Pyruvate
    (D) Lactic acid
    (E) Glucose

1. Location of cellular respiration in prokaryotes

2. End product of anaerobic metabolism in muscle cells

3. Location of glycolysis in eukaryotes

Questions 4-6

    (A) Anaphase II
    (B) Metaphase I
    (C) Prophase II
    (D) Metaphase II
    (E) Prophase I

4. Stage of meiosis during which recombination of genetic material occurs

5. Stage of meiosis during which pairs of homologous chromosomes align at the center of the cell

6. Stage of meiosis during which sister chromatids are separated

Questions 7-9

    (A) Reasoning/insight
    (B) Imprinting
    (C) Classical conditioning
    (D) Habituation
    (E) Instinct

7. A simple kind of learning involving loss of sensitivity to unimportant stimuli

8. Geese recognize a ticking clock as "mother" if exposed to it during a critical period shortly after hatching

9. Fish are given food at the same time as a tap on their glass bowl and soon learn to approach when a tap sounds even in the absence of food

Questions 10-12

    (A) Small intestine
    (B) Large intestine
    (C) Stomach
    (D) Esophagus
    (E) Mouth

10. Structure where most digestion and absorption of nutrients occurs

11. Structure where starch digestion first takes place

12. Structure with the lowest pH

GO ON TO THE NEXT PAGE

Directions: Each of the questions or incomplete statements below is followed by five suggested answers or completions. Some questions pertain to a set that refers to a laboratory or experimental situation. For each question, select the one choice that is the best answer to the question and then fill in the corresponding oval on the answer sheet.

13. Homologous structures, which have similar underlying structures but may have different functions, are formed by

    (A) divergent evolution
    (B) speciation
    (C) segregation
    (D) convergent evolution
    (E) stabilizing selection

14. Hemoglobin is a protein in red blood cells that binds and carries oxygen and some carbon dioxide. Its affinity for oxygen changes as blood travels from the lungs to the body tissues and back to the lungs again. One could expect hemoglobin to have

    (A) a high carbon dioxide affinity in the lungs and a low oxygen affinity in the tissues
    (B) a low carbon dioxide affinity in the lungs and a high oxygen affinity in the tissues
    (C) a high oxygen affinity in the lungs and a low oxygen affinity in the tissues
    (D) a low oxygen affinity in the lungs and a high oxygen affinity in the tissues
    (E) a high oxygen affinity in the lungs and a high carbon dioxide affinity in the lungs

15. Which of the following RNA sequences would be transcribed from the DNA sequence ATGCCTAGGAC?

    (A) TACGGATCCTG
    (B) UAGCGAUCCUG
    (C) AUGCCUAGGAC
    (D) UACGGAUCCUG
    (E) GCAUUCGAAGU

16. Arthropods can be characterized by all of the following EXCEPT

    (A) a hard exoskeleton
    (B) a water vascular system
    (C) jointed appendages
    (D) molting
    (E) segmented body

17. Which of the following are functions of the kidney?

    I. filtration of blood to remove wastes
    II. blood pressure regulation
    III. pH regulation

    (A) I only
    (B) I and II only
    (C) I and III only
    (D) II and III only
    (E) I, II, and III

18. In chickens, the allele for long tail feathers (T) is dominant over the allele for short tail feathers (t). If a pure-breeding long-tailed chicken (TT) mates with a pure-breeding short-tailed chicken (tt), what percentage of their offspring (if mated with the correct genotype) could give rise to chickens with short tails?

    (A) 25%
    (B) 50%
    (C) 75%
    (D) 100%
    (E) unable to determine from the information given

GO ON TO THE NEXT PAGE

19. All of the following could be considered density-dependent factors affecting population growth EXCEPT

    (A) limited nutrients
    (B) climate temperature
    (C) build-up of toxins
    (D) predation
    (E) limited water

20. The best definition of a species is

    (A) a group of organisms that occupy the same niche
    (B) a population that works together to defend itself from predators
    (C) a group of organisms that can mate with each other
    (D) a population that preys on other populations
    (E) a population in which all members benefit from the association in some way

21. Which of the following contains blood poor in oxygen?

    I. Right ventricle
    II. Pulmonary vein
    III. Pulmonary artery

    (A) I only
    (B) II only
    (C) III only
    (D) I and II only
    (E) I and III only

22. An organism appears to be a segmented worm. Upon observation it is determined that the organism has a closed circulation, a mouth and an anus, and does NOT have an exoskeleton. The organism most likely belongs to the phylum

    (A) mollusca
    (B) annelida
    (C) echinodermata
    (D) arthropoda
    (E) chordata

23. Which of the following substances are produced by the light reactions of photosynthesis?

    (A) ATP and NADPH
    (B) ATP and glucose
    (C) NADH and glucose
    (D) ATP and NADH
    (E) NADPH and glucose

24. Consider the following graph of substrate concentration vs. product formation. Assume enzyme concentration to be constant. Why does the graph level off at high substrate concentrations?

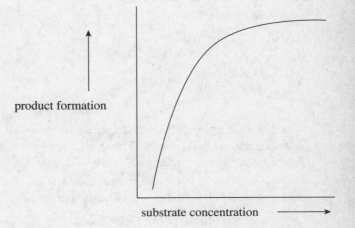

product formation

substrate concentration

    (A) All the enzyme is used up, and product formation cannot occur without it.
    (B) There is no more substrate to be converted into product.
    (C) Substrate concentration, exceeds enzyme concentration, and all active sites are saturated.
    (D) The reaction has run to completion.
    (E) An inhibitor has been added, and it has slowed down the rate of product formation.

GO ON TO THE NEXT PAGE

25. A bird that feeds on both insects and berries would be classified as a

    I. primary consumer
    II. secondary consumer
    III. tertiary consumer

    (A) I only
    (B) II only
    (C) III only
    (D) I and II only
    (E) II and III only

26. Which of the following chemical formulas could represent a monosaccharide?

    (A) $C_6H_6O_6$
    (B) $C_3H_6O_3$
    (C) $C_6H_{12}O_3$
    (D) $C_5H_{10}O_{10}$
    (E) CH_2O_4

27. A population of birds lives in an area with many insects upon which it feeds. The insects live inside trees, burrowing into the bark. Over many hundreds of years, the average beak size in the bird population has increased. This is due to

    (A) increased fitness of the birds, leading to speciation
    (B) decreased fitness of the insects, allowing the birds to catch them more easily
    (C) increased fitness of large-beaked birds, leading to evolution
    (D) decreased fitness of small-beaked birds, leading to speciation
    (E) random mutation and genetic recombination

28. The location on an enzyme where a substrate binds is called the

    (A) binding site
    (B) reaction center
    (C) allosteric site
    (D) lock-and-key model
    (E) active site

29. Human cells maintain concentration gradients across their plasma membranes, such that there is a high sodium concentration outside the cell and a high potassium concentration inside the cell. Suppose that within the cell membrane are sodium "leak" channels. These channels would allow sodium to

    (A) move out of the cell by simple diffusion
    (B) move into the cell by simple diffusion
    (C) move out of the cell by facilitated diffusion
    (D) move into the cell by facilitated diffusion
    (E) move into the cell by active transport

30. The role of decomposers in the nitrogen cycle is to

    (A) fix atmospheric nitrogen into ammonia
    (B) incorporate nitrogen into amino acids and organic compounds
    (C) convert ammonia to nitrate, which can then be absorbed by plants
    (D) denitrify ammonia, thus returning nitrogen to the atmosphere
    (E) release ammonia from organic compounds, thus returning it to the soil

31. All of the following are true about the endocrine system EXCEPT

    (A) it relies on chemical messengers that travel through the bloodstream
    (B) it is a control system that has extremely rapid effects on the body
    (C) the hormones affect only certain "target" organs
    (D) it is involved in maintaining body homeostasis
    (E) its organs secrete hormones directly into the bloodstream, rather than through ducts

GO ON TO THE NEXT PAGE ➤

32. Two organisms live in close association with each other. One organism is helped by the association, whereas the other is neither helped nor harmed. Which of the following terms best describes this relationship?

    (A) Mutualism
    (B) Commensalism
    (C) Symbiosis
    (D) Parasitism
    (E) Predator-prey relationship

33. Cardiac output (the amount of blood pumped out of the heart in one minute) and blood pressure are directly proportional. Which of the following graphs best depicts the relationship between cardiac output and blood pressure?

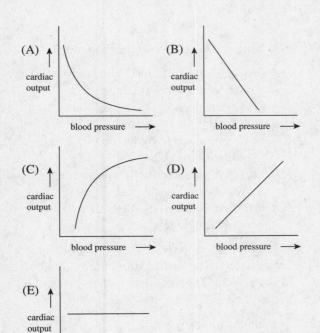

Questions 34-36 refer to the following diagram.

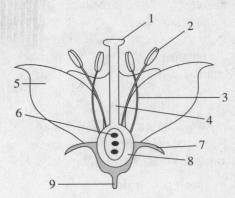

34. Location where male haploid cells are produced

    (A) 1
    (B) 2
    (C) 3
    (D) 6
    (E) 8

35. Sticky structure where pollen grains can attach and germinate

    (A) 1
    (B) 2
    (C) 4
    (D) 6
    (E) 8

36. Structure which, when fertilized, develops into fruit

    (A) 1
    (B) 2
    (C) 5
    (D) 6
    (E) 8

GO ON TO THE NEXT PAGE

Questions 37-38

Tropisms refer to movements made by plants toward or away from certain stimuli. "Positive" tropisms refer specifically to movements toward a stimulus, whereas "negative" tropisms refer to movements made away from a stimulus.

37. A plant growing on the shady side of a building bends around the corner of the building toward the sunlight. This is an example of

    (A) negative geotropism
    (B) negative phototropism
    (C) positive phototropism
    (D) positive hydrotropism
    (E) negative hydrotropism

38. The stem and leaves of the plant grow up, away from the soil. This is an example of

    (A) negative geotropism
    (B) positive geotropism
    (C) negative phototropism
    (D) positive hydrotropism
    (E) negative hydrotropism

Questions 39-43 refer to the following diagram.

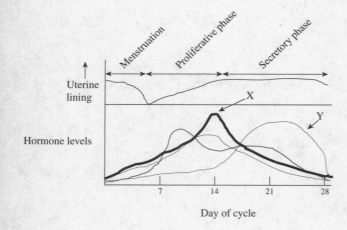

Day of cycle

39. The hormone labeled X in the diagram is often used in over-the-counter diagnostic tests to determine when ovulation has occurred. This hormone is

    (A) estrogen
    (B) progesterone
    (C) FSH
    (D) LH
    (E) testosterone

40. Based on the peak levels of hormone X, on what day of the cycle is ovulation most likely to occur?

    (A) Day 21
    (B) Day 14
    (C) Day 12
    (D) Day 25
    (E) Day 28

41. The hormone labeled Y in the diagram is

    (A) progesterone, secreted by the corpus luteum after ovulation has occurred
    (B) progesterone, secreted by the ovary after ovulation has occurred
    (C) estrogen, secreted by the corpus luteum after ovulation has occurred
    (D) estrogen, secreted by the ovary after ovulation has occurred
    (E) estrogen, secreted by the follicle before ovulation occurs

42. Immediately after fertilization, the zygote begins to undergo rapid cell division. This process is known as

    (A) blastulation
    (B) gastrulation
    (C) neurulation
    (D) implantation
    (E) cleavage

GO ON TO THE NEXT PAGE

43. From which of the primary germ layers does the nervous system develop?

    (A) Endoderm
    (B) Mesoderm
    (C) Ectoderm
    (D) Enteroderm
    (E) Epidermis

Questions 44-46

A barren, rocky community near a lake has virtually no vegetation or animal life. After a period of approximately 75 years, the community boasts a wide variety of flora and fauna, including deciduous trees, deer, and raccoon.

44. The process which has taken place can best be described as

    (A) progression
    (B) succession
    (C) evolution
    (D) habitation
    (E) colonization

45. The stable community of deciduous trees and animals is known as the

    (A) final community
    (B) climax community
    (C) apex community
    (D) summit community
    (E) composite community

46. Usually the first organisms to colonize rocky areas are lichen. These are known as the

    (A) primary community
    (B) starter community
    (C) colony organisms
    (D) pioneer organisms
    (E) settler organisms

Questions 47-50 refer to the following experiment.

Diuretics are substances that help eliminate water from the body. The effects of various substances were tested on several volunteers. All volunteers had a mass of 70 kg. They drank nothing for eight hours before the test and urinated just prior to ingesting the test substance. The three substances (water, caffeine, and salt) were tested on three separate days. The results are shown in the tables below.

Table 1

volunteer	amount caffeine ingested (in 100 ml water)	volume urine collected after 1 hour
A	50 mg	302 ml
B	100 mg	492 ml
C	150 mg	667 ml
D	200 mg	863 ml

Table 2

volunteer	amount sodium chloride ingested (in 100 ml water)	volume urine collected after 1 hour
A	.9 g	201 ml
B	1.8 g	162 ml
C	2.7 g	125 ml
D	3.6 g	82 ml

Table 3

volunteer	volume water ingested	volume urine collected after 1 hour
A	100 ml	230 ml
B	200 ml	240 ml
C	300 ml	252 ml
D	400 ml	263 ml

GO ON TO THE NEXT PAGE

47. Which of the following substances could be classified as a diuretic?

    I. Caffeine
    II. Sodium
    III. Water

    (A) I only
    (B) II only
    (C) I and II only
    (D) II and III only
    (E) I, II, and III

48. Which graph best represents the change in urine volume when ingesting caffeine?

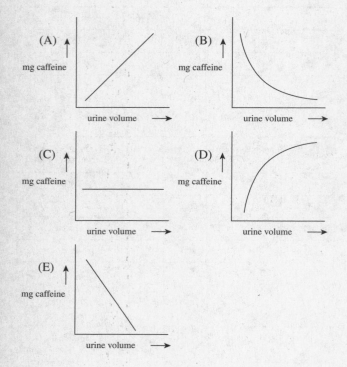

49. The purpose of ingesting the plain water (Table 3) was to

    (A) rehydrate the volunteers
    (B) dissolve the substances
    (C) act as a control
    (D) flush out the kidneys
    (E) act as a positive test substance

50. Based on the results in Table 2, if a volunteer were to ingest 4.5 g sodium chloride dissolved in 100 ml water, what would be the approximate predicted urine volume collected after one hour?

    (A) 20 ml
    (B) 30 ml
    (C) 40 ml
    (D) 50 ml
    (E) 60 ml

Questions 51-53 refer to the following information on heredity.

Hemophilia is a disorder in which blood fails to clot. John, a male hemophiliac, marries Jane, a normal woman, and together they have four children, two boys (Mark and Mike) and two girls (Molly and Mary). None of the children display the symptoms of hemophilia. Mark, Mike, Molly, and Mary all marry normal individuals and have children. None of Mark's or Mike's children, male or female, display symptoms of hemophilia, but the sons of Molly and Mary all display symptoms of hemophilia while the daughters of Molly and Mary do not.

51. Which of the following best explains the reason that Mark, Mike, Molly, and Mary do not display symptoms of hemophilia, even though their father, John, is a hemophiliac?

    (A) Hemophilia is an X-linked disorder, and John can pass on only his Y chromosome.
    (B) Hemophilia is an X-linked disorder and even though Molly and Mary received a hemophiliac X chromosome from John, Jane gave them a normal X chromosome.
    (C) Hemophilia is a Y-linked disorder and therefore cannot be displayed in females.
    (D) Hemophilia is a Y-linked disorder and Mark and Mike must have received an X chromosome from John.
    (E) Hemophilia is an X-linked disorder, and even though Mark and Mike received a hemophiliac X chromosome from John, Jane gave them a normal X chromosome.

GO ON TO THE NEXT PAGE

52. If one of Mike's daughters marries a normal man, what is the probability that one of their children will display symptoms of hemophilia?

    (A)   0%
    (B)   25%
    (C)   50%
    (D)   75%
    (E)   100%

53. Which of the following individuals are heterozygous for hemophilia?

    (A) John, Mark, and Mike
    (B) Mark, Mike, Molly, and Mary
    (C) John and Jane
    (D) Molly and Mary
    (E) Mark and Mike

Questions 54-57

A volunteer was injected intravenously with several test substances to determine the effect of each substance on normal body variables. The results are shown in Table 1. Assume that enough time was allowed between injections so that the substances do not interfere with one another.

Table 1

variable	baseline values	values after injecting substance A	values after injecting substance B	values after injecting substance C	values after injecting substance D
serum Ca^{++}	2.3 mmol/ L	2.3 mmol/ L	3.0 mmol/ L	2.3 mmol/ L	2.3 mmol/ L
serum Na^+	135 mmol/ L	135 mmol/ L	136 mmol/ L	135 mmol/ L	147 mmol/ L
serum glucose	5.6 mmol/ L	3.3 mmol/ L	5.6 mmol/ L	7.4 mmol/ L	5.6 mmol/ L

54. Based on the information in Table 1, which of the following is most likely substance B?

    (A) Calcitonin
    (B) Insulin
    (C) Parathyroid hormone
    (D) Glucagon
    (E) Aldosterone

55. Based on the information in Table 1, which of the following is most likely substance A?

    (A) Glucagon
    (B) Aldosterone
    (C) Calcitonin
    (D) Parathyroid hormone
    (E) Insulin

56. Under what conditions might substance D be released normally?

    (A) Soon after a meal
    (B) When blood pressure is low
    (C) Between meals
    (D) When there has been limited intake of dietary calcium
    (E) When dietary calcium is in excess

57. All of the following changes in variable values are significant EXCEPT

    (A) the change in serum glucose when substance A is injected
    (B) the change in serum Na^+ when substance D is injected
    (C) the change in serum Ca^{++} when substance B is injected
    (D) the change in serum glucose when substance C is injected
    (E) the change in serum Na^+ when substance B is injected

Questions 58-60

Three different cell types were observed under the microscope. The observations are summarized in Table 1.

Table 1

Cell type	Nucleus?	Cell wall?	Chloroplasts?
A	No	Yes	No
B	Yes	Yes	No
C	Yes	Yes	Yes

GO ON TO THE NEXT PAGE

The three cell types were grown in separate cultures with plenty of oxygen and nutrients available. Figure 1 shows their rates of growth. At Time 1, oxygen was no longer available to the cells.

Figure 1

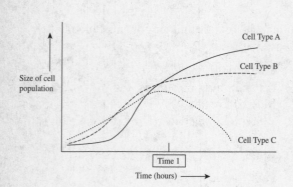

58. Based on the information in Table 1, which of the following is the most likely classification of cell Type A?

    (A) Fungi
    (B) Plant
    (C) Bacteria
    (D) Animal
    (E) Protist

59. Which of the following equations is cell Type C able to run?

    I. $C_6H_{12}O_6 + 6 O_2 \rightarrow 6 CO_2 + 6 H_2O + ATP$
    II. $H_2O + light \rightarrow O_2 + ATP + NADPH$
    III. $6 CO_2 + 6 H_2O + ATP + NADPH \rightarrow C_6H_{12}O_6$

    (A) I only
    (B) II only
    (C) I and III only
    (D) II and III only
    (E) I, II, and III

60. Consider Figure 1. Which of the following statements best describes the reason for the difference between the curves for cell Type B and cell Type C?

    (A) Cell Type B is unable to survive in the presence of oxygen, while cell Type C can ferment.
    (B) The products of fermentation in cell Type C are toxic to the cells and they are dying.
    (C) Cell Type B is an obligate aerobe while cell Type C is able to ferment.
    (D) Cell Type B is a facultative anaerobe, while cell Type C is an obligate aerobe.
    (E) Cell Type C is an obligate aerobe, while cell Type B is an obligate anaerobe.

**If you are taking the Biology-E test, continue with questions 61-80.
If you are taking the Biology-M test, go to question 81 now.**

BIOLOGY-E TEST

Directions: Each of the questions or incomplete statements below is followed by five suggested answers or completions. Some questions pertain to a set that refers to a laboratory or experimental situation. For each question, select the one choice that is the best answer to the question and then fill in the corresponding oval on the answer sheet.

Questions 61-64

    (A) Tundra
    (B) Taiga
    (C) Tropical rain forest
    (D) Deciduous forest
    (E) Desert

61. The driest of all terrestrial biomes, characterized by low and unpredictable precipitation

62. Coniferous forests, characterized by long, cold winters and short, wet summers

63. Biome characterized by great diversity of flora and fauna and high levels of precipitation

64. Northern areas, characterized by permafrost, extremely cold temperatures, and few trees

65. Plants that have true roots, stems, and leaves, as well as flowers and seeds enclosed in fruit, are classified as

    (A) bryophytes
    (B) tracheophytes
    (C) gymnosperms
    (D) angiosperms
    (E) endosperms

66. Which of the following indicates that animals have internal biological clocks?

    (A) A mouse kept in constant darkness shows a daily rhythm of activity.
    (B) A rooster crows whenever the sun rises in both winter and summer.
    (C) An owl kept in constant light drifts away from a 24-hour cycle.
    (D) Some species of birds can sense fluctuations in the Earth's magnetic field.
    (E) A squirrel whose night and day are artificially reversed soon adapts to its new schedule.

67. Which of the following correctly lists the phylogenic hierarchy?

    (A) Domain, kingdom, phylum, family, class, order, genus, species
    (B) Phylum, family, order, domain, class, kingdom, species, genus
    (C) Kingdom, domain, family, order, class, phylum, genus, species
    (D) Domain, kingdom, phylum, class, order, family, genus, species
    (E) Family, kingdom, order, domain, phylum, genus, class, species

68. A rattlesnake would be classified as a

    (A) tertiary consumer and a heterotroph
    (B) secondary consumer and an autotroph
    (C) producer and an autotroph
    (D) producer and a heterotroph
    (E) primary consumer and a heterotroph

69. At some point in their development, chordates possess all of the following EXCEPT

    (A) a dorsal hollow nerve cord
    (B) a notochord
    (C) gill slits
    (D) postanal tail
    (E) an exoskeleton

GO ON TO THE NEXT PAGE

Questions 70-73

A population of birds (Population A) on a remote, isolated island is studied to determine beak length. The resulting data are plotted in Figure 1.

Figure 1

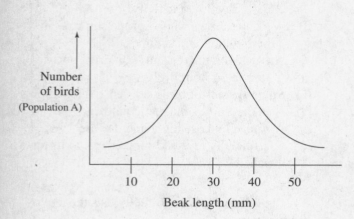

Suppose that 200 years later, the beaks of the birds on the island were again measured (Population B). The data, when plotted, yielded a graph as in Figure 2.

Figure 2

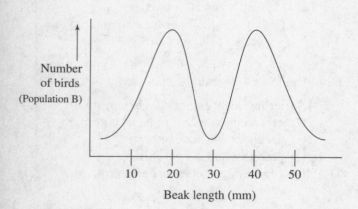

70. What is the average beak length (in cm) of the birds in Figure 1 ?

   (A) 30 cm
   (B) 15 cm
   (C) 5 cm
   (D) 3 cm
   (E) 1 cm

71. What is the most likely reason for the difference in distribution of beak lengths between the data plotted in Figure 1 and the data plotted in Figure 2 ?

   (A) All birds with beaks of 30 mm flew to a new island over the 200-year time span.
   (B) Birds with beaks of 30 mm were selected against.
   (C) Predators consumed birds with beaks of 40 mm.
   (D) Predators consumed birds with beaks of 20 mm.
   (E) Birds with beaks of 30 mm were selected for extinction.

72. Suppose that a researcher studying Population B found that birds with beaks of 20 mm were unable to mate with birds that had 40 mm beaks. These two groups of birds would now be classified as

   (A) occupying different niches
   (B) separate species
   (C) competitors
   (D) predators
   (E) separate populations

73. How would beak length in the bird population change after another 200-year time span?

   (A) The average beak length would return to 30 mm.
   (B) The average beak length would shift to 40 mm.
   (C) The average beak length would shift to 20 mm.
   (D) The differences in beak length would be more pronounced.
   (E) It is not possible to determine how beak length might change.

GO ON TO THE NEXT PAGE

Questions 74-78

Acid rain is formed after the burning of fossil fuels releases compounds containing nitrogen and sulfur into the atmosphere. Sunlight and rain bring about chemical reactions that convert these compounds into nitric acid and sulfur dioxide, which combine with water droplets to form acid rain. Acid rain typically has a pH of approximately 5.5.

The higher acidity of soil and water affects many living organisms adversely. As the pH of lake water falls, fish become ill and die. Table 1 shows the effects of pH on the size of adult fish.

Table 1

pH of lake	Average length of fish (cm)	Average mass of fish (g)
7.5	30 cm	454 g
7.0	28 cm	450 g
6.5	29 cm	453 g
6.0	25 cm	401 g
5.5	20 cm	288 g
5.0	17 cm	127 g
4.5	all fish dead	all fish dead

Mycorrhizal fungi, which form a mutualistic association with many plant roots, are particularly sensitive to the effects of acid rain. These fungi facilitate the absorption of water and nutrients by the plants; in turn, the plants provide sugars and amino acids without which the fungi could not survive.

74. The effect of acid rain on fish size is best represented by which of the following graphs?

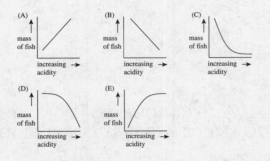

75. The relationship between mycorrhizal fungi and plants can best be described as one in which
   (A) one partner benefits from the association and the other partner is harmed
   (B) one partner benefits from the association and the other partner is neither harmed nor helped
   (C) one partner preys upon the other partner
   (D) both partners benefit from the association
   (E) neither partner benefits from the association

76. If the pH of the soil were 7.0, what would be the effect on the mycorrhizal fungi and plants?
   (A) The fungi would survive but the plant would be harmed.
   (B) The fungi would be harmed but the plant would survive.
   (C) The fungi would be slightly harmed and the plant would be slightly harmed.
   (D) Neither the fungi nor the plant would survive.
   (E) Neither the fungi nor the plant would be harmed.

77. What might be the best strategy to prevent ecological damage due to acid rain?
   (A) Stock the lakes with bigger fish so that they can resist the effects of the acid better
   (B) Reduce the amount of fossil fuels that are burned
   (C) Supply plants with excess phosphorus and water
   (D) Supply fungi with excess sugars and amino acids
   (E) Add alkalines to soil and water to neutralize the acid

78. Fungi are classified as
   (A) prokaryotic decomposers
   (B) eukaryotic producers
   (C) eukaryotic decomposers
   (D) eukaryotic autotrophs
   (E) prokaryotic consumers

GO ON TO THE NEXT PAGE

Questions 79-80

The following graphs show the growth of two closely related species of paramecia, both when grown alone (Figure 1) and when grown together (Figure 2). Both species consume bacteria as their food source and reproduce by binary fission as often as several times a day.

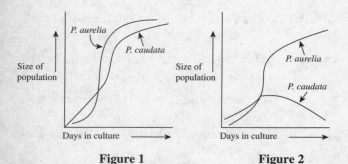

Figure 1   **Figure 2**

79. The data in Figure 2 indicate that

    (A) *P. aurelia* is preying on *P. caudata*

    (B) *P. aurelia* is a better competitor than *P. caudata*

    (C) *P. aurelia* and *P. caudata* are in a symbiotic relationship

    (D) *P. aurelia* is a parasite of *P. caudata*

    (E) *P. aurelia* grew better when combined with *P. caudata* than it did when grown alone

80. Paramecia are members of the kingdom

    (A) fungi

    (B) animalia

    (C) archaea

    (D) protista

    (E) plantae

STOP

IF YOU FINISH BEFORE TIME IS CALLED, YOU MAY CHECK YOUR WORK ON THE ENTIRE BIOLOGY-E TEST ONLY. DO NOT TURN TO ANY OTHER TEST IN THIS BOOK.

BIOLOGY-M TEST

If you are taking the Biology-M test, continue with questions 81–100.
Be sure to start this section of the test by filling in oval 81 on your answer sheet.

Directions: Each of the questions or incomplete statements below is followed by five suggested answers or completions. Some questions pertain to a set that refers to a laboratory or experimental situation. For each question, select the one choice that is the best answer to the question and then fill in the corresponding oval on the answer sheet.

81. All of the following are true about RNA EXCEPT

    (A) it is single-stranded
    (B) its bases are adenine, thymine, guanine, and uracil
    (C) it has a sugar-phosphate backbone
    (D) its sugar is ribose
    (E) it is found in the both the nucleus and the cytoplasm of the cell

82. The function of the Golgi apparatus is to

    (A) package and store proteins for secretion
    (B) synthesize proteins
    (C) function in cellular respiration
    (D) help the cell expel waste
    (E) digest foreign substances

83. A eukaryotic cell that has a cell wall but lacks chloroplasts would be classified as a

    (A) bacteria
    (B) chordate
    (C) plant
    (D) fungus
    (E) bacteria

84. All of the following could give rise to new species EXCEPT

    (A) variations in antler size between male and female reindeer
    (B) an earthquake that physically separates a population of lizards into two separate groups
    (C) divergent evolution
    (D) evolution of a population of cats such that they can no longer mate with their ancestors
    (E) a massive flood that separates a population of frogs onto opposite sides of a large lake

85. A retrovirus requires which of the following enzymes in order to integrate its genome with its host's genome?

    (A) Host's RNA polymerase
    (B) RNA dependent RNA polymerase
    (C) DNA dependent RNA polymerase
    (D) DNA dependent DNA polymerase
    (E) RNA dependent DNA polymerase

86. Which of the following groups have the most in common with one another?

    (A) Members of the same kingdom
    (B) Members of the same genus
    (C) Members of the same phylum
    (D) Members of the same class
    (E) Members of the same family

87. Which of the following individuals is the LEAST fit in evolutionary terms?

    (A) A 45-year-old male with a terminal disease who has fathered three children
    (B) A 20-year-old man who has fathered one child
    (C) A 35-year-old woman with four children
    (D) A healthy 4-year-old child
    (E) A 25-year-old woman with one child, who has had a tubal ligation to prevent future pregnancies

GO ON TO THE NEXT PAGE

Questions 88-92

Most bacteria can be grown in the laboratory on agar plates containing glucose as their only carbon source. Some bacteria require additional substances, such as amino acids, to be added to the growth medium. Such bacteria are termed *auxotrophs*. These bacteria are denoted by the amino acid they require followed by a "-" in superscript (e.g., arg⁻). Bacteria that do not require that particular amino acid can be indicated by a "+" in superscript.

Different strains of bacteria were grown on several plates containing a variety of nutrients. Figure 1 shows the colonies (numbered) that grew on each plate. The supplements in each plate are indicated.

Figure 1

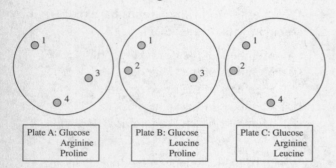

In a second experiment, Colony 1 was mixed with soft agar and spread over a plate so that an even lawn of bacteria grew. Bacterial lawns appear cloudy on agar plates. A single drop of an unknown organism was placed in the center of the bacterial lawn, and after 24 hours, a clear area known as a "plaque" appeared at that spot. The clear area continued to expand at a slow rate. Although new colonies could be grown from samples taken from the lawn, attempts to grow new colonies from samples taken from the plaque area were unsuccessful.

88. Referring to Figure 1, what is the genotype of Colony 3 ?

    (A) arg⁺, leu⁺, pro⁺
    (B) arg⁺, leu⁻, pro⁺
    (C) arg⁺, leu⁺, pro⁻
    (D) arg⁻, leu⁻, pro⁺
    (E) arg⁻, leu⁻, pro⁻

89. Is Colony 1 an auxotroph?

    (A) Yes, it is able to grow in the presence of the three amino acids being tested.
    (B) Yes, it can only grow if glucose is present.
    (C) No, it is able to grow in the absence of glucose.
    (D) No, it is able to grow in the absence of any additional amino acids.
    (E) The data available are insufficient to determine the answer.

90. Which structures could be observed in a sample of Colony 2 ?

    I.   Nuclei
    II. Ribosomes
    III. Mitochondria

    (A) I only
    (B) II only
    (C) I, and III
    (D) II and III only
    (E) I, II, and III

91. If a liquid culture medium containing glucose, leucine, and proline was inoculated with Colony 4, would bacterial growth be observed?

    (A) No, Colony 4 is an arginine auxotroph (arg⁻).
    (B) No, Colony 4 cannot grow in the presence of leucine.
    (C) Yes, Colony 4's genotype is leu⁻, pro⁻.
    (D) Yes, Colony 4 requires only glucose to grow.
    (E) The data available are insufficient to make a prediction.

92. What is the most likely reason for the clearing (the plaque) in the lawn of bacteria in the second experiment?

    (A) The unknown organism is bacterial Colony 2, and these bacteria are eating the bacteria from Colony 1 forming the lawn.
    (B) The unknown organism is a virus that is infecting the bacteria and causing them to lyse (killing them).
    (C) The drop placed in the center of the lawn contained a strong acid that destroyed the bacteria at that spot.
    (D) Bacteria are very delicate and the disturbance caused them to die.
    (E) The unknown organism began producing threonine, which is toxic to Colony 1.

GO ON TO THE NEXT PAGE

Questions 93-96

In 1910, a small town on the East Coast of the United States relied primarily on agriculture to support its economy. In the mid-1930s, a steel mill was built, and the economy shifted from being agriculturally supported to being industrially supported. The steel mill released a lot of smog and soot into the air, which collected on the bark of trees in a wooded area near the outskirts of town. Over a period of ten years the bark gradually darkened, then maintained a constant dark color.

A variety of animals and insects lived in the wooded area. In particular, a certain species of moth served as the primary food source for a population of birds. The moths lay their eggs in the bark of the trees and, thus, must spend a fair amount of time sitting on the tree trunks. Table 1 presents data on the moth population.

Table 1

Year	% white moths	% black moths
1910	95	5
1920	95	5
1930	95	5
1940	50	50
1950	20	80
1960	5	95

93. The wings of the moths and the wings of the birds are both used for flight (similar functions); however, their underlying structures are very different. Moth wings and bird wings are thus classified as

    (A) homologous structures
    (B) autologous structures
    (C) divergent structures
    (D) analogous structures
    (E) emergent structures

94. What is the most likely explanation for the shift in the percentage of black moths in the population?

    (A) The white moths no longer blended with the color of the tree bark and, thus, were selected for.
    (B) The black moths blended better with the color of the tree bark and, thus, were selected for.
    (C) The black moths blended better with the color of the tree bark and, thus, were selected against.
    (D) The white moths blended better with the color of the tree bark and, thus, were selected against.
    (E) The black moths did not blend with the color of the tree bark and, thus, were selected against.

95. If a seed from one of the trees was planted in an area far from the steel mill, what color would the bark of the tree be?

    (A) Black, because the parent tree had black bark
    (B) White, because the gene causing black bark was mutated due to environmental pollution
    (C) Black, because the gene causing white bark was mutated due to environmental pollution
    (D) White, because the black bark was an acquired characteristic and is therefore not passed on to progeny
    (E) The color of the bark is not able to be determined.

96. Birds track their prey visually, whereas bats rely on sonar to locate their food. If the bird population were replaced with a bat population in 1940, what would be the ratio of white moths to black moths?

    (A) 95% white, 5% black
    (B) 80% white, 20% black
    (C) 50% white, 50% black
    (D) 20% white, 80% black
    (E) 5% white, 90% black

GO ON TO THE NEXT PAGE

Questions 97-100

Dialysis tubing is a semipermeable membrane. It allows small molecules, such as water, to pass through easily, while larger molecules, such as sucrose, are restricted. Movement of molecules across the tubing is due to concentration gradients. In an experiment designed to study osmosis, several pieces of dialysis tubing were filled with sucrose solutions of varying concentration and placed in beakers containing distilled water. The rate and direction of water movement was determined by weighing the bags before and after placing them in the distilled water. The data are recorded below.

Table 1

Tube number	Tube contents (beaker contents)	Mass (g) 0 minutes	Mass (g) 15 minutes	Mass (g) 30 minutes	Mass (g) 45 minutes	Mass (g) 60 minutes
1	Distilled water (distilled water)	22.3 g	22.4 g	22.2 g	22.3 g	22.3 g
2	10% sucrose (distilled water)	24.8 g	25.3 g	25.7 g	26.4 g	26.9 g
3	40% sucrose (distilled water)	25.1 g	26.3 g	27.5 g	28.9 g	29.6 g
4	Distilled water (40% sucrose)	22.7 g	21.3 g	20.5 g	19.8 g	18.7 g

97. Why does the mass of Tube 3 increase while the mass of Tube 4 decreases?

(A) Water is moving into Tube 3, and sucrose is moving into Tube 4.
(B) Water is moving into Tube 4, and sucrose is moving into Tube 3.
(C) Water is moving into Tube 3, and water is moving out of Tube 4.
(D) Sucrose is moving into Tube 3, and sucrose is moving out of Tube 4.
(E) Sucrose is moving out of Tube 3, and water is moving out of Tube 4.

98. Why does the mass of Tube 1 remain relatively unchanged throughout the experiment?

(A) The dialysis tubing in Tube 1 is defective and does not allow water to cross.
(B) There is no concentration gradient to drive the movement of sucrose.
(C) The dialysis tubing broke, allowing the tube contents to mix with the beaker contents.
(D) There is no concentration gradient to drive the movement of water.
(E) The experimenter failed to record the data properly.

99. Which of the following graphs best illustrates the relationship between Tube 2 and Tube 3?

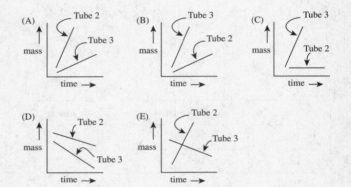

100. Cell membranes are also semipermeable, allowing water but not other substances to cross easily. A red blood cell placed in a 0.9% NaCl solution will neither swell nor shrivel. Based on this knowledge, and the information presented in Table 1, what would happen to a red blood cell placed in a 20% NaCl solution?

(A) Water would be drawn out of the cell and the cell would swell.
(B) Water would be drawn into the cell and the cell would swell.
(C) Water would be drawn out of the cell and the cell would shrivel.
(D) Water would be drawn into the cell and the cell would shrivel.
(E) No change would occur to the cell.

STOP

IF YOU FINISH BEFORE TIME IS CALLED, YOU MAY CHECK YOUR WORK ON THE ENTIRE BIOLOGY-M TEST ONLY. DO NOT TURN TO ANY OTHER TEST IN THIS BOOK.

HOW TO SCORE THE PRINCETON REVIEW
BIOLOGY E/M SUBJECT TEST 1

When you take the real exam, the proctors will collect your test booklet and bubble sheet and send your answer sheet to New Jersey where a computer looks at the pattern of filled-in ovals on your answer sheet and gives you a score. We couldn't include even a small computer with this book, so we are providing this more primitive way of scoring your exam.

Determining Your Score

STEP 1   Determine how many questions you got right and how many you got wrong on the test. Remember, questions that you do not answer do not count as either right answers or wrong answers.

STEP 2   List the number of right answers here.

(A) _____

STEP 3   List the number of wrong answers here. Now divide that number by 4. (Use a calculator if you're feeling particularly lazy.)

(B) _____ ÷ 4 = (C) _____

STEP 4   Subtract the number of wrong answers divided by 4 from the number of correct answers. Round this score to the nearest whole number. This is your raw score.

(A) – (C) = _____

STEP 5   To determine your real score, take the number from Step 4 above and look it up in the Scoring Grid on page 402. For example, if your raw score is 53, find your exam score by going to 50 in the left-hand column and then moving to the right 4 spaces to the "3" column. Your exam score would be 630.

PRACTICE SAT BIOLOGY SUBJECT TEST 1
SCORING GRID

	0	1	2	3	4	5	6	7	8	9
0	0	330	340	350	360	370	380	380	390	390
10	400	400	410	410	420	420	430	430	440	440
20	450	450	460	460	470	470	480	480	490	490
30	500	500	510	510	520	520	530	530	540	550
40	560	560	570	570	580	580	590	590	600	600
50	610	610	620	630	630	640	650	650	660	660
60	670	670	680	680	690	700	700	710	720	720
70	730	730	740	750	760	770	780	790	800	800
80	800	N/A	N/A	N/A	N/A	N/A	N/A	N/A	N/A	N/A

Chapter 17
Practice SAT Biology
E/M Subject Test 1:
Answers and
Explanations

Answers and Explanations

Question	Answer	Explanation
1	B	Prokaryotes (Domains Bacteria and Archaea) have no membrane-bound organelles, so all reactions and processes occur in the cytoplasm. You should have been able to eliminate choices C, D, and E because they did not describe locations.
2	D	When muscle cells run out of oxygen and switch to anaerobic metabolism (glycolysis only) to make ATP, the end product is lactic acid. Yeast can also switch to anaerobic metabolism; their end product is ethanol. You should have been able to eliminate choices A and B because they are not products.
3	B	Eukaryotes possess organelles and as such divide the location of their cellular processes among them. Glycolysis occurs in the cytoplasm, whereas the Krebs cycle and electron transport occur in the mitochondria. As in Question 1, you should have eliminated choices C, D, and E.
4	E	Recombination occurs when the homologous chromosomes are paired and crossing over can take place. This occurs during prophase I of meiosis. Remember that recombination occurs during prophase, and this would help you eliminate choices A, B, and D.
5	B	After prophase I, the homologous chromosomes remain paired and align at the center of the cell, on the "metaphase plate." (The prefix *meta* means "middle." Use this fact to help you elimate choices A, C, and E.) During metaphase II, the individual, unpaired chromosomes align at the cell center.
6	A	During meiosis, the chromosomes remain replicated (i.e., remain as two joined sister chromatids) for the entire first set of divisions. The whole point to the second set of meiotic divisions is to separate the sister chromatids. This takes place during anaphase II.
7	D	Habituation involves becoming accustomed to certain stimuli that are not harmful or important. For example, if you walk down the hallway and a friend jumps out at you and you get scared, that is a normal reaction to a startling stimulus. However, if this happens every time you walk down the hallway, you get accustomed to it and no longer are startled. You have become *habituated* to the stimulus. Note that for Questions 7–9, you just had to know the basic definitions of these types of learning. Most of the classification-type questions are like that.
8	B	Some animals do not have an instinctive sense for who their mother is and will bond with any object they are exposed to during a certain time period after their birth. The object "imprints" on their minds, and thereafter, even if exposed to their real mother, they will still treat the object as Mom.

Question	Answer	Explanation
9	C	Conditioning involves the association of and response to one stimulus with a second, different stimulus. The best example is Ivan Pavlov's dogs. He rang a bell when he fed them, and the dogs salivated in response to the food. Soon, all he had to do was ring the bell, and the dogs would salivate, even in the absence of food.
10	A	Most digestion and absorption occur in the small intestine. A very small amount of digestion (starch only) takes place in the mouth, and a very small amount of digestion takes place in the stomach (acid hydrolysis of food and some protein digestion). As with Questions 7–9, Questions 10–11 require the same type of knowledge—memorization of basic facts.
11	E	Saliva contains the enzyme amylase, which breaks down starch.
12	C	Cells in the stomach secrete hydrochloric acid, which keeps the pH of the stomach around 1–2. The other regions of the digestive tract maintain a fairly neutral pH.
13	A	Divergent evolution occurs when the same ancestral organism is placed into different environments and must then adapt to function in these different environments. Thus the same original structures evolve separately and "diverge" from one another. Examples of homologous structures are the arm of a man, the wing of a bat, and the flipper of a whale. All have the same basic bone structure but vastly different functions. The opposite of divergent evolution is convergent evolution, in which vastly different organisms are placed into the same environment and must adapt to perform similar functions with different structures. Convergent evolution produces analogous structures, examples of which are the wings of bats, the wings of birds, and the wings of butterflies. Speciation is often the result of divergent evolution, not the cause of it.
14	C	The job of the blood is to carry oxygen from the lungs, where it is plentiful, to the tissues, where it is not. Thus hemoglobin should have a high affinity for oxygen in the lungs so it can bind oxygen (choices A, B, and D could be eliminated) and a low oxygen affinity in the tissues (so it can release the oxygen where it is needed). The reverse is true for carbon dioxide. Hemoglobin has a high carbon dioxide affinity in the tissues and a low carbon dioxide affinity in the lungs.
15	D	In RNA, the base thymine (T) is replaced with uracil (U), so choice A can be immediately eliminated. Further, A will always pair with U, and G will always pair with C. The only choice that has the bases paired correctly is choice D.

Question	Answer	Explanation
16	B	Choices A, C, D, and E all describe characteristics of the phylum arthropoda. A water vascular system is a characteristic of the phylum echinodermata, the "spiny skinned" animals such as sea stars and sea urchins. Their water vascular system ends in tube feet that play a role in locomotion and feeding. Don't forget your LEAST/EXCEPT/NOT technique of circling the word "EXCEPT" and drawing a vertical line through the answer choices to help you remember to choose the incorrect statement.
17	E	The kidney's primary role is to filter blood to remove wastes (statement I is true, and choice D is eliminated), but it is also involved to a fair extent in blood pressure regulation (through renin and aldosterone, so II is true and choices A and C are eliminated) and in pH regulation (through excretion of hydrogen ions, so III is true and choice B is eliminated).
18	D	If a pure-breeding long-tailed chicken (TT) mates with a pure-breeding short-tailed chicken (tt), all of their offspring (the F1 generation) will have the genotype Tt (and have long tails). Thus all of them, if mated with the correct genotype (Tt or tt), could produce offspring with short tails. Draw some quick Punnett squares to prove it to yourself.
19	B	Density-dependent factors are those that get more significant as the size of the population increases. Limited nutrients and water, toxic waste build-up, and predation are all issues that are of greater concern to a large population than to a small one. Only choice B, climate temperature, is not more worrisome to a large group than to a small one. It will affect all populations equally, regardless of their size. Remember your LEAST/EXCEPT/NOT technique.
20	C	Two populations are considered separate species when they are so different from one another that they can no longer mate and produce viable offspring. Thus, organisms that can mate with each other must be of the same species.
21	E	Blood that is poor in oxygen returns from the body to the right side of the heart (I is true, so choices B and C are eliminated), then travels through the pulmonary artery (III is true, so choices A and D are eliminated) to get to the lungs, where it picks up oxygen again. This oxygen-rich blood returns to the left side of the heart through the pulmonary vein (II is false) and is pumped back out to the body through the aorta.
22	B	The characteristics described are those of the phylum annelida, the best example of which is the earthworm. Mollusks have external shells (snails), echinoderms and arthropods have exoskeletons (sea stars, crustaceans, insects), and chordates have endoskeletons and, in any case, are not worms.

Question	Answer	Explanation
23	A	The light reactions of photosynthesis convert solar energy to usable energy in the form of ATP (choices C and E are eliminated) and NADPH (a reduced electron carrier). The ATP and NADPH (i.e., energy) produced during these reactions are used later during the Calvin cycle to fix carbon dioxide into carbohydrates, like glucose. Because glucose is a product of the light-independent reactions, choice B could be eliminated. Remember that NAD$\underline{P}$H belongs with $\underline{p}$hotosynthesis to eliminate choice D.
24	C	When the concentration of substrate far exceeds the concentration of enzyme (remember, the question states that enzyme concentration is assumed to be constant), all the enzyme active sites are saturated with substrate, and the product is being formed at its maximum rate. The only way to increase product formation at this point is to increase the concentration of the enzyme. Note that enzymes should not be used up in the course of the reaction (A is wrong). Furthermore, product formation is still occurring, just at a stable rate (B and D are wrong). There is no reason to assume an inhibitor has been added; the rate of product formation remains constant.
25	D	Berries are plant products (i.e., primary producers), thus any organism that eats berries is a primary consumer, or an herbivore (I is true, choices B, C, and E can be eliminated). Notice at this point that the only remaining choices (A and D) do not contain option III, therefore, option III is false. Secondary consumers, carnivores and omnivores (e.g., birds) eat primary consumers (e.g., bugs), thus II is also true, and choice A can be eliminated. Tertiary consumers are carnivores (e.g., cats) that eat other carnivores (e.g., birds, secondary consumers). III is false, as we saw earlier.
26	B	Monosaccharides have the general molecular formula $C_nH_{2n}O_n$, as in glucose, which is $C_6H_{12}O_6$. The only formula that fits this rule is choice B.
27	C	A change in a population that occurs over a long period of time is evolution. This alone is a good tip-off that choice C, the only choice that mentions evolution, is correct. Speciation has not occurred, only a change in the characteristic of the birds, thus choices A and D can be eliminated. Any change in the fitness of the insects would change the characteristics of the insect population, not the bird population (B is wrong), and random mutation would not produce a specific, directed effect (E is wrong). Birds with large beaks had greater fitness because they could more easily obtain food, thus they had an advantage over birds with smaller beaks, which died out as time passed.
28	E	The other choices do not describe substrate binding sites on an enzyme.

Question	Answer	Explanation
29	D	Break this question down one piece at a time. First, the question states that there is a high sodium concentration outside the cell. This means sodium wants to move into the cell (where concentration is lower). Choices A and C can be eliminated because they state that sodium would move out of the cell. Active transport requires ATP, and because there is no ATP involved, choice E can be eliminated. Last, because sodium moves across the membrane with the help of a channel, it is moving by facilitated diffusion (choice B is eliminated).
30	E	Decomposers take organic material and break it down into its individual compounds, thus returning these compounds back to the earth. The other processes listed are carried out by other organisms: nitrogen fixing bacteria (choice A), heterotrophs and autotrophs (choice B), and other soil bacteria (choices C and D).
31	B	The endocrine system is a body control system, but it is NOT rapid. The fastest hormone in the body is adrenaline, and even that takes a few seconds, compared to the nervous system's milliseconds. Most hormones operate in the minutes to hours range. The other choices regarding the endocrine system are all true. Remember your LEAST/ EXCEPT/NOT technique!
32	B	This symbiotic relationship describes commensalism. In mutualism both partners benefit, in parasitism and predator-prey relationships one partner benefits while the other is harmed, and symbiosis is just a general term used to describe close living arrangements.
33	D	Relationships that are directly proportional have linear graphs with a positive slope.
34	B	Male haploid cells (pollen grains or microspores) are produced on the anther (#2 in the diagram), which is at the tip of the filament (#3 in the diagram).
35	A	Pollen grains stick to the stigma (#1 in the diagram), which is supported by the style (#4 in diagram).
36	E	The pollen fertilizes the ovule (female haploid cells, or megaspores, #6 in the diagram); once fertilized, the ovary (#8 in the diagram) develops into a fruit.
37	C	The prefix *photo* refers to light; because the plant is growing toward light we can eliminate choices A, D, and E. "Positive" means growing toward, so choice B can be eliminated.
38	A	The prefix *geo* refers to the earth, or soil; thus we can eliminate choices C, D, and E. Because the plant is growing away from the earth, this is a negative tropism and we can eliminate choice B.
39	D	A surge in LH is what causes ovulation and is measured in the ovulation prediction kits. Estrogen and progesterone affect the uterus, not the ovary, and FSH causes development of a follicle (A, B, and C are wrong). Testosterone is a male hormone (E is wrong).

Question	Answer	Explanation
40	B	Because we know hormone X is peaking at ovulation time, a quick look at the graph shows hormone X peaking at about Day 14 of the cycle.
41	A	The rise in hormone Y occurs after ovulation (choice E is wrong) and coincides with formation of the corpus luteum (choices B and D are wrong). The primary hormone secreted by the corpus luteum is progesterone.
42	E	Rapid cell division after fertilization is known as cleavage. Blastulation is the formation of a hollow ball of cells (A is wrong), gastrulation is formation of the three primary germ layers (B is wrong), neurulation is development of the nervous system (C is wrong), and implantation is when the morula (solid ball of cells) burrows into the uterine lining (D is wrong).
43	C	You should remember the prefixes *ecto*, *meso*, and *endo* for the primary germ layers and therefore eliminate choices D and E right away. The ectoderm forms the skin, hair, nails, mouth lining, and nervous system. The mesoderm forms muscle, bone, blood vessels, and organs (B is wrong). The endoderm forms inner linings and glands (A is wrong).
44	B	The development of a thriving ecosystem from a barren area is known as succession. Note that evolution usually has a much longer time frame than succession.
45	B	The climax community is the final, stable community in succession. The key word here is "stable." That should tip you off that this is the end of the process, or the " climax."
46	D	The first organisms to colonize a barren area are known as the pioneer organisms.
47	A	Diuretics help eliminate water (i.e., increase urine production) from the body. From the data tables, the only substance that increases urine production significantly is caffeine. Don't forget the I, II, III technique here; even just knowing that option I is true allows you to eliminate two (choices B and D) of the five choices.
48	A	Again, from the data tables, there is a directly proportional (i.e., linear) relationship between the amount of caffeine ingested and the volume of urine produced. As caffeine consumption increases, so does urine volume. The only graph that shows this relationship is choice A.
49	C	Because the caffeine and the sodium chloride were dissolved in water, plain water was consumed as a control, to make sure the effects seen were due to the added substances and not the water. Questions about experimental controls come up fairly frequently on the SAT Biology E/M Subject Test; make sure you know the definition for a control and how to spot it in the experiment.

Question	Answer	Explanation
50	C	From Table 2, an increase in sodium chloride of 0.9 g results in a decrease in urine volume of approximately 40 ml. When 3.6 g sodium chloride are ingested, 82 ml urine is produced; thus if 4.5 g sodium chloride were to be ingested, the expected urine volume would be 40 ml less, approximately 40 ml.
51	B	As soon as you see "Hemophilia," you should be thinking "X-linked disorder." Then use the technique for avoiding the temptation trap, which is particularly dangerous here, because the passage and the questions are confusing, and it's very tempting to just guess blindly. Resist! Take the paragraph apart piece by piece, sentence by sentence. Write out genotypes as you read through, and construct Punnett squares to help you see probability. Out of this family, the only members that express this condition are males. This is a tip-off for X-linked disorders, which are more common in males because they have only a single X chromosome. (In any case, you should remember the two most common X-linked disorders: hemophilia and color blindness.) John's genotype is YX^h. He passed his Y chromosome to Mark and Mike; they also received a normal X from Jane, thus they do not have hemophilia, nor can they pass it on to their kids. Molly and Mary received X^h from John but also received a normal X from Jane, thus they are carriers of hemophilia but do not display its symptoms.
52	A	Because Mike does not carry the gene for hemophilia (see above), he cannot pass it on to his children, and they in turn cannot pass it on to their children.
53	D	Mark and Mike do not carry the gene for hemophilia (see solution to 51 above), thus we can eliminate choices A, B, and E. Jane is normal, so choice C is eliminated as well.
54	C	From Table 1, substance B caused an increase in serum calcium levels, which is the effect that parathyroid hormone has on the body.
55	E	Again, from Table 1, substance A caused a decrease in serum glucose levels, which is the effect that insulin has on the body.
56	B	Substance D causes an increase in serum sodium, which is the effect aldosterone has on the body. Aldosterone is released when blood pressure is low, because excess sodium will have the effect of causing water retention, which will increase blood volume, which will increase blood pressure. (Note: Even if you did not know this, you should have been able to eliminate the other choices.)
57	E	The change in serum sodium after injection of Substance B is insignificant. All other choices cause significant change from the baseline values of the variables being measured. Don't forget the LEAST/EXCEPT/NOT technique.
58	C	Cell Type A has no nucleus. The only organisms that do not have nuclei are bacteria (Domains Bacteria and Archaea).

Question	Answer	Explanation
59	E	Cell Type C has a nucleus, a cell wall, and chloroplasts and therefore most likely comes from a plant. Equations II and III are the equations for photosynthesis and would occur in plants (choices A, B, and C are eliminated), and equation I is the equation for cellular respiration, which also occurs in plants (choice D is eliminated).
60	D	This is a great question to do some answer predicting on. At Time 1 the oxygen was removed from the cultures and cell Type C died. Clearly it is an obligate aerobe. Thus we can eliminate choices A, B, and C. Because cell Type B was growing well in the presence of oxygen, it cannot be an obligate anaerobe, thus choice E is eliminated. Cell Type B must be a facultative anaerobe, using oxygen when it is available and fermenting when oxygen is not available. The decrease in growth of cell Type B after Time 1 is most likely because energy is produced during fermentation than during aerobic metabolism.

Biology-E Test

Question	Answer	Explanation
61	E	These are the characteristics of desert.
62	B	These are the characteristics of taiga.
63	C	These are the characteristics of tropical rain forest.
64	A	These are the characteristics of tundra.
65	D	Flowering plants are angiosperms. Gymnosperms are conifers (naked seed plants; C is wrong), bryophytes are mosses (A is wrong), and tracheophytes are non-seed producing plants (ferns; B is wrong). "Endosperm" is not a classification for plants.
66	A	If an organism's environment remains absolutely constant, and that organism still exhibits regular rhythms of activity, there must be some internal "clock" that keeps it on schedule (C and E are wrong). Roosters vary the time of their crow as the sun varies the time it rises (B is wrong). The magnetic field has nothing to do with internal clocks (D is wrong).
67	D	Remember: "Dumb King Philip Came Over From Germany—So?" or make up your own!
68	A	Rattlesnakes are clearly heterotrophs (only photosynthetic organisms are autotrophs), so we can eliminate choices B and C. Rattlesnakes are carnivores, not producers (D is wrong) or primary consumers (herbivores, so E is wrong).

Question	Answer	Explanation
69	E	Remember your LEAST/EXCEPT/NOT technique. There are four features present in all chordates—dorsal nerve cords (choice A), notochords (choice B), gill slits (choice C), and postanal tails (choice D). Note that some of these features may be found only in embryonic or larval stages. The "wrong" answer is choice E—not all chordates (for example, sea squirts and lancelets) have a bony endoskeleton.
70	D	The question asks for the average beak length in cm, but the graph gives it in mm. Average beak length is 30 mm. 10 mm = 1 cm; therefore, 30 mm = 3 cm. Read the questions carefully!
71	B	Clearly the birds with 30 mm beaks were not surviving too well. There is no reason to assume they flew to another island; remember, they are on a remote, isolated island. There may not be another island near enough to fly to (A is wrong). If predators consumed birds with 20 mm or 40 mm beaks, they would not be the prevalent populations in Figure 2 (C and D are wrong), and if birds with 30 mm beaks were selected for, the population would not have been divided (E is wrong).
72	B	The defining characteristic for speciation is an inability to interbreed.
73	E	Just because we have some information about how the population changed in the last 200 years, it doesn't tell us how it may change in the next 200 years. It would depend on how the environment changed during that time period.
74	D	As the acidity increases (pH goes down), the average mass of the fish decreases. However, it does not decrease linearly; rather, it stays constant for a while, then gradually drops off, then rapidly drops off as acidity becomes severe. The best representation of this is choice D.
75	D	The plant benefits by easier availability of water and phosphorus, and the fungi benefit by receiving amino acids and sugars. Another term for this type of relationship is *mutualism*.
76	E	pH 7.0 is neutral, thus neither the plant nor the fungi would be harmed.
77	B	The best way to prevent damage from acid rain would be to prevent its formation by reducing the burning of the fossil fuels that cause it. There is no guarantee that bigger fish will resist the acidity any better than smaller fish (A is wrong), supplying plants with excess phosphorus will not help them take it up any easier (C is wrong), supplying fungi with sugars and amino acids will not help them overcome the effects of acid soil (D is wrong), and, even if alkalines will neutralize acid, they might be just as harmful to the environment (E is wrong)!
78	C	Fungi are eukaryotes (A and E are eliminated), and they are not photosynthetic (B and D are eliminated).

Question	Answer	Explanation
79	B	Clearly *P. aurelia* can compete better and get more food that *P. caudata*; thus it will grow while *P. caudata* is competed to extinction. Choice A is highly unlikely, because the food source the paramecia prefer is bacteria, not each other. This is not a symbiotic relationship but a competitive one (C and D are eliminated), and the data contradict choice E.
80	D	Paramecia are single-celled eukaryotes, members of kingdom Protista.

Biology-M Test

Question	Answer	Explanation
81	B	RNA bases do not include thymine; they are adenine, guanine, cytosine, and uracil. All other statements about RNA are correct. Remember the LEAST/EXCEPT/NOT technique!
82	A	Ribosomes synthesize protein (B is wrong), mitochondria function in respiration (C is wrong), vacuoles help expel waste (D is wrong), and lysosomes function in digestion (E is wrong).
83	D	Choices A and E are prokaryotic and can be eliminated. Chordates have no cell walls (B is wrong), and plants have chloroplasts (C is wrong).
84	A	The defining characteristic for speciation is an inability to interbreed. Choices B, C, D, and E could all ultimately produce two different populations that lack the ability to mate. Choice A would not lead to an inability to mate. Remember this is a LEAST/EXCEPT/NOT question.
85	E	A retrovirus has an RNA genome, so its polymerase must be able to read RNA (DNA-dependent choices C and D can be eliminated). Furthermore, retroviruses go through the lysogenic life cycle, and so must insert their genome into their host's genome. Because all other organisms have a DNA genome, a DNA copy of the viral (RNA) genome must be synthesized. A DNA polymerase is needed (choices A and B can be eliminated). Note that the host's RNA polymerase is DNA dependent, the same answer as choice C.
86	B	The members that have the most in common with one another are the members near the bottom of the hierarchy. Of the choices given, genus is the closest to the bottom of the hierarchy.
87	D	Anyone who has produced offspring has demonstrated their fitness. Regardless of how healthy a child is, he has not yet produced offspring to prove his fitness. Use the LEAST/EXCEPT/NOT technique.

Question	Answer	Explanation
88	C	The only plate that Colony 3 cannot grow on is Plate C, which lacks proline. Thus Colony 3 requires proline to grow and is a proline auxotroph (pro⁻). This eliminates choices A, B, and D. Choice E is incorrect because Colony 3 does not require arginine or leucine to grow; it can grow just fine in the absence of these amino acids, as is indicated on plates A and B.
89	D	Colony 1 can grow on any of the plates, thus it does not require any additional amino acids. Auxotrophs require additional supplements to their growth media.
90	B	Because these are bacterial colonies, they would not have any membrane-bound organelles, and thus no nuclei (choices A, C, and E can be eliminated) or mitochondria (choice D can be eliminated). Bacteria do have ribosomes to synthesize proteins.
91	A	It really helps to predict an answer BEFORE you look at the answer choices. Sometimes looking at the choices first can confuse your thinking and lead you to a trap, but if you have an idea of the correct answer before you look at the choices, you will be less tempted. Colony 4 cannot grow in the absence of arginine as is evidenced by Plate B. Thus, because the liquid medium does not contain arginine, no bacterial growth would be observed.
92	B	Again, try to predict an answer first. Clear spots on lawns of bacteria are due to infection by viruses that cause lysis of the bacteria. Even if this was not obvious to you, you should have been able to eliminate the other choices. There is no reason to assume Colony 2 would prey on Colony 1 (A is wrong); strong acid would lyse and destroy the bacteria immediately, not after 24 hours (C is wrong); bacteria are not delicate, they can grow just about anywhere, under any conditions (D is wrong); and there is no data to support the fact that threonine may be toxic to the bacteria or that the "unknown organism" was producing it.
93	D	Structures with similar functions but different underlying structures are the result of vastly different organisms being placed into similar environments and having to adapt to the same stresses with different starting materials. These are termed "analogous structures" and are the result of convergent evolution. (See also Question #13.)
94	B	Because the percentage of black moths is increasing, they must be selected for. This eliminates C and E. Because the percentage of white moths is decreasing, they must be selected against, eliminating choice A. Choice D is wrong because white moths would not blend better against dark tree bark.
95	D	The original parent had white bark. The change in bark color is the result of an accumulation of soot on the tree. This is an acquired characteristic and would not be passed on to offspring. Seedlings that grew far from the plant would not be exposed to soot in the air and would not experience discoloration of their bark.

Question	Answer	Explanation
96	C	The reason the percentage of black moths increased was because they were no longer visible against the now darkened bark of the trees. Because the white moths were more easily seen by the birds, their numbers declined. However, because bats rely on sonar to locate prey instead of vision, darker coloring would not give the moths any advantage, and the population percentages would stay at the point they were at when the birds were replaced by bats, a fifty-fifty split.
97	C	Sucrose cannot cross the dialysis membrane, so it cannot cause any effect on the mass of the tubes. This eliminates choices A, B, D, and E.
98	D	Because movement across the membrane relies strictly on concentration gradients, the fact that there is no gradient in Tube 1 would prevent the movement of water into or out of the tube. Thus there would be no change in mass.
99	B	The gradient in Tube 3 is much larger than the gradient in Tube 2, thus water would be expected to enter more rapidly. This is confirmed by the data in Table 1. A linear graph should show two lines with positive slopes, and the slope of Tube 3's line should be greater than the slope of Tube 2's line.
100	C	The fact that the cell does not swell or shrivel in 0.9% NaCl implies that there is no concentration gradient. A cell in a 20% NaCl solution would experience similar stresses to a dialysis tube filled with water sitting in a beaker filled with a more concentrated solution, such as Tube 4. The data indicate that Tube 4 lost mass, thus water exited the tube, and the same would happen to the red blood cell.

Chapter 18
Practice SAT Biology
E/M Subject Test 2

BIOLOGY E/M
SUBJECT TEST 2

Your responses to the Biology E/M Subject Test 2 questions must be filled in on the Test 2 part of your answer sheet (at the back of the book). Marks on any other section will not be counted toward your Biology E/M Subject Test score.

When your supervisor gives the signal, turn the page and begin the Biology E/M Subject Test. There are 100 numbered ovals on the answer sheet. There are 60 questions in the core Biology test, 20 questions in the Biology-E section, and 20 questions in the Biology-M section. Therefore, use only ovals 1-80 (for Biology-E) OR ovals 1-60 plus 81-100 (for Biology-M) for recording your answers.

FOR BOTH BIOLOGY-E AND BIOLOGY-M, ANSWER QUESTIONS 1–60

Directions: Each set of lettered choices below refers to the numbered statements immediately following it. Select the one lettered choice that BEST answers each question or BEST fits each statement, and then fill in the corresponding oval on the answer sheet. A choice may be used once, more than once, or not at all in each set.

Questions 1-4

    (A) Hair
    (B) Epidermis
    (C) Cuticle
    (D) Guard cell
    (E) Sweat gland

1. Permits gas exchange and transpiration in leaves

2. Layer that restricts evaporation in humans

3. Layer that restricts evaporation in plants

4. Important thermoregulatory structure in humans

Questions 5-8

    (A) DNA
    (B) tRNA
    (C) mRNA
    (D) rRNA
    (E) RNA polymerase

5. Translated to synthesize protein

6. Transports amino acids during protein synthesis

7. Passed on to progeny cells during cell division

8. Includes a structure known as the "anticodon"

GO ON TO THE NEXT PAGE

Questions 9-12

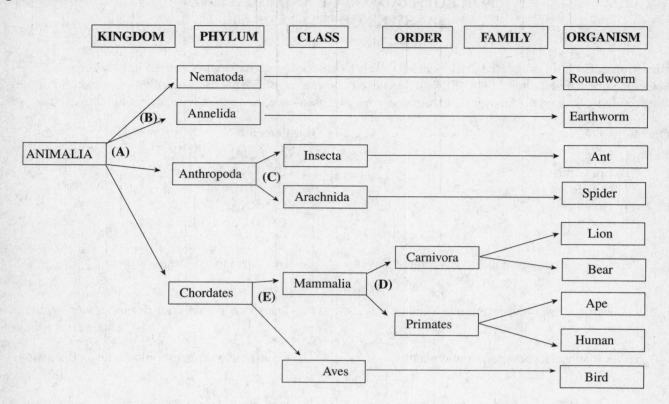

| KINGDOM | PHYLUM | CLASS | ORDER | FAMILY | ORGANISM |

9. Separates animals with nails from animals with claws

10. Separates segmented worms from worms with no segmentation

11. Separates animals with feathers from animals with hair

12. Separates animals with exoskeletons from animals with no exoskeletons

GO ON TO THE NEXT PAGE

Questions 13-16

(A) Predation
(B) Commensalism
(C) Interspecific competition
(D) Mutualism
(E) Parasitism

13. An albino plant with vascular connections to a green plant of the same species that drains food from the green plant

14. Algae that grows on the shell of a turtle; the turtle is not harmed

15. A tapeworm in the intestine of a human

16. A population that prevents other populations from using a particular limited resource

Directions: Each of the questions or incomplete statements below is followed by five suggested answers or completions. Some questions pertain to a set that refers to a laboratory or experimental situation. For each situation, select the one choice that is the best answer to the question and then fill in the corresponding oval on the answer sheet.

17. Which biome contains maples, squirrels, and black bears?

(A) Tundra
(B) Tropical rain forest
(C) Temperate grasslands
(D) Taiga
(E) Deciduous forest

18. A man who is color blind marries a normal woman, and together they have a daughter who is not color blind. If the daughter marries a man with normal vision, what is the probability of their firstborn child being a son who is color blind?

(A)   0%
(B)   25%
(C)   50%
(D)   75%
(E) 100%

19. All of the following are needed for photosynthesis EXCEPT

(A) light
(B) glucose
(C) chlorophyll
(D) water
(E) carbon dioxide

20. Black coat color in horses is caused by a dominant allele, while white coat color is due to the recessive allele. Two black horses produce a foal with a white coat. If they were to produce a second foal, what would be the probability of the second foal having a black coat?

(A) 0
(B) 1/4
(C) 1/2
(D) 3/4
(E) 1

21. If one ribose molecule were bonded to one adenine molecule and one phosphate molecule, we would have a

(A) ribosome
(B) nucleotide
(C) nucleic acid
(D) ATP
(E) ADP

GO ON TO THE NEXT PAGE

22. Consider this pedigree:

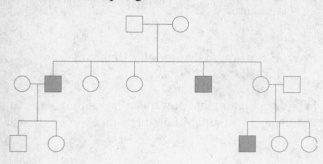

    The allele causing the disorder (shaded individuals are affected) can best be described as

    (A) autosomal dominant
    (B) autosomal recessive
    (C) X-linked dominant
    (D) X-linked recessive
    (E) There is not enough information to determine.

23. Which of the following is/are true for a resting human?

    I. Systolic blood pressure of 180 mm Hg
    II. Heart rate of 60–80 beats per minute
    III. Body temperature of 37° C

    (A) I only
    (B) II only
    (C) I and II
    (D) II and III only
    (E) I, II, and III

24. A researcher has a black guinea pig and wishes to determine if it carries a recessive allele for white hair. Both of the guinea pig's parents are black. Which of the following would be the best method for the researcher to use?

    (A) Mate the guinea pig with another black guinea pig and look for white offspring
    (B) Look for white hairs on the guinea pig
    (C) Mate the guinea pig with a white guinea pig and look for white offspring
    (D) Observe the chromosomes of a hair cell from a black hair
    (E) See if the guinea pig has any white siblings

25. A community includes seven different populations with various degrees of interbreeding. Population 1 shares genes only with Population 2. Population 2 shares genes only with Population 1. Population 3 has no gene flow with other populations. Population 4 shares genes only with Population 5. Population 5 shares genes with Population 4, Population 6, and Population 7. Population 6 shares genes with Population 5 and Population 7. Population 7 shares genes with Population 5 and Population 6. Which population(s) is (are) most likely to evolve after a change in its environment?

    (A) Populations 1 and 2
    (B) Population 3
    (C) Population 4
    (D) Population 5
    (E) Populations 6 and 7

26. Which of the following could be reasons for infertility in a woman who is ovulating normally?

    I. Blocked uterine tube
    II. Large amounts of FSH released just prior to ovulation
    III. Large amounts of LH released just prior to ovulation

    (A) I only
    (B) II only
    (C) I and II only
    (D) II and III only
    (E) I, II, and III

GO ON TO THE NEXT PAGE

27. What fragments would be produced if the following plasmid were to be digested with *Eco*RI and *Hind*III to completion?

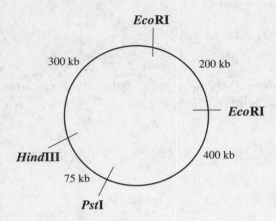

(A) 200 kb and 300 kb
(B) 200 kb, 300 kb, and 475 kb
(C) 600 kb, 475 kb, 375 kb, and 500 kb
(D) 200 kb, 300 kb, 400 kb, and 75 kb
(E) 200 kb and 775 kb

28. Human ABO blood typing is determined by the proteins present on red blood cells. The gene that codes for these proteins has three alleles: I^A, I^B, and i. I^A codes for protein type A, I^B codes for protein type B, and i codes for the absence of protein. I^A and I^B are codominant and i is recessive to both I^A and I^B. A woman with blood type A and a man with blood type AB marry and produce children. Which of the following blood types is NOT possible in their children?

(A) Type A
(B) Type B
(C) Type O
(D) Type AB
(E) All blood types are possible in their children.

29. Which organism is the LEAST closely related to the others?

(A) Lizard
(B) Frog
(C) Turtle
(D) Alligator
(E) Snake

30. Which of the following organelles would be present in a eukaryote but NOT in a prokaryote?

I. Nucleus
II. Mitochondria
III. Ribosome

(A) I only
(B) II only
(C) I and II only
(D) II and III only
(E) I, II, and III

Questions 31-33 refer to the following diagram of a human heart.

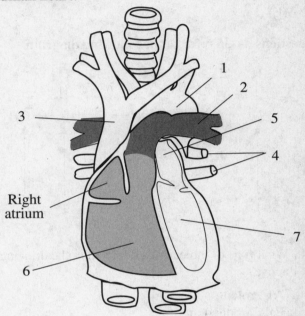

31. Which of the following represents the correct sequence of heart structures that blood would pass through when traveling from the right atrium to the lungs and then to the left ventricle?

(A) 3, 2, 4, 5, 7
(B) 6, 2, 1, 4, 5
(C) 3, 2, 1, 5, 7
(D) 6, 2, 3, 4, 5
(E) 6, 2, 4, 5, 7

GO ON TO THE NEXT PAGE

32. Which structures carry blood rich in oxygen?

    (A) 2, 3, 4
    (B) 3, 5, 7
    (C) 4, 5, 6
    (D) 1, 5, 7
    (E) 2, 4, 5

33. Which structure returns blood poor in oxygen to the heart?

    (A) 1
    (B) 2
    (C) 3
    (D) 4
    (E) 5

Questions 34-36 refer to the following diagram.

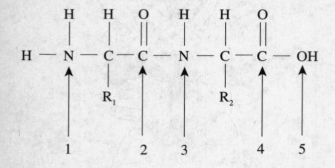

34. What type of molecule is depicted in the drawing above?

    (A) Protein
    (B) Carbohydrate
    (C) Lipid
    (D) Nucleic acid
    (E) Starch

35. If we were to continue adding to this molecule to increase its size, to which atom would the next portion be bonded?

    (A) 1
    (B) 2
    (C) 3
    (D) 4
    (E) 5

36. The synthesis of this molecule also results in the production of

    (A) carbon dioxide
    (B) water
    (C) lipids
    (D) ATP
    (E) NADH

Questions 37-39 refer to the following diagram of marine biomes.

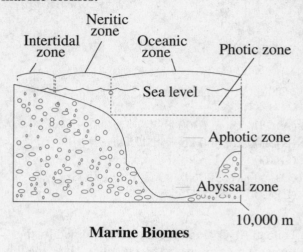

Marine Biomes

37. Which of the following is the area of least productivity?

    (A) Intertidal zone
    (B) Oceanic zone
    (C) Photic zone
    (D) Aphotic zone
    (E) Neritic zone

38. Organisms that live in the abyssal zone would need all of the following adaptations EXCEPT

    (A) ability to withstand extreme pressures
    (B) well-developed eyes
    (C) tolerance of cold temperatures
    (D) ability to survive in areas of low nutrient density
    (E) ability to utilize limited resources

GO ON TO THE NEXT PAGE

39. Organisms that live in the intertidal zone might have which of the following characteristics?

    I.   Ability to conduct photosynthesis
    II. Tolerance of periodic drought
    III. Tolerance of a wide range of temperatures

    (A) I only
    (B) II only
    (C) I and III only
    (D) II and III only
    (E) I, II, and III

Questions 40-43

Because some fruits contain enzymes that act as proteases, various fruit extracts were tested for use as possible meat tenderizers. The extracts were tested over a range of pH values. Below is a graph of relative effectiveness (compared to distilled water) vs. pH.

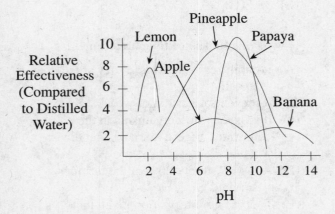

40. Which fruit extract operates over the broadest pH range?

    (A) Lemon
    (B) Pineapple
    (C) Papaya
    (D) Apple
    (E) Banana

41. Over which pH range does pineapple extract operate at no less than 50% of its maximum effectiveness?

    (A) pH 4 to pH 10
    (B) pH 2 to pH 12
    (C) pH 6 to pH 8
    (D) pH 7 to pH 11
    (E) pH 10 to pH 14

42. Which fruit extract is most effective at a neutral pH?

    (A) Lemon
    (B) Banana
    (C) Papaya
    (D) Pineapple
    (E) Apple

43. What does it mean when a fruit extract has a relative effectiveness of 1 ?

    (A) It is 100% more effective than water.
    (B) It is 10% as effective as water.
    (C) It is 1% as effective as water.
    (D) It is equally as effective as water.
    (E) It is equally concentrated as water.

Questions 44-47

A self-pollinating plant with orange flowers and alternating leaf arrangement produces 47 plants with red flowers and alternating leaves, 103 plants with orange flowers and alternating leaves, and 51 plants with yellow flowers and alternating leaves.

44. The allele for yellow flower color is

    (A) recessive
    (B) dominant
    (C) incompletely dominant
    (D) incompletely recessive
    (E) codominant

45. If a yellow-flowered offspring were self-pollinated, what would the resulting plants' flowers look like?

    (A) 100% yellow
    (B) 100% red
    (C) 100% orange
    (D) 50% yellow, 50% red
    (E) 75% red, 25% yellow

GO ON TO THE NEXT PAGE

46. The genotype of the original parent plant is

    (A) heterozygous for both flower color and leaf arrangement
    (B) homozygous for both flower color and leaf arrangement
    (C) homozygous for flower color and heterozygous for leaf arrangement
    (D) heterozygous for flower color and homozygous for leaf arrangement
    (E) heterozygous for flower color but unable to determine genotype for leaf arrangement

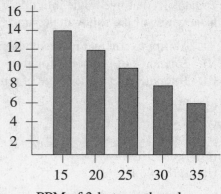

Number of surviving termites

PPM of 2-butoxyethanol

47. Suppose the original parent plant is cross-pollinated with a plant that has red flowers and non-alternating leaves. All of the resulting offspring have non-alternating leaves. Which of the following is/are true?

    I. None of the offspring have orange flowers.
    II. The allele for alternating leaves is recessive.
    III. Approximately half of the offspring have red flowers.

    (A) I only
    (B) II only
    (C) III only
    (D) I and III only
    (E) II and III only

Questions 48-50

2-butoxyethanol, a substance found in a general household cleaner, was tested for toxicity to termites. Solutions were made that contained various parts per million (PPM) of 2-butoxyethanol, and 15 mL of each of these diluted solutions was mixed with 150 g of wood chips. Twenty mature termites were added to the wood chips, and the number surviving after 24 hours was determined and recorded. The following graph presents the results.

48. At which dose does 50% of the termite population survive?

    (A) 15 PPM
    (B) 20 PPM
    (C) 25 PPM
    (D) 30 PPM
    (E) 35 PPM

49. How is this substance toxic to termites?

    (A) It paralyzes their jaws so they are unable to eat.
    (B) It prevents digestion of wood.
    (C) It kills the microorganisms in the termites' digestive tracks that digest wood.
    (D) At 40 PPM only 20% of the termites survive.
    (E) There is no information given that describes the mechanism of toxicity.

50. Based on the data for 20 PPM 2-butoxyethanol, what concentration of solution would be required to kill the entire 20-member termite population?

    (A) 40 PPM
    (B) 50 PPM
    (C) 60 PPM
    (D) 70 PPM
    (E) 80 PPM

GO ON TO THE NEXT PAGE

Questions 51-54

The following experiment was performed to test the effect of an auxin on plant growth. The auxin was dissolved in a gelatin block; gelatin does not affect the biological activity of the auxin. Several plant seedlings were prepared as described below and growth was measured every five days.

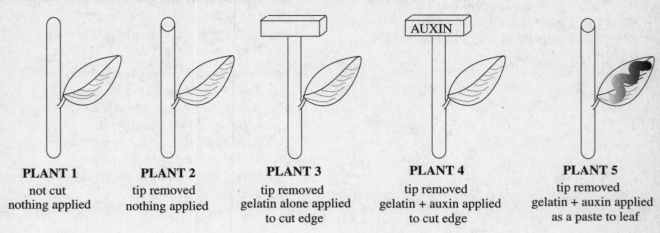

PLANT 1	**PLANT 2**	**PLANT 3**	**PLANT 4**	**PLANT 5**
not cut nothing applied	tip removed nothing applied	tip removed gelatin alone applied to cut edge	tip removed gelatin + auxin applied to cut edge	tip removed gelatin + auxin applied as a paste to leaf

Plant	Growth after 5 days	Growth after 10 days
1	15 mm	29 mm
2	4 mm	9 mm
3	5 mm	10 mm
4	14 mm	31 mm
5	8 mm	20 mm

51. Based on the results of the experiment, one can conclude that the tip of the plant contains

(A) gelatin
(B) water
(C) auxin
(D) paste
(E) nothing significant

52. Which of the following plants in the experiment acted as a control?

  I. Plant 1
 II. Plants 2 and 3
III. Plant 5

(A) I only
(B) II only
(C) III only
(D) I and II only
(E) I, II, and III

GO ON TO THE NEXT PAGE

53. What proves that auxin is necessary for plant growth?

    (A) Plant 1 grew faster than Plants 2 or 3.
    (B) Plant 4 grew faster than Plants 2 or 3.
    (C) Plant 5 grew faster than Plant 1.
    (D) Plant 3 grew faster than Plant 2.
    (E) Plant 4 grew faster than Plant 5.

54. In a separate experiment, an auxin/gelatin block applied to only half the cut edge of the tip caused the plant to grow and bend in the opposite direction. For example, if the auxin/gelatin block was applied to the left side of the cut edge, the plant grew and bent toward the right. Which of the following is the most likely explanation for this observation?

    (A) Sunlight caused the plant to bend.
    (B) The plant exhibited gravitropism.
    (C) Auxin stimulated cell division on the opposite side of the plant.
    (D) Auxin stimulated cell division on the same side of the plant.
    (E) Auxin stimulated cell growth toward a light source.

Questions 55-58 refer to the following experiment performed on frog oocytes.

Unfertilized frog oocytes were bathed in a neutral, isotonic solution (Frog Ringer's solution) to prevent changes in volume due to osmosis. The Frog Ringer's solution was supplemented with radiolabeled amino acids. A sample of oocytes was taken every 30 minutes and assayed for radioactivity.

At Time 1, the oocytes were fertilized. Samples were taken at five-minute intervals after fertilization and assayed for radioactivity. The results are presented in the graph below.

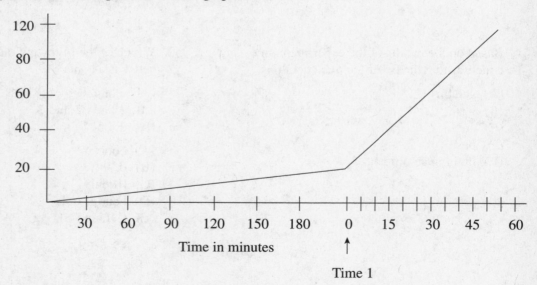

55. The radioactivity measured after fertilization was taken up by

(A) being incorporated into DNA
(B) being incorporated into proteins
(C) attaching to the cell membrane
(D) endocytosis
(E) associating with carbohydrates

56. How could a control be created for this experiment?

(A) Immerse the oocytes in non-radiolabeled Frog Ringer's solution prior to fertilization
(B) Sample the oocytes at five–minute intervals prior to fertilization
(C) Sample the oocytes at 30–minute intervals after fertilization
(D) Divide the oocytes into two groups, immerse one group in non-radiolabeled Frog Ringer's solution and one group in radiolabeled solution
(E) Divide the oocytes into two groups, fertilize one group, and simulate fertilization in the other, but do not actually introduce sperm into the oocytes

57. Based on the results of the experiment, the process most likely occurring after fertilization is

(A) DNA replication
(B) organogenesis
(C) protein synthesis
(D) RNA transcription
(E) endocytosis

58. The Frog Ringer's solution in the experiment is described as being isotonic. An isotonic solution

(A) has more DNA than another solution
(B) has more protein than another solution
(C) is more concentrated than another solution
(D) is less concentrated than another solution
(E) is equally concentrated to another solution

Questions 59-60

A group of 10 newly hatched chicks was separated into two smaller groups containing five chicks each. One group (Group A) was left with the mother hen, the other group (Group B) was taken shortly after hatching and kept with a mother goose. The chicks in Group A displayed normal behavior and followed the mother hen around. The chicks in Group B followed the mother goose around and exhibited goose like behavior, such as swimming. After one week, Group B was reunited with the mother hen, but ignored her, and instead continued to follow the mother goose around the barnyard.

59. The behavior exhibited by the chicks in Group B is

(A) imprinting
(B) instinct
(C) insight
(D) habituation
(E) conditioning

60. If exposed to a mother pig during the period shortly after hatching, the chicks in Group B would exhibit

(A) pig like behavior
(B) goose like behavior
(C) chick like behavior
(D) unique behavior
(E) unknown behavior

If you are taking the Biology-E test, continue with questions 61-80.

If you are taking the Biology-M test, go to question 81 now.

BIOLOGY-E TEST 2

Directions: Each of the questions or incomplete statements below is followed by five suggested answers or completions. Some questions pertain to a set that refers to a laboratory or experimental situation. For each question, select the one choice that is the best answer to the question and then fill in the corresponding oval on the answer sheet.

61. Which of the following organisms is able to regulate its own body temperature?

    (A) Frog
    (B) Fish
    (C) Snake
    (D) Sparrow
    (E) Turtle

62. A virus is considered a parasite because it

    I.   harms its host
    II. kills its host
    III. cannot reproduce outside its host

    (A) I only
    (B) II only
    (C) I and III only
    (D) II and III only
    (E) I, II, and III

63. An organism that feeds at several trophic levels is

    (A) a carnivore
    (B) an omnivore
    (C) a primary consumer
    (D) an herbivore
    (E) a primary producer

64. Yeast are cultured in a flask of nutrient broth under anaerobic conditions. The yeast that are most fit are those that

    (A) ferment the fastest
    (B) consume less of the limited oxygen supply
    (C) survive the longest
    (D) produce the most ATP
    (E) produce the most buds

65. A mushroom is most like a

    (A) moss
    (B) fern
    (C) yeast
    (D) pine
    (E) seaweed

66. In a certain ecosystem, the primary producers represent 100,000 kcal of energy. Assuming a 10% transfer of energy between trophic levels, how much energy is available to the fourth trophic level?

    (A)   10 kcal
    (B)   100 kcal
    (C)   1,000 kcal
    (D)   10,000 kcal
    (E) 100,000 kcal

67. Which of the following represents the proper ecological hierarchy?

    (A) Population → community → ecosystem → biosphere
    (B) Ecosystem → community → population → biosphere
    (C) Population → ecosystem → community → biosphere
    (D) Biosphere → ecosystem → population → community
    (E) Community → population → biosphere → ecosystem

GO ON TO THE NEXT PAGE

Questions 68-69

The following data table shows the number of different amino acids in the beta hemoglobin chain of various organisms compared to the human beta chain.

Organism	Number of different amino acids
Human	0
Mouse	27
Frog	68
Monkey	11
Lamprey	125
Chicken	35
Gibbon	2

68. To which of the following organisms are humans most closely related, based on hemoglobin amino acid sequence?

   (A) Mouse
   (B) Monkey
   (C) Chicken
   (D) Gibbon
   (E) Lamprey

69. Human hemoglobin and gorilla hemoglobin are even more closely related than the organisms shown in the table; they differ by only a single amino acid. Yet humans and gorillas are considered to be separate species. This is because

   (A) their hemoglobin chains differ by a single amino acid
   (B) human hemoglobin and gorilla hemoglobin have different functions
   (C) they are unable to interbreed
   (D) they are the result of convergent evolution
   (E) they are the result of parallel evolution

GO ON TO THE NEXT PAGE

Questions 70-71 refer to the diagram below.

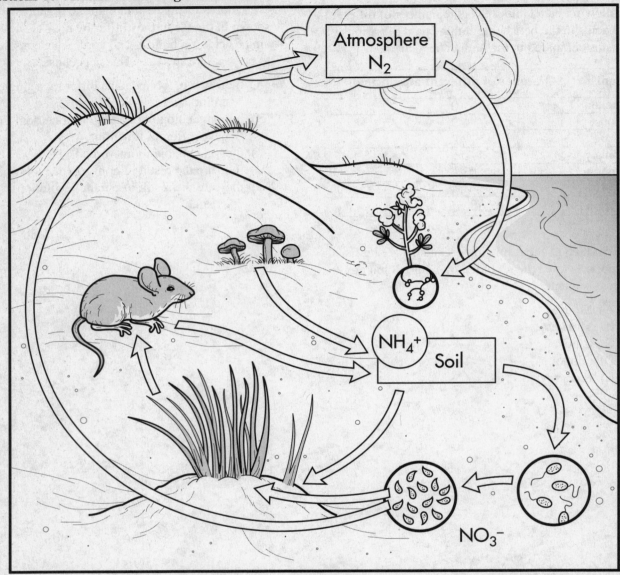

Nitrogen Cycle

70. Can both animals and plants obtain their nitrogen from the atmosphere?

    (A) Yes, both animals and plants take in nitrogen during respiration.
    (B) Yes, most of the nitrogen in the cycle is in the atmosphere.
    (C) No, only plants can take in nitrogen from the atmosphere.
    (D) No, they must consume it through eating or uptake from the soil.
    (E) No, they must obtain it through symbiotic relationships.

71. Bacteria in the soil are

    (A) primary producers
    (B) primary consumers
    (C) secondary consumers
    (D) tertiary consumers
    (E) decomposers

Questions 72-73 refer to the following structures.

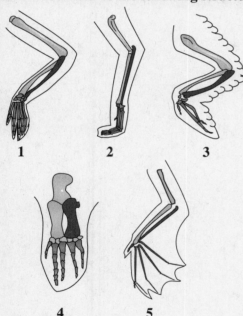

1   2   3

4   5

72. Which of these structures would be used for grasping?

    (A) 1
    (B) 2
    (C) 3
    (D) 4
    (E) 5

73. All of the structures are the result of

    (A) mutation
    (B) succession
    (C) convergent evolution
    (D) divergent evolution
    (E) regression

Questions 74-75 refer to the following diagrams.

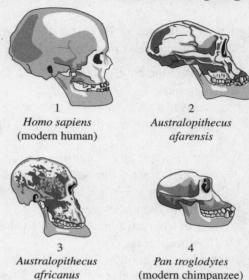

1
Homo sapiens
(modern human)

2
Australopithecus afarensis

3
Australopithecus africanus

4
Pan troglodytes
(modern chimpanzee)

74. Based on physical similarity, which skulls appear to be most closely related?

    (A) 1 and 2
    (B) 1 and 3
    (C) 2 and 3
    (D) 2 and 4
    (E) 1 and 4

75. What is the most advantageous difference between the ancestral primate skulls and the modern human skull?

    (A) Forward-facing eyes
    (B) Increased brain capacity
    (C) Loss of canine teeth
    (D) Loss of brow ridge
    (E) Reduction in jaw size

GO ON TO THE NEXT PAGE

Questions 76-77

Six pairs of bald eagles were released into the wild in Indiana. Four of the pairs of birds successfully nested and raised young. Two of the pairs nested near an industrial complex that released waste products (PCBs) into a nearby lake. These birds laid eggs, but the embryos failed to develop.

76. Which of the following is the LEAST likely reason for the failure of the embryos to develop?

   (A) Mutations in the embryos halted their development.
   (B) The adult birds failed to exhibit proper nesting behavior and did not care for the eggs.
   (C) The contaminated lake water that the birds consumed affected the development of their young.
   (D) The sperm of the males were affected by the PCBs in such a way that they were unable to fertilize the eggs.
   (E) Indiana is not a good location for bald eagles to mate and reproduce.

77. The eggshells of the embryos that failed to develop were tested and were found to contain more PCBs than the nearby plants and insects. This is due to

   (A) biological accumulation
   (B) increased levels of PCBs in the lake
   (C) the resistance of the insects to PCBs
   (D) failure of the plants to take up PCBs
   (E) absorption of PCBs from the nesting site into the eggshell

Questions 78-80 refer to the following data obtained for a rabbit population over a period of several years.

Year	Number of rabbits
1	4
2	17
3	62
4	245

78. Which of the following graphs best represents the data on rabbit population size?

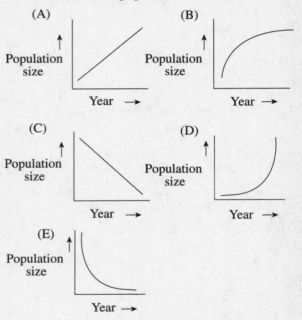

79. Assuming unlimited resources, what would be the approximate expected rabbit population in Year 5 ?

    (A) 5,000
    (B) 1,000
    (C) 500
    (D) 300
    (E) 100

80. Ultimately, the amount of nutrients and other resources would become limiting. What would happen to the rabbit population at that time?

    I. It would reach the carrying capacity of the environment.
    II. It would continue to grow indefinitely.
    III. It would engage in intraspecific competition.

    (A) I only
    (B) II only
    (C) I and II only
    (D) I and III only
    (E) I, II, and III

STOP

IF YOU FINISH BEFORE TIME IS CALLED, YOU MAY CHECK YOUR WORK ON THE ENTIRE BIOLOGY-E TEST.

BIOLOGY-M TEST 2

If you are taking the Biology-M test, continue with questions 81-100.
Be sure to start this section of the test by filling in oval 81 on your answer sheet.

Directions: Each of the questions or incomplete statements below is followed by five suggested answers or completions. Some questions pertain to a set that refers to a laboratory or experimental situation. For each question, select the one choice that is the best answer to the question and then fill in the corresponding oval on the answer sheet.

81. An animal cell placed into a 0.9% solute solution would do which of the following?

    (A) Remain unchanged
    (B) Swell and burst
    (C) Shrivel
    (D) Swell and divide
    (E) Release solute by exocytosis

82. When during cell division do chromosomes move to opposite poles of the cell?

    (A) When the centrioles replicate
    (B) After the nuclear membrane disintegrates
    (C) Immediately following DNA replication
    (D) When the DNA condenses
    (E) Immediately after the centromere splits

83. Convergent evolution can result in all of the following EXCEPT

    (A) structures that have similar functions
    (B) behaviors that are similar
    (C) different species that resemble one another
    (D) production of a single species from two
          originally different species
    (E) niches that are similar

84. What structure is common to ALL cell types?

    (A) Chloroplast
    (B) Plasma membrane
    (C) Cell wall
    (D) Mitochondria
    (E) Flagella

85. A buck with a large, impressive rack of antlers sires four offspring, three males and one female. The three male offspring also have large, impressive antlers, but before being able to reproduce, two of the male offspring get their antlers tangled in a low-hanging tree and are caught and killed by wolves. A second buck with a smaller set of antlers sires three male offspring; all of these males have smaller antlers like their father. They are more effective at escaping predators and successfully reproduce. In terms of evolution, which of the original bucks is more fit?

    (A) The buck with the larger antlers because he sired more offspring.
    (B) The buck with the smaller antlers because more of his offspring survived.
    (C) The buck with the larger antlers because he will be more successful at attracting a mate and continuing to reproduce.
    (D) The buck with the smaller antlers because he is more effective at escaping predators and will continue to reproduce.
    (E) Both bucks are equally fit.

GO ON TO THE NEXT PAGE

Questions 86-89 refer to the following experiment.

A population of ampicillin-resistant bacteria (Strain 1) is grown in a laboratory and is infected with a virus. The bacterial population begins to decline as the virus initially goes through the lytic cycle, then rebounds as the virus integrates into the bacterial chromosome to begin the lysogenic cycle.

The bacteria reproduce normally until they are heat-shocked. The rapid increase in temperature causes the virus to remove itself from the bacterial genome and enter the lytic cycle. Within several hours all bacteria are dead and a free virus is found in high concentration in the bacterial growth medium.

This free virus is used to infect a population of bacteria that is sensitive to ampicillin (Strain 2). After the expected decrease and rebound of this bacterial population (as above), the rebounded population was found to be ampicillin-resistant.

86. Evolution of a bacterial population occurs much more rapidly than evolution of a human population. This is because

(A) the bacteria are smaller and thus more susceptible to change
(B) the bacterial life cycle is short and many new generations can be produced quickly
(C) humans do not evolve
(D) humans can only reproduce during a portion of their life cycle, whereas bacteria can reproduce throughout their entire life cycle
(E) bacteria do not require oxygen to survive

87. The acquisition of ampicillin resistance by bacterial Strain 2 is due to

(A) evolution
(B) speciation
(C) conjugation
(D) transformation
(E) transduction

88. The bacterial culture is constantly infused with oxygen to ensure a high rate of reproduction among the bacteria and a healthy population. One evening the oxygen delivery system gets clogged and the bacteria receive no oxygen, yet they survive and continue to reproduce, just at a slower rate. These bacteria can be classified as

(A) obligate aerobes
(B) obligate anaerobes
(C) tolerant anaerobes
(D) facultative anaerobes
(E) simple anaerobes

89. Which of the following increase genetic diversity in bacteria?

  I. Conjugation
 II. Transformation
III. Crossing over

(A) I only
(B) I and II only
(C) III only
(D) II and III only
(E) I, II, and III

GO ON TO THE NEXT PAGE

Questions 90-93 refer to the following experiment involving human liver cells.

Aspartate aminotransferase (AAT) is an enzyme produced in liver cells that catalyzes an important step in the metabolism of amino acids. The production of AAT is dependent upon various hormonal stimuli. Human liver cells were cultured; half the cultured cells were used to measure the amount of AAT mRNA present, and half were used to measure the amount of AAT present. Measurements were taken at five-minute intervals following hormonal stimulation of the cells. Figure 1 shows the results of this experiment.

Figure 1

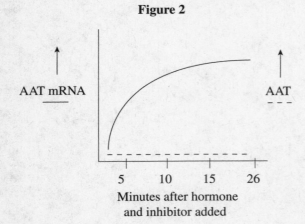

Minutes after hormone added

The experiment was repeated, this time adding an inhibitor of protein synthesis along with the hormone. Figure 2 shows the results of this experiment.

Figure 2

90. Figure 2 shows that AAT is a(n)

(A) protein
(B) hormone
(C) lipid
(D) inhibitor
(E) amino acid

91. Figure 1 shows that the hormone is needed to

(A) induce protein synthesis
(B) induce RNA transcription
(C) induce DNA replication
(D) inhibit protein synthesis
(E) induce cell division

92. The enzyme that transcribes mRNA is a protein, and the enzyme that produces AAT is a protein. However, in the presence of an inhibitor of protein synthesis, mRNA production occurs unhindered while AAT production is inhibited (Figure 2). This is because

(A) mRNA production does not require an enzyme
(B) mRNA is not a protein
(C) the enzyme needed to make mRNA is not a protein
(D) the enzyme needed to make mRNA still needs to be translated
(E) the enzyme needed to make mRNA is already present in the cell

93. Consider Figure 1. If radiolabeled uracil were added to the cultured liver cells BEFORE the addition of hormone, and the mRNA and AAT were analyzed at one-minute intervals to determine the presence of radioactivity, at what time would radioactivity first be detected?

(A) Immediately upon addition of hormone
(B) 1 minute after addition of hormone
(C) 3 minutes after addition of hormone
(D) 8 minutes after addition of hormone
(E) 20 minutes after addition of hormone

GO ON TO THE NEXT PAGE

Questions 94-96 refer to the following experiment.

ß-galactosidase (ß-gal) is a bacterial enzyme used in the metabolism of lactose. Three different groups of human intestinal bacteria were cultured in a glucose-based medium. At Time 1, the bacteria were transferred to media containing lactose as a nutrient source instead of glucose. At Time 2, the bacteria were returned to the glucose-based medium. Samples of bacteria were removed at five-minute intervals and tested for the presence of ß-gal. The results are presented below.

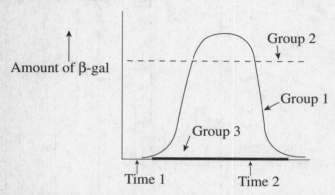

94. What could account for the delay in ß-gal production after Time 1 seen in Group 1 ?

(A) An inability to synthesize ß-gal
(B) Transcription of ß-gal mRNA
(C) Continued use of glucose as a nutrient
(D) Replication of the bacterial DNA
(E) Infection by a virus

95. Why is it an advantage to intestinal bacteria to be able to induce ß-gal production in this way?

(A) Humans do not consume foods containing lactose all the time.
(B) It prevents toxic buildup of lactic acid.
(C) ß-gal is harmful to bacteria.
(D) It prevents the bacteria from using glucose as a nutrient source.
(E) Lactose is harmful to bacteria.

96. Which of the following could be reasons for the inability of Group 3 to produce ß-gal?

I. Error in DNA replication
II. Error in RNA transcription
III. Error in protein translation

(A) I only
(B) III only
(C) I and II only
(D) II and III only
(E) I, II, and III

Questions 97-100

Situation 1: A species of moth is preyed on by bats. Over hundreds and hundreds of years, the moths develop a sophisticated pattern of flying when they hear the screech of a bat. This helps them escape danger. Other changes occur as well, and when an attempt is made to mate the current moth with its ancestor moth, no viable eggs are produced.

Situation 2: A species of frogs is living in a pond near an earthquake fault line. A sizable earthquake separates the frog population into two separate populations. After hundreds and hundreds of years, the two groups are unable to mate.

97. Consider Situation 2. Because the two groups of frogs are unable to mate, they are now considered to be different

(A) populations
(B) communities
(C) species
(D) organisms
(E) amphibians

98. A similarity between Situation 1 and Situation 2 is

(A) reproductive isolation
(B) genetic drift
(C) increased fitness
(D) geographic separation
(E) competition

GO ON TO THE NEXT PAGE

99. Another term used to describe what happened in Situation 2 is

(A) survival of the fittest
(B) convergent evolution
(C) divergent evolution
(D) stabilizing selection
(E) directional selection

100. If the earthquake in Situation 2 left one group of frogs without a water source, would the frogs be able to survive and reproduce?

(A) No, frogs are amphibians and can live only in water.
(B) No, frog eggs must be laid in water because they lack a shell.
(C) Yes, because amphibians frogs can live on both land and water.
(D) Yes, frogs have a thick scaly skin, which protects them from dehydration.
(E) Yes, the frogs would quickly adapt to the new environment.

STOP
IF YOU FINISH BEFORE TIME IS CALLED, YOU MAY CHECK YOUR WORK ON THE ENTIRE BIOLOGY-M TEST.

HOW TO SCORE THE PRINCETON REVIEW
BIOLOGY E/M SUBJECT TEST 2

When you take the real exam, the proctors will collect your test booklet and bubble sheet and send your answer sheet to New Jersey where a computer looks at the pattern of filled-in ovals on your answer sheet and gives you a score. We couldn't include even a small computer with this book, so we are providing this more primitive way of scoring your exam.

Determining Your Score

STEP 1   Determine how many questions you got right and how many you got wrong on the test. Remember, questions that you do not answer do not count as either right answers or wrong answers.

STEP 2   List the number of right answers here.

(A) _____

STEP 3   List the number of wrong answers here. Now divide that number by 4. (Use a calculator if you're feeling particularly lazy.)

(B) _____ ÷ 4 = (C) _____

STEP 4   Subtract the number of wrong answers divided by 4 from the number of correct answers. Round this score to the nearest whole number. This is your raw score.

(A) − (C) = _____

STEP 5   To determine your real score, take the number from Step 4 above and look it up in the Scoring Grid on page 442. For example, if your raw score is 53, find your exam score by going to 50 in the left-hand column and then moving to the right 4 spaces to the "3" column. Your exam score would be 630.

PRACTICE SAT BIOLOGY SUBJECT TEST 2
SCORING GRID

	0	1	2	3	4	5	6	7	8	9
0	0	330	340	350	360	370	380	380	390	390
10	400	400	410	410	420	420	430	430	440	440
20	450	450	460	460	470	470	480	480	490	490
30	500	500	510	510	520	520	530	530	540	550
40	560	560	570	570	580	580	590	590	600	600
50	610	610	620	630	630	640	650	650	660	660
60	670	670	680	680	690	700	700	710	720	720
70	730	730	740	750	760	770	780	790	800	800
80	800	N/A	N/A	N/A	N/A	N/A	N/A	N/A	N/A	N/A

Chapter 19
Practice SAT Biology E/M Subject Test 2: Answers and Explanations

ANSWERS AND EXPLANATIONS

Question	Answer	Explanation
1	D	The guard cells are found near the openings in the leaf called stomates. Stomates allow gas exchange to occur (notably oxygen and carbon dioxide), and while they are open water leaves through transpiration. You should have immediately eliminated choices A and E, because they are not leaf structures.
2	B	Start by eliminating structures that are not layers, such as choices A, D, and E. Because humans do not have a cuticle as an outer layer (that's a plant layer), choice C can also be eliminated.
3	C	Using the same strategy as above, eliminate choices A, D, and E, which are not layers. Plants have an epidermis, but the layer that restricts evaporation is the cuticle.
4	E	As always, eliminate first. Choices C and D are not found in humans and can be eliminated. A thermoregulatory structure is one that helps control temperature. The epidermis (choice B) prevents loss of water, but does not really aid in thermoregulation (that's the job of the dermis), so eliminate choice B as well. You may be tempted by choice A, because hair plays a minor thermoregulatory role in humans (its role is much more important in other animals), but a sweat gland is a major thermoregulatory structure.
5	C	For this question, you really have to know the definition of *translate* and know which type of nucleic acid gets translated. Eliminate choice E first, because it is not a nucleic acid (it's an enzyme). You should also be able to eliminate choice A fairly easily, if you know that RNA, and not DNA, is the nucleic acid that is translated. Finally, you should know that mRNA (messenger RNA) is the nucleic acid that is read (translated) to synthesize protein.
6	B	You should again be able to eliminate choices E and A, as above. The type of RNA that carries amino acids is tRNA. Remember *t* for "transport."
7	A	The only type of nucleic acid that is passed on to offspring (progeny—don't fall into the camouflage trap) is DNA.
8	B	Remember that the choices given for the classification questions can be used more than once. tRNA includes the anticodon that base-pairs with a codon in mRNA.
9	D	For these diagram questions, start at the right-hand side of the diagram and work toward the left until you get to a letter (answer choice) that separates the animals described in the question. Beginning on the right, find the animals with nails (apes and humans) and the animals with claws (lions and bears). Then work toward the left until you find the common branch from which these species originated. The split into orders Carnivora and Primates separated these animals.
10	B	On the right, find segmented worms (earthworm) and nonsegmented worms (roundworm), and again work toward the left. The split occurs at phylum Nematoda (nonsegmented worms) and phylum Annelida (segmented worms).

Question	Answer	Explanation
11	E	On the right, the animals with feathers are birds and animals with hair include lions, bears, apes, and humans. Working toward the left, the split that separates birds from the rest is the one that separates class Mammalia from class Aves.
12	A	This is the most difficult of the four questions. Animals with exoskeletons are ants and spiders; all the rest have endoskeletons (lions, bears, apes, humans, and birds) or no skeletons (roundworms and earthworms). If you work toward the left, you find the choices D and E only divide up the animals with endoskeletons but do not separate them from the animals with exoskeletons. Choice C only subdivides phylum Arthropoda; it does not make the separation asked for in the question. This leaves only choices A and B, and choice B separates segmentation from no segmentation; neither of these animals has a skeleton at all. The correct answer is A, which divides phylum Arthropoda (animals with exoskeletons) from phylums Nematoda and Annelida (animals with no exoskeletons).
13	E	If the albino plant is draining food from the green plant, the green plant is being harmed (being deprived of nutrition). Therefore, you can eliminate choices that do NOT cause harm: choice B (commensalism) and choice D (mutualism). Choice C can be eliminated because it discusses competition between two different species (interspecific) and the plants are of the same species. The choice falls between A and E. E is a better choice because the green plant is not being killed by the albino plant and predators generally kill their prey.
14	B	Because the turtle is not being harmed, eliminate choices that cause harm to one of the parties involved, such as choices A and E. Choice C may not directly cause harm to one of the species involved, but neither are the algae and turtle competing for anything; choice C can be eliminated. Eliminate choice D, because in mutualism both parties must benefit from the association, and while the algae may benefit, the turtle does not.
15	E	Again, the human is being harmed by the tapeworm, so eliminate choices in which no harm is done (choices B and D). The human is not preyed on by the tapeworm (choice A is eliminated), and neither are the human and tapeworm competing (choice C is eliminated).
16	C	For a population to prevent another population from using a resource, the first population must be a better competitor. Choice C is the only one that deals with competition.
17	E	Maples are deciduous trees (they lose their leaves); this is the best tip-off for choice E. You should be able to eliminate choice A (tundra has only small shrubby plants) and choice D (taiga is coniferous forest) easily. Tropical rain forest (choice B) and temperate grasslands (choice C) do not have black bears.

Question	Answer	Explanation
18	B	This is a typical genetics probability question with a twist. *Make sure you read the questions carefully!* You should know that color blindness is caused by an X-linked recessive allele. The only way the color blind man can produce a daughter is if he passes on his X chromosome; therefore, the daughter, even though normal, must be a carrier of color blindness. The daughter marries a normal man, meaning that he does not carry the allele for color blindness on his X chromosome. For them to produce a son, he must pass on his Y chromosome (so it doesn't really matter what his X is like, anyway) and the probability of him passing on his Y is 50%. The final probability lies with the daughter and whether she passes on her normal X or her color blind X to her son; this is also a 50% probability. It's very tempting to choose choice C; however, here's the twist: The question asks for the probability that BOTH events (male child AND color blind) occur TOGETHER. The easiest way to solve this is to a the Punnett square. |	X^c	X
X	XX^c	XX
Y	X^cY	XY | The four possibilities in offspring are XX^c (carrier daughter), XX (normal daughter), X^cY (color blind son), and XY (normal son). The probability of producing a color blind son is 1 out of 4, or 25%.
19	B	First of all, remember that this is a LEAST/EXCEPT/NOT question. Circle the word "EXCEPT" and draw a vertical line through the answer choices to remind yourself that you are looking for the "wrong" answer, in this case, the word that doesn't fit with the description in the question. Basically, the process of photosynthesis involves using a green pigment called chlorophyll (choice C) to capture light energy (choice A). Water (choice D) is used to convert the light energy into chemical energy (ATP and NADPH). This chemical energy is used to convert carbon dioxide (choice E) into carbohydrates. Glucose (choice B) is an end product of photosynthesis. It isn't needed in the course of the reactions.

Question	Answer	Explanation
20	D	Again, make sure you read the question carefully and know *exactly* what you're being asked. If black coat color in horses is the dominant phenotype, and both parental horses are black, then they must have at least one allele for black coat color. Because white coat color is the recessive phenotype, it can be caused only by a homozygous recessive genotype. The fact that the parental horses produced a white foal indicates that they must BOTH be heterozygous for coat color, each having an allele for white coat color as well as black. In the Punnett square below, B represents the dominant allele (causing black coat color) and b represents the recessive allele (causing white coat color). The probability of these horses producing a foal with a black coat is 75%, or 3 out of 4. <table><tr><td></td><td>B</td><td>b</td></tr><tr><td>B</td><td>BB</td><td>Bb</td></tr><tr><td>b</td><td>Bb</td><td>bb</td></tr></table> Note that the fact that we're asked about the second foal produced doesn't really matter. Each time the parental horses mate they have the same probability of producing black foals (75%) or white foals (25%). The coat color of previous offspring does not change the probability.
21	B	You should immediately recognize ribose as being the sugar used in RNA nucleotides, thereby eliminating choice A. Because the question asks about a single ribose molecule, you can eliminate choice C as well. Nucleic acids are made up of many nucleotides, containing many ribose molecules. Choices D and E are very tempting because they have adenine in them, and the question asks about ribose bonded to adenine. However, ATP stands for adenosine triphosphate—which means it has three phosphates—and ADP stands for adenosine diphosphate—which means it has two phosphates. The question specifies that only a single phosphate is included. The best answer is choice B—a nucleotide.
22	D	First, the disorder skips generations (the parents of affected individuals do not display the disorder) so it is recessive, and choices A and C can be eliminated. Furthermore, all affected individuals are male, indicating that the disorder is sex-linked, and choice B can be eliminated. Finally, because the disease does not pass from father to son, it must be X-linked, and choice E can be eliminated.

Question	Answer	Explanation
23	D	Remember your I, II, III technique—eliminate answer choices as you determine options I, II, or III to be true or false. Let's look at option I. Normal blood pressure in a resting human is about 120/80 mm Hg. The higher number (120 mm Hg) is the systolic blood pressure. Option I is false. 180 mm Hg is much too high a systolic blood pressure for a resting human. Knowing that I is false, we can eliminate choices A, C, and E. Of the remaining choices (B and D), both contain option II, so option II must be true. When you're taking the real SAT II, don't waste time thinking about option II; move right ahead to option III. For the purposes of this discussion, however, let's take a look. Option II is a heart rate of 60–80 beats per minute. This is true for a resting human. Continuing with option III: Humans do maintain a body temperature of around 37° C at rest (it increases during exercise). Because option III is true, choice B can be eliminated, leaving D as the correct answer choice.

Question	Answer	Explanation
24	C	Whenever you're trying to determine the genotype of an organism that has a dominant phenotype, the best thing to do is something called a test cross. A test cross is a mating between the organism with the unknown genotype and an organism with the recessive phenotype. (Organisms that display the recessive phenotype MUST have the homozygous recessive genotype; the genotype of this organism is known.) Then, you just look at the offspring produced. If the organism with the unknown genotype were homozygous dominant, all the offspring would have the dominant phenotype. If, however, the organism with the unknown genotype were heterozygous, half the offspring would have the dominant phenotype and half would have the recessive phenotype. Look at the two possible Punnett squares: |	D	D
d	Dd	Dd
d	Dd	Dd | This is the Punnett square that would result if the genotype of the unknown organism were homozygous dominant. Note that all offspring from this test cross display the dominant phenotype. |	D	d
d	Dd	dd
d	Dd	dd | This is the Punnett square that would result if the genotype of the unknown organism were heterozygous. Note that half the offspring from this test cross display the dominant phenotype and half display the recessive phenotype. Knowing this, let's take a look at the answer choices. You should be able to eliminate choice D quickly—all chromosomes look physically alike, regardless of the alleles they carry. Choice B should also be eliminated relatively quickly—just because there are a few white hairs on the guinea pig doesn't mean that it carries the recessive allele. There could be other causes for the occasional white hair. Choice E would give us some information, but not enough to determine if our unknown guinea pig were heterozygous or homozygous. In other words, if the guinea pig did have white siblings, it would tell us that the guinea pig's parents were heterozygous (that's the only way they could produce white offspring), and it tells us that the guinea pig has a chance of carrying the recessive allele for white hair, but it doesn't tell us for sure that it is carrying the recessive allele. It comes down to a choice between answer choice A and answer choice C. Choice C describes a test cross and is the correct answer. The problem with choice A is that you'd be mating your unknown guinea pig with another unknown guinea pig—not a great way to figure something out. The idea is to mate your unknown with a known—then you know what to expect and can use those results to determine the unknown genotype. Note that you should be familiar with a test cross and what it can tell you—and now you are.

Question	Answer	Explanation
25	D	This question is intimidating because it seems so complex. Remember to take the question apart piece by piece—don't guess at an answer until you are sure what the question is asking! The best way to tackle this question is to draw a diagram of the interactions of the populations with one another. It might look something like this: The question goes on to ask which population is most likely to evolve after a change—in other words, which population can best adapt to its new environment. You should know that evolution requires genetic variability, which is achieved through random mutation and through exchange of genetic material with other organisms (sexual reproduction). Clearly, the population that will be most likely to evolve is the one in which there is the greatest genetic variability. In this situation, that population is Population 5, because it interacts with the most other populations.
26	A	Infertility can be caused by anything that prevents the meeting of sperm and egg, including things that prevent sperm or egg survival. Remember also that this is a I, II, III style question—eliminate answer choices as you work through the options. Option I is true. The egg must travel through the uterine tube toward the uterus, and the sperm must travel through the uterine tube toward the egg. If the tube is blocked, travel cannot occur and the sperm and egg would not meet. (You can now eliminate choices B and D.) Options II and III are false. Large amounts of FSH and LH are normally released prior to ovulation; the LH surge is, in fact, what triggers ovulation. These could not be reasons for infertility. (Eliminate choices C and E.)
27	B	Note that the plasmid has *Eco*RI sites, a *Hind*III site, and a *Pst*I site. Because only *Eco*RI and *Hind*III are used, only those sites will be cut; the *Pst*I site will effectively be ignored. To "digest to completion" means that the plasmid will be cut completely at those restriction sites. Three fragments will be produced, each corresponding to the distance (in kb) between the *Eco*RI and *Hind*III sites.

Question	Answer	Explanation
28	C	You should be familiar with the rules for blood typing in humans, but if you aren't, this question gives you the basics. Because the alleles I^A and I^B are codominant, a man with blood type AB can only have the genotype $I^A I^B$. The woman with blood type A could have either $I^A I^A$ or $I^A i$ as her genotype. Here are the Punnett squares: |	I^A	I^A
-------	-----------	-----------
I^A	$I^A I^A$	$I^A I^A$
I^B	$I^A I^B$	$I^A I^B$ | This is the Punnett square that would result if the genotype of the type A woman was $I^A I^A$. Offspring would have either type A or type AB blood. |	I^A	i
-------	-----------	----------
I^A	$I^A I^A$	$I^A i$
I^B	$I^A I^B$	$I^B i$ | This is the Punnett square that would result if the genotype of the type A woman was $I^A i$. Offspring would have type A, type B, or type AB blood. Because type O blood is the recessive phenotype, it requires the homozygous recessive genotype (in this case, ii) in order to be displayed. This is the only blood type not possible in their children. A quick way to solve this question is to recognize that type O requires the homozygous recessive genotype, and for that to happen, each parent must donate a recessive i allele. Because the type AB man does not carry the recessive allele, this is not possible.
29	B	Remember your LEAST/EXCEPT/NOT technique. Lizards, turtles, alligators, and snakes are all members of the class Reptilia. Frogs, however, are members of class Amphibia.
30	C	This is a I, II, III–style question, so eliminate choices as you eliminate options. Option I is true. Eukaryotes have nuclei and prokaryotes do not. You can eliminate choices B and D. Option II is also true. Eukaryotes have mitochondria, and prokaryotes do not. You can eliminate choice A. Option III is false. Prokaryotes do have ribosomes; they need to synthesize proteins just as eukaryotes do. Eliminate choice E. The thing to remember about prokaryotes is that they have no membrane-bound organelles. Ribosomes are not membrane-bound and ARE found in prokaryotes.

Question	Answer	Explanation
31	E	You need to know the pathway that blood takes through the heart and some basic heart anatomy (names of chambers and vessels). Beginning at the right atrium, the next chamber blood enters is the right ventricle, which on this diagram is labeled "6." Because choices A and C do not start with "6" they can be eliminated. All of the remaining choices then contain structure 2 (the pulmonary artery), which is the next structure in sequence. From the pulmonary artery, blood flows to the lungs, then returns to the heart through the pulmonary veins, labeled "4" on the diagram. This eliminates choices B and D. Note that you don't have to worry about the rest of the sequence, because you have already eliminated all other answer choices (although "5," the left atrium, and "7," the left ventricle, are the correct structures in sequence).
32	D	Oxygen-poor blood returns to the right side of the heart through the superior and inferior vena cavae. The superior vena cava is labeled "3," so choices A and B can be eliminated. The right side of the heart (which includes the right ventricle, "6") sends oxygen-poor blood to the lungs through the pulmonary artery, structure "2" (choices C and E are eliminated). Structures 1 (the aorta), 5 (the left atrium), and 7 (the left ventricle), all carry blood rich in oxygen.
33	C	As mentioned in Question 32 above, blood is returned to the heart through the superior and inferior vena cavae. The superior vena cava in this diagram is labeled "3."
34	A	You should immediately recognize this molecule as a protein.
35	D	When a new amino acid is added to a protein, it is added at the carbon atom on the far right of the molecule. The OH group already attached to this carbon is lost as part of a water molecule.
36	B	As described in Question 35 above, to attach two amino acids together, the OH group attached to the carbon of the first amino acid and the H attached to the nitrogen of the second amino acid leave as water.
37	D	The area of least productivity in the ocean is the area that does not receive any sunlight, so photosynthesis cannot occur. The area without any sunlight is called the aphotic zone.
38	B	The abyssal zone is characterized by extremely high water pressure, extreme cold, darkness, and very low nutrient density. Organisms that live here must be able to tolerate all of those conditions. Well-developed eyes would not be useful, because there is no light in this deepest part of the ocean. Remember, this is a LEAST/EXCEPT/NOT question. Circle the word "EXCEPT" and draw a vertical line to remind yourself to choose the "wrong" answer.

Question	Answer	Explanation
39	E	The intertidal zone receives plenty of sunshine, periodically dries up (when the tide goes out), and has large fluctuations in temperature because of the changes in water depth. Organisms that live here may have characteristics that help them survive those conditions. Options I, II, and III are all true. Don't forget to eliminate answer choices as you decide whether an option is true or false.
40	B	Pineapple appears to have some effectiveness from pH 2 up to pH 12. None of the other fruit extracts operate over such a wide range.
41	A	Pineapple extract's maximum effectiveness is approximately 10. 50% of that is 5. The pH range where pineapple extract operates at at least 5 or better is pH 4 to pH 10.
42	D	Pineapple is maximally effective at pH 7, which is a neutral pH. pHs from 0 to 7 are acidic, and pHs from 7 to 14 are basic, or alkaline.
43	D	The graph shows relative effectiveness of the extracts when compared with distilled water. If an extract had a relative effectiveness of 1, that means it is equally as effective as the distilled water.
44	C	Upon reading this experiment, you should note that the plant with orange flowers produced plants with red flowers, plants with orange flowers, and plants with yellow flowers. The blended phenotype (orange flowers) is a tip-off for incomplete dominance in flower color, and the parent plant, with orange flowers, must have both the red allele and the yellow allele (is heterozygous). The plant produced 25% red flowers, 50% orange flowers, and 25% yellow flowers. If the allele for yellow flower color were recessive, the heterozygous parent plant would have produced 75% orange flowers and 25% yellow flowers (choice A is eliminated). If it were dominant, the resulting offspring would be 75% yellow flowers and 25% orange flowers (choice B is eliminated). There is no such thing as "incompletely recessive" (choice D is eliminated), and codominance between red and yellow would not produce a blended phenotype, it would produce plants that had both red and yellow flowers, but no orange.
45	A	The only way plants can have yellow flowers is if they are homozygous for yellow allele. If a plant is homozygous for a particular trait and is self-pollinated, it can only produce plants with that trait.
46	D	We know that the plant must be heterozygous for flower color, because that's the only way you can get orange flowers (the blended phenotype). Choices B and C can be eliminated. Furthermore, the plant must be homozygous for leaf arrangement because all progeny plants look like the parent plant. If the self-pollinated parent plant had been heterozygous for leaf arrangement, we would have expected to see different phenotypes in the offspring (choices A and E can be eliminated).

Question	Answer	Explanation
47	E	This question really needs to be broken down a step at a time, and the I, II, III technique applied. First, let's consider the genotype of the parent plant. If it has red flowers, its genotype for flower color must be homozygous (RR). Furthermore, a cross between a plant homozygous for alternating leaves (the original plant) and this plant (with non-alternating leaves) produces plants that all have nonalternating leaves. This tells us two things: First, the allele for nonalternating leaves must be dominant (otherwise all progeny plants would have alternating leaves), and second, the plant with nonalternating leaves must be homozygous (otherwise some progeny plants would have nonalternating leaves, and some would have alternating leaves). Let's look at the Punnett squares. You can draw two separate Punnett squares, one for flower color and one for leaf arrangement: <table><tr><td></td><td>R</td><td>R</td></tr><tr><td>R</td><td>RR</td><td>RR</td></tr><tr><td>Y</td><td>RY</td><td>RY</td></tr></table> This is the Punnett square for flower color. <table><tr><td></td><td>N</td><td>N</td></tr><tr><td>n</td><td>Nn</td><td>Nn</td></tr><tr><td>n</td><td>Nn</td><td>Nn</td></tr></table> This is the Punnett square for leaf arrangement. N represents nonalternating leaves, and n represents alternating leaves. Now let's look at option I. Looking at the Punnett square for flower color, we see that some of the offspring will have orange flowers, so option I is false. You can eliminate answer choices A and D. Option II is true (we discussed that above); you can eliminate choice C. Option III is also true. Looking again at the Punnett square for flower color, about half the offspring should have red flowers. Choice B is eliminated.
48	C	The experiment started with groups of 20 termites each, and 50% of that is 10 termites. The dose that allows 10 termites (or 50% of the termite population) to survive is 25 PPM 2-butoxyethanol.
49	E	This question is an excellent example of the temptation trap. The experiment description really doesn't tell us anything about how this substance kills the termites, just that it does kill the termites. Choices A, B, and C may be true, but we don't know for sure. The tempting choice is choice D, because that is a true statement. Expecting the graph to continue the pattern it shows, a dose of 40 PPM would leave only 4 termites alive, or 20% of the original population. However, even though it's a true statement, it doesn't answer the question. The best choice is choice E.
50	B	A dose of 20 PPM kills 40% of the population. $40\% \times 2.5 = 100\%$, so 20 PPM $\times$ 2.5 = 50 PPM.

Question	Answer	Explanation
51	C	Plant 1, the intact plant, grows at a rate of about 3 mm per day. Removal of the tip, as in Plant 2, reduces that growth to only about 1 mm per day. However, returning the auxin to the cut plant (as in Plant 4) restores the growth to about 3 mm per day.
52	D	First, this is a I, II, III–style question, so you will be eliminating answer choices as you work through the options. Second, you should always be able to identify the control or controls in an experiment; this comes up very frequently on the SAT Biology E/M Subject Test. Option I is true. Plant 1 was left in its natural state. You can eliminate choices B and C. Option II is also true. Neither Plant 2 nor Plant 3 is treated with the test substance (auxin), but they are subjected to the other conditions the test plants are subjected to. You can eliminate choice A. Option III is false. Plant 5 is testing the effects of auxin when it is applied at a location other than the tip of the plant. You can eliminate choice D. NOTE: Don't get careless and mix up your option numbers with your plant numbers! It's an easy mistake to make.
53	B	First go through the answer choices and eliminate obviously wrong ones, such as choices C and D. The data table given shows that Plant 5 grew more slowly than Plant 1, and that the growth of Plants 2 and 3 are about the same. To prove that auxin is necessary for plant growth, we have to show that when it is present plant growth occurs, and when it is absent, growth does not occur, or is much slower. Choice A is true, but it doesn't show the necessity for auxin, you can eliminate it. Choice E is true, but again, doesn't show the necessity for auxin, because auxin is present on both plants.
54	D	Because light is not mentioned in the question at all, we can eliminate choices that have light as the reason for growth, such as choices A and E. We can also eliminate choice B, because movement toward the earth is not described. For a plant to bend to the right, cells on the left side of the plant must grow faster than cells on the right. For a plant to bend to the left, the opposite must occur; cells must grow faster on the right than on the left. In the question, auxin applied to half the plant causes the plant to bend in the opposite direction; for example, auxin on the left stimulates bending to the right. Bending to the right means growth on the left; therefore, auxin must stimulate growth on the same side of the plant to which it is attached.
55	B	Radiolabeled amino acids would be incorporated into proteins.
56	E	Remember that a control is subjected to everything the experimental group is, except for the item being tested. The experiment in this case is testing the effect of fertilization on protein synthesis. A control group should be exposed to everything the experimental group is except for the actual fertilization.

Question	Answer	Explanation
57	C	Of the choices available, you should be able to eliminate choice E (endocytosis) first. There is no evidence to support this. As for the remaining choices, be careful not to come to conclusions too quickly based on your prior knowledge. In other words, you know that after fertilization occurs the zygote undergoes rapid cell division. This means that DNA will be replicated, RNA will be transcribed, proteins will be synthesized, and ultimately, organogenesis will occur. So in effect, choices A, B, C, and D are all occurring. The question, however, asks specifically for the process that is most likely occurring based on the results of the experiment. Because the experiment measures the amount of a radiolabeled amino acid present in the cells after fertilization, it is most directly measuring the rate of protein synthesis, making C a better choice than the others.
58	E	The experiment description explains that the oocytes were placed into Frog Ringer's solution to prevent changes in volume caused by to osmosis. The only way that osmosis can be prevented is to make sure that the solution the cells are suspended in is equally concentrated to the cells themselves.
59	A	Remember that any type of behavior in newborn animals that depends on exposure to an object during a critical time period (such as right after hatching) is called imprinting.
60	A	For imprinting to occur, the only critical thing is the time period of exposure. The object the chicks are exposed to doesn't matter; whatever it is, they will attempt to imitate it. Because the chicks in this question were exposed to a pig during the critical period, they would exhibit piglike behavior.

Biology-E Test

Question	Answer	Explanation
61	D	A sparrow is the only animal out of that group that is endothermic.
62	C	Remember the I, II, III technique! Statement I is true; parasites (including viruses) harm their hosts (eliminate choices B and D). Not all parasites kill their hosts—you didn't die from the last viral cold you had, did you? Statement II is false (eliminate choice E). Last, statement III is true; a parasite requires a host for *something*, in the case of a virus it is to reproduce (eliminate choice A).
63	B	The easiest choice to eliminate is E; primary producers do not feed at *any* trophic level. They support all other trophic levels by using solar energy to produce carbohydrates from carbon dioxide. Choices C and D mean the same thing. Primary consumers eat the primary producers (essentially plants) and therefore are called herbivores. Because there cannot be two correct answer choices, both C and D can be eliminated. Of the two remaining choices, both could be correct. Carnivores as well as omnivores can feed at several trophic levels. However, we know for a fact that all omnivores feed at at least two trophic levels (they eat primary producers as well as primary or secondary consumers), making choice B better than choice A.

Question	Answer	Explanation
64	E	The definition of fitness describes an organism that is successful at passing its genes on to the next generation. Because yeast reproduce by budding, the yeast that produce the most buds are the most successful at passing their genes on and are therefore the most fit.
65	C	Mushrooms belong to kingdom Fungi, as do yeast; therefore, mushrooms and yeast will have the most in common. Mosses (choice A), ferns (choice B), and pines (choice D) are all members of kingdom Plantae. Seaweeds (choice E) are members of kingdom Protista.
66	B	If 100,000 kcal are available at the first trophic level (the primary producers), then 10,000 kcal are available to the second trophic level, 1,000 kcal to the third trophic level, and 100 kcal to the fourth trophic level.
67	A	The biosphere is the highest level of organization, so choices D and E can be eliminated. Populations represent a lower level of organization than ecosystems, so choice B can also be eliminated. Finally, a community is the next step up from populations, choice A is correct and C is wrong.
68	D	Because the human hemoglobin and the gibbon hemoglobin differ by only two amino acids, these two organisms (of the ones listed) are the most closely related.
69	C	The defining factor in considering two organisms as separate species is their inability to interbreed. If humans and gorillas cannot interbreed, then they are separate species, regardless of the similarity in their hemoglobin amino acid sequence.
70	D	Looking at the diagram, we see that plants take up nitrogen from the soil or obtain it through nitrogen-fixing bacteria in their roots, and animals obtain nitrogen by eating plants. Choice A is true; animals and plants do take in nitrogen during respiration. However, choice A should be eliminated, because this nitrogen is in a form that is not usable by animals and plants. Choice B is true but doesn't really answer the question and should be eliminated. Choice C is false; plants cannot take nitrogen directly from the atmosphere. It must first be fixed by symbiotic root bacteria or converted into ammonia. Choice E is true for plants but not for animals, and can therefore be eliminated.
71	E	Bacteria anywhere are essentially decomposers. The only exceptions are the photosynthetic cyanobacteria.
72	A	Structure #1 is a human arm and hand, which can be used for grasping.

Question	Answer	Explanation
73	D	Divergent evolution produces structures that are similar in basic structure (look at the skeletal pattern in each of the limbs) but that may differ in function. Note that mutation (choice A) may have produced the changes that ultimately led to evolution, but choice D is a better, more accurate answer. Succession (choice B) describes the change from barren land to a stable climax community. Convergent evolution (choice C) produces organisms with similar functions but with different basic structures. Regression (choice E) makes no sense at all. It is not a term that describes anything to do with evolution; in fact, it means the opposite of evolution.
74	D	The *A. afarensis* skull and the *P. troglodytes* skulls have the same forward-jutting jaw, the same enlarged brow ridge, and the same general skull shape.
75	B	Having forward-facing eyes (choice A) was certainly an advantage as it increased visual depth perception. However, because all the skulls have forward-facing eyes, this does not represent a difference between ancient primates and modern humans. Loss of the canine teeth, loss of the brow ridge, and a reduction in jaw size (choices C, D, and E) are also apparent differences, but none is as helpful as the increased brain capacity.
76	E	Remember this is a LEAST/EXCEPT/NOT question—you're looking for the "wrong" answer. Choices A through D all describe possible reasons for the failure of embryo development. However, choice E is false, because four pairs (of the six pairs of bald eagles released) successfully nested and raised young.
77	A	Because the higher trophic levels feed on the lower trophic levels, toxins tend to accumulate in the higher trophic levels. Eagles are top carnivores and would exhibit a lot of toxin accumulation, more so than plants or insects. Choice B may be true but doesn't answer the question—don't fall into the temptation trap. Choice C is not mentioned in the passage, and the plants do take up DDT (choice D is eliminated). The DDT in the eggs came from the eagles themselves, not from absorption.
78	D	Because the population is obviously growing bigger, choices C and E, which depict declining populations, can be eliminated. Take a look at the number of rabbits in each year—it's growing exponentially (choice A can be eliminated) and hasn't yet leveled off (choice B can be eliminated).
79	B	If the resources are unlimited, the population can continue growing exponentially. In the first year, there were 4 rabbits. In the second year, there were approximately 4×4 (4^2), or 16 rabbits. In the third year, there were $4 \times 4 \times 4$ (4^3) rabbits, about 64. In the fourth year, there were approximately $4 \times 4 \times 4 \times 4$ (4^4) rabbits, or about 256. Following this pattern, we can assume in the fifth year there would be approximately $4 \times 4 \times 4 \times 4 \times 4$ (4^5), or 1024 rabbits. This number is closest to choice B.

Question	Answer	Explanation
80	D	This is a I, II, III–style question, so remember to eliminate answer choices as you work through the options. If the nutrients and other resources are "limiting," they will limit the population size and it will reach the "carrying capacity" of the environment. Option I is therefore true, and choice B can be eliminated. Option II directly contradicts option I; if option I is true, then option II must be false; choices C and E can be eliminated. Option III is also true. If nutrients and other resources are limited, the rabbits will compete with one another (intraspecific competition) for these limited nutrients; choice A can be eliminated. The stronger rabbits will survive, the weaker will die off, and the population will stabilize at its carrying capacity.

Biology-M Test

Question	Answer	Explanation
81	A	You should know that animal cells are approximately as concentrated as (isotonic to) a 0.9% solute solution. If the cells are placed in such a solution, there will be no osmosis, so the cell will neither swell nor shrink.
82	E	The centromere is the structure that holds the sister chromatids (the replicated DNA) together. As soon as the centromere splits (in anaphase), the sister chromatids (new chromosomes) are pulled to the opposite sides of the cell in preparation for cytokinesis.
83	D	Convergent evolution is the evolution of two totally separate species along similar lines, so that they both produce features that have similar functions. It can result in everything described, but it cannot make the two different species into a single species. Remember, the species were originally very different, and their underlying structures are still different. They just share some common behaviors and features. (Remember also that this is a LEAST/EXCEPT/NOT question—you're looking for the "wrong" answer.)
84	B	All cell types have a plasma membrane. Chloroplasts (choice A) are found only in photosynthetic organisms, cell walls (choice C) are found in plants, bacteria, and fungi only, mitochondria (choice D) are found in all eukaryotic cells but not in prokaryotic cells, and flagella (choice E) is only found on certain cells to aid in their movement, such as sperm cells or paramecia.
85	B	Remember, the key to fitness is not how many children you produce or how long you live, but how much you contribute to the next generation's gene pool. Because the buck with smaller antlers sired three surviving offspring, and the buck with larger antlers sired only two surviving offspring, the buck with smaller antlers is more "fit" in the evolutionary sense.
86	B	Evolution will always occur faster in an organism that has short generation times, simply because it is replicating its DNA more frequently and, thus, has a greater chance of mutations occuring.

Question	Answer	Explanation
87	E	Know your terms for genetic variability in bacteria! Transduction is the transfer of DNA (and therefore of new traits, such as resistance to an antibiotic) through viral infection. Choice A, evolution, *is* true—the bacterial population has evolved. However, the question asks for the more specific answer. The bacteria are not a new species; they have simply acquired a new trait (choice B is eliminated). Conjugation (choice C) is the transfer of DNA between two different strains of bacteria and requires that the two different strains be mixed together at some point. This did not occur in the experiment. Transformation (choice D) is a situation in which bacteria take up naked DNA from the environment; again, this did not occur here.
88	D	Organisms that use oxygen when it is available and survive by fermenting when oxygen is not available are classified as facultative anaerobes. You should have at least been able to eliminate choices A and B; the word *obligate* implies that they MUST be a certain way (e.g., always aerobic or always anaerobic), and these bacteria are able to switch.
89	B	Remember the I, II, III technique! Again, you need to know the definitions of these terms. Conjugation is the transfer of DNA between two strains of bacteria and leads to genetic diversity. Therefore, option I is true, and choices C and D can be eliminated. Transformation means the bacteria acquire DNA from the environment; this also leads to genetic diversity. Because option II is also true, choice A can be eliminated. Crossing over is a phenomenon associated with meiosis, which bacteria do *not* undergo. Option III is false, eliminating choice E.
90	A	Even without looking at Figure 2, the experiment description states that AAT is an enzyme, and enzymes are proteins. Figure 2 confirms this, because when an inhibitor of protein synthesis was added to the mix, no AAT was made.
91	B	By looking at the two figures, you should be able to eliminate choices C, D, and E, because these processes are not monitored in the experiment. Because mRNA transcription is the first process to occur after addition of hormone, it seems likely that this is the process the hormone is stimulating.
92	E	An inhibitor of protein synthesis will affect the production of new proteins only, not previously existing proteins. Because the enzyme needed to make the mRNA is already present, it is available to transcribe the AAT mRNA. Choices A and C are contradicted by the question, which states that mRNA production is run by an enzyme and that the enzyme is a protein. Choice B is true; however, the enzyme needed to make mRNA *is* a protein, and this is what the question is asking about. Don't fall into the temptation trap—be sure you know what the question is asking before you choose an answer! Choice D is false—if this enzyme still needed to be translated, no mRNA production could occur and the figure shows that mRNA production *is* occurring.

Question	Answer	Explanation
93	B	Radiolabeled uracil would be incorporated into mRNA and so would be detected as soon as mRNA were present—at approximately one minute after the addition of hormone.
94	B	Choice A is false; clearly the bacteria are able to produce ß-gal as shown in the figure. Choice C is also false. The bacteria cannot continue to use glucose because they were switched to a lactose-based medium. There is no reason to assume that the switch to lactose-based medium would induce DNA replication (eliminated choice D), and there has been no infection by a virus (eliminate choice E). It takes a little bit of time for the enzyme ß-gal (which is a protein) to be produced, because the mRNA for this enzyme is not normally present. The mRNA is transcribed when the enzyme is needed (such as when the bacteria are in lactose), and the time it takes the mRNA to be transcribed is the delay seen in production of ß-gal.
95	A	Because humans consume lactose-containing foods irregularly, it makes sense for the bacteria to expend the energy only to make this enzyme when it is needed. None of the choices B, C, D, or E make any sense. Producing the enzyme ß-gal would not prevent buildup of lactic acid. It's not as though the lactose spontaneously converts to lactic acid and the enzyme would prevent this. ß-gal cannot be harmful to bacteria (choice C). If it were, they might die. Over time, the ability to make ß-gal would be lost, because the bacteria that had this ability would die out. The bacteria are still able to use glucose as a nutrient source (choice D). They were grown in glucose originally and were returned to glucose at the end of the experiment. Finally, lactose is a nutrient. It is not harmful to bacteria (choice E).
96	E	An error in any of these processes could result in a nonfunctional protein. Option I, an error in DNA replication, could cause a mutation in the ß-gal gene, leading to defective mRNA and a defective protein. Option II, an error in RNA transcription, could produce a defective mRNA, resulting in a defective protein. Option III, an error in protein synthesis, could definitely produce a defective protein. Remember the I, II, III technique.
97	C	This is the definition of a species!
98	A	Of the choices given, the only one the two groups have in common is that they are now reproductively isolated—in other words, they are no longer able to interbreed. Genetic drift (choice B) occurs when random events eliminate certain genes from a population; this has not occurred in either situation. Increased fitness (choice C) may have occurred with the moths in the first situation, but not with the frogs in the second. Geographic separation (choice D) occurred with the frogs, but not with the moths, and competition (choice E) is not mentioned in either situation.

Question	Answer	Explanation
99	C	Divergent evolution often leads to speciation (C is correct, and B, the opposite, can be eliminated). Survival of the fittest (choice A) may have occurred but is not stated so specifically in the passage. Stabilizing selection (choice D) and directional selection (choice E) happen to a single population and usually do not separate it into two new species.
100	B	One of the main issues that separates frogs from reptiles is that reptile eggs have a shell that prevents them from dehydrating and can therefore live away from a water source. Be careful of tempting, correct-sounding answer choices! The first part of choice A is true; frogs are amphibians, but that means they can live both in water and land. Choice C is true, but doesn't address the issue of reproduction. Choice D is false; frogs lack the scaly skin of reptiles, which is why they need to be around water, and choice E is unlikely. Maybe over a long period of time the frogs could adapt, but switching from a partially aquatic to a completely terrestrial lifestyle would require many significant changes and would take a very long time.

About the Author

Judene Wright holds a Master's Degree in Physiology and Biophysics from the University of California, Irvine, and a Master's Degree in Education from Azusa Pacific University. Judene is a senior lecturer in Biology with The Princeton Review, is a Biology master trainer and "ubertrainer" for The Princeton Review's MCAT course, has developed The Princeton Review SAT II Biology E/M preparatory course, has worked extensively on the Biology materials for the MCAT course, and is currently the National Content Director of the MCAT Program for The Princeton Review.

Judene Wright also teaches Anatomy, Physiology, Biochemistry, and general Biology at several universities and community colleges in California. When not involved in lecturing, developing, editing, training, or teaching, she breathes and spends time with her four children and her husband.

Practice Test Form

Completely darken bubbles with a No. 2 pencil. If you make a mistake, be sure to erase mark completely. Erase all stray marks.

The Princeton Review

1.

YOUR NAME: _____
(Print)   Last   First   M.I.

SIGNATURE: _____ DATE: ___ / ___ / ___

HOME ADDRESS: _____
(Print)   Number and Street

_____
City   State   Zip Code

PHONE NO.: _____
(Print)

SAT Biology E/M Test 1

1. Ⓐ Ⓑ Ⓒ Ⓓ Ⓔ
2. Ⓐ Ⓑ Ⓒ Ⓓ Ⓔ
3. Ⓐ Ⓑ Ⓒ Ⓓ Ⓔ
4. Ⓐ Ⓑ Ⓒ Ⓓ Ⓔ
5. Ⓐ Ⓑ Ⓒ Ⓓ Ⓔ
6. Ⓐ Ⓑ Ⓒ Ⓓ Ⓔ
7. Ⓐ Ⓑ Ⓒ Ⓓ Ⓔ
8. Ⓐ Ⓑ Ⓒ Ⓓ Ⓔ
9. Ⓐ Ⓑ Ⓒ Ⓓ Ⓔ
10. Ⓐ Ⓑ Ⓒ Ⓓ Ⓔ
11. Ⓐ Ⓑ Ⓒ Ⓓ Ⓔ
12. Ⓐ Ⓑ Ⓒ Ⓓ Ⓔ
13. Ⓐ Ⓑ Ⓒ Ⓓ Ⓔ
14. Ⓐ Ⓑ Ⓒ Ⓓ Ⓔ
15. Ⓐ Ⓑ Ⓒ Ⓓ Ⓔ
16. Ⓐ Ⓑ Ⓒ Ⓓ Ⓔ
17. Ⓐ Ⓑ Ⓒ Ⓓ Ⓔ
18. Ⓐ Ⓑ Ⓒ Ⓓ Ⓔ
19. Ⓐ Ⓑ Ⓒ Ⓓ Ⓔ
20. Ⓐ Ⓑ Ⓒ Ⓓ Ⓔ
21. Ⓐ Ⓑ Ⓒ Ⓓ Ⓔ
22. Ⓐ Ⓑ Ⓒ Ⓓ Ⓔ
23. Ⓐ Ⓑ Ⓒ Ⓓ Ⓔ
24. Ⓐ Ⓑ Ⓒ Ⓓ Ⓔ
25. Ⓐ Ⓑ Ⓒ Ⓓ Ⓔ
26. Ⓐ Ⓑ Ⓒ Ⓓ Ⓔ
27. Ⓐ Ⓑ Ⓒ Ⓓ Ⓔ

28. Ⓐ Ⓑ Ⓒ Ⓓ Ⓔ
29. Ⓐ Ⓑ Ⓒ Ⓓ Ⓔ
30. Ⓐ Ⓑ Ⓒ Ⓓ Ⓔ
31. Ⓐ Ⓑ Ⓒ Ⓓ Ⓔ
32. Ⓐ Ⓑ Ⓒ Ⓓ Ⓔ
33. Ⓐ Ⓑ Ⓒ Ⓓ Ⓔ
34. Ⓐ Ⓑ Ⓒ Ⓓ Ⓔ
35. Ⓐ Ⓑ Ⓒ Ⓓ Ⓔ
36. Ⓐ Ⓑ Ⓒ Ⓓ Ⓔ
37. Ⓐ Ⓑ Ⓒ Ⓓ Ⓔ
38. Ⓐ Ⓑ Ⓒ Ⓓ Ⓔ
39. Ⓐ Ⓑ Ⓒ Ⓓ Ⓔ
40. Ⓐ Ⓑ Ⓒ Ⓓ Ⓔ
41. Ⓐ Ⓑ Ⓒ Ⓓ Ⓔ
42. Ⓐ Ⓑ Ⓒ Ⓓ Ⓔ
43. Ⓐ Ⓑ Ⓒ Ⓓ Ⓔ
44. Ⓐ Ⓑ Ⓒ Ⓓ Ⓔ
45. Ⓐ Ⓑ Ⓒ Ⓓ Ⓔ
46. Ⓐ Ⓑ Ⓒ Ⓓ Ⓔ
47. Ⓐ Ⓑ Ⓒ Ⓓ Ⓔ
48. Ⓐ Ⓑ Ⓒ Ⓓ Ⓔ
49. Ⓐ Ⓑ Ⓒ Ⓓ Ⓔ
50. Ⓐ Ⓑ Ⓒ Ⓓ Ⓔ
51. Ⓐ Ⓑ Ⓒ Ⓓ Ⓔ
52. Ⓐ Ⓑ Ⓒ Ⓓ Ⓔ
53. Ⓐ Ⓑ Ⓒ Ⓓ Ⓔ
54. Ⓐ Ⓑ Ⓒ Ⓓ Ⓔ

55. Ⓐ Ⓑ Ⓒ Ⓓ Ⓔ
56. Ⓐ Ⓑ Ⓒ Ⓓ Ⓔ
57. Ⓐ Ⓑ Ⓒ Ⓓ Ⓔ
58. Ⓐ Ⓑ Ⓒ Ⓓ Ⓔ
59. Ⓐ Ⓑ Ⓒ Ⓓ Ⓔ
60. Ⓐ Ⓑ Ⓒ Ⓓ Ⓔ

E Section

61. Ⓐ Ⓑ Ⓒ Ⓓ Ⓔ
62. Ⓐ Ⓑ Ⓒ Ⓓ Ⓔ
63. Ⓐ Ⓑ Ⓒ Ⓓ Ⓔ
64. Ⓐ Ⓑ Ⓒ Ⓓ Ⓔ
65. Ⓐ Ⓑ Ⓒ Ⓓ Ⓔ
66. Ⓐ Ⓑ Ⓒ Ⓓ Ⓔ
67. Ⓐ Ⓑ Ⓒ Ⓓ Ⓔ
68. Ⓐ Ⓑ Ⓒ Ⓓ Ⓔ
69. Ⓐ Ⓑ Ⓒ Ⓓ Ⓔ
70. Ⓐ Ⓑ Ⓒ Ⓓ Ⓔ
71. Ⓐ Ⓑ Ⓒ Ⓓ Ⓔ
72. Ⓐ Ⓑ Ⓒ Ⓓ Ⓔ
73. Ⓐ Ⓑ Ⓒ Ⓓ Ⓔ
74. Ⓐ Ⓑ Ⓒ Ⓓ Ⓔ
75. Ⓐ Ⓑ Ⓒ Ⓓ Ⓔ
76. Ⓐ Ⓑ Ⓒ Ⓓ Ⓔ
77. Ⓐ Ⓑ Ⓒ Ⓓ Ⓔ
78. Ⓐ Ⓑ Ⓒ Ⓓ Ⓔ
79. Ⓐ Ⓑ Ⓒ Ⓓ Ⓔ
80. Ⓐ Ⓑ Ⓒ Ⓓ Ⓔ

M Section

81. Ⓐ Ⓑ Ⓒ Ⓓ Ⓔ
82. Ⓐ Ⓑ Ⓒ Ⓓ Ⓔ
83. Ⓐ Ⓑ Ⓒ Ⓓ Ⓔ
84. Ⓐ Ⓑ Ⓒ Ⓓ Ⓔ
85. Ⓐ Ⓑ Ⓒ Ⓓ Ⓔ
86. Ⓐ Ⓑ Ⓒ Ⓓ Ⓔ
87. Ⓐ Ⓑ Ⓒ Ⓓ Ⓔ
88. Ⓐ Ⓑ Ⓒ Ⓓ Ⓔ
89. Ⓐ Ⓑ Ⓒ Ⓓ Ⓔ
90. Ⓐ Ⓑ Ⓒ Ⓓ Ⓔ
91. Ⓐ Ⓑ Ⓒ Ⓓ Ⓔ
92. Ⓐ Ⓑ Ⓒ Ⓓ Ⓔ
93. Ⓐ Ⓑ Ⓒ Ⓓ Ⓔ
94. Ⓐ Ⓑ Ⓒ Ⓓ Ⓔ
95. Ⓐ Ⓑ Ⓒ Ⓓ Ⓔ
96. Ⓐ Ⓑ Ⓒ Ⓓ Ⓔ
97. Ⓐ Ⓑ Ⓒ Ⓓ Ⓔ
98. Ⓐ Ⓑ Ⓒ Ⓓ Ⓔ
99. Ⓐ Ⓑ Ⓒ Ⓓ Ⓔ
100. Ⓐ Ⓑ Ⓒ Ⓓ Ⓔ

Practice Test Form

Completely darken bubbles with a No. 2 pencil. If you make a mistake, be sure to erase mark completely. Erase all stray marks.

1.

YOUR NAME: _____
(Print)   Last   First   M.I.

SIGNATURE: _____   DATE: ___/___/___

HOME ADDRESS: _____
(Print)   Number and Street

_____
City   State   Zip Code

PHONE NO.: _____
(Print)

SAT Biology E/M Test 2

1. (A) (B) (C) (D) (E)
2. (A) (B) (C) (D) (E)
3. (A) (B) (C) (D) (E)
4. (A) (B) (C) (D) (E)
5. (A) (B) (C) (D) (E)
6. (A) (B) (C) (D) (E)
7. (A) (B) (C) (D) (E)
8. (A) (B) (C) (D) (E)
9. (A) (B) (C) (D) (E)
10. (A) (B) (C) (D) (E)
11. (A) (B) (C) (D) (E)
12. (A) (B) (C) (D) (E)
13. (A) (B) (C) (D) (E)
14. (A) (B) (C) (D) (E)
15. (A) (B) (C) (D) (E)
16. (A) (B) (C) (D) (E)
17. (A) (B) (C) (D) (E)
18. (A) (B) (C) (D) (E)
19. (A) (B) (C) (D) (E)
20. (A) (B) (C) (D) (E)
21. (A) (B) (C) (D) (E)
22. (A) (B) (C) (D) (E)
23. (A) (B) (C) (D) (E)
24. (A) (B) (C) (D) (E)
25. (A) (B) (C) (D) (E)
26. (A) (B) (C) (D) (E)
27. (A) (B) (C) (D) (E)

28. (A) (B) (C) (D) (E)
29. (A) (B) (C) (D) (E)
30. (A) (B) (C) (D) (E)
31. (A) (B) (C) (D) (E)
32. (A) (B) (C) (D) (E)
33. (A) (B) (C) (D) (E)
34. (A) (B) (C) (D) (E)
35. (A) (B) (C) (D) (E)
36. (A) (B) (C) (D) (E)
37. (A) (B) (C) (D) (E)
38. (A) (B) (C) (D) (E)
39. (A) (B) (C) (D) (E)
40. (A) (B) (C) (D) (E)
41. (A) (B) (C) (D) (E)
42. (A) (B) (C) (D) (E)
43. (A) (B) (C) (D) (E)
44. (A) (B) (C) (D) (E)
45. (A) (B) (C) (D) (E)
46. (A) (B) (C) (D) (E)
47. (A) (B) (C) (D) (E)
48. (A) (B) (C) (D) (E)
49. (A) (B) (C) (D) (E)
50. (A) (B) (C) (D) (E)
51. (A) (B) (C) (D) (E)
52. (A) (B) (C) (D) (E)
53. (A) (B) (C) (D) (E)
54. (A) (B) (C) (D) (E)

55. (A) (B) (C) (D) (E)
56. (A) (B) (C) (D) (E)
57. (A) (B) (C) (D) (E)
58. (A) (B) (C) (D) (E)
59. (A) (B) (C) (D) (E)
60. (A) (B) (C) (D) (E)

E Section

61. (A) (B) (C) (D) (E)
62. (A) (B) (C) (D) (E)
63. (A) (B) (C) (D) (E)
64. (A) (B) (C) (D) (E)
65. (A) (B) (C) (D) (E)
66. (A) (B) (C) (D) (E)
67. (A) (B) (C) (D) (E)
68. (A) (B) (C) (D) (E)
69. (A) (B) (C) (D) (E)
70. (A) (B) (C) (D) (E)
71. (A) (B) (C) (D) (E)
72. (A) (B) (C) (D) (E)
73. (A) (B) (C) (D) (E)
74. (A) (B) (C) (D) (E)
75. (A) (B) (C) (D) (E)
76. (A) (B) (C) (D) (E)
77. (A) (B) (C) (D) (E)
78. (A) (B) (C) (D) (E)
79. (A) (B) (C) (D) (E)
80. (A) (B) (C) (D) (E)

M Section

81. (A) (B) (C) (D) (E)
82. (A) (B) (C) (D) (E)
83. (A) (B) (C) (D) (E)
84. (A) (B) (C) (D) (E)
85. (A) (B) (C) (D) (E)
86. (A) (B) (C) (D) (E)
87. (A) (B) (C) (D) (E)
88. (A) (B) (C) (D) (E)
89. (A) (B) (C) (D) (E)
90. (A) (B) (C) (D) (E)
91. (A) (B) (C) (D) (E)
92. (A) (B) (C) (D) (E)
93. (A) (B) (C) (D) (E)
94. (A) (B) (C) (D) (E)
95. (A) (B) (C) (D) (E)
96. (A) (B) (C) (D) (E)
97. (A) (B) (C) (D) (E)
98. (A) (B) (C) (D) (E)
99. (A) (B) (C) (D) (E)
100. (A) (B) (C) (D) (E)

Our Books Help You Navigate the College Admissions Process

Find the Right School

Best 368 Colleges, 2009 Edition
978-0-375-42872-2 • $21.95/C$25.00

Complete Book of Colleges, 2009 Edition
978-0-375-42874-6 • $26.95/C$32.00

College Navigator
978-0-375-76583-4 • $12.95/C$16.00

America's Best Value Colleges, 2008 Edition
978-0-375-76601-5 • $18.95/C$24.95

Guide to College Visits
978-0-375-76600-8 • $20.00/C$25.00

Get In

Cracking the SAT, 2009 Edition
978-0-375-42856-2 • $19.95/C$22.95

Cracking the SAT with DVD, 2009 Edition
978-0-375-42857-9 • $33.95/C$37.95

Math Workout for the SAT
978-0-375-76433-2 • $16.00/C$23.00

Reading and Writing Workout for the SAT
978-0-375-76431-8 • $16.00/C$23.00

11 Practice Tests for the SAT and PSAT, 2009 Edition
978-0-375-42860-9 • $19.95/C$22.95

12 Practice Tests for the AP Exams
978-0-375-76584-1 • $19.95/C$24.95

Cracking the ACT, 2008 Edition
978-0-375-76634-3 • $19.95/C$22.95

Cracking the ACT with DVD, 2008 Edition
978-0-375-76635-0 • $31.95/C$35.95

Crash Course for the ACT, 3rd Edition
978-0-375-76587-2 • $9.95/C$12.95

Fund It

Paying for College Without Going Broke, 2009 Edition
978-0-375-42883-8 • $20.00/C$23.00

Available at Bookstores Everywhere
PrincetonReview.com

The Princeton Review

AP Exams

**Cracking the AP Biology Exam,
2009 Edition**
978-0-375-42884-5 • $18.00/C$21.00

**Cracking the AP Calculus AB & BC Exams,
2009 Edition**
978-0-375-42885-2 • $19.00/C$22.00

**Cracking the AP Chemistry Exam,
2009 Edition**
978-0-375-42886-9 • $18.00/C$22.00

**Cracking the AP Computer Science A & AB,
2006–2007**
978-0-375-76528-5 • $19.00/C$27.00

**Cracking the AP Economics Macro & Micro
Exams, 2009 Edition**
978-0-375-42887-6 • $18.00/C$21.00

**Cracking the AP English Language &
Composition Exam, 2009 Edition**
978-0-375-42888-3 • $18.00/C$21.00

**Cracking the AP English Literature &
Composition Exam, 2009 Edition**
978-0-375-42889-0 • $18.00/C$21.00

**Cracking the AP Environmental
Science Exam, 2009 Edition**
978-0-375-42890-6 • $18.00/C$21.00

**Cracking the AP European History Exam,
2009 Edition**
978-0-375-42891-3 • $18.00/C$21.00

**Cracking the AP Physics B Exam,
2009 Edition**
978-0-375-42892-0 • $18.00/C$21.00

**Cracking the AP Physics C Exam,
2009 Edition**
978-0-375-42893-7 • $18.00/C$21.00

**Cracking the AP Psychology Exam,
2009 Edition**
978-0-375-42894-4 • $18.00/C$21.00

**Cracking the AP Spanish Exam,
with Audio CD, 2009 Edition**
978-0-375-76530-8 • $24.95/$27.95

**Cracking the AP Statistics Exam,
2009 Edition**
978-0-375-42848-7 • $19.00/C$22.00

**Cracking the AP U.S. Government
and Politics Exam, 2009 Edition**
978-0-375-42896-8 • $18.00/C$21.00

**Cracking the AP U.S. History Exam,
2009 Edition**
978-0-375-42897-5 • $18.00/C$21.00

**Cracking the AP World History Exam,
2009 Edition**
978-0-375-42898-2 • $18.00/C$21.00

SAT Subject Tests

**Cracking the SAT Biology E/M Subject Test,
2009–2010 Edition**
978-0-375-42905-7 • $19.00/C$22.00

**Cracking the SAT Chemistry Subject Test,
2009–2010 Edition**
978-0-375-42906-4 • $19.00/C$22.00

**Cracking the SAT French Subject Test,
2009–2010 Edition**
978-0-375-42907-1 • $19.00/C$22.00

**Cracking the SAT U.S. & World History
Subject Tests, 2009–2010 Edition**
978-0-375-42908-8 • $19.00/C$22.00

**Cracking the SAT Literature Subject Test,
2009–2010 Edition**
978-0-375-42909-5 • $19.00/C$22.00

**Cracking the SAT Math 1 & 2 Subject Tests,
2009–2010 Edition**
978-0-375-42910-1 • $19.00/C$22.00

**Cracking the SAT Physics Subject Test,
2009–2010 Edition**
978-0-375-42911-8 • $19.00/C$22.00

**Cracking the SAT Spanish Subject Test,
2009–2010 Edition**
978-0-375-42912-5 • $19.00/C$22.00

Don't Stop Now

We've got even more great info online.

PrincetonReview.com offers an array of online tools to help you prepare for various college admissions exams. The Princeton Review represents the very best in test preparation, and we're committed to ensuring that you have the tools you need to succeed.

More Test Prep—If you're looking to excel on your SAT, ACT, SAT Subject Tests, or AP exams, you're in the right place. We offer private tutoring, small group tutoring, classroom courses, and online courses, as well as various other books to help you prepare.

More Practice—If you need to get ready for the SAT or ACT and you prefer independent study and want a flexible schedule, we recommend one of our online courses. *Online Private Tutoring* for the SAT is our most personalized and comprehensive online option. Our *LiveOnline*, *Online*, or *ExpressOnline* options for the SAT and ACT will help you prepare when and where you need.

More Books—If you like this book, you might want to check out some other books we offer:

The Best 368 Colleges
Cracking the ACT
College Matchmaker
Complete Book of Colleges

More Fat Envelopes—We know more than just tests. We know a lot about college admissions, too. We'll help you find the school that best meets your needs.

To learn more about any of our private tutoring programs, Small Group Tutoring, classroom courses, or online courses, call **800-2Review** (800-273-8439) or visit **PrincetonReview.com**